Small Summaries for Big Data

The massive volume of data generated in modern applications can overwhelm our ability to conveniently transmit, store, and index it. For many scenarios, building a compact summary of a dataset that is vastly smaller enables flexibility and efficiency in a range of queries over the data, in exchange for some approximation.

This comprehensive introduction to data summarization, aimed at practitioners and students, showcases the algorithms, their behavior, and the mathematical underpinnings of their operation. The coverage starts with simple sums and approximate counts, building to more advanced probabilistic structures such as the Bloom filter, distinct value summaries, sketches, and quantile summaries. Summaries are described for specific types of data, such as geometric data, graphs, and vectors and matrices. The authors offer detailed descriptions of, and pseudocode for, key algorithms that have been incorporated in systems from companies such as Google, Apple, Microsoft, Netflix, and Twitter.

GRAHAM CORMODE is Professor of Computer Science at the University of Warwick, doing research in data management, privacy, and big data analysis. Previously he was a principal member of technical staff at AT&T Labs-Research. His work has attracted more than 14,000 citations and has appeared in more than 100 conference papers and 40 journal papers and been awarded 30 US patents. Cormode is the corecipient of the 2017 Adams Prize for Mathematics for his work on statistical analysis of big data. He has edited two books on applications of algorithms and coauthored a third.

KE YI is a professor in the Department of Computer Science and Engineering, Hong Kong University of Science and Technology. He obtained his PhD from Duke University. His research spans theoretical computer science and database systems. He has received the SIGMOD Best Paper Award (2016), a SIGMOD Best Demonstration Award (2015), and a Google Faculty Research Award (2010). He currently serves as an associate editor of *ACM Transactions on Database Systems*, and has also previously served for *IEEE Transactions on Knowledge and Data Engineering*.

Small Summaries for Big Data

Graham Cormode

University of Warwick

Ke Yi

Hong Kong University of Science and Technology

CAMBRIDGE
UNIVERSITY PRESS

CAMBRIDGE
UNIVERSITY PRESS

University Printing House, Cambridge CB2 8BS, United Kingdom

One Liberty Plaza, 20th Floor, New York, NY 10006, USA

477 Williamstown Road, Port Melbourne, VIC 3207, Australia

314–321, 3rd Floor, Plot 3, Splendor Forum, Jasola District Centre, New Delhi – 110025, India

79 Anson Road, #06–04/06, Singapore 079906

Cambridge University Press is part of the University of Cambridge.

It furthers the University's mission by disseminating knowledge in the pursuit of education, learning, and research at the highest international levels of excellence.

www.cambridge.org
Information on this title: www.cambridge.org/9781108477444
DOI: 10.1017/9781108769938

First published 2020

A catalogue record for this publication is available from the British Library.

ISBN 978-1-108-47744-4 Hardback

Cambridge University Press has no responsibility for the persistence or accuracy of URLs for external or third-party internet websites referred to in this publication and does not guarantee that any content on such websites is, or will remain, accurate or appropriate.

Contents

Acknowledgments

We thank the many colleagues and friends who have read drafts of this volume, and provided feedback and suggestions. These include Edith Cohen, Gil Einziger, Floris Geerts, Zengfeng Huang, Piotr Indyk, Nikolai Karpov, Edo Liberty, Lee Rhodes, Justin Thaler, Andrew Twigg, Pavel Veselý, Zhewei Wei, and Qin Zhang. The authors are also grateful for the research funding that supported some of the effort in writing this volume. Graham Cormode acknowledges European Research Council grant ERC-2014-CoG 647557, and Ke Yi acknowledges Hong Kong Research Grants Council grants 16202317 and 16201318.

1

Introduction

"Space," it says, "is big. Really big. You just won't believe how vastly, hugely, mindbogglingly big it is. I mean, you may think it's a long way down the road to the chemist's, but that's just peanuts to space, listen..."

Douglas Adams, *The Hitchhiker's Guide to the Galaxy*

1.1 Small Summaries for Big Data

Data, to paraphrase Douglas Adams, is big. Really big. Moreover, it is getting bigger, due to increased abilities to measure and capture more information. Sources of big data are becoming increasingly common, while the resources to deal with big data (chiefly, processor power, fast memory, and slower disk) are growing at a slower pace. The consequence of this trend is that we need more effort in order to capture and process data in applications. Careful planning and scalable architectures are needed to fulfill the requirements of analysis and information extraction on big data. While the "big" in big data can be interpreted more broadly, to refer to the big potential of such data, or the wide variety of data, the focus of this volume is primarily on the scale of data.

Some examples of applications that generate large volumes of data include the following:

Physical Data. The growing development of sensors and sensor deployments has led to settings where measurements of the physical world are available at very high dimensionality and at a great rate. Scientific measurements are the cutting edge of this trend. Astronomy data gathered from modern telescopes can easily generate terabytes of data in a single night. Aggregating large quantities of astronomical data provides a substantial big data challenge to

1

support the study and discovery of new phenomena. The volume of data from particle physics experiments is also enormous: each experiment can generate many terabytes of readings, which can dwarf what is economically feasible to store for later comparison and investigation.

Medical Data. It is increasingly feasible to sequence entire genomes. A single genome is not so large – it can be represented in under a gigabyte – but considering the entire genetic data of a large population represents a big data challenge. This may be accompanied by increasing growth in other forms of medical data, based on monitoring multiple vital signs for many patients at fine granularity. Collectively, this leads to the area of data-driven medicine, seeking better understanding of disease, and leading to new treatments and interventions, personalized for each individual patient.

Activity Data. We commonly capture large amounts of human activity data. Online social networks record not just friendship relations but interactions, messages, photos, and interests. Location datasets are also more available, due to mobile devices that can obtain GPS information. Other electronic activities, such as patterns of website visits, email messages, and phone calls, can be collected and analyzed. Collectively, this provides ever-larger collections of activity information. Service providers who can collect such data seek to make sense of it in order to identify patterns of behavior or signals of behavioral change, and opportunities for advertising and marketing.

Business Data. Businesses are increasingly able to capture more and complex data about their customers. Online stores can track millions of customers as they explore their site, and seek patterns in purchasing and interest, with the aim of providing better service and anticipating future needs. The detail level of data is getting finer and finer. Previously, data would be limited to just the items purchased, but now extends to more detailed shopping and comparison activity, tracking the whole path to purchase.

Across all of these disparate settings, certain common themes emerge. The datasets in question are large, and growing. The applications seek to extract patterns, trends, or descriptions of the data. Scalability and timeliness of response are vital in many of these applications.

In response to these needs, new computational paradigms are being adopted to deal with the challenge of big data. Large-scale distributed computation is a central piece: the scope of the computation can exceed what is feasible on a single machine, and so clusters of machines work together in parallel. On top of these architectures, parallel algorithms are designed that can take the complex task and break it into independent pieces suitable for distribution over multiple machines.

A central challenge within any such system is how to compute and represent complex features of big data in a way that can be processed by many single machines in parallel. One answer is to be able to build and manipulate a compact summary of a large amount of data, modeled as a mathematical object. This notion of a small summary is the subject of study of this work. The idea of a summary is a natural and familiar one. It should represent something large and complex in a compact fashion. Inevitably, a summary must dispense with some of the detail and nuance of the object that it is summarizing. However, it should also preserve some key features of the object in an accurate fashion.

There is no single summary that accurately captures all properties of a dataset, even approximately. Thus, at the heart of the study of small summaries are the questions of *what should be preserved* and *how accurately can it be preserved*. The answer to the first question determines which of many different possible summary types may be appropriate, or indeed whether any compact summary even exists. The answer to the second question can determine the size and processing cost of working with the summary in question.

Another important question about summaries for big data is how they can be constructed and maintained as new data items arrive. Given that it is typically not feasible to load all the data into memory on one machine, we need summaries that can be constructed incrementally. That is, we seek summaries that can be built by observing each individual data item in turn, and updating the partial summary. Or, more strongly, we seek summaries such that summaries of different subsets of data built on different machines can be combined together to obtain a single summary that accurately represents the full dataset.

Note that the notion of summarization is distinct from that of *compression*. In general, lossless compression is concerned with identifying regularity and redundancy in datasets to provide a more compact exact representation of the data. This is done for the purpose of compactly storing the data, or reducing the data transmission time. However, in general, there is no guarantee of significant size reduction from compression. The compressed form is also typically difficult to analyze, and decompression is required in order to work with the data. In contrast, summarization is intended to provide a very significant reduction in the size of the data (sometimes several orders of magnitude), but does not promise to reconstruct the original data, only to capture certain key properties. Lossy compression methods fall in between, as they can provide guaranteed size reductions. They also aim to allow an approximate reconstruction of the original data with some limited loss of fidelity: typically, based on the human perception of multimedia data, such as audio or video. Summarization aims to provide only small loss of fidelity, but measured along other dimensions; summaries do not necessarily provide a way to reconstruct even an approximation of the original input.

As a first example of summarization, consider a data set consisting of a large collection of temperature readings over time. A suitable summary might be to keep the sum of all the temperatures seen, and the count. From this summary given by two numbers, we can extract the average temperature. This summary is easy to update incrementally, and can also be combined with a corresponding summary of different data by computing the overall sum and count. A different summary retains only the maximum and minimum temperature observed so far. From this, we can extract the range of temperatures observed. This too is straightforward to maintain under updates, and to merge across multiple subsets. However, neither summary is good at retrieving the median temperature, or some other properties of the statistical distribution of temperatures. Instead, more complex summaries and maintenance procedures are required.

This work aims to describe and explain the summaries that have been developed to deal with big data, and to compare summaries for similar goals in terms of the forms of data that they accept, and their flexibility of use. It follows a fairly technical approach, describing each summary in turn. It lists the type of data that can be summarized, and what operations can be performed on the summary to include more data in it, and to extract information about the summarized data. We assume some familiarity with mathematical and computer science concepts, but provide some necessary background in subsequent sections.

1.2 Preliminaries

This section lays down some of the basics of working with summaries: the kinds of data that they can take as inputs; the operations that may be performed on the summaries during their use; and the types of guarantees they provide over their output.

1.2.1 Data Models

In this volume, we focus on datasets that arise from the aggregation of many small pieces of data. That is, the challenge arises from the scale of billions or trillions of simple observations. This matches the motivating applications described previously: high-frequency sensor readings, social network activities, transactions, and so on all have a moderate number of different types, but potentially huge quantities of each type. The summaries we describe will operate on a large number of "tuples" of a common type, which collectively describe a complex whole.

The types of data we consider are therefore each quite simple, and it is their scale that presents the challenge for summarization. We describe the types of data in somewhat abstract terms, with the understanding that these can be mapped onto the specific applications when needed.

Set Data. The simplest form of data we consider is a set of items. That is, the input forms a set A, as a subset of some universe of possible items U. For example, U could be the set of 64-bit integers (denoting, perhaps, serial numbers of items), and each item x in the data is then some particular 64-bit integer.

A very basic summary over set data is a random sample. A random sample is a quite general-purpose summary in the sense that it is useful for answering many possible questions about the underlying set A, although the accuracy may not be satisfactory. For example, a basic query that we may wish to pose on a set A is whether a particular item x is present in A, i.e., a *membership* query; or, for two sets A and B, how similar (the notion will be made more precise later) they are. Random samples can be used in place of the full datasets for answering these queries, but clearly will frequently make errors. The majority of the work on data summarization is thus devoted to constructing summaries targeted at certain specific queries, usually with (much) better accuracies than random samples.

Problems on sets often get more challenging if the same item may be fed into the summary multiple times, while A is still considered as a set, i.e., duplicates should be removed. In this case, even counting the cardinality of A becomes nontrivial, if we do not want the summary to store every distinct input item.

Multiset Data. With set data, we typically assume the semantics that an item is either present or absent from the set. Under the multiset semantics, each item has a multiplicity. That is, we count the number of occurrences of each item. Again, the input is supported over a set U. Now, queries of interest relate to the multiplicity of items: how many occurrences of x are there in the data? Which items x occur most frequently?

It is sometimes convenient to think of multiset data as defining a vector of values, v. Then v_x denotes the multiplicity of item x in the input. Natural queries over vectors include asking for the (Euclidean) norm of the vector, the distance between a pair of vectors, or the inner-product between two vectors. The accuracy of such estimators is often expressed in terms of the ℓ_p norm of the vector, $\|v\|_p$, where

$$\|v\|_p = \left(\sum_{i \in U} |v_i|^p \right)^{1/p}.$$

Important special cases include the Euclidean norm, $\|v\|_2$, and the Manhattan norm, $\|v\|_1$ (the sum of absolute values). We may also abuse notation and make reference to the ℓ_0 norm, sometimes called the Hamming norm, which is defined as $\|v\|_0 = |\{i : v_i \neq 0\}|$. This counts the number of nonzero entries in the vector v, i.e., the number of *distinct* items in the multiset. When dealing with skewed data, that is, where a few items have much larger count than others, we sometimes give bounds in terms of the residual ℓ_p norm. This is denoted as $\|v\|_p^{\text{res}(k)}$, where, if we reindex v so that v_i is the ith largest (absolute) value, then

$$\|v\|_p^{\text{res}(k)} = \left(\sum_{i=k+1}^{|U|} |v_i|^p \right)^{1/p}.$$

That is, the ℓ_p norm after removing the k largest entries of v.

Weighted Multiset Data. More generally, input describing a multiset may arrive with corresponding weights. This can represent, for example, a customer buying several instances of the same item in a single transaction. The multiplicity of the item across the whole input is the sum of all weights associated with it. The vector representation of the multiset naturally models the weighted case well, where v_i is the sum of weights of item i processed by the summary. The preceding queries all make sense over this style of input – to find the total weight for a given item, or the items with the largest total weights. Guarantees for summaries may be expressed in terms of vector norms such as $\|v\|_2$ or $\|v\|_1$. Different summaries can cope with different constraints on the weights: whether the weights should be integral, or can be arbitrary.

Of some concern is whether a summary allows *negative* weights. A negative weight corresponds to the removal of some copies of an item. Some summaries only tolerate nonnegative weights (the positive weights case), while others allow arbitrary positive and negative weights (which we call the general weights case). Lastly, a few summaries work in the "strict" case, where positive and negative weights are permitted, provided that the final weight of every item is nonnegative when the summary is interrogated. By contrast, in the general case, we allow the multiplicity of an item to be negative. For the positive weights and strict cases, guarantees may be given in terms of $W = \|v\|_1$, the sum of the weights. Some summaries have guarantees in terms of $W^{\text{res}(k)} = \|v\|_1^{\text{res}(k)}$, the weight of the input (in the positive weight or strict case) after removing the k heaviest weights.

Matrices. Going beyond vectors, we may have data that can be thought of as many different vectors. These can be naturally collected together as large matrices. We are typically interested in $n \times d$ matrices M where both n and d are considerably large. In some cases, one or other of n and d is not so large, in which case we have a "short, fat matrix" or a "tall, skinny matrix," respectively.

As with the vector case, the constraints on the data can affect what is possible. Are the entries in the matrix integer or real valued? Is each entry in the matrix seen once only, or subject to multiple additive updates? Are entries seen in any particular order (say, a row at time), or without any order? Guarantees may be given in terms of a variety of matrix norms, including entrywise norms, such as the Frobenius norm,

$$\|M\|_F = \sqrt{\sum_{i,j} M_{i,j}^2},$$

or the p-norm, taken over unit norm vectors x,

$$\|M\|_p = \sup_{\|x\|_p=1} \|Mx\|_p.$$

Ordered Data. When U has a total order – namely, given any two items, we can compare them and determine which is the greater and which is the lesser under the order – we can formulate additional queries. For example, *how many occurrences of items in a given range are there (range queries)?*; *what is the median of the input?*; and more generally, *what does the data distribution look like on U?*

Some summaries manipulate items only by comparison, that is, given two items, checking whether one is greater or less than the other, or the two are equal. These summaries are said to be *comparison based*. They thus do not need to assume a fixed universe U beforehand, which is useful when dealing with, e.g., variable-length strings or user-defined data types.

Geometric Data. Multidimensional geometric data naturally arise in big data analytics. Any point on earth is characterized by latitude and longitude; a point in space has three coordinates. More importantly, many types of multidimensional data can be interpreted and analyzed geometrically, although they are not inherently geometric by nature. For example, we may see readings which include temperature, pressure, and humidity. In data mining, various features can be extracted from an object, which map it to a high-dimensional point.

Over such data, the summary may support range queries, which could generalize one-dimensional ranges in different ways such as axis-parallel rectangles, half-spaces, or simplexes. Moreover, one could ask for many interesting geometric properties to be preserved by the summary, for example, the diameter, the convex hull, the minimum enclosing ball, pairwise distances, and various clusterings.

Graph Data. A graph represents a different kind of multidimensional data, where each input item describes an edge in a graph. Typically, the set of possible nodes V is known upfront, and each edge is a member of $V \times V$. However, in some cases V is defined implicitly from the set of edges that arrive. Over graphs, typical queries supported by summaries may be to approximate the distance between a pair of nodes, determine the number of connected components in the graph, or count the number of a particular subgraph, such as counting the number of triangles.

1.2.2 Operations on Summaries

For uniformity of presentation, each summary we describe typically supports the same set of basic operations, although these have different meanings for each summary. These basic operations are INITIALIZE, UPDATE, MERGE, and QUERY. Some summaries additionally have methods to CONSTRUCT and COMPRESS them.

INITIALIZE. The INITIALIZE operation for a summary is to initialize a new instance of the summary. Typically, this is quite simple, just creating empty data structures for the summary to use. For summaries that use randomization, this can also involve drawing the random values that will be used throughout the operation of the summary.

UPDATE. The UPDATE operation takes a new data item, and updates the summary to reflect this. The time to do this UPDATE should be quite fast, since we want to process a large input formed of many data items. Ideally, this should be faster than reading the whole summary. Since UPDATE takes a single item at a time, the summary can process a stream of items one at a time, and only retain the current state of the summary at each step.

Many summaries described in this book support not only adding a new item to the summary, but also deleting a previously inserted item. To maintain uniformity, we treat a deletion as an UPDATE operation with a negative multiplicity. Examples include the Count-Min Sketch (Section 3.4), Count Sketch (Section 3.5), and the AMS Sketch (Section 3.6). This usually follows from the fact the summary is a linear transformation of the multiplicity vector representing the input, and such summaries are often called *linear sketches*. This concept is discussed in more detail toward the end of the book (Section 9.3.4).

MERGE. When faced with a large amount of data to summarize, we would like to distribute the computation over multiple machines. Performing a sequence of UPDATE operations does not guarantee that we can parallelize the action of the summary, so we also need the ability to MERGE together a pair of summaries to obtain a summary of the union of their inputs. This is possible in the majority of cases, although a few summaries only provide an UPDATE operation and not a MERGE. MERGE is often a generalization of UPDATE: applying MERGE when one of the input summaries consists of just a single item usually reduces to the UPDATE operation. In general, a MERGE operation is slower than UPDATE, since it requires reading through both summaries in full.

QUERY. At various points, we want to use the summary to learn something about the data that are summarized. We abstract this as QUERY, with the understanding that the meaning of QUERY depends on the summary: different summaries capture different properties of the data. In some cases, QUERY takes parameters, while for other summaries, there is a single QUERY operation. Some summaries can be used to answer several different types of query. In this presentation, we typically pick one primary question to answer with the QUERY operation, and then discuss the other ways in which the summary can be used.

CONSTRUCT. We can always construct a summary by adding items one by one into the summary using the UPDATE and MERGE operations. However, for a few summaries, UPDATE is expensive, complicated, or even impossible. In these cases, we will describe how to CONSTRUCT the summary from the given input in an offline setting.

Compress. Some summaries also provide an additional operation which seeks to Compress the data structure. This is the case when the effect of Update and Merge operations allows the size of the summary to grow. In this case, Compress will aim to reduce the size of the summary as much as possible, while retaining an accurate representation. However, since the time cost for this operation may be higher than Update, it is not performed with every Update operation, but on a slower schedule, say after some number of Update operations have been performed.

A Simple Example: Counts, Sums, Means, Variances. We give an illustration of how these operations apply to the simple case of keeping counts. These give a first example of a summary allowing us to track the number of events that have been observed. Counters also easily allow us to track the sum of a sequence of weights, find their mean, and compute the observed variance/standard deviation.

We will illustrate the use of a counter c, and a sum of weights w, as well as a sum of squared weights s. The Initialize operation sets all of these to zero. Given an update of an item i, with a possible weight w_i, we can Update c by incrementing it: $c \leftarrow c + 1$. The sum of weights is updated as $w \leftarrow w + w_i$, and the sum of squared weights as $s \leftarrow s + w_i^2$. To Merge together two counter summaries, we can simply sum the corresponding values: the merge of c_1 and c_2 is $c_1 + c_2$, the merge of w_1 and w_2 is $w_1 + w_2$, and the merge of s_1 and s_2 is $s_1 + s_2$. We can apply different Query operations to obtain different aggregates: the total count of all the updates and the total sum of all the weights are simply the final values of c and w, respectively. The mean weight is given by w/c, and the variance of the weights is $s/w - (w/c)^2$.

1.2.3 Models of Computation

Traditionally, computer science has focused on the random access machine (RAM) model of computation to study algorithms and data structures. This abstraction is a good match for single-threaded computation on a single machine, but other models are required to fit computation on large volumes of data. The summaries that we describe are flexible and can be implemented in a variety of different settings.

The Streaming Model. The streaming model of computation considers data that arrive as a massive sequence of discrete observations, which collectively describe the data. For example, we might think of the data as describing a vector, by giving a list of increments to entries in the vector (initially zero) in some arbitrary order. Since we require our summaries to support an UPDATE operation, we can usually make each piece of information about the data the subject of an UPDATE operation to build a summary of the whole data in the streaming model. This assumes that there is a single (centralized) observer; variants involving multiple, distributed observers can also be accommodated, as described in the following paragraphs.

Parallel Processing. When subsets of one dataset are observed in parallel, we can have each parallel thread perform UPDATE operations to build their own summaries of part of the data. Data can be assigned to each thread in some fashion: round-robin scheduling, or hash partitioning, for example. To collect all the observations, we can then MERGE together the summaries. Some extra effort may be needed to handle synchronization and coordination issues, which we assume would be taken care of within the parallel system.

Distributed Processing. Summaries can likewise be used in systems that handle datasets that are distributed over multiple machines. Multiple UPDATE operations can build a local summary, and these summaries can then be combined with MERGE operations by a central entity to allow QUERY operations on the global summary. This can easily be implemented within various distributed frameworks, such as the MapReduce model within the Apache Hadoop and Spark systems.

1.2.4 Implementations of Summaries

In many cases, the summaries that we describe are relatively simple to implement. The pseudocode to outline each of the operations is often only a few lines long. Consequently, they can be implemented with relative ease from scratch. However, there are some subtleties, such as the use of suitable random hash functions, or the reliance on lower-level data structures with efficient maintenance operations. It is therefore preferable to rely on preexisting implementations for some or all of the summary functions.

Fortunately, there are many implementations and libraries freely available online, particularly for the most well-known summaries (such as Bloom-Filter). Inevitably, these are of varying quality and reliability, and adopt a number of different languages and coding styles. Throughout the main section of the book, we will make reference to the Apache DataSketches library as a main reference for implementations. This is a well-established project to provide flexible implementations of the most important summaries in Java. It includes several carefully engineered features, such as internal memory management to avoid overheads from the default heap management and garbage collection routines. The project was initiated within Yahoo!, then open sourced, and most recently transitioned to the Apache Software Foundation. The home for this project is `https://datasketches.github.io/`. After DataSketches, the stream-lib library (also in Java) also has many Java implementations of summaries, with multiple contributors (`https://github.com/addthis/stream-lib`). The Algebird library from Twitter has many implementations of summaries in the Scala language (`https://github.com/twitter/algebird`).

1.2.5 Output Guarantees: Approximation and Randomization

Necessarily, any summary must lose fidelity in its description of the data. In many cases, we cannot expect a summary to answer every QUERY with perfect accuracy (unless the summary only supports a few fixed simple queries like sum and variance as just discussed). If this were the case, it may be possible to carefully choose a battery of queries so that we would be able to recover almost every detail of the original input. This intuition can be formalized to prove strong lower bounds on the size of any summary that hopes to provide such strong guarantees. More detail on reasoning about the size of a summary to answer certain queries is given in Section 10.

Therefore, in order to provide a summary that is more compact than the original data, we must tolerate some loss of accuracy. There are two natural ways that this is formalized: approximation and randomization. Most summaries we describe will include one or both of these.

Approximation. Often the answer to a QUERY is numerical. Rather than the exact answer, it is often sufficient to provide some approximation of the answer. A *relative error approximation* gives an answer that is guaranteed to be within a fixed fraction of the true answer. For example, a 2-approximation is guaranteed to be at most twice the true answer. An *additive approximation* provides an answer that is guaranteed to be within some fixed amount of the true answer (this amount may depend on other properties of the input, such as the total size of the input). For example, a summary might guarantee to approximate the fraction of N input items satisfying a particular condition, up to additive error $0.01 \cdot N$.

Often, the quality of the approximation is a tunable parameter, which affects the size of the summary, and the time to perform operations on it. In this case, we may express the quality of approximation in terms of a parameter ε.

This may lead to a $(1 + \varepsilon)$ relative error approximation, or an ε additive error, where the size of the summary is then expressed as a function of ε.

Randomization. There are many cases where guaranteeing a correct answer requires a very large summary, but allowing a small probability of error means that we create a much smaller summary. This typically works by making some random choices during the operation of the summary, and providing some probabilistic analysis to show that the summary provides a correct answer sufficiently often. Typically, the quality of a randomized summary is expressed in terms of a parameter δ, with the understanding that the probability of the summary failing to provide a correct answer is δ. The space used by the summary, and the time to perform operations upon it, is then expressed in terms of δ.

For most summaries, it is possible to set δ to be very small, without significantly increasing the size of the summary. Then this guarantee holds except with a vanishingly small probability, say 10^{-20}, comparable to the probability that there is a CPU error sometime during the processing of the data. Note that the probability analysis will depend only on the random choices made by the algorithm – there are no assumptions that the input data are "random" in any way.

Approximation and Randomization. In many cases, the summaries described adopt both randomization *and* approximation, based on parameters ε and δ. The interpretation of this guarantee is that "the summary provides a $(1 + \varepsilon)$ approximation, with probability at least $1 - \delta$." With probability δ, this approximation guarantee does not hold.

1.3 Summaries in Applications

In this section, we outline a few examples of data processing, and describe how summaries with certain properties might be able to help overcome the resource challenges. We refer to various different types of summaries that are discussed in detail in later chapters.

1.3.1 Data Center Monitoring

Consider a large data center, supporting millions of users who cause the execution of billions of processes. Each process consumes a variety of resources: CPU, bandwidth, memory, disk usage, etc. These processes are distributed over tens of thousands of machines, where each machine has many processors, and each processor has multiple cores. Each process may be placed over multiple cores throughout the center. The data center operators would like to build a 'dashboard' application that provides information on the overall behavior of the center. It should provide information on the processes that are consuming a large fraction of resources.

To exactly track the amount of resources used is itself a potentially costly operation. The total amount of information involved is nontrivial: for each thread on each core, we will keep at least tens of bytes, enough to identify the process and to record its resource consumption in multiple dimensions. Multiplied by billions of processes, this is tens to hundreds of gigabytes of state information. Storing this amount of information is no great challenge. However, communicating this level of data potentially incurs an overhead. Suppose we wish to gather statistics every second. Then a simplistic approach could communicate a hundred gigabytes of data a second to a monitoring node. This requires substantial network bandwidth to support: approaching a terabit, if this dataset is to pass over a single link. This speed even taxes memory access times, which can comfortably cope with up to only ten gigabytes per second. Thus, implementing the simple exact tracking solution will require some amount of effort to parallelize and distribute the monitoring.

An alternative is to adopt a lightweight approximate approach. Here, we allow a little imprecision in the results in order to reduce the amount of information needed to be shipped around. This imprecision can easily be made comparable to the measurement error in tracking the results. For example, we can adopt a summary such as the Count-Min Sketch or the SpaceSaving structure to track resource usage accurate up to 0.01%. The summary can be bounded in size to around 100KB. We can build a summary of the activity on a single machine, and ship it up to an intermediate node in the network. This node can collect summaries from a large number of machines, and MERGE these together to obtain a single summary that combines the results from all the inputs. These merged summaries can be passed on to the monitor, which can further MERGE all received summaries to obtain a single 100KB summary of the whole network. From this compact summary, the processes with high resource usage can be easily extracted.

The communication costs of this approach are much reduced: if we have 10,000 machines in the data center, with 100 intermediate nodes, the maximum bandwidth required is just 10MB/s: each node receives 100 summaries of 100KB each, and combines these to a single summary; the monitor receives these 100 summaries. Other cost regimes can be achieved by organizing the data transfer in others ways, or adjusting other parameters of the data collection. The cost reductions are achieved due to the use of summaries, which prune away insignificant information, and because we are able to perform *in-network aggregation*: rather than wait to the end to reduce the information, we can use the MERGE property of summaries to combine them at intermediate stages.

Another advantage of using summaries in this setting is that it is easy to reason about their properties, and accuracy: we have the assurance that the size of the summary remains fixed no matter how many MERGE operations we perform, and that the accuracy guarantees remain correspondingly fixed. While it would be possible to design implementations that apply pruning to the collection of exact counts, it would require some effort and analysis to understand the tradeoffs between amount of pruning and the resulting accuracy. By adopting summary techniques, this trade-off is already well understood.

1.3.2 Network Scanning Detection

Consider the operator of a large data network, over which a large amount of Internet traffic passes. Within this network, it is important to identify unusual or suspicious behavior, as this can be indicative of an attack or the spread of unwanted software (viruses, worms, etc.). There has been much study of the signals that can be mined in the networking context to identify such activity. Here, we focus on a relatively simple case, of detecting port scan activity.

A port scan is when a single host tries to connect to a large number of different machines on different ports, in the hope of finding an open port, which can potentially be used to attack the machine. Although such scans may represent a large number of distinct connections, in terms of the total bandwidth or number of packets, they can represent a very small fraction, and so can be easily lost among the overall traffic. Simple techniques, such as sampling, may be unable to detect the presence of port scan activity. Keeping logs of the whole traffic for off-line analysis is rarely practical: the information is huge, and arrives at a very high rate (terabytes per hour).

A first approach is to track for each active host on the network the number of distinct (IP address, port) combinations that it tries to connect to. When this becomes large, it is indicative that the host is performing a port scan. One way to do this is to make use of the BloomFilter data structure. We can keep one BloomFilter for each host, along with a counter initialized to zero. This allows us to compactly store the set of (IP address, port) combinations that the host has connected to. For every connection that is seen, we can test whether it is already stored in the set: if not, then we add it to the set, and increase the counter. If we want to detect accurately when a host has made more than 1,000 distinct connections, say, then a BloomFilter of size approximately 1KB will suffice. For cases where we see a moderate number of distinct hosts – say, a few million – then this approach will suffice, consuming only a few gigabytes of fast memory in total.

However, in cases where we have more limited resources to devote to the monitoring process, and where there are a greater number of hosts active in the network, a more compact solution may be required. A more advanced approach is to combine types of summaries to obtain accurate identification of port scan activity. We would like to adopt a summary such as Count-Min Sketch or SpaceSaving, as in the previous example. However, these are good at identifying those items that have large absolute weights associated with them: this would find those hosts that use a large amount of bandwidth, which is distinct from port scanning. Rather, we would like these summaries to allow us to find those hosts that have a large number of distinct connections. This can be accomplished by modifying the summaries: replacing the counters in the summaries with distinct counters.

Understanding the impact of combining two summaries is somewhat complex. However, this approach has been applied successfully in a number of cases [228, 161, 77], allowing efficient identification of all hosts that are responsible for more than a given fraction of distinct connections with a summary totaling only megabytes in size. Further discussion is given in Section 9.4.3.

1.3.3 Service Quality Management

Consider an organization that hosts a large number of services for many different customers. Each customer has a set of service level agreements (SLAs) that determine the level of service they are guaranteed by contract. The hosting organization needs to monitor the behavior of all services, to ensure that all the SLAs are met. Such agreements are typically of the form "95% of responses are made within 100ms." The organization would therefore like to track the adherence to these SLAs across its different customers. While exact tracking may be required in some cases, it is also helpful to allow lightweight approximate tracking to identify when there is a danger of not meeting these agreements, and to respond accordingly by adjusting parameters or deploying more resources.

For SLAs of this form, we need to be able to track the quantiles of the monitored quantity. That is, for the previous example, given the series of response times, we need to identify what is the 95th percentile of this series, and how it compares to 100ms. We can maintain a list of all response times in sorted order, and periodically probe this list to check this quantile. However, this requires a lot of storage, and can be slow to update as the list grows.

Instead, we can make use of summaries which support quantile queries. Example summaries include the GK and Q-Digest summaries. These have differing properties. Q-Digest works when the number of possible values is bounded. So, if we have response times measured to microsecond accuracy, then it is suitable to use Q-Digest. On the other hand, if we have a very large range of possible values, GK can be used. The space of Q-Digest remains bounded, no matter how many items are summarized by the summary, or how many times we perform MERGE operations to combine different summaries. Meanwhile, the GK summary may grow (logarithmically) with the size of its input in the worst case.

In other situations, we might have additional requirements for the monitoring. For example, we might want to track not just the full history of response times, but rather a moving window of response times: what is the 95th percentile of the responses in the last hour. A crude approach is to start a fresh summary periodically – say, every five minutes – and to maintain multiple summaries in parallel. This imposes a greater overhead on the monitoring process. A more refined approach is to partition time into buckets – say, five minute intervals – and track a summary for each bucket separately. Then we can MERGE the summaries for multiple such buckets to get the summary for a recent window. However, this still only approximates the desired window size. More complex solutions can be used to generate a summary for any window size that gives a stronger guarantee of accuracy – see Section 9.2.2.

1.3.4 Query Optimization

In database management systems, datasets are organized into relations, where each relation has a number of fields. Queries perform operations on relations, such as selecting records with particular field values, joining relations based on matching values, and applying aggregates such as count and sum. For most nontrivial queries, there are multiple ways to perform a query, and the system wants to pick the one with the lowest (estimated) cost. Here, the "cost" of a query execution plan may be the time taken to perform it, the amount of disk access, or other measure.

Summary techniques have been adopted by many different database systems to allow approximation of the cost of different plans, and hence the selection of one that is believed to be cheap. Most commonly, basic summaries, such as a count and sum of numeric values, are maintained. For low cardinality attributes (ones taking on a small number of different values), it is natural to keep a count of the frequency of each value. For attributes with more possible values, a RandomSample of items is kept for each field in a relation, to allow simple statistics to be estimated. A common basic question is to estimate the *selectivity* of a particular predicate – that is, to estimate how many records in a relation satisfy a particular property, such as being equal to a particular constant, being less than some value, or falling in some range. A RandomSample is a natural way to accurately estimate these values; more sophisticated schemes take account of weights associated with items, such as WeightedRandomSample.

More recently, database systems have adopted more complex summary methods. To summarize numeric attributes, a histogram describing how it is distributed can be useful, and the most common type of histogram is an *equi-depth histogram*, where the bucket boundaries are quantiles of the item distribution. Some systems may simply recompute the quantiles of the field periodically (either exactly, or by making a summary of the current values); others may maintain a summary as records are added and deleted to the relation. Other statistics on the values in the relation, such as the number of distinct values, and estimations of the join size between two relations, may be maintained using appropriate summaries.

1.3.5 Ad Impression Monitoring and Audience Analysis

Online advertising has made it possible for advertisers to obtain more detailed information about who has seen their adverts, in comparison to traditional broadcast media. Each day, billions of adverts are shown to users of the web and apps by ad publishers, and tracking these "impressions" presents a substantial data management challenge. The same ad may be shown to the same user multiple times, but that should only be counted once (or the count capped). Advertisers also want to know which demographic have seen their ad – females aged 18–35 working in white collar jobs with a university level education, say. Current advertising networks have reasonably accurate profiles of web users based on information gathered and inferred about them. But allowing questions about different ads and different demographics in real time stretches the ability of large-scale data management systems.

There has been considerable success in using summaries to answer these kind of queries. This is a situation where an approximate answer is acceptable – advertisers want to know with reasonable precision how many have seen their advert, but the numbers are large enough that error of 1% or so can be tolerated. For the basic question of tracking the number of different people who have seen an advert, methods such as the KMV and HLL summaries answer this directly and effectively, at the cost of a few kilobytes per advert. Very small space for this tracking is important when millions of ads may be in rotation from a single publisher.

A simple way to deal with queries that ask for different subpopulations is to keep a summary for each combination of possible demographic group and ad. This quickly becomes unscalable as the number of demographic groups grows exponentially with the number of features stored on each user. The question to be answered is, for each ad, to look at the different demographics of viewers (male/female, age group, education level and so on) and to find the cardinality of the intersection of the desired sets – the female, 18 to 35 year old, university-educated viewers of the previous example. It turns out that it is possible to estimate the size of these intersections from the aforementioned KMV and HLL summaries. That is, given a summary for the number of distinct female viewers and another for the number of distinct university-educated viewers, we can combine these to obtain an estimate for the number of female, university-educated viewers. The accuracy of these intersection estimates can degrade quickly, particularly when the size of the intersection is small compared to the total number of distinct views of the ad. Nevertheless, the results can be effective, and have formed the technical underpinning of a number of businesses formed around this question. The benefits are that arbitrary questions can be answered almost instantaneously from combining a number of small summaries. This is dramatically faster than any database system that has to rescan the raw view data, even if indexes are available and preprocessing is done on the data.

1.4 Computational and Mathematical Tools

Throughout, we assume familiarity with basic computational and mathematical tools, such as the big-Oh ($O(\cdot)$) notation to express the asymptotic growth behavior of time and space bounds. We also assume familiarity with standard data structures, such as heaps, queues, and lists. The description of properties of summaries makes use of standard probabilistic analysis and tail bounds. For convenience, we list the forms of the tail bounds that we make use of (for more details, see the standard randomized algorithms texts such as [191, 185]).

Fact 1.1 (Markov inequality) *Given a nonnegative random variable X with expectation $\mathsf{E}[X]$, we have*

$$\Pr[X > k\mathsf{E}[X]] \leq \frac{1}{k}$$

Further Discussion. Throughout this book, we avoid requiring proofs to be read in order to understand the ideas introduced. For those wanting to understand more details, we provide optional material, marked out from the rest of the text. We begin this optional material with a simple proof of the Markov inequality.

The Markov inequality can be proved using some basic rules of probability. Consider the event that $X > c$ for some constant $c > 0$. For any value of x, we have $cI(x \geq c) < x$, where $I(b)$ is 1 if b evaluates to true, and 0 otherwise. This can be checked by considering the two cases $x \geq c$ and $x < c$. We can apply this to the variable X to get $cI(X \geq c) < X$, and take the expectation of both sides:

$$cE[I(X \geq c)] = c\Pr[X \geq c] < E[X].$$

Rearranging, and substituting $c = kE[X]$, we obtain the inequality in the quoted form.

The variance of X is

$$\text{Var}[X] = E[(X - E[X])^2] = E[X^2] - (E[X])^2,$$

while the covariance of two random variables X and Y is

$$\text{Cov}[X, Y] = E[XY] - E[X]E[Y].$$

The variance satisfies several properties that we make use of:

Fact 1.2 (Properties of variance) *Given a random variable X and constants a, b, we have*

$$\text{Var}[aX + b] = a^2\text{Var}[X].$$

Given n random variables X_i, we have

$$\text{Var}\left[\sum_{i=1}^{n} X_i\right] = \sum_{i=1}^{n} \text{Var}[X_i] + \sum_{1 \leq i < j \leq n} \text{Cov}[X_i, X_j]$$

When the n random variables X_i are uncorrelated *(have zero covariance), we have*

$$\text{Var}\left[\sum_{i=1}^{n} X_i\right] = \sum_{i=1}^{n} \text{Var}[X_i]$$

Applying the Markov inequality to the variance of X, we obtain the Chebyshev inequality:

Fact 1.3 (Chebyshev inequality) *Given any random variable X, we have*

$$\Pr[|X - \mathsf{E}[X]| > k] \le \frac{\mathsf{Var}[X]}{k^2}$$

Chernoff bounds arise from applying the Markov inequality to exponential functions of variables. We use two forms of Chernoff bounds, the (additive) Chernoff–Hoeffding bound, and the relative Chernoff bound.

Fact 1.4 (Additive Chernoff–Hoeffding bound) *Given n independent random variables $X_1 \ldots X_n$ such that there are bounds $a_i \le X_i \le b_i$ for each X_i, we write $X = \sum_{i=1}^{n} X_i$. Then*

$$\Pr[|X - \mathsf{E}[X]| > k] \le 2 \exp\left(\frac{-2k^2}{\sum_{i=1}^{n}(b_i - a_i)^2}\right).$$

A Bernoulli random variable X with a single parameter p is such that $\Pr[X = 1] = p$, $\Pr[X = 0] = (1 - p)$. Hence, $\mathsf{E}[X] = p$.

Fact 1.5 (Multiplicative Chernoff bound) *Given independent Bernoulli random variables $X_1 \ldots X_n$, such that $X = \sum_{i=1}^{n} X_i$ and $\mathsf{E}[X] = \sum_{i=1}^{n} \mathsf{E}[X_i] = \mu$, then, for $0 < \beta \le 1$, and $0 \le \rho \le 4$,*

$$\Pr[X \le (1 - \beta)\mu] \le \exp\left(\frac{-\beta^2 \mu}{2}\right)$$

$$\Pr[X \ge (1 + \rho)\mu] \le \exp\left(\frac{-\rho^2 \mu}{4}\right).$$

Further Discussion. We do not provide detailed proofs of all Chernoff bounds, but for a flavor, we describe one case to show how the proof builds on basic ideas such as the previously stated Markov inequality. Let $\Pr[X_i = 1] = p_i$ so that $\mathsf{E}[X] = \sum_{i=1}^{n} p_i = \mu$. We seek to bound $\Pr[X > (1 + \rho)\mu]$. We introduce a (positive) parameter t, and apply an exponential function to both sides of the inequality. This does not change the probability, so

$$\Pr[X > (1 + \rho)\mu] = \Pr[\exp(tX) > \exp(t(1 + \rho)\mu)].$$

By the Markov inequality, we have

$$\Pr[\exp(tX) > \exp(t(1 + \rho)\mu)] \le \mathsf{E}[\exp(tX)] / \exp(t(1 + \rho)\mu). \quad (1.1)$$

The rest of the proof aims to simplify the form of this expression. Observe that, from the definition of X and by the independence of the X_is,

$$E[\exp(tX)] = E\left[\exp\left(t\sum_{i=1}^{n} X_i\right)\right] = \prod_{i=1}^{n} E[\exp(tX_i)].$$

The expectation of $\exp(tX_i)$ is a summation of two cases: X_i is zero with probability $1 - p_i$, giving a contribution of $\exp(0) = 1$; or X_i is one with probability p_i, giving a contribution of $\exp(t)$. Thus,

$$\prod_{i=1}^{n} E[\exp(tX_i)] = \prod_{i=1}^{n} ((1 - p_i) + p_i e^t).$$

Using the usual expansion of the exponential function and the fact that $t > 0$,

$$\exp(p_i(e^t - 1)) = 1 + (p_i(e^t - 1)) + \ldots > 1 - p_i + p_i e^t$$

so we can write

$$\prod_{i=1}^{n}(1 - p_i + p_i e^t) \le \prod_{i=1}^{n} \exp(p_i(e^t - 1)) = \exp\left(\sum_{i=1}^{n} p_i(e^t - 1)\right)$$
$$= \exp(\mu(e^t - 1)).$$

Substituting this back into (1.1), we obtain

$$Pr[X > (1 + \rho)\mu] \le \exp(\mu(e^t - 1) - \mu t(1 + \rho))$$
$$\le \exp(\mu(-\rho t + t^2/2 + t^3/6 + \ldots)).$$

At this point, we can choose the value of t to give the final form of the bound. In this case, we can pick $t = \frac{2}{5}\rho$. One can verify that for this choice of t in the range $0 \le \rho < 4$, we have $\exp(\mu(-\rho t + t^2/2 + t^3/6 + \ldots)) < \exp(\rho^2 \mu/4)$.

Last, we sometimes make use of a simple bound, which allows us to reason about the probability of any one of multiple events.

Fact 1.6 (Union bound)

$$Pr[A \cup B] \le Pr[A] + Pr[B].$$

Note that we do not require the events A and B to be independent. This fact follows immediately from the fact that $Pr[A \cup B] = Pr[A] + Pr[B] - Pr[A \cap B]$. We often use this fact to argue about the probability of success of an algorithm that relies on many events being true. That is, if there are n "bad events", $B_1 \ldots B_n$, but each one is very unlikely, we can argue that the probability of *any* bad event happening is at most $Pr[\cup_{i=1}^{n} B_i] \le \sum_{i=1}^{n} Pr[B_i]$, by repeated application of Fact 1.6. If each $\Pr[B_i]$ is sufficiently small – say, $\Pr[B_i] = 1/n^2$ – then the probability of any of them happening is still very small, in this case, at most $\sum_{i=1}^{n} 1/n^2 = 1/n$.

Another idea often used in arguing for the correctness of a randomized algorithm is the *principle of deferred decisions*. A simple application of this principle, as used in Section 2.2, is to sample an item uniformly at random from two sets S_1 and S_2, of sizes n_1 and n_2, respectively. The direct way of doing so is to simply sample an item from all the $n_1 + n_2$ items uniformly at random. However, we could also do it in two steps: we first decide which one of the two sets to choose the sample from: S_1 should be picked with probability $\frac{n_1}{n_1+n_2}$ while S_2 should be picked with probability $\frac{n_2}{n_1+n_2}$. In the second step, which the algorithm may choose to do at a later time, is to pick an item from the chosen set uniformly at random. The correctness of this principle follows easily from the fact that, for any two events A and B,

$$\Pr[A \cap B] = \Pr[A]\Pr[B \mid A].$$

1.4.1 A Chernoff Bounds Argument

A standard application of the Chernoff bound is to take multiple estimates of a quantity, and combine them to pick an estimate that is good with high probability. Specifically, we have estimates, each of which is a "good" estimate of a desired quantity with at least a constant probability. However, it's not possible to tell whether or not an estimate is good just by looking at it. The goal is to combine all these to make an estimate that is "good" with high probability. The approach is to take the *median* of enough estimates to reduce the error. Although it is not possible to determine which estimates are good or bad, sorting the estimates by value will place all the "good" estimates together in the middle of the sorted order, with "bad" estimates above and below (too low or too high). Then the only way that the median estimate can be bad is if more than half of the estimates are bad, which is unlikely. In fact, the probability of returning a bad estimate is now exponentially small in the number of estimates.

The proof makes use of the Chernoff bound from Fact 1.5. Assume that each estimate is good with probability at least $7/8$. The outcome of each estimate is an independent random event, so in expectation only $1/8$ of the estimates are bad. Thus the final result is only bad if the number of bad events exceeds its expectation by a factor of 4. Set the number of estimates to be $4\ln(1/\delta)$ for some desired small probability δ. Since whether each estimate is "good" or "bad" can be modeled by a Bernoulli random variable with expectation $1/8$, then this setting is modeled with $\rho = 3$ and $\mathsf{E}[X] = 1/2\ln(1/\delta)$. Hence,

$$\Pr[X \geq 2\log(1/\delta)] \leq \exp(-9/8\ln(1/\delta)) < \delta.$$

This implies that taking the median of $O(\log(1/\delta))$ estimates reduces the probability of finding a bad final estimate to less than δ.

1.4.2 Hash Functions

Many summaries make use of *hash functions*, which are functions picked at random from a family $\mathcal{F}$ containing many possible hash functions, where each maps onto some range R. In order to provide the guarantees on the summary, we typically require that the family of functions satisfies some properties. The most common property is that the family is t-wise independent. This means that (over the random choice of the hash function), the probability of seeing any t values appears uniform: given any t distinct items $x_1, \ldots x_t$, and any t values in the output of the function $y_1, \ldots y_t \in R^t$, we have

$$\Pr_{f \in \mathcal{F}} [f(x_1) = y_1, f(x_2) = y_2, f(x_t) = y_t] = \frac{1}{|R|^t}.$$

A simple family of functions that meets this requirement[1] is the family of polynomials,

$$\mathcal{F} = \left\{ \sum_{i=1}^{t} c_i x^{i-1} \mod p \mod |R| \right\},$$

where p is a (fixed) prime number and c_i range over all (nonzero) values modulo p. Thus, to draw a function from this family, we simply pick the t coefficients c_1 to c_t uniformly from the range $1 \ldots p - 1$. Further discussion and code for efficient implementations of these functions is given by Thorup and Zhang [219, 221].

The reason for this analysis of the degree of independence of hash functions is to quantify the "strength" of the functions that is required. In many cases, it is shown that summaries require only two-wise (pairwise) or four-wise independent hash functions. In other cases, the analysis makes the assumption that the hash functions are "fully independent" for convenience of analysis, even though this assumption is technically unrealistic: hash functions that guarantee to act independently over very many items require a lot of space to represent. In practice, functions without this strict guarantee are used, without any reported problem.

---

[1] Strictly speaking, the actual probability for this family can be very slightly larger than $\frac{1}{|R|^t}$, but this does not affect the analysis or practical use in any significant way.

Where fully independent hash functions are needed, some widely adopted hash function (without full independence) is typically used. *Cryptographic* hash functions are ones that are designed to provide hash values that are very difficulty to invert: given the hash value, it should be impossible to find what input it was applied to, short of trying all possibilities. Well-known examples include MD5, SHA-1, and SHA-3. However, such functions tend to be much slower than pairwise independent hash functions, as they apply multiple rounds of expensive operations to their inputs in order to mask the contents. This can be a bottleneck in high-performance systems. Instead, *noncryptographic* hash functions may be most suitable. These do not aim to provide the level of noninvertibility of the cryptographic counterparts; rather, they seek to ensure that the output appears random given the input. They are constructed based on combining parts of their input through fast operations (such as exclusive-or and bit shifts) with carefully chosen constants. A popular example is the *murmurhash* function,[2] which can be implemented using a small number of fast low-level bit-manipulation operations, and has been found to be very effective for applications such as those discussed here.

As a rough guide, the simplest pairwise independent hash functions are the fastest, and can be evaluated many hundreds of millions of times per second on a single processor core. Four-wise independence is about half the speed of pairwise. Murmurhash is of comparable speed, while SHA-1 and MD5 are about four times slower. Some example numbers from experiments on a commodity CPU indicate that pairwise hash functions can easily process in excess of 500 million 32-bit keys in one second, while four-wise hash functions can manage 250 million, murmurhash 200 million, and SHA-1/MD5 around 50 million. This indicates that cryptographic hash functions can be 10 times slower than simple pairwise hashing.

1.5 Organization of the Book

This book is primarily intended as an introduction and reference for both researchers and practitioners whenever the need for some kind of data summarization arises. It is broken into two main parts. The first part of the book introduces the principle examples of the algorithms and data structures that form the summaries of interest. For each summary described in detail in the main text, we provide description under several standard headings. We first provide a **Brief Summary** of the summary to describe its general properties

---

[2] https://github.com/aappleby/smhasher.

and operation. The bulk of the description is often in describing the details of the **Operations on the Summary** (such as INITIALIZE, UPDATE, and QUERY). These are illustrated with an **Example** and described in pseudocode where appropriate, to give a more formal outline of the key operations. Sometimes **Implementation Issues** and **Available Implementations** are also discussed. More detailed analysis, including technical explanations of summary properties, is given under **Further Discussion**, with the intention that the reader can achieve a basic understanding and be able to use the summary without reading this part. Finally, some **History and Background** are outlined with links to further reading and alternative approaches.

The second part of the book looks at more complex summary techniques for specific kinds of data (such as geometric, graph, or matrix data) that combine or build upon the fundamental summaries. It also describes how to modify summary techniques to accommodate weights and time decay. Here, we relax the constraints on the presentation, and provide more general high-level descriptions of the summaries and their applications. We also discuss lower bounds, which provide limitations on what it is possible to summarize within a certain amount of memory space.

PART I

Fundamental Summary Techniques

2
Summaries for Sets

This chapter studies some fundamental and commonly used summaries for sets. The input consists of items drawn from a universe U, which define the set A to be summarized. By definition, a set does not contain duplicated items, but the input to the summary may or may not contain duplicates. Some summaries are able to remove duplicates automatically, while others treat each item in the input as distinct from all others. This will be pointed out explicitly when each summary is described.

The summaries described in this chapter address the following tasks:

- Approximately large quantities with few bits: the MorrisCounter (Section 2.1)
- Maintaining a random sample of unweighted items: the RandomSample (Section 2.2)
- Maintaining random samples where items in the set also have (fixed) weights: the WeightedRandomSample and PrioritySample summaries (Sections 2.3 and 2.4)
- Estimating the number of distinct items in a collection: the KMV and HLL summaries (Sections 2.5 and 2.6).
- Approximately representing the members of a set in a compact format: the BloomFilter (Section 2.7)

2.1 Morris Approximate Counter

Brief Summary. The very first question one could ask about a set is its cardinality. When no duplicates are present in the input, counting the items in the set A can be trivially done with a counter of $\log |A|$ bits. The MorrisCounter summary provides an approximate counter using even fewer bits. Instead of increasing the counter for every item, a random process determines when to increase the counter, as a function of the current state of the counter.

Note that the MorrisCounter cannot deal with duplicates in the input; please use the summaries described in Sections 2.5 and 2.6 if this is the case.

Algorithm 2.1: MorrisCounter: UPDATE ()

---

1 Pick y uniform over $[0,1]$;
2 **if** $y < b^{-c}$ **then** $c \leftarrow c+1$;

Algorithm 2.2: MorrisCounter: QUERY ()

---

1 **return** $(b^c - 1)/(b - 1)$;

Operations on the Summary. The MorrisCounter summary is simply a counter c, with a parameter $1 < b \leq 2$, that can be thought of as the (number) base over which the counter operates. The INITIALIZE (b) operation sets the counter to 0 and locks in the value of b. The UPDATE operation updates the counter when a new item is added to A. Specifically, UPDATE increases c by 1 with probability b^{-c}, and leaves it unchanged otherwise. Informally, we expect b items for this counter to go from 1 to 2, then a further b^2 to reach 3, b^3 more to reach 4, and so on in a geometric progression. This justifies the fact that the QUERY operation shown in Algorithm 2.2 provides an estimated count as $\frac{b^c-1}{b-1}$.

The analysis of this summary indicates that setting $b = 1 + 2\varepsilon^2\delta$ is sufficient to provide ε-relative accuracy of counts with probability at least $1 - \delta$. When $|A| = n$, this suggests that the counter c should go up to $\log((b-1)n)/\log b = O\left(\frac{1}{\varepsilon^2\delta} \log \varepsilon^2\delta n\right)$, and therefore requires $O(\log 1/\varepsilon + \log 1/\delta + \log\log \varepsilon^2\delta n)$ bits. This can be much more compact than the $\lceil \log n + 1 \rceil$ bits required to keep an exact count of up to n items when n is very large indeed.

Algorithm 2.3: MorrisCounter: MERGE (c_a, c_b)

---

1 $\alpha = \min(c_a, c_b), \beta = \max(c_a, c_b)$;
2 **for** $j \leftarrow 0$ **to** $\alpha - 1$ **do**
3   Pick y uniform over $[0,1]$;
4   **if** $y < b^{j-\beta}$ **then** $\beta \leftarrow \beta + 1$;
5 **return** β;

To MERGE together two MorrisCounter summaries that used the same base b, we can pick the larger of the two counters as the primary, and use the smaller to determine whether to further increase it. Let β denote the current count of the larger counter, and α denote the smaller counter. We perform α tests to determine whether to increment β. We increment β with probability

$b^{i-\beta}$ for i from 0 to $\alpha - 1$. This corresponds to stepping through the α items that prompted increments in the smaller counter. Algorithm 2.3 details the MERGE algorithm, incrementing the larger counter based on the appropriate conditional probabilities implied by the smaller counter.

Example. We set $b = 2$, and consider a stream of nine items. The following table shows a sample state of the counter after each of these.

Timestep	1	2	3	4	5	6	7	8	9
c	1	1	1	2	2	3	3	3	3

After nine items, the counter records 3, which corresponds to an estimate of 7.

Given two MorrisCounter summaries using base 2 that both contain 3, we MERGE by starting with a counter of 3. We first increment this with probability $2^{0-3} = 1/8$; say this test does not pass. Then we increment with probability $2^{1-3} = 1/4$. Suppose in this example, the test passes, so we now have a counter of 4. Finally, we increment with probability $2^{2-4} = 1/4$ (note, we use the current value of the counter). In our example, this test does not pass, so we conclude with a merged counter with count of 4, representing an estimate of 15.

Implementation Issues. To draw a random value with probability b^{-c}, it is convenient to choose b based on a power of two, such as $b = 1 + 1/(2^{\ell} - 1)$ for some integer ℓ. The test with probability $1/b$ passes with probability $(2^{\ell} - 1)/2^{\ell}$, which can be done by generating ℓ uniform random bits — for example, if not all of the bits are zero. The test with probability b^{-c} passes if c instances of the previous test pass. This requires a lot of randomness, and so can be approximated using a single floating-point random value tested against b^{-c}.

Further Discussion. The analysis of the expectation of the estimate $\frac{b^c-1}{b-1}$ under a sequence of UPDATE operations essentially shows that at each step, the expected change in the estimated count is one. Formally, let X_n denote the output of the counter after n UPDATE operations, and let C_n denote the value of the stored count c. Then, inductively,

$$E[X_n] = \sum_c \Pr[C_n = c]\frac{b^c - 1}{b - 1}$$

$$= \sum_c \left(\Pr[C_{n-1} = c - 1]b^{-c} + \Pr[C_{n-1} = c](1 - b^{-c})\right)\frac{b^c - 1}{b - 1}$$

$$= \sum_c \Pr[C_{n-1} = c] \left(b^{-c} \frac{b^{c+1} - 1}{b - 1} + (1 - b^{-c}) \frac{b^c - 1}{b - 1} \right)$$

$$\text{(regrouping the terms)}$$

$$= \sum_c \Pr[C_{n-1} = c] \frac{b^c - 1}{b - 1} + 1$$

$$= \mathsf{E}[X_{n-1}] + 1.$$

Therefore, since $X_0 = 0$, we have that $\mathsf{E}[X_n] = n$. For the variance, we first define $Y_n = X_n + \frac{1}{b-1}$ and compute

$$\mathsf{E}[Y_n^2] = \sum_c \Pr[C_n = c] \left(\frac{b^c}{b - 1} \right)^2$$

$$= \sum_c \Pr[C_{n-1} = c] \left(b^{-c} \left(\frac{b^{c+1}}{b - 1} \right)^2 + (1 - b^{-c}) \left(\frac{b^c}{b - 1} \right)^2 \right)$$

$$= \sum_c \Pr[C_{n-1} = c] \left(\left(\frac{b^c}{b - 1} \right)^2 + \frac{b^{-c}}{(b - 1)^2} \left((b^{c+1})^2 - (b^c)^2 \right) \right)$$

$$\text{(regrouping)}$$

$$= \mathsf{E}[Y_{n-1}^2] + \sum_c \Pr[C_{n-1} = c] \frac{b^{-c}}{(b - 1)^2} (b^{c+1} - b^c)(b^{c+1} + b^c)$$

$$= \mathsf{E}[Y_{n-1}^2] + (b + 1) \sum_c \Pr[C_{n-1} = c] \frac{b^c}{b - 1}$$

$$= \mathsf{E}[Y_{n-1}^2] + (b + 1)\mathsf{E}[Y_{n-1}]$$

$$= \mathsf{E}[Y_{n-1}^2] + (b + 1)(n - 1)$$

$$= \mathsf{E}[Y_0^2] + (b + 1) \sum_{i=0}^{n-1} i.$$

Thus, since $Y_0 = \frac{1}{b-1}$, we have

$$\mathsf{E}[X_n^2] = \mathsf{E}\left[\left(Y_n - \frac{1}{b - 1} \right)^2 \right] \leq \mathsf{E}[Y_n^2 - Y_0^2] = \frac{1}{2}(b + 1)n(n - 1),$$

and so

$$\mathsf{Var}[X_n] \leq \frac{1}{2}(b + 1)n^2 - n^2 = \frac{1}{2}(b - 1)n^2.$$

Via the Chebyshev inequality, we then have

$$\Pr[|X_n - n| \geq \varepsilon n] \leq \frac{1}{2}(b-1)n^2/\varepsilon^2 n^2 = \frac{b-1}{2\varepsilon^2}.$$

Therefore, if we choose $b \leq 1 + 2\varepsilon^2\delta$, we have the desired bound. Alternately, we can take $b \leq 1 + \varepsilon^2$ to have this hold with probability at most $1/2$. Then taking the median of $O(\log 1/\delta)$ estimates will reduce the error probability to δ, via the Chernoff bounds argument of Section 1.4.1.

To merge two MorrisCounter summaries, it is helpful to think of the random decision of whether to update the counter as being determined by a random variable Y that is uniform over the range $[0, 1]$. The test at a step with probability b^{-c} is passed when $Y < b^{-c}$, i.e., $\Pr[Y < b^{-c}] = b^{-c}$. Associate the ith update with such a random variable, Y_i. Then fix these choices over the series of updates, that is, imagine that there is a fixed y_i value associated with each update. Now imagine taking the sequence of updates associated with the second (smaller) counter, and applying them as updates to the first (larger) counter, with this now fixed set of y_i values. The result is an updated counter that reflects the full set of updates and has the correct distribution.

We now argue that there is enough information in the smaller counter that describes the set of y_i values observed to exactly simulate this process, without explicit access to them. First, consider those UPDATE events that did not change the value of the smaller counter. These must have been associated with y_i values greater than b^{-c}, where c is the value of the larger counter: since the smaller counter ended with a value at most c, these updates could not have had such a small y_i value, else they would have changed the counter. This leaves the UPDATE events that caused the smaller counter to increase from j to $j + 1$. Here, the corresponding Y value must have been less than b^{-j}. Beyond this, we have no information. Since the Y random variable is uniform, conditioned on the fact that $y_i < b^{-j}$, Y_i is uniform in the range $[0, b^{-j}]$. Therefore, the probability that Y_i is below b^{-c} is $b^{-c}/b^{-j} = b^{j-c}$. It is acceptable to make this randomized test at the time of the merge, by invoking the principle of deferred decisions.

History and Background. The notion of the approximate counter was first introduced by Morris in 1977 [189]. It is sometimes regarded as the first nontrivial streaming algorithm. A thorough analysis was presented by Flajolet in 1985 [104]. The analysis presented here follows that of Gronmeier and

Sauerhoff [125]. The generalization to addition of approximate counters does not appear to have been explicitly considered before. The summary is considered a basic tool in handling very large data volumes, and can be applied in any scenario where there are a large number of statistics to maintain, but some inaccuracy in each count can be tolerated – for example, in maintaining counts of many different combinations of events that will instantiate a machine learned model. An early application of the MorrisCounter was to count the frequencies of combinations of letters in large collections of text with few bits per counter. Such frequency counts can be used to give more effective data compression models, even with approximate counts. Some additional historical notes and applications are described by Lumbroso [175].

2.2 Random Sampling

Brief Summary. A random sample is a basic summary for a set that can be used for a variety of purposes. Formally, a RandomSample (without replacement) of size s of a set A is a subset of s items from A (assuming $|A| \geq s$, and treating all members of A as distinct) such that every subset of s items of A has the same probability of being chosen as the sample.

The random sampling algorithms described in this section cannot handle duplicates in the input, i.e., if the same item appears multiple times, they will be treated as distinct items, and they will all get the chance to be sampled. If the multiplicities should not matter, please see *distinct sampling* in Section 3.9.

Operations on the Summary. Let S be the random sample. In order to UPDATE and MERGE random samples, we also need to store n, the cardinality of the underlying set A, together with S. To INITIALIZE the summary with a set A of size s, we set $S = A$ and $n = s$. To UPDATE the summary with a new item x (which is not in A yet), we first increment n by 1. Then, with probability s/n, we choose an item currently in S uniformly at random and replace it by x; and with probability $1 - s/n$, we discard x. Algorithm 2.4 implements the UPDATE procedure by keeping the sampled items S in an array indexed from 1 to s. This way, the decision whether to add the new item and which existing

---

Algorithm 2.4: RandomSample: UPDATE (x)

1 $n \leftarrow n + 1$;
2 Pick i uniformly from $\{1, \ldots, n\}$;
3 **if** $i \leq s$ **then** $S[i] \leftarrow x$;

---

item to replace can be combined by generating one random number. This also ensures that items in S are randomly permuted (for this to be true, we need to have randomly permuted S in the INITIALIZE step, too).

Algorithm 2.5: RandomSample: MERGE $((S_1, n_1), (S_2, n_2))$

---

1   $k_1 \leftarrow 1, k_2 \leftarrow 1$;
2   **for** $i \leftarrow 1$ **to** s **do**
3   Pick j uniformly over $\{1, \ldots, n_1 + n_2\}$;
4   **if** $j \leq n_1$ **then**
5         $S[i] \leftarrow S_1[k_1]$;
6         $k_1 \leftarrow k_1 + 1$;
7         $n_1 \leftarrow n_1 - 1$;
8   **else**
9         $S[i] \leftarrow S_2[k_2]$;
10        $k_2 \leftarrow k_2 + 1$;
11        $n_2 \leftarrow n_2 - 1$;
12   **return** $(S, n_1 + n_2 + s)$;

Next we describe how to MERGE two random samples S_1 and S_2, drawn from two sets A_1 and A_2 of cardinality n_1 and n_2, respectively. We proceed in s rounds, outputting one sampled item in each round. In the ith round, with probability $n_1/(n_1 + n_2)$ we randomly pick an item x in S_1 to the new sample, then remove x from S_1 and decrement n_1 by 1; with probability $n_2/(n_1 + n_2)$, we randomly pick an item x from S_2 to output to the sample, then remove it from S_2 and decrement n_2. Algorithm 2.4 implements the MERGE procedure, assuming that the two samples are stored in uniformly random order. Then the MERGE simply builds the new sample by picking the next element from either S_1 or S_2 step by step.

Example. Suppose we are given a sequence of 10 items numbered from 1 to 10 in order. The random sample is initialized to contain the first three items after random permutation, say, [1, 3, 2]. Further suppose that the random numbers generated in line 2 of Algorithm 2.4 are 2, 5, 3, 3, 7, 9, 1. Then, the content of the array S will be as follows after each item has been processed by UPDATE.

After INITIALIZE: [1, 3, 2];
After item 4: [1, 4, 2];
After item 5: [1, 4, 2];
After item 6: [1, 4, 6];

After item 7: [1, 4, 7];
After item 8: [1, 4, 7];
After item 9: [1, 4, 7];
After item 10: [10, 4, 7];

Further Discussion. To see why UPDATE and MERGE draw a random sample, we relate random sampling to random shuffling, where an array A is randomly permuted in a way such that each permutation is equally likely. Then a random sample can be obtained by picking the first s items in the permutation.

One method for doing random shuffling is the *Fisher–Yates shuffle*. Given an array A (indexed from 1 to n), the procedure works as follows.

Algorithm 2.6: Fisher–Yates shuffle

---
1 **for** $i \leftarrow 1$ **to** n **do**
2 $\quad$ Pick j randomly from $\{1, \ldots, i\}$;
3 $\quad$ Exchange $A[i]$ and $A[j]$;

By an easy induction proof, we can show that every permutation is possible by the preceding procedure. On the other hand, the procedure generates exactly $n!$ different sequences of random numbers, each with probability $1/n!$, so every permutation must be equally likely. Now, we see that if we only keep the first s items of A, each iteration of the Fisher–Yates shuffle algorithm exactly becomes the UPDATE algorithm described earlier.

To see that MERGE is also correct, imagine a process that permutes all the items in A_1 and A_2 randomly and chooses the first s of them, which form a random sample of size s from $A_1 \cup A_2$. Using the principle of deferred decisions, the first item in the permutation has probability $n_1/(n_1+n_2)$ of being from A_1, and conditioned upon this, it is a randomly picked item from S_1. This is exactly how the MERGE algorithm picks the first sampled item for $A_1 \cup A_2$. Carrying out this argument iteratively proves the correctness of the algorithm.

The preceding algorithms maintain a random sample without replacement. If a random sample with replacement is desired, one can simply run s independent instances of the preceding algorithm, each maintaining a random sample of size 1 without replacement.

History and Background. The UPDATE algorithm is referred to as the *reservoir sampling* algorithm in the literature, first formalized by Knuth [160], who attributes it to Alan G. Waterman. The preceding shuffling algorithm was first described by Fisher and Yates in 1938, and later formalized by Durstenfeld [94]. The reservoir sampling algorithm has been frequently rediscovered (and used as an interview question for technical positions), but the proof being offered often only proves that the procedure samples each item with probability s/n. This is only a necessary condition for the sample to be a random sample. One can also use the definition of random sample, that is, every subset of s items is equally likely to be in the sample, but the correspondence to the Fisher–Yates shuffle yields the cleanest proof. Vitter [229] made a comprehensive study of the reservoir sampling algorithm. In particular, he considered the case where there is a constant-time "skip" operation that can be used to skip a given number of items in the input, and gave optimal reservoir sampling algorithms in this setting. The MERGE algorithm for merging two random samples appears to be folklore.

The applications of random sampling are so broad as to defy a concise summation. Suffice it to say many statistical applications take a random sample of data on which to evaluate a function of interest. Random samples are used with many computer systems to estimate the cost of different operations and choose which method will be most efficient. Many algorithms use random samples of the input to quickly compute an approximate solution to a problem in preference to the slower evaluation on the full data.

Available Implementations. A version of reservoir sampling is implemented in the DataSketches library, with discussion at `https://datasketches.github.io/docs/Sampling/ReservoirSampling.html`. Experiments on commodity hardware show that speeds of tens of millions of UPDATE operations per second are achievable. Performing a MERGE depends on the size of the sample, but takes less than 1ms for samples of size tens of thousands.

2.3 Weighted Random Sampling

Brief Summary. In many situations, each item $x \in A$ is associated with a positive weight $w_x > 0$. Naturally, when we maintain a random sample of size s over weighted items, we would like to include an item i in the sample with probability proportional to w_i. In this section, we describe a WeightedRandomSample that achieves this goal. More precisely, since a probability cannot be greater than 1, item x will be included in the sample with probability $p_x = \min\{1, w_x/\tau\}$, where τ is the unique value such that $\sum_{x \in A} p_x = s$. Note that the value of τ solely depends on the weights of the items. This is assuming $s \le n$, where n is the size of the underlying set A from which the sample is drawn. If $s > n$, we take all elements in A as the sample and set $\tau = 0$. We refer to τ as the *sampling threshold*, as all items with weight greater than τ are guaranteed to be in the sample. Note that when all weights are 1, we have $\tau = n/s$, so $p_x = 1/\tau = s/n$ for all x, and the WeightedRandomSample degenerates into a RandomSample.

Similar to a RandomSample, the WeightedRandomSample cannot handle duplicates in the input, i.e., each distinct item can be added to the WeightedRandomSample only once with a given weight, which can no longer be changed.

The most important QUERY on a WeightedRandomSample is to ask for the total weight of all items in some subset $Q \subseteq A$. If Q were given in advance, the problem would be trivial, as we can check if an item is in Q when the item is inserted to the summary. In many practical situations, Q is not known in advance. For example, in Internet traffic analysis, an item is an IP packet with various attributes such as source IP, source port, destination IP, destination port, etc., while the packet size is the weight. Very often, many analytical questions are ad hoc and will be asked after the data stream has passed. For example, a customer might be interested in the total traffic volume of a certain application that uses a specific source port and destination port. He or she might further narrow down the query to the traffic between two specific network domains. Such exploratory studies require a summary that supports estimating the total weight of an arbitrary subset.

Operations on the Summary. Let S be the random sample. In addition, for each item $x \in S$, we maintain an adjusted weight $\tilde{w}_x = w_x/p_x$. In fact, the original weight w_x and the sampling probability p_x need not be maintained; just maintaining $\tilde{w}_x$ would be sufficient. To INITIALIZE the summary with a set A of size s, we set $S = A$ and $\tilde{w}_x = w_x$ for all $x \in S$. We split S into a subset of *large* items $L = \{x \in S \mid \tilde{w}_x > \tau\}$ and the *small* items $T = S \setminus L$. Items in L are sorted by their adjusted weights. We will maintain the invariant that $\tilde{w}_x = \tau$ for all $x \in T$, so for items in T, there is no need to record their adjusted weights explicitly. Initially, the sampling threshold τ is 0, so $T = \emptyset$, $L = S = A$, and $\tilde{w}_x = w_x$ for all $x \in L$.

The procedure to UPDATE the sample with a new item y with weight w_y is described in Algorithm 2.7. The details are a little more involved than the unweighted case, since it has more cases to handle based on whether items have weight above or below τ. The basic idea is to take a WeightedRandom-Sample of size s out of the $s + 1$ items, which consist of the s items in the summary plus the new one to be inserted. In this process, for the new item, we use its original weight, while for items in the current sample, we use their adjusted weights. This ensures that items survive in the sample with the correct probabilities.

We will build a set X (implemented as an array) with items outside of T and L whose weights we know are smaller than the new threshold $\tau' > \tau$. To start, if w_y is less than the current threshold τ, we set $X \leftarrow \{y\}$; otherwise item y is considered large, and so we set $X \leftarrow \emptyset$ and insert y into L (lines 3 through 6). Then, we are going to move items from the current L to X until L contains only items with weights greater than the new threshold τ. For that purpose, we will maintain the sum W of adjusted weights in $X \cup T$. The sum of T is known as $\tau|T|$ (line 2), to which we add w_y if $w_y < \tau$ (line 6).

Algorithm 2.7: WeightedRandomSample: UPDATE (y)

1   $X \leftarrow \emptyset, \tilde{w}_y = w_y$;
2   $W \leftarrow \tau|T|$;
3   **if** $w_y > \tau$ **then** insert y into L;
4   **else**
5      $X \leftarrow \{y\}$;
6      $W \leftarrow W + \tilde{w}_y$;
7   **while** $L \neq \emptyset$ *and* $W \geq (s - |L|)(\min_{h \in L} \tilde{w}_h)$ **do**
8      $h \leftarrow \arg\min_{h \in L} \tilde{w}_h$;
9   move h from L to X;
10     $W \leftarrow W + \tilde{w}_h$;
11   $\tau \leftarrow W/(s - |L|)$;
12   generate r uniformly random from $[0, 1]$;
13   $i \leftarrow 1$;
14   **while** $i \leq |X|$ *and* $r \geq 0$ **do**
15     $r \leftarrow r - (1 - \tilde{w}_{X[i]}/\tau)$;
16     $i \leftarrow i + 1$;
17   **if** $r < 0$ **then** remove $X[i - 1]$ from X;
18   **else** remove an item from T chosen uniformly at random;
19   $T \leftarrow T \cup X$;

Then we remove items in L in the increasing order of their weights. Let the current smallest item in L be h. We move h from L to X if setting $\tau' = \tilde{w}_h$ is not enough to reduce the sample size to s, i.e.,

$$W/\tilde{w}_h + |L| \geq s, \tag{2.1}$$

which is the same as the condition checked in line 7. Whenever (2.1) is true, we move h from L to X while adding $\tilde{w}_h$ to W (lines 9 and 10). We repeat this step until L is empty or (2.1) is violated. Then we can compute the new threshold so that

$$W/\tau' + |L| = s,$$

i.e., $\tau' = W/(s - |L|)$ (line 11).

The remaining task is to find an item to delete so that each item remains in the sample with the right probability. More precisely, items in L must all remain in the sample, while an item $x \in T \cup X$ should remain with probability $\tilde{w}_x/\tau'$, i.e., it should be deleted with probability $1 - \tilde{w}_x/\tau'$. Recall that all items in T have the same adjusted weights, so the implementation can be made more efficient as described in lines 12 through 18. Here, the value of r chosen uniformly in $[0, 1]$ is used to select one to delete.

The running time of the UPDATE algorithm can be analyzed quite easily. Inserting an item in to the sorted list L takes $O(\log s)$ time. The rest of the algorithm takes time proportional to $|X|$, the number of items being moved from L to T. Since an item is moved at most once, the amortized cost is just $O(1)$.

One can see that if all items have weight 1, then L is always empty; $\tau = s/n$, where n is the total number of items that have been added; and Algorithm 2.7 does indeed degenerate into Algorithm 2.4.

To merge two samples $S_1 = (\tau_1, T_1, L_1)$ and $S_2 = (\tau_2, T_2, L_2)$, one can insert items from one sample to the other (using their adjusted weights) by repeatedly calling UPDATE, which would take $O(s \log s)$ time. Observing that the bottleneck in Algorithm 2.7 is to insert the new item into the sorted list L (line 3), we can improve the running time to $O(s)$ by first inserting all items in L_2 in a batch, and then inserting the items in T_2 one by one, as described in Algorithm 2.8. To insert all items in L_2, we first merge L_1 and L_2 into one combined sorted list. Since both L_1 and L_2 are already sorted, the merge takes $O(s)$ time. Then we iteratively reduce the sample size back to s, following the same procedure as in the UPDATE algorithm. Next, we insert all items of T_2 one by one using the same UPDATE algorithm. One trick is that if we make sure $\tau_1 \geq \tau_2$ (swapping S_1 and S_2 if needed), then the adjusted weight of all the items to be inserted, which is τ_2, is always smaller than the current $\tau \geq \tau_1$, so we will never need to insert them into L, saving the $O(\log s)$ cost in the UPDATE algorithm.

Algorithm 2.8: WeightedRandomSample: MERGE $(S_1 = (\tau_1, T_1, L_1),$
$S_2 = (\tau_2, T_2, L_2), \tau_1 \geq \tau_2)$

---

1 merge L_1 and L_2 into L;
2 $T \leftarrow T_1, W \leftarrow \tau_1 |T|$;
3 **for** $d \leftarrow 1$ **to** $|L_2|$ **do**
4      $X \leftarrow \emptyset$;
5   run lines 7–19 of Algorithm 2.7 replacing s with $s + |L_2| - d$;
6 **for** $d \leftarrow 1$ **to** $|T_2|$ **do**
7      $X \leftarrow \{T_2[d]\}$;
8      $W \leftarrow W + \tau_2$;
9   run lines 7–19 of Algorithm 2.7;
10 **return** $S = (\tau, T, L)$;

For any subset $Q \subseteq A$, let $w(Q) = \sum_{x \in Q} w_x$. One can QUERY a WeightedRandomSample S for $w(Q)$ for an arbitrary subset $Q \subseteq A$, by simply returning $\tilde{w}(Q) = \sum_{x \in S \cap Q} \tilde{w}_x$, that is, we simply add up all adjusted weights of the items in the sample that fall in Q. This turns out to be an unbiased estimator of the true total weight $w(Q)$ with strong guarantees on the variance, as discussed later.

Example. Suppose we are to maintain a weighted random sample of size $s = 4$ over a sequence of eight items numbered from 1 to 8 in order. The following example shows one possible execution of the UPDATE algorithm, together with the contents of $\tau, T, L,$ and X. We use the notation $x : w_x$ to denote an item x with weight w_x or adjusted weight $\tilde{w}_x$. Note that all items in T have the same adjusted weight τ.

INITIALIZE: $\tau = 0, L = [2 : 1, 3 : 3, 1 : 4, 4 : 8], T = \emptyset$;
UPDATE $(5 : 3)$:   Add $5 : 3$ to L: $L = [2 : 1, 3 : 3, 5 : 3, 1 : 4, 4 : 8]$
                 New $\tau = 7/2, X = [2 : 1, 3 : 3, 5 : 3]$
                 Deletion probabilities: $2 : 5/7, 3 : 1/7, 5 : 1/7$
                 Suppose item 3 is deleted
                 $T = \{2, 5\}, L = [1 : 4, 4 : 8]$;
UPDATE $(6 : 5)$:   Add $6 : 5$ to L : $L = [1 : 4, 6 : 5, 4 : 8]$
                 New $\tau = 16/3, X = [1 : 4, 6 : 5]$
                 Deletion probabilities: $2 : 11/32, 5 : 11/32, 1 : 1/4, 6 : 1/16$
                 Suppose item 5 is deleted
                 $T = \{1, 2, 6\}, L = [4 : 8]$;
UPDATE $(7 : 1)$:   Add $7 : 1$ to X : $X = [7 : 1]$
                 New $\tau = 17/3, X = [7 : 1]$

Deletion probabilities: $1 : 1/17, 2 : 1/17, 6 : 1/17, 7 : 14/17$
Suppose item 7 is deleted
$T = \{1, 2, 6\}, L = [4 : 8]$;
UPDATE $(8 : 7)$:   Add $8 : 7$ to $L : L = [8 : 7, 4 : 8]$
New $\tau = 8, X = [8 : 7, 4 : 8]$
Deletion probabilities:
$1 : 7/24, 2 : 7/24, 6 : 7/24, 8 : 1/8, 4 : 0$
Suppose item 1 is deleted
$T = \{2, 4, 6, 8\}, L = \emptyset$.

Next, suppose we want to merge two weighted samples $S_1 = (\tau_1 = 4, T_1 = \{1, 2\}, L_1 = \{3 : 5, 4 : 6\})$ and $S_2 = (\tau_2 = 3, T_2 = \{5\}, L_2 = \{6 : 4, 7 : 4, 8 : 11\})$. We first merge L_1 and L_2 into L, and then perform the deletions iteratively, as follows.

Merge L_1, L_2: $T = \{1, 2\}, L = [6 : 4, 7 : 4, 3 : 5, 4 : 6, 8 : 11]$;
$s = 6$:   New $\tau = 21/4, X = [6 : 4, 7 : 4, 3 : 5]$
Deletion probabilities:
$1 : 5/21, 2 : 5/21, 6 : 5/21, 7 : 5/21, 3 : 1/21$
Suppose item 1 is deleted
$T = \{2, 6, 7, 3\}, L = [4 : 6, 8 : 11]$;
$i = 5$:   New $\tau = 27/4, X = [4 : 6]$
Deletion probabilities:
$2 : 2/9, 6 : 2/9, 7 : 2/9, 3 : 2/9, 4 : 1/9$
Suppose item 7 is deleted
$T = \{2, 6, 3, 4\}, L = [8 : 11]$;
$i = 4$:   New $\tau = 9, X = \emptyset$
Deletion probabilities: $2 : 1/4, 6 : 1/4, 3 : 1/4, 4 : 1/4$
Suppose item 3 is deleted
$T = \{2, 6, 4\}, L = [8 : 11]$.

Next, we insert items in T_2 one by one, each with weight $\tau_2 = 3$.

UPDATE $(5 : 3)$: $X = [5 : 3], W = 30$
New $\tau = 10, X = [5 : 3]$
Deletion probabilities: $2 : 1/10, 6 : 1/10, 4 : 1/10, 5 : 7/10$
Suppose item 5 is deleted
$T = \{2, 6, 4\}, L = [8 : 11]$;

Further Discussion. There is no clear generalization of the classical random sample definition that "every subset of size s is sampled with equal probability" to the weighted case. Nevertheless, the WeightedRandomSample we have described has the following nice properties, which are sufficient to derive strong statistical properties regarding the estimation of an arbitrary subset sum.

(i) Inclusion probabilities proportional to size (IPPS). Each item x is sampled with probability $p_x = \min\{1, w_x/\tau\}$, where τ is the unique value such that $\sum_{x \in A} \min\{1, w_x/\tau\} = s$ if $s < n$; otherwise, $\tau = 0$, meaning that all items are sampled. A sampled item is associated with adjusted weight $\tilde{w}_x = w_x/p_x$. Set $\tilde{w}_x = 0$ if x is not sampled. It is easy to see that $\mathsf{E}[\tilde{w}_x] = w_x$, and $\tilde{w}_x$ is known as the Horvitz–Thompson estimator.

(ii) The sample size is at most s. Together with (i), this means that the sample size must be $\min\{s, n\}$.

(iii) No positive covariances, i.e., for any two distinct $x, y \in A, \mathsf{Cov}[\tilde{w}_x, \tilde{w}_y] \leq 0$.

Let $\textsc{Sample}_s(I)$ be a procedure that takes a sample of size s from a set of weighted items I so that properties (i) through (iii) are satisfied. It turns out such a $\textsc{Sample}_s$ can be constructed recursively, as follows. Let $I_1, \ldots, I_m$ be disjoint nonempty subsets of I, and let $s_1, \ldots, s_m \geq s$. Then

$$\textsc{Sample}_s(I) = \textsc{Sample}_s\left(\bigcup_{i=1}^{m} \textsc{Sample}_{s_i}(I_i)\right). \tag{2.2}$$

Here, when running $\textsc{Sample}$ on a sample produced by another call to $\textsc{Sample}$, we simply treat the adjusted weights of the items as if they were their original weights. We omit the correctness proof of this recurrence, which can be found in [58]. Here, we only show how it leads to the $\textsc{Update}$ and $\textsc{Merge}$ algorithms described earlier.

First, the trivial base case of $\textsc{Sample}_s$ is when I has at most s items, in which case $\textsc{Sample}_s(I) = I$. We need another base case when I has $s+1$ items, denoted $\textsc{Sample}_{s,s+1}$. In this case, an item needs to be deleted at random with appropriate deletion probabilities. To determine the deletion probabilities, we first find the correct value of τ. Then item x should be sampled with probability $p_x = \max\{1, w_x/\tau\}$, i.e., should be deleted with probability $1 - p_x$. After a randomly chosen item has been dropped, we compute the adjusted weights of the remaining items as $\tilde{w}_x = w_x/p_x$, which is τ if $w_x \leq \tau$, and w_x if $w_x > \tau$.

To use this for the $\textsc{Update}$ algorithm, we specialize (2.2) with $m = 2$, $s_1 = s_2 = s, I_1 = A, I_2 = \{y\}$. Note that $\textsc{Sample}_s(I_2) = \{y\}$. Then the

UPDATE algorithm becomes exactly $\text{SAMPLE}_{s,s+1}$, by treating the adjusted weights of items in $\text{SAMPLE}_s(A)$ as their weights. To reduce the running time, we exploit the previous observation, maintaining the items in two lists T and L. All items in T have the same adjusted weights τ, while items in L have their adjusted weights equal to their original weights.

To compute a merged sample $\text{SAMPLE}_s(A)$ from $\text{SAMPLE}_s(A_1)$ and $\text{SAMPLE}_s(A_2)$, where $A = A_1 \cup A_2, A_1 \cap A_2 = \emptyset$, recurrence (2.2) says that we can simply run SAMPLE_s on $\text{SAMPLE}_s(A_1) \cup \text{SAMPLE}_s(A_2)$, treating their adjusted weights as their weights. To do so, we insert each item in $\text{SAMPLE}_s(A_2)$ into $\text{SAMPLE}_s(A_1)$ one by one by the UPDATE algorithm. The MERGE algorithm described earlier is just a more efficient implementation of this process.

Now we discuss the statistical properties of the subset sum estimator $\tilde{w}(Q) = \sum_{x \in S \cap Q} \tilde{w}_x$. First, because item x is sampled with probability p_x, and when it is sampled, its adjusted weight is set to w_x/p_x, and to 0 otherwise. Thus we have

$$\mathsf{E}[\tilde{w}_x] = p_x \cdot w_x/p_x = w_x,$$

i.e., $\tilde{w}_x$ is an unbiased estimator of w_x. Because each $\tilde{w}_x$ is unbiased, the unbiasedness of $\tilde{w}(Q)$ follows trivially. The variance of $\tilde{w}(Q)$ enjoys the following three forms of guarantees.

1. *Average variance:* Consider all the subsets $Q \subseteq A$ of size $m \le n$. Their average variance is

$$V_m = \frac{\sum_{Q \subseteq A, |Q|=m} \mathsf{Var}[\tilde{w}(Q)]}{\binom{n}{m}}.$$

It has been shown [216] that

$$V_m = \frac{m}{n} \left(\frac{n-m}{n-1} \Sigma V + \frac{m-1}{n-1} V\Sigma \right),$$

where

$$\Sigma V = \sum_{x \in A} \mathsf{Var}[\tilde{w}_x],$$

$$V\Sigma = \mathsf{Var}\left[\sum_{x \in A} \tilde{w}_x \right].$$

It is known [206] that the IPPS property (i) uniquely minimizes ΣV under a given sample size s. Also, as seen earlier, $\tilde{w}_x$ is either τ

(when $w_x \leq \tau$ and x is sampled) or w_x (when $w_x \geq \tau$, in which case x must be sampled). Since τ is deterministic, $\sum_{x \in A} \tilde{w}_x$ is also deterministic due to property (ii). So $V\Sigma = 0$. Therefore, we conclude that V_m is minimized simultaneously for all values of m, among all sampling schemes under a given sample size s.

2. *Expected variance:* Let W_p denote the expected variance of a random subset Q including each item $x \in A$ independently with some probability p. It is also shown [216] that

$$W_p = p((1 - p)\Sigma V + pV\Sigma).$$

Thus by the same reasoning, W_p is minimized for all values of p.

3. *Worst-case variance:* Combining the IPPS property (i) and the nonpositive covariance property (iii), we can also bound $\mathsf{Var}[\tilde{w}(Q)]$ for any particular Q. Since each individual $\tilde{w}_x$ is w_x/p_x with probability p_x and 0 otherwise, its variance is $\mathsf{Var}[\tilde{w}_x] = w_x^2(1/p_x - 1)$. Observing that $\tau \leq w(A)/s$, so $p_x = \max\{1, w_x/\tau\} \geq \min\{1, sw_x/w(A)\}$. If $p_x = 1$, then $\mathsf{Var}[\tilde{w}_x] = 0$. Otherwise, we must have $p_x \geq sw_x/w(A)$, and we can give two bounds on $\mathsf{Var}[\tilde{w}_x]$:

$$\mathsf{Var}[\tilde{w}_x] < w_x^2/p_x \leq w_x w(A)/s, \tag{2.3}$$

or

$$\mathsf{Var}[\tilde{w}_x] < w_x^2 \left(\frac{w(A)}{sw_x} - 1\right) = \left(\frac{w(A)}{2s}\right)^2 - \left(w_x - \frac{w(A)}{2s}\right)^2$$

$$\leq \left(\frac{w(A)}{2s}\right)^2. \tag{2.4}$$

Combining with the nonpositive covariance property, we have $\mathsf{Var}[\tilde{w}(Q)] \leq \sum_{x \in Q} \mathsf{Var}[\tilde{w}_x]$. Plugging in (2.3) and (2.4) respectively yields a weight-bounded variance $\mathsf{Var}[\tilde{w}(Q)] \leq w(Q)w(A)/s$, and a cardinality-bounded variance $\mathsf{Var}[\tilde{w}(Q)] \leq |Q|(w(A)/2s)^2$.

History and Background. The development of the algorithms and analysis largely follows that of Cohen et al. [58], where it is referred to as variance optimal, or VarOpt sampling. The UPDATE algorithm described in the preceding has an amortized time cost of $O(\log s)$. This can be improved to $O(\log \log s)$ if we assume that the weights are integers or finite-precision floating-point numbers, by storing L in a priority queue that supports fast updates (see the work of Thorup [220]). It can also be shown that if the stream is randomly ordered, then the amortized cost will be $O(1)$. The MERGE algorithm is not explicitly described in [58], though.

This version of weighted sampling was designed for the problem of sampling effectively from massive streams of network data. Here, uniform sampling of data connections would tend to overrepresent the many small flows and miss the important large flows. Simply picking out the largest flows would not give a full picture of the entire distribution. Weighted sampling allows the range of different flow sizes to be better represented, and volume-based queries (what fraction of network traffic is of a particular type, or headed to a particular set of destinations) to be answered accurately. Further examples in the networking domain are discussed by Duffield et al. [91].

> **Available Implementations.** VarOpt sampling is implemented in the DataSketches library, and is discussed at `https://datasketches` `.github.io/docs/Sampling/VarOptSampling.html`, with routines implemented for UPDATE and MERGE procedures. The implementation also provides lower and upper bounds on the estimations of subset sums.

2.4 Priority Sampling

Brief Summary. A PrioritySample is also a random sample over a set A of weighted items, which can be used to estimate the total weight of an arbitrary subset, as supported by a WeightedRandomSample. The variance achievable by a PrioritySample is slightly worse than that of WeightedRandomSample. However, its simpler implementation often makes it a preferable choice in practice.

Operations on the Summary. For each item $x \in A$ with weight w_x, we generate an independent uniformly distributed random number $\alpha_x \in (0, 1)$, and set its *priority* to $q_x = w_x/\alpha_x$. A PrioritySample S of size s consists of the s items of the highest priority. The threshold τ is the $(s + 1)$st highest priority. The summary simply stores these items, their weights and priorities, as well as the threshold τ. We can store them in a priority queue so that new items can be added to the summary easily in $O(\log s)$ time. Merging two such summaries can be also easily done in $O(s)$ time using the linear-time heap building algorithm [63].

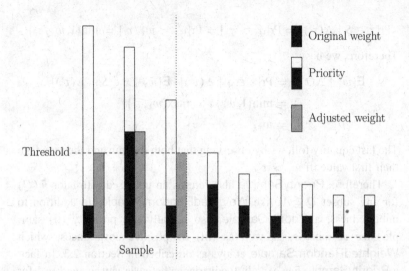

Figure 2.1 Priority sampling of size $s = 3$ from a set of nine weighted items.

For any subset $Q \subseteq A$, we can QUERY a PrioritySample S for $w(Q)$ in a similar way as on a WeightedRandomSample, by returning $\tilde{w}(Q) = \sum_{x \in S \cap Q} \tilde{w}_x$. The only difference is that the adjusted weight $\tilde{w}_x$ is defined as $\tilde{w}_x = \max\{w_i, \tau\}$. This is also an unbiased estimator of $w(Q)$, but its variance is slightly worse than WeightedRandomSample, as discussed later.

Example. A graphical example of a PrioritySample is shown in Figure 2.1.

Further Discussion. We now show that for any x, $\tilde{w}_x$ is an unbiased estimator of w_x. In fact, we will prove a stronger result, that $\mathsf{E}[\tilde{w}_x] = w_x$ regardless of the values of all $\alpha_y, y \in A, y \neq x$. Let τ' be the sth highest of the priorities $q_y, y \in A, y \neq x$. More formally, we will show

$$E[\tilde{w}_x \mid \Lambda(\tau')] = w_x, \qquad (2.5)$$

where $\Lambda(\tau')$ is the event that τ' is the sth highest in $\{q_y : y \in A, y \neq x\}$. Proving (2.5) for any value τ' implies that $\mathsf{E}[\tilde{w}_x] = w_x$.

We first analyze the probability that item x is picked into the sample S, conditioned on $\Lambda(\tau')$. If $q_x < \tau'$, there are at least s priorities higher than q_x, so x will not be picked. If $q_x > \tau'$, then τ' becomes the $(s+1)$st priority among all priorities, so $\tau = \tau'$ and x will be picked into S. Thus,

$$\Pr[x \in S \mid \Lambda(\tau')] = \Pr[q_x > \tau'] = \Pr[\alpha_x < w_x/\tau'] = \min\{1, w_x/\tau'\}.$$

Therefore, we have

$$\mathsf{E}[\tilde{w}_x \mid \Lambda(\tau')] = \Pr[x \in S \mid \Lambda(\tau')] \cdot \mathsf{E}[\tilde{w}_x \mid x \in S \cap \Lambda(\tau')]$$
$$= \min\{1, w_x/\tau'\} \cdot \max\{w_x, \tau'\}$$
$$= w_x.$$

The last equality follows by observing that both the min and the max take their first value iff $w_x > \tau'$.

Therefore, PrioritySample also returns an unbiased estimator $\tilde{w}(Q)$ for any subset $Q \subseteq A$, like WeightedRandomSample. In addition to unbiasedness, a PrioritySample also trivially has property (ii) sample size at most s, as well as (iii) no positive covariances, which WeightedRandomSample enjoys as described in Section 2.3. In fact, a PrioritySample has exactly 0 covariance between any $\tilde{w}_x$ and $\tilde{w}_y$, for $x \neq y$ (see [92] for a proof).

However, the variance of PrioritySample is slightly worse than that of WeightedRandomSample in the following two aspects. First, PrioritySample does not have property (i) IPPS. Although we have shown that conditioned on $\Lambda(\tau')$, the probability that x is sampled into S is indeed proportional to w_x, it does not imply that the overall sampling probability is proportional to w_x. Therefore, PrioritySample does not achieve the minimum ΣV that WeightedRandomSample achieves. Nevertheless, as shown in [215], a PrioritySample with sample size $s+1$ can achieve a ΣV that is as good as the minimum ΣV achievable by a WeightedRandomSample with sample size s. Thus, the difference between the two sampling methods in terms of ΣV is really negligible.

Second, we know from Section 2.3 that WeightedRandomSample has $V\Sigma = 0$. However, for a PrioritySample, we have $V\Sigma = \Sigma V$ (because the covariances are 0). So, it has larger variances for larger subsets Q.

2.5 k Minimum Values (KMV) for Set Cardinality

Brief Summary. Similar to the MorrisCounter, the KMV summary also counts the number of elements in the set being summarized. But unlike the MorrisCounter, the KMV summary is able to remove duplicates in the input automatically. In other words, KMV summarizes a multiset A of items and can be used to report the approximate number of distinct items observed, i.e., to approximate the size of the support set. The accuracy of the approximation determines the size of the summary, and there is a small probability (δ) of giving an answer that is outside the desired approximation guarantee (ϵ). The summary works by applying a hash function to the input items and keeping information about the k distinct items with the smallest hash values. The size of the summary, k, is determined by the accuracy parameters ϵ and δ.

Operations on the Summary. One instance of a KMV summary can be represented as a list of hash values and corresponding items that led to those hash values.

Algorithm 2.9: KMV: INITIALIZE (k)

---

1 Pick hash function h, and store k;
2 Initialize list $L = \emptyset$ for k item, hash pairs;

The INITIALIZE operation picks a hash function h mapping onto a range $1 \ldots R$, and creates an empty list capable of holding up to k hashes and items.

Algorithm 2.10: KMV: UPDATE (x)

---

1 **if** $x \notin L$ **then**
2    $L \leftarrow L \cup \{(x, h(x))\}$;
3   **if** $|L| > k$ **then** Remove item x with largest hash value $h(x)$ from L;

Each UPDATE operation receives an item and applies the function h to it. If the item is already present in the list, it is dropped and need not be stored. If the hash value is among the k smallest hash values, the item and its hash value are stored in the list, and the list pruned to retain only the k smallest. We use set notation to refer to the list of items L, augmented so that we can find the kth largest hash value (Algorithm 2.11). This can be supported with a heap data structure, linked to a hash table to test for presence of an item.

Algorithm 2.11: KMV: QUERY ()

---

1 $v_k \leftarrow$ largest hash value in L;
2 **return** $(k - 1) * R / v_k$

To QUERY the summary for the estimated number of distinct items seen, find the kth smallest hash value seen so far, as v_k, and compute the estimate as $R(k - 1)/v_k$. If there are fewer than k values stored, then these represent the set of distinct items seen, and so the exact answer can be given.

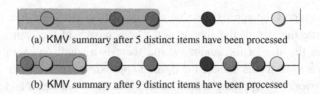

(a) KMV summary after 5 distinct items have been processed

(b) KMV summary after 9 distinct items have been processed

Figure 2.2 KMV summary with $k = 3$.

To MERGE together two summaries (where, we require that both were built using the same hash function h) and obtain a summary of the union of the inputs, the two lists are merged, and the set of distinct pairs of hashes and items is found. The k pairs corresponding to the k smallest hash values are retained.

Example. Figure 2.2 shows a schematic representation of the KMV summary as items are processed, with $k = 3$. Different items are shown as different colored balls, with each ball being represented as its hash value, smallest on the left and largest on the right. Figure 2.2a shows the status after five distinct items have been observed. The highlighted items, corresponding to the three smallest hash values, are stored in the summary. As more items arrive (Figure 2.2b), the summary is updated: two new items enter the k smallest, and only information about the current k smallest is stored. In this example, the ratio R/v_k is approximately 4 (the kth smallest hash value falls about 1/4 of the way along the range), and so the estimate given is $2 \times 4 = 8$, which is close to the true answer of 9.

Further Discussion. The initial properties of KMV can be understood as follows. Suppose that the input domain is the range $1 \ldots M$, and the output range R is chosen to be M^3. This is large enough that hash collisions are so unlikely we can discount them. Let the hash function h be chosen from a family of pairwise independent hash functions.

We now study the chance that the estimated answer D' is much larger than the true answer, $|A|$. Suppose $R(k - 1)/v_k > (1 + \epsilon)|A|$ for some $\epsilon < 1$. This implies that at least k items from the input had a hash value that was below a value $\tau := R(k - 1)/(1 + \epsilon)|A|$, i.e., v_k was smaller than it should have been. We prefer to have the dependence on ϵ in the numerator rather than the denominator, so we upper bound this value of τ using the fact that $\epsilon < 1$:

$$\tau = \frac{R(k-1)}{(1+\epsilon)|A|} \leq \frac{R(k-1)}{|A|}\left(1 - \frac{\epsilon}{2}\right).$$

Considering a single item x, the probability that its hash value is below this threshold τ is at most

$$\frac{1}{R} \cdot \left(1 - \frac{\epsilon}{2}\right)\frac{(k-1)R}{|A|} = \left(1 - \frac{\epsilon}{2}\right)\frac{k-1}{|A|} := p.$$

Note that technically, this probability should be slightly increased by a small amount of $1/M$, to account for rounding of the hash values; however, this does not significantly affect the analysis, so we gloss over this quantity in the interest of keeping the expressions clear to read.

For the analysis, we create Bernoulli random variables X_i for each of the distinct items, indexed from 1 up to $|A|$, to indicate the event that the item's hash value is below τ. Each of these is 1 with probability at most p. Let Y be the sum of these $|A|$ random variables: a necessary condition for the estimate being too large is $Y \geq k$. We compute

$$\mathsf{E}[Y] = |A|p \leq \left(1 - \frac{\epsilon}{2}\right)(k-1).$$

The variance of Y can be computed as the sum of variances of the X_is. Each $\mathsf{Var}[X_i] \leq p(1-p)$, and these are (pairwise) independent, so

$$\mathsf{Var}[Y] = |A|p(1-p) \leq \left(1 - \frac{\epsilon}{2}\right)(k-1).$$

We can then apply the Chebyshev inequality, to conclude that

$$\Pr[Y \geq k] \leq \Pr\left[|Y - \mathsf{E}[Y]| > \frac{\epsilon}{2}k\right] \leq 4\frac{\mathsf{Var}[Y]}{\epsilon^2 k^2} \leq \frac{4}{\epsilon^2 k}.$$

The analysis for the case that the estimate falls below $(1-\epsilon)|A|$ is very similar. This occurs when fewer than k items hash *below*

$$\frac{(k-1)R}{(1-\epsilon)|A|} \geq (1+\epsilon)\frac{(k-1)R}{|A|}.$$

As before, the probability of this can be bounded using the Chebyshev inequality over a summation of Bernoulli random variables with parameter $p' := (1+\epsilon)(k-1)/|A|$. The estimate is too small when more than k of these events occur out of the $|A|$ trials. Thus we can similarly show that the probability of this undesirable outcome is bounded by $\frac{1}{\epsilon^2 k}$.

Combining these two probabilities, we have that

$$\Pr[|R(k-1)/v_k - |A|| \leq \epsilon|A|] \leq \frac{5}{\epsilon^2 k}.$$

To make this at most $1/4$, we choose $k = 20/\epsilon^2$. To reduce the probability to δ, we repeat the process $4 \log 1/\delta$ times with different hash functions and take the median estimate (following the argument of Section 1.4.1). This implies that we need space to store $80/\epsilon^2 \log 1/\delta$ items in total.

A tighter analysis was provided by [27]. They study higher moments of the estimator, under the assumption of fully random hash functions, and show that the estimator is unbiased. They show in particular that the variance of this estimator is proportional to $|A|^2/k$, and so setting k to $1/\epsilon^2$ guarantees that the standard deviation is proportional to $\epsilon|A|$, which bounds the expected absolute error. Thus the asymptotic performance is essentially the same: to give an ϵ relative error, a summary of size proportional to $1/\epsilon^2$ is needed, but the true constants of proportionality are smaller than the preceding basic analysis would indicate.

Unions, Intersections, and Predicates. The MERGE operation corresponds to computing a summary of the union of the sets being combined. The correctness of this process is easy to see: since the hash values of items can be treated as fixed, the KMV summary of the union of the sets is defined by the k smallest hash values of items in the union, which can be found from the k smallest hash values of the two input sets. These in turn are given by the KMV summaries of these sets.

For intersections between sets, we can look to the intersection of their corresponding summary. Specifically, we can count the number of elements in the intersection of the corresponding KMV summaries. Roughly speaking, we expect the fraction of elements in the intersection of the two summaries to be proportional to the overall fraction of elements in the intersection. That is, for sets A and B it should be proportional to $\frac{|A \cap B|}{|A \cup B|}$. Let ρ be the observed fraction of elements intersection, i.e., $\rho = i/k$, where i is the number of intersecting elements. We use this to scale the estimate obtained for the size of the union. The variance of this estimator can be shown to scale according to $|A \cap B| \cdot |A \cup B|/k$ [27]. That is, if we pick $k \propto 1/\epsilon^2$, the error (standard deviation) will be bounded by $\epsilon \sqrt{|A \cap B| \cdot |A \cup B|}$. Since we do not know how big $|A \cap B|$ will be in advance, this can be bounded by $\epsilon|A \cup B|$ in the worst case, i.e., the (additive) error in estimating an intersection scales at worst in accordance with the size of the union of the sets.

The idea for the intersection can be applied to other concepts. Suppose we want to estimate the number of distinct items in the input that satisfy a particular property (i.e., a predicate). Then we can see what fraction of items stored in the summary satisfy the property, and then scale the estimated number of distinct items by this fraction. Again, the error scales with $\epsilon |A \cup B|$ in the worst case, so this will not work well when the desired property is very rare. This should not be surprising: if the property is rare, then it is unlikely that any of the items within the summary will possess it, and hence our estimate will be 0.

Generalization to Multisets. We can generalize the summary to track information about the multiplicity of items in a multiset. The approach is natural: we additionally keep, for each item stored in the summary, the number of times it has occurred. This is useful when we wish to additionally pose queries that involve the multiplicity of items: for example, we could ask how many items occur exactly once in the data (this statistic is known as the *rarity*), and estimate this based on the fraction of items in the summary that occur exactly once. This can be addressed using the previous approach for counting the number of items satisfying a given property.

The summary can still operate correctly when the input stream includes operations that delete an item, as well as just insertions of items. We keep track of the multiplicity of each item in the summary and remove any whose count reaches zero after a deletion operation. This can have the effect of bringing the size of the summary down below k. To ensure a correct estimate, we must keep track of the least value of the kth smallest hash value that has been maintained, m_k. We must ensure that the summary contains information about all items in the input that hash below m_k. Consequently, even when the summary has fewer than k items in it, we cannot fill it up with elements from the input that hash above m_k. Instead, we must use the summary with the current "effective" value of k, i.e., the number of items that hash below m_k. This may mean that in a very dynamic situation, where there are a large number of deletions, the effective value of k may become very small, meaning that the summary gives poor accuracy. There are summaries that can cope with such deletions, which are described later in Section 2.6, at the cost of using more space.

Implementation Issues. In our description, we have stated that we should keep the original items in addition to the hashed values. For the basic uses of the summary, this is not necessary, and we can retain only the hash values to perform the estimation of set, union, and intersection sizes. It is only when applying predicate tests that we also need to keep the original items, so that the tests can be applied to them. Thus, the space can be reduced to the size of the hash values, which should depend on the expected maximum number of distinct items, rather than the size of the input items. This can be very space efficient when the input items are very large, e.g., long text strings. Additional space efficiency can be obtained based on the observation that as the number of distinct items increases, the fraction of the hash range occupied decreases: the hash values of the stored items begin with a prefix of zero bits. This prefix can therefore be omitted, to reduce the size of the stored hashes.

History and Background. The KMV summary was introduced in the work of Bar-Yossef et al. [19]. This paper introduced a selection of algorithms for tracking the number of distinct items in a stream of elements. Of these, the KMV has had the most impact, as it blends space efficiency with simplicity to implement. A version of KMV with $k = 1$ was first proposed by Cohen [56]. The idea can be seen as related to the work of Gibbons and Tirthapura [113] which also uses the idea of hash functions to select a set of items from the input based on their hash value. This in turn is conceptually (though less clearly) related to the earliest work on distinct counting, due to Flajolet and Martin [107]. The tighter analysis of the KMV summary is due to Beyer et al. [27]. This proposed an unbiased version of the estimator (previous presentations used a biased estimator) and analyze its higher moments under the assumption of fully random hash functions. A generalization of KMV is presented by Dasgupta et al. [81] in the form of the theta-sketch framework. This generalizes KMV by considering sketching methods defined by a threshold θ derived from the stream that is used to maintain a set of hash values of stream elements below the threshold. It is instantiated by different choices of function to determine the threshold θ. The framework can naturally handle MERGE (union) operations, as well as estimate the cardinality of intersections and more general set expressions.

Available Implementations. The DataSketches library provides an implementation of the KMV summary within the more general framework of θ-sketches. Concurrent versions are also implemented that can efficiently parallelize the computation. Experiments on commodity hardware show that the sketch can process tens of millions of UPDATE operations per second in a single thread. Evaluation of standard error shows that a summary with k around ten thousand is sufficient to obtain relative error of 1% with high probability.

2.6 HyperLogLog (HLL) for Set Cardinality

Brief Summary. Like KMV, the HLL summary also summarizes a multiset A of items in order to approximate the number of distinct items observed, but in a very bit-efficient way. It tracks information about hashed values of input items, and uses this to build an accurate approximation of the counts. Different summaries can be combined to estimate the size of the union of their inputs, and from this, the size of the intersection can also be estimated.

Algorithm 2.12: HLL: INITIALIZE (m)

---

1 Pick hash functions h, g and store m;
2 $C[1] \dots C[m] \leftarrow 0$;

Operations on the Summary. The HLL summary is stored as an array of m entries. Each input item is mapped by a hash function to an entry, and a second hash function is applied; the array entry keeps track of statistics on the hash values mapped there. Specifically, it tracks the largest number of leading zeros in the binary encoding of evaluations of the hash function. The INITIALIZE function creates the two hash functions, h to map to entries in the array, and g to remap the items. It initializes the array of size m to all zeros (Algorithm 2.12).

Algorithm 2.13: HLL: UPDATE (x)

---

1 $C[h(x)] \leftarrow \max(C[h(x)], z(g(x)))$;

To UPDATE a summary with item x, we make use of the function $z(\cdot)$, which returns the number of leading zeros in the binary representation of its argument. For example, $z(1010)$ is 0 (applied to the 4-bit binary input 1010, corresponding to the integer 12), while $z(0001)$ is 3. The new item is mapped under h to an entry in the array, and we test whether $z(g(x))$ is greater than the current item. If so, we update the entry to $z(g(x))$. This is expressed in Algorithm 2.13.

To MERGE two summaries built using the same parameters ($h()$, $g()$, and m), we merge the arrays in the natural way: for each array entry, take the maximum value of the corresponding input arrays.

Algorithm 2.14: HLL: QUERY ()

---

1 $X \leftarrow 0$;
2 **for** $j \leftarrow 1$ **to** m **do** $X \leftarrow X + 2^{-C[j]}$;
3 **return** $(\alpha_m m^2 / X)$;

To QUERY the summary for the approximate number of distinct items, we extract an estimate for the number of distinct items mapped to each array entry, and then combine these to get an estimate for the total number. Specifically, for each entry of the matrix, we take 2 raised to the power of this value, and then take the harmonic mean of these values. This is shown in Algorithm 2.14. The estimate is then an appropriately rescaled value of this estimate, based on a constant $\alpha_m = 0.7213/(1 + 1.079/m)$, discussed later.

Example. We show a small example with $m = 3$. Consider five distinct items a, b, c, d, e, with the following hash values:

x	a	b	c	d	e
$h(x)$	1	2	3	1	3
$g(x)$	0001	0011	1010	1101	0101

From this, we obtain the following array:

3	2	1

Applying the QUERY function, we obtain $X = 7/8$, and choosing $\alpha_m = 0.5305$, we get an estimate of the number of distinct items as 5.45, which is close to the true result of 5.

Further Discussion. The central intuition behind the HLL summary is that tracking the maximum value of $z(g(x))$ gives information about the number of distinct items mapped to that array entry. If we assume that g appears sufficiently random, then we expect half the hashed items seen to have 0 as their first bit (and hence have $z(g(x)) = 1$). Similarly, we expect a quarter of the items to have two leading zeros, an eighth to have three, and so on. Inverting this relationship, if we see a value of ρ in an array entry, then we interpret this as most likely to have been caused by 2^ρ distinct items. As storing the value ρ only takes $O(\log \rho) = O(\log \log n)$ bits, where n is the number of distinct elements, this leads to the "log log" in the name of the summary.

Applying this argument to each of the array entries in turn, we have an estimate for the number of distinct items mapped to each entry. The most direct way to combine these would be to sum them, but this has high variability. Instead, we take advantage of the property of the hash function h as mapping items approximately uniformly to each array entry. So we can interpret each of the estimates obtained as an estimate of

n/m, where n is the number of distinct items. We could directly average these, but instead we adopt the harmonic mean, which is more robust to outlying values. The harmonic mean of m values x_i is $\left(\frac{1}{m}\sum_{i=1}^{m} x_i^{-1}\right)^{-1}$. In Algorithm 2.14, X computes the needed sum of values, so the harmonic mean is given by m/X. This is our estimate for n/m, so we scale this by a further factor of m to obtain m^2/X as the estimate. However, this turns out to be biased, so the factor α_m is used to rescale out the bias.

A full discussion of the analysis of this estimator is beyond the scope of this presentation (see the original paper [105] for this). This shows that α_m should be picked to be $\frac{1}{2\ln 2}\left(1 + \frac{1}{m}(3\ln 2 - 1)\right)$, i.e., $0.7213/(1 + 1.079/m)$, for m larger than 100. In this case, the bias of the estimator is essentially removed. The variance of the estimator is shown to approach $1.08/m$ as m increases, and is bounded for all $m \geq 3$. Thus the estimator achieves ϵ relative error with constant probability provided $m \geq 1/\epsilon^2$, by the Chebyshev inequality. The probability of exceeding this bound can be driven down to δ by performing $O(\log 1/\delta)$ independent repetitions and taking the median, following the Chernoff bounds argument (Section 1.4.1). However, it is argued by Flajolet et al. [105] that the central limit theorem applies, and the estimator follows a Gaussian distribution; in this case, increasing m by a factor of $O(\log 1/\delta)$ is sufficient to achieve the same result. Therefore, the HLL summary takes a total of $O(1/\varepsilon^2 \log(1/\delta) \log\log n)$ *bits*. This is more bit efficient than the KMV summary, which keeps $O(1/\varepsilon^2 \log(1/\delta))$ hash values, amounting to $O(1/\varepsilon^2 \log(1/\delta) \log n)$ bits.

Intersections. Since the HLL summary can give an accurate estimate of the size of the union of two sets, it can also estimate the size of their intersection. We take advantage of the identity $|A \cap B| = |A| + |B| - |A \cup B|$, and form our estimate of $|A \cap B|$ from the corresponding estimates of $|A|, |B|$, and $|A \cup B|$. The error then depends on the size of these quantities: if we estimate $|A|$ and $|B|$ with relative error ϵ, then the error in $|A \cap B|$ will also depend on $\epsilon(|A| + |B|)$. Hence if $|A|$ or $|B|$ is large compared to $|A \cap B|$, the error will overwhelm the true answer.

The same principle can be extended to estimate higher-order intersections, via the principle of inclusion–exclusion:

$$|A \cap B \cap C| = |A \cup B \cup C| + |A \cap B| + |A \cap C| + |B \cap C|$$
$$- |A| - |B| - |C|.$$

Indeed, arbitrary expressions can be decomposed in terms of unions alone: $|(A \cap B) \cup C| = |A \cup C| + |B \cup C| - |A \cup B \cup C|$. However, the number of terms in these expressions increases quickly, causing the error to rise accordingly.

Handling Deletions. The HLL summary cannot support deletions directly as it only keeps the maximum of all the $z(g(x))$s ever seen. However, one can easily support deletions, though at the cost of using more space. The idea is for each possible value of $z(g(x))$, we keep track of the number of xs that correspond to this value, i.e., we use a two-dimensional array C where $C[i, j] = |x : h(x) = i, z(g(x)) = j|$. This makes the summary a linear sketch of the data, so it can support arbitrary deletions. However, the total space needed increases substantially to $O(1/\varepsilon^2 \log(1/\delta) \log^2 n)$ bits.

Implementation Issues. Due to its wide adoption, the HLL summary has been subject to much scrutiny, and hence a number of engineering issues have been suggested to further increase its usefulness.

Hash Function Issues. We have described the HLL summary in terms of two hash functions, h and g. However, implementations typically use a single hash function f, and derive the two values from this. Assume that m is chosen to be a power of two, and that $\log_2 m = b$. Also assume that g is chosen to map onto a domain of 2^d bits. Then $h(x)$ can be taken as the first b bits of a hash function, and g taken as the last d bits, providing that the single hash function f provides at least $b + d$ bits. Implementations have tended to look at specific choices of parameters: Flajolet et al. [105] study $d = 32$, meaning that each value of $z(g(x))$ can be represented in 5 bits. For larger cardinalities, Heule et al. [132] use $d = 64$, and so store 6 bits for each array entry. Choosing $d = 32$ is sufficient to handle inputs with billions of entries (hundreds of billions if m is large enough that each array entry is unlikely to exceed 32 zeros in the g hash value), while $d = 64$ allows accurate counting up to the trillions. The space of the summary is $O(m \log \log n)$ bits, but as these implementations show, $\log \log n$ can be effectively treated as a constant: choosing $d = 2^8$ (so storing 8-bit values) is enough to count to $2^{256} = 10^{77}$, larger than most natural quantities.

The analysis of the algorithm requires assuming that the hash functions used are as good as a random function (i.e., fully random). Hence, simple hash functions (pairwise or k-wise independent) are insufficient for this purpose. Instead, stronger noncryptographic hash functions are used in practice (Section 1.4.2).

High-End Correction. When dealing with large cardinalities, there is the possibility of hash collisions under g. That is, assuming that g maps onto 2^d bits, there may be items $x \neq y$ such that $g(x) = g(y)$. The result is to underestimate the number of distinct items. One solution is to make a correction to the estimate, if the estimate is so large that this is a possibility. The original HLL paper [105] uses the correction that if the estimate E is more than $2^{2^d}/4$, then the new estimate is $\log_2(1 - E/2^{2^d})/2^{2^d}$. This expression for the correction comes from considering the probability of such collisions. However, a more direct approach is simply to increase d to the point where such collisions are unlikely: given n distinct items, the expected number of collisions is approximately $n/2^{1+2^d}$, so increasing d by 1 is usually sufficient to eliminate this problem.

Low-End Correction. The opposite problem can occur with small counts. This is more significant, since in many applications it is important to obtain more accurate estimates for small counts. However, the HLL summary shows a notable bias for small counts. In particular, consider an empty summary with m entries. The harmonic mean of the estimates is 1, and so the estimate is approximately $0.7m$, much larger than the true value. Instead, we can use a different estimator, based on the number of entries in the summary that are nonzero (indicating that some item has updated them). After seeing n distinct items, the probability that an entry in the array is empty is $(1 - 1/m)^n$, assuming a random mapping of items to entries. This is well approximated by $\exp(-n/m)$. So we expect a $\exp(-n/m)$ fraction of the array entries to be empty. If we observe that there are V empty entries in the array, then we make our estimator to be $m\ln(m/V)$, by rearranging this expression. This correction can be used when it is feasible to do so, i.e., when V is nonzero. This estimator is known as LinearCounting, since it works well when the number of distinct items n is at most linear in m.

More advanced approaches can be used when this correction cannot be applied but the estimate is still small. Heule et al. [132] empirically measure the bias, and build a mapping from the estimated value based on tabulated values, and using these to interpolate a "corrected" estimate. This can be applied when the initial estimate indicates that n is small, e.g., when it appears to be below $5m$. Storing and accessing this mapping comes at some extra space cost, but this can be less significant if there are a large number of instances of HLL being run in parallel (to count different subsets of items), or if this look-up table can be stored in slower storage (slow memory or disk) and only accessed relatively rarely.

Sparse Representation for Small Counts. When space is at a high premium, as may be the case when a large number of HLL summaries are deployed in parallel to count a large number of different quantities, it is desirable to further compact the summary. Observe that when n is small, the number of entries of the array that are occupied is correspondingly small. In this case, it is more space efficient to store in a list information about only the nonempty entries. Further space reductions are possible by storing the list in sorted order and encoding the entries based on differences between subsequent entries in a bit-efficient variable-length encoding. However, this complicates the implementation, which has to convert between formats (array based and list based) and handle more cases. There is considerable scope for further encodings and optimizations here, which are described and evaluated at greater length in the literature.

History and Background. The development of the HLL sketch spans three decades, and due to its popularity, additional variations and implementation issues continue to be discussed. The central idea, of mapping items under a hash function and looking at the number of leading zeros in the hash value, was introduced by Flajolet and Martin in 1983 [106]. In this early paper, some key techniques were introduced, such as defining estimators based on different statistics of the z function and combining multiple estimators with the arithmetic average. This process was called Probabilistic Counting with Stochastic Averaging, or PCSA for short. A simple analysis to show that a similar algorithm gives a constant factor approximation with bounded independence hash functions is given by Alon et al. [11]. The work on LogLog counting, nearly 20 years later [93], is similar to HLL, but computes the (arithmetic) mean of the array entries first (with some truncation and restriction to reduce variance), then raises 2 to this power to obtain the estimate. The variation of using the hypergeometric mean was introduced by Flajolet et al. in 2007 [105] and shown to be very effective. Further commentary on the evolution of the data structure is given by Lumbroso [175]. A different branch of this work is due to Lang [166], who proposed a different approach to compressing the Flajolet–Martin sketch. The resulting approach is comparable in speed to HLL, while being very space efficient.

The summary has been used widely in practice, and a subsequent paper [132] studies multiple engineering optimizations to provide a more effective implementation. The "low-end correction" makes use of the LinearCounting algorithm, due to Whang et al. [232]. The example uses of the summary given by Heule et al. [132] include speeding up database queries that ask for the number of distinct elements in group-by queries (within the

PowerDrill system [128]); and within tools for analyzing massive log files to apply distinct counting, e.g., number of distinct advertising impressions [203] or distinct viewers of online content [50].

Theoretically speaking, the KMV and HLL are not the best summaries for approximately counting the number of distinct items. After a long line of research, the problem has been finally settled by Kane et al. [153], who gave a summary of $O(1/\varepsilon^2 + \log\log n)$ bits. Their summary returns a $(1 + \varepsilon)$-approximation to the distinct count with constant probability. It can also be updated in $O(1)$ time. To boost the success probability to $1 - \delta$, the standard approach is to take the median of $O(\log(1/\delta))$ independent instances of the summary. Interestingly, it has been recently shown that one can further improve this to using only $O(1/\varepsilon^2 \log(1/\delta) + \log n)$ bits [29]. This bound is optimal in all the parameters ε, δ, and n.

Available Implementations. Implementations of HLL are available in various software libraries and systems, such as stream-lib, the Redis database, and Algebird, part of Twitter's Summingbird streaming data processing tool. The DataSketches library implements HLL and several variants, such as the corrections due to Heule et al. [132], and with choices of 4, 6, or 8 bits per bucket, to accommodate different anticipated cardinalities. Processing speeds of tens of millions of UPDATE operations per second are easily achievable. An implementation of Lang's "Compressed Probabilistic Counting" [166] is also available in the library for comparison.

2.7 Bloom Filters for Set Membership

Brief Summary. The BloomFilter summarizes a set A of items in a compact (bit-efficient) format. Given a candidate item as a query, it answers whether the item is in A or not. It provides a one-sided guarantee: if the item is in the set, then it will always respond positively. However, there is the possibility of false positives. The probability of a false positive can be bounded as a function of the size of the summary and $|A|$: as the latter increases, false positives become more likely. The summary keeps a bit string, entries of which are set to one based on a hash function applied to the updates. In its simplest form, only insertions are allowed, but generalizations also allow deletions. The BloomFilter handles duplicates in the input automatically.

Operations on the Summary. The BloomFilter summary consists of a binary
string B of length m and k hash functions $h_1 \dots h_k$, which each independently
map elements of U to $\{1, 2, \dots m\}$. The INITIALIZE operation creates the string
B initialized to all zeros and picks the k hash functions. If the size of the set A is
expected to be n, a good choice of m and k is $m = 10n$ and $k = m/n \ln 2 = 7$;
the following analysis will give more guidance on how to set these parameters.

Algorithm 2.15: BloomFilter: UPDATE (i)

---

1 **for** $j \leftarrow 1$ **to** k **do**
2 $\quad \lfloor \; B[h_j(i)] \leftarrow 1;$

For each UPDATE operation to insert an element i into the set A, the
BloomFilter sets $B[h_j(i)] = 1$ for all $1 \leq j \leq k$, as shown in Algorithm 2.15.
Hence each update takes $O(k)$ time to process.

Algorithm 2.16: BloomFilter: QUERY (x)

---

1 **for** $j \leftarrow 1$ **to** k **do**
2 $\quad \lfloor \;$ **if** $B[h_j(x)] = 0$ **then return** false;
3 **return** true

The QUERY operation on a BloomFilter summary takes an element x from
U and tries to determine whether it was previously the subject of an UPDATE
operation, i.e., whether $x \in A$. The QUERY operation inspects the entries
$B[h_j(x)]$, where x would be mapped to if it were inserted. If there is some
$j \in [k]$ for which $B[h_j(x)] = 0$, then the item is surely not present: UPDATE
would have set all of these entries to 1, and no other operation ever changes
this. Otherwise, it is concluded that x is in A. Hence, Algorithm 2.16 inspects
all the locations where x is mapped, and returns false if any one of them is 0.

From this description, it can be seen that the data structure guarantees
no false negatives, but may report false positives. False positives occur if
a collection of other items inserted into the summary happens to cause the
corresponding entries $B[h_j(x)]$ to be 1, but x itself is never actually inserted.

Algorithm 2.17: BloomFilter: MERGE (B_a, B_b)

---

1 **for** $i \leftarrow 1$ **to** m **do**
2 $\quad \lfloor \; B_a[i] \leftarrow \max(B_a[i], B_b[i]);$

To MERGE two BloomFilter summaries, they must be built with the same
parameters, i.e., with the same size m, the same number of hash functions k,
and the same set of hash functions $h_1 \dots h_k$. The resulting BloomFilter is the

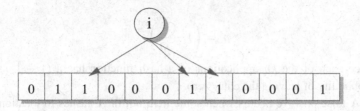

Figure 2.3 Bloom filter with $k = 3$, $m = 12$.

bitwise OR of the two bitstrings. That is, the new B has $B[j] = 1$ if this entry was 1 in either of the input summaries, and is 0 if this entry was 0 in both. Algorithm 2.17 takes a pass through the two input summaries and merges the second into the first.

Example. A simple example is shown in Figure 2.3: an item i is mapped by $k = 3$ hash functions to a filter of size $m = 12$, and these entries are set to 1.

Further Discussion. A basic rule-of-thumb is that the size of the Bloom-Filter in bits should be roughly proportional to the size of the set S that is to be summarized. That is, the summary cannot encode a very large set in space dramatically smaller than the innate size of the set. However, the filter can be much smaller than explicitly representing the set A, either by listing its members, or storing them in a hash table. This is particularly pronounced when the identifiers of the elements are quite large, since the BloomFilter does not explicitly store these. If the size of the set A is expected to be n, allocating $m = 10n$ (i.e., 10 bits per item stored) and $k = 7$ gives a false positive probability of around 1%. To understand the relation between these parameters in more detail, we present further detailed analysis as follows.

Detailed Analysis of BloomFilter. The false positive rate can be analyzed as a function of $|A| = n$, m, and k: given bounds on n and m, optimal values of k can be set. We follow the outline of Broder and Mitzenmacher [40] to derive the relationship between these values. For the analysis, the hash functions are assumed to be fully random. That is, the location that an item is mapped to by any hash function is viewed as being uniformly random over the range of possibilities and fully independent of the other hash functions. Consequently, the probability that any entry of B is zero after n distinct items have been seen is given by

$$p' = \left(1 - \frac{1}{m}\right)^{kn}$$

since each of the kn applications of a hash function has a $(1 - 1/m)$ probability of leaving the entry zero.

A false positive occurs when some item not in A hashes to locations in B that are all set to 1 by other items. For an arbitrary item not in A, this happens with probability $(1 - \rho)^k$, where ρ denotes the fraction of bits in B that are set to 0. In expectation, ρ is equal to p', and it can be shown that ρ is very close to p' with high probability. Given fixed values of m and n, it is possible to optimize k, the number of hash functions. Small values of k keep the number of 1s lower, but make it easier to have a collision; larger values of k increase the density of 1s. The false positive rate is

$$q = \left(1 - \left(1 - \frac{1}{m}\right)^{kn}\right)^k \approx \left(1 - e^{-kn/m}\right)^k = \exp\left(k \ln\left(1 - e^{kn/m}\right)\right).$$

(2.6)

The smallest value of q as a function of k is given by minimizing the exponent. This in turn can be written as $-m/n \ln(p) \ln(1 - p)$, for $p = e^{-kn/m}$, and so by symmetry, the smallest value occurs for $p = 1/2$. Rearranging gives $k = (m/n) \ln 2$.

This has the effect of setting the occupancy of the filter to be 0.5, that is, half the bits are expected to be 0 and half 1. This causes the false positive rate to be $q = (1/2)^k = (0.6185)^{m/n}$. To make this probability at most a small constant, it is necessary to make $m > n$. Indeed, setting $m = cn$ gives the false positive probability at 0.6185^c: choosing $c = 9.6$, for example, is sufficient to make this probability less than 1%.

Other Operations on BloomFilter *Summaries.* The semantics of the MERGE operator is to provide a BloomFilter summary of the union of the two sets summarized by each input summary. It is also possible to build a summary that corresponds to the intersection of the input sets, by taking the bitwise AND of each bit in the bitstrings, instead of the bitwise OR. That is, if we were to keep the two BloomFilter summaries and test whether x was present in both, we would check the locations $h_j(x)$ in each summary. If there is any such location in either summary that is 0, then we would conclude x is not present in both. This is equivalent to taking the bitwise AND of each of these locations, and checking them all. So the BloomFilter summary that is formed as the bitwise

AND of the two input summaries will give the same response for every query x.

The summary as described so far only allows UPDATE operations that insert an item into the set A. More generally, we might like to allow deletions of elements as well. There are two possible semantics for deletions. If we treat A as a set, then a deletion of element x ensures that x is not stored in the set any more. If we treat A as a multiset, then each element in the set has a multiplicity, such that insertions increase that multiplicity, and deletions decrement it (down to 0). In both cases, to handle deletions we will replace the bitstring B with a collection of counters, but how we use these counters will differ.

We first consider the set semantics. The data structure looks much the same as before, except each bit is replaced with a small counter. Here, an UPDATE operation corresponding to an insert of i first performs a QUERY to test whether i is already represented in the summary. If so, nothing changes. Otherwise, the operation increments the counter $B[h_j(i)]$ for $h_1 \ldots h_k$. Likewise, an UPDATE that is a deletion of i also checks whether i is stored in the summary. If so, the operation decrements the counters $B[h_j(i)]$. Otherwise, nothing changes. Lastly, the QUERY operation remains as shown in Algorithm 2.16: it checks all locations where i is mapped, and returns false if any is 0. The interpretation of the summary is that each counter stores the number of distinct items that have been mapped there. Insertions increase these counts, while deletions decrease these counts. Because multiple insertions of the same item do not alter the structure, these counters do not need to grow very large. However, note that it is now possible to have false negatives from this structure: an insertion of an item that is not present in the structure may not lead to counter increments if there is a false positive for it. The subsequent deletion of this item may lead to zero values, causing false negatives for other items. Analysis shows that counters with a bit depth of only 4 bits will suffice to keep accurate summaries without overflow. This analysis is due to Fan et al., who dub this variant of the BloomFilter the "counting Bloom Filter" [101].

The case for the multiset semantics is simpler to describe, but requires more space in general. Instead of a bitmap, the Bloom filter is now represented by an array of counters. When performing an UPDATE that inserts a new copy of i, we increase the corresponding counters by 1, i.e., $B[h_j(i)] \leftarrow B[h_j(i)] + 1$. Likewise, for an UPDATE that removes a copy of i, we decrease the corresponding counters by 1. Now the transform is linear, and so it can process arbitrary streams of update transactions. The number of entries needed in the array remains the same, but now the entries are counters (represented with 32 or 64 bits) rather than single bits, and these counters may now need to represent a large number of elements. This variation is referred to as a spectral Bloom filter, and is described by Cohen and Matias, who also discuss space efficient ways to implement the counters [60].

History and Background. The BloomFilter summary, named for its inventor [31], was first proposed in 1970 in the context of compactly representing information. One of the first applications was to compactly represent a dictionary for spell-checking [181]. Its attraction is that it is a compact and fast alternative to explicitly representing a set of items when it is not required to list out the members of the set. Interest in the structure was renewed in the late 1990s, in the context of tracking the content of caches of large data in a network [101]. Subsequently, there has been a huge interest in using BloomFilter summaries for a wide variety of applications, and many variations and extensions have been proposed. Broder and Mitzenmacher provide a survey of some of these uses [40, 184], but there have been many more papers published on this summary and its variants in the interim.

A common theme of applications of Bloom filters is that they require that a small fraction of false positives must be acceptable, or that it be feasible to double-check a positive report (at some additional cost) using a more authoritative reference. For example, they can be used to avoid storing items in a cache, if the item has not been previously accessed. That is, we use a Bloom filter to record item accesses, and only store an item if it has been seen at least once before. In this example, the consequence of false positives is just that a small number of unpopular items ends up being cached, which should have minimal impact on system performance. This exemplar is now found in practice in many large distributed databases, such as Google BigTable, Apache Cassandra, and HBase. These systems keep a Bloom filter to index distributed segments of sparse tables of data. The filter records which rows or columns of the table are stored and can use a negative response to avoid a costly look-up on disk or over the network.

Another example is from web browsers, which aim to protect their users from malware by warning about deceptive or dangerous sites. This check requires looking up the web site address (URL) in a database of known problematic URLs, and reporting if a match is found. This database is sufficiently large that it is not convenient to keep locally on the (mobile) device. Instead, the browser can keep a Bloom filter encoding the database to check URLs against. Most URLs visited do not trigger the Bloom filter, and so do not affect the behavior. When the Bloom filter reports a potential positive, it can be checked against the centralized database with a look-up over the network. This slows things down, but so long as false positives are sufficiently rare, then the impact is minimal. Thus, the correct response is found for each URL, while the common case (the URL is allowed) is made fast. The space is kept low, based on a Bloom filter of a few megabytes in size. This approach has been adopted by browsers including Chrome and Firefox. Current versions have adopted variant summaries, which trade off a higher time for queries and reduced capacity to handle updates (since the sets are not updated more than once a day) for reduced size.

Other examples of Bloom filters in practice range from speeding up actions in blockchain implementations to providing private collection of browsing statistics [99]. Given these applications, it is likely that Bloom filters are the most widely used of the summaries discussed in this book, after "classical" summaries based on random sampling.

Available Implementations. Given its ubiquity, many implementations of the BloomFilter are available online, across a wide range of languages. The code hosting site GitHub lists over a thousand references to Bloom-Filter (https://github.com/search?q=bloom+filter), in languages including Java, JavaScript, C, C++, Go, Python, and more. The implementation from stream-lib (https://github.com/addthis/stream-lib/tree/master/src/main/java/com/clear spring/analytics/stream/membership) takes around 100 lines of Java, although the core logic for UPDATE and QUERY are a handful of lines each. Likewise, Algebird (https://github.com/twitter/algebird/blob/develop/algebird-core/src/main/scala/com/twitter/algebird/BloomFilter.scala) provides a flexible Scala implementation.

3

Summaries for Multisets

This chapter turns to multisets, namely, each item in the set A to be summarized is associated with a multiplicity representing its number of occurrences, and queries to the multiset relate to the multiplicity of items. Recall from Section 1.2.1 that a convenient way to represent a multiset is to use a vector v, where v_x denotes the multiplicity of x. In this chapter, we assume that the input consists of (x, w) pairs, where x is an item drawn from a universe U, and w is the weight. For simplicity, we assume the weights are integers, but generalization to real numbers is often possible. Some summaries only allow positive weights, while others allow both positive and negative weights, where negative weights correspond to deletion of items from the multiset. The multiplicity of x, v_x, is thus the sum of all the weights of x in the input. We assume every v_x to be nonnegative whenever the summary is queried.

Error guarantees for queries over a multiset often depend on $\|v\|_p$, the ℓ_p-norm of the vector v, where $\|v\|_p = \left(\sum_i v_i^p \right)^{1/p}$. The most commonly used norms are the ℓ_1-norm (which is simply the total weight of all items) and the ℓ_2-norm.

The summaries covered in this chapter solve the following problems:

- Testing whether two multisets contain the exact same set of items and frequencies: the Fingerprint summary (Section 3.1).
- Tracking the high-frequency items over weighted positive updates: the MG and SpaceSaving summaries (Sections 3.2 and 3.3).
- Estimating the frequencies of items over weighted positive and negative updates under different error guarantees: the Count-Min Sketch and Count Sketch summaries (Sections 3.4 and 3.5).
- Estimating the Euclidean norm of the vector of frequencies of a mulitset: the AMS Sketch (Section 3.6).

- Estimating arbitrary Minkowski (ℓ_p) norms of a multiset: the ℓ_p sketch (Section 3.7).
- Exactly recovering the items and (integer) frequencies for a multiset that has a bounded number of elements after a sequence of insertions and deletions: the SparseRecovery summary (Section 3.8).
- Sampling near-uniformly from the set of distinct items in a multiset with (integer) frequencies: the ℓ_0-sampler structure (Section 3.9).
- Sampling near-uniformly from a multiset with arbitrary weights, according to a class of weighting functions: the ℓ_p-sampler structure (Section 3.10).

3.1 Fingerprints for Testing Multiset Equality

Brief Summary. A Fingerprint summary represents a large multiset of items as a very compact hash value. Given two Fingerprint summaries, if the summaries are different, then the corresponding multisets must differ, while if the summaries are identical, then with high probability we conclude that the corresponding multisets are identical. The probability of a false positive – of erroneously concluding that two distinct sets are identical – is governed by the size of the summary, and can be made vanishingly small. Fingerprint summaries of two multisets can be combined to generate a Fingerprint of the *sum* of the multisets, i.e., where multiplicities of the same item are added.

Algorithm 3.1: Fingerprint: UPDATE (x, w)

---

1   $f \leftarrow (f + w\alpha^x) \bmod p$;

Operations on the Summary. For now, we assume that the universe U from which items are drawn is the integer domain $U = [u] = \{0, 1, \ldots, u - 1\}$. The Fingerprint summary can be thought of as a (possibly large) integer number f in the range 0 to $p - 1$, where p is a fixed prime number greater than u. It also requires a randomly chosen value α. To INITIALIZE an empty summary, we fix a prime number $p > u$ and set f to 0. We also choose α uniformly at random in the range 1 to $p - 1$. To UPDATE the summary with a new item x, we set $f \leftarrow (f + \alpha^x) \bmod p$. If x has an associated weight w (which can be either positive or negative), then this UPDATE becomes $f \leftarrow (f + w\alpha^x) \bmod p$. Algorithm 3.1 shows how to UPDATE the Fingerprint summary with an item x of weight w.

Algorithm 3.2: Fingerprint: MERGE (f_a, f_b)

---

1 **return** $(f_a + f_b)$ mod p;

To MERGE two **Fingerprint** summaries, f_a and f_b, with the same parameters (i.e., both have the same p and α values), the merged summary is given by $(f_a + f_b)$ mod p. Thus, the MERGE operation shown in Algorithm 3.2 simply has to return the sum, modulo p. As indicated earlier, to QUERY whether two summaries represent the same multiset, we report true if the corresponding summaries are identical, and false otherwise.

Example. For a simple example, we pick $p = 13$ and $\alpha = 3$. Given input of the item 4, we compute the **Fingerprint** summary as 3^4 mod $13 = 3$. Consider the input consisting of the set $\{1, 2\}$. The **Fingerprint** summary of this input is $3^1 + 3^2$ mod $13 = 12$, which is different from the previous **Fingerprint** summary, as desired. However, the input $\{5, 10\}$ also has the **Fingerprint** summary $3^5 + 3^{10}$ mod $13 = 12$, a collision. This is due in part to the small value of p: choosing larger p values makes such collisions increasingly unlikely.

Implementation Issues. Computing α^x can be done efficiently by the method of *exponentiation by squaring*, that is, we first compute $\alpha, \alpha^2, \alpha^4, \alpha^8, \ldots,$ in succession, and then pick the right collection of terms to make up α^x, depending on the location of ones in the binary representation of x. All computations are done modulo p, so that the intermediate results can be kept no larger than p^2.

Alternative Fingerprint Construction. If the weight w is usually small, there is another fingerprint construction that is more efficient. We similarly pick some prime $p > u$ and a random number α in the range 1 to $p - 1$. The operations, however, are slightly different. To INITIALIZE an empty summary, we set f to 1 (as opposed to 0). To UPDATE the summary with an item x with weight w, we set $f \leftarrow f \cdot (\alpha + x)^w$ mod p. Using the exponentiation by squaring technique, this fingerprint thus requires $O(\log w)$ time to update. In particular, if each update only adds a single item, this fingerprint can be updated in $O(1)$ time.

However, if w is negative (i.e., deleting items from the summary), things become a bit tricky as we need to set $f \leftarrow f \cdot (\alpha + x)^w$ mod p. Here, the exponentiation should be done in the finite field $[p]$. More precisely, we first need to compute $(\alpha + x)^{-1}$, which is the value $y \in [p]$ such that

$(\alpha + x) \cdot y \mod p = 1$. This can be done using Euclid's gcd algorithm [159] in $O(\log p)$ time. Then we use exponentiation by squaring to compute y^{-w}.

Finally, to MERGE two such fingerprints f_a and f_b, we simply compute $f_a \cdot f_b \mod p$.

Further Discussion. To understand the properties of the Fingerprint summary, consider the frequency vector representation of the multiset. For a frequency vector v, the Fingerprint summary is given by

$$f(v) = \sum_{i \in U} v_i \alpha^i \mod p.$$

The analysis of this summary relies on the fact that it can be viewed as a polynomial in α of degree at most u. Such a polynomial can have at most u roots (values of α where it evaluates to zero). Technically, we are evaluating this polynomial over the finite field $[p]$. Testing whether two multisets D and D' are equal, based on the fingerprints of their corresponding frequency vectors, $f(v)$ and $f(v')$, is equivalent to testing the identity $f(v) - f(v') = 0$. Based on the definition of f, if the two multisets are identical, then the fingerprints will be identical. But if they are different and the test still passes, the fingerprint will give the wrong answer. Treating $f()$ as a polynomial in α, $f(v) - f(v')$ has degree no more than u, so there can only be u values of α for which $f(v) - f(v') = 0$. Effectively, the fingerprint is the evaluation of this polynomial at a randomly chosen value of α; it can only result in 0 when we are unlucky and choose an α, which happens to be a root of this polynomial. But we can bound the probability of this event. Specifically, if p is chosen to be at least u/δ, the probability (based on choosing a random α) of having picked a root is at most δ, for a parameter δ. This requires the modular arithmetic operations to be done using $O(\log u + \log 1/\delta)$ bits of precision, which is feasible for most reasonable choices of U and δ. This analysis also assumes that the coefficients of the polynomial f are representable within the field, i.e., all v_i are less than p. This means that p should be chosen such that $p \geq \max\{u/\delta, v_i, i \in [u]\}$.

Viewing the Fingerprint summary through the lens of polynomials, it is then clear why the UPDATE and MERGE operations are as stated: an UPDATE computes the change in $f(v)$ caused by the change in v, while MERGE takes advantage of the fact that the Fingerprint of the sum of two vectors is the sum of the corresponding Fingerprint summaries.

The preceding analysis also applies to the second fingerprint, by observing that it evaluates the following polynomial:

$$f(v) = \prod_{i \in U} (\alpha - i)^{v_i} \mod p.$$

This polynomial has degree $\sum_i v_i$. Thus if we choose $p \geq \sum_i v_i / \delta$, then the probability that this fingerprint fails is at most δ.

So far, we have assumed that the input item identifiers x are integers, since the argument is all based on evaluating polynomials over the finite field $[p]$. However, it is natural to allow x to be drawn from an arbitrary domain U. We just require a suitable hash function that will map U to a large enough integer domain. Ideally, the size of the integer domain should be polynomial in the number of distinct items seen. That is, if there are n different input items, then mapping to a domain of size n^3 means that with high probability there will be no hash collisions. This affects the choice of p, but only by a constant factor in terms of bit length.

The Fingerprint summary does require that all the item frequencies v_i are integral. Fractional values can be tolerated, if these can be rescaled to be integral. Arbitrary real values are not allowed, since these conflict with the analysis over finite fields.

History and Background. The idea of a compact hash function to test equality or inequality of sets or vectors has been used many times in computer science. Many different forms of hash function are possible, but we adopt this form to define the Fingerprint summary due to its ability to support both UPDATE and MERGE operations quite efficiently. Note that while these appear similar to the family of hash functions described in Section 1.4.2, they are distinct: in Section 1.4.2, we compute a polynomial of degree t, where the coefficients are chosen randomly (then fixed), and the variable x is the single data item; here, we compute a polynomial of potentially much higher degree, where the data determine the coefficients, and the variable x is chosen randomly (then fixed). The form of hash used here is inspired by the style of "rolling hash" function used in the Karp–Rabin string matching algorithm [157], and its generalization by Lipton [173]. Applications are broad: fingerprints can be used anywhere that a checksum would be useful, to check correct storage or transmission of data. They can also be applied to find large matching pieces of data in files that have changed, and so reduce the communication cost of sending the new version, such as in the rsync protocol [225], also used by systems like Dropbox and Amazon S3. Fingerprints are also used by some of other summary constructions, such as SparseRecovery (Section 3.8).

3.2 Misra–Gries (MG)

Brief Summary. The Misra–Gries (MG) summary maintains a subset of items from a multiset v, with an associated weight for each item stored. It answers point queries approximately: the answer to a query x is the weight associated with x in the summary, if x is stored, and 0 otherwise. Given a parameter ε, the summary stores $1/\varepsilon$ items and weights, and guarantees that for any point query x, the additive error from its true weight v_x is at most $\varepsilon \|v\|_1$. This summary only supports updates with positive weights.

Operations on the Summary. The MG summary is represented as a collection of pairs: items drawn from the input x and associated weights w_x, which will be an approximation of its true weight v_x. To INITIALIZE an empty MG summary, it suffices to create an empty set of tuples, with space to store $k = 1/\varepsilon$. Each UPDATE operation of an item x with weight w (which must be positive) tries to include x in the summary. If x is already stored with weight w_x, then UPDATE increases this weight to $w_x + w$. If not, provided there is room in the summary (i.e., there are fewer than k distinct items stored with nonzero weights), then a new tuple (x, w) is added to the summary. Else, there are already k tuples in the summary. Let m be the smallest weight among all these tuples and w itself. Then the UPDATE operation reduces all weights in the summary by m. If $w - m$ is still positive, then it can add the tuple $(x, w - m)$ to the summary: some tuple in the summary must have had its weight reduced to 0, and so can be overwritten with x.

Algorithm 3.3: MG: UPDATE $((x, w))$

---

1 **if** $i \in T$ **then**
2     $w_x \leftarrow w_x + w$;
3 **else**
4     $T \leftarrow T \cup \{x\}$;
5     $w_x \leftarrow w$;
6   **if** $|T| > k$ **then**
7        $m = \min(\{w_x : x \in T\})$;
8   **forall** $j \in T$ **do**
9           $w_j \leftarrow w_j - m$;
10   **if** $w_j = 0$ **then** $T \leftarrow T \setminus \{j\}$;

Pseudocode to illustrate the UPDATE operation is given in Algorithm 3.3, making use of set notation to represent the operations on the set of stored items T: items are added and removed from this set using set union and set subtraction respectively, and we allow ranging over the members of this set (thus implementations will have to choose appropriate data structures that allow the efficient realization of these operations). We also assume that each item j stored in T has an associated weight w_j. For items not stored in T, we define w_j to be 0, which does not need to be explicitly stored. Lines 6 to 10 handle the case when we need to find the minimum weight item and decrease weights by this much. The inner for-loop performs this decrease and removes items with weight 0.

The MERGE of two MG summaries is a generalization of the UPDATE operation. Given two summaries constructed using the same parameter k, first merge the component tuples in the natural way: if x is stored in both summaries, its merged weight is the sum of the weights in each input summary. If x is stored in only one of the summaries, it is also placed in the merged summary with the same weight. This produces a new MG summary with between k and $2k$ tuples, depending on the amount of overlap of items between the two input summaries. To reduce the size back to k, we sort the tuples by weight, and find the $k + 1$st largest weight, w_{k+1}. This weight is subtracted from *all* tuples. At most k tuples can now have weight above zero: the tuple with the $k+1$st largest weight, and all tuples with smaller weight, will now have weight 0 or below, and so can be discarded from the summary. The preceding UPDATE procedure can therefore be seen as the case of MERGE where one of the summaries contains just a single item.

Algorithm 3.4: MG: MERGE (T_a, T_b)

---

1 $T \leftarrow T_a$;
2 **forall** $j \in T_b$ **do**
3   **if** $j \in T$ **then** $w_j \leftarrow w_j + w_{b,j}$;
4   **else**
5          $T \leftarrow T \cup \{j\}$;
6          $w_j \leftarrow w_{b,j}$;

7 **if** $|T| > k$ **then**
8      $w_{k+1} \leftarrow k + 1$st largest weight ;
9   **forall** $j \in T$ **do**
10         $w_j \leftarrow w_j - w_{k+1}$;
11   **if** $w_j \leq 0$ **then** $T \leftarrow T \setminus \{j\}$;

Algorithm 3.4 shows the pseudocode to MERGE two MG summaries T_a and T_b together. Line 3 captures the case when j is present in both, and computes the new weight as the sum of the two weights. Lines 7 through 11 then reduce the size of the merged summary to k by reducing weights and removing items with nonpositive weights.

To QUERY for the estimated weight of an item x, we look up whether x is stored in the summary. If so, QUERY reports the associated weight w_x as the estimate; otherwise, the weight is assumed to be 0. Comparing the approximate answer given by QUERY, and the true weight of x (the sum of all weights associated with x in the input), the approximate answer is never more than the true answer. This is because the weight associated with x in the summary is the sum of all weights for x in the input, less the various decreases due to MERGE and UPDATE operations. The MG summary also ensures that this estimated weight is not more than εW below the true answer, where W is the sum of all input weights. A tighter guarantee provided is that this error is at most $(W - M)/(k + 1)$, where M is the sum of the counters in the structure, and k is the number of counters.

Example. Consider the input sequence

$$a, b, a, c, d, e, a, d, f, a, d$$

interpreted as a sequence of items of weight 1. If we UPDATE each item in turn into a MG summary of size k=3, we obtain at the end

a	d	-
2	1	0

There are two points where counts are decremented: on the UPDATE for the first d, and on the UPDATE for the f. Our final estimate of a is 2, which underestimates the true count by 2, which meets the bound of $(W - M)/(k + 1) = (11 - 3)/4 = 2$.

If we MERGE this summary with the MG summary

b	c	d
3	1	2

the final MG summary we obtain is

a	b	d
1	2	2

Further Discussion. To understand the guarantees of the MG summary, we study the effect of each operation in turn. First, consider a summary subject to a sequence of UPDATE operations alone. Let W be the sum of the input weights, and let M denote the sum of the weights stored by the summary. Consider the impact of decreasing the m value during an UPDATE operation. This impacts the weight of $k + 1$ items: the k items in the summary, and the new item that is the subject of the UPDATE. Consequently, we can "spread" the impact of this reduction across $k + 1$ items. The total impact is to increase the difference between W and M (the sum of stored weights) by $(k + 1) \cdot m$. Thus, at any point, the error in the estimated weight of an item is at most $(W - M)/(k + 1)$. This is because this difference, $(W - M)$, arises only from reductions in count to items during the UPDATE operations. Even if one item lost weight during all of these, the same weight loss was shared by k others (possibly different each time). So no item can suffer more than a $1/(k + 1)$ fraction of the total weight loss, $(W - M)$.

A similar argument holds in the case of MERGE operations. Let W_a and W_b denote the total weights of inputs summarized by the two MG summaries to be merged, and M_a, M_b represent the corresponding sum of weights stored in the summary. Following the MERGE operation, the new weight of the summary is M_{ab}, which is at most the sum $M_a + M_b$. The MERGE operation means that the difference $(M_a + M_b) - M_{ab}$ is at least $(k+1)w_{k+1}$: we subtract w_{k+1} from the $k+1$ largest weights (ignoring the impact on the smaller weights). Rearranging, we have $w_{k+1} \leq \frac{1}{k+1}(M_a + M_b - M_{ab})$. The amount of additional error introduced by the MERGE into each estimated weight is at most w_{k+1}. If we assume (inductively) that the prior error from the two summaries is $(W_a - M_a)/(k + 1)$ and $(W_b - M_b)/(k + 1)$ respectively, then the new error is at most

$$\frac{1}{k + 1} ((W_a - M_a) + (W_b - M_b) + (M_a + M_b - M_{ab}))$$

$$= \frac{1}{k + 1}(W_a + W_b - M_{ab}) = (W_{ab} - M_{ab})/(k + 1).$$

Consequently, the MERGE operation also preserves the property that the query error is bounded by at most a $1/(k+1)$ fraction of the difference between the sum of true weights and the sum of weights stored in the summary. Even in the worst case, when the weight of items stored in the summary is zero, this guarantees error of at most $W/(k + 1) \leq \varepsilon W$. In general, the bound can be stronger. Let $W^{\text{res}(t)}$ denote the *residual weight* of the input after removing the t heaviest items (as defined in Section 1.2.1). We can show a bound on the error in terms of $W^{\text{res}(t)}$ for $t < k$. Let Δ denote the largest error in estimating the weight of any item. By the preceding analysis, we have that $\Delta \leq (W - M)/(k + 1)$, and so $M \leq W - \Delta(k + 1)$. Let w_i denote the (true) weight of the ith heaviest item. The estimated weight of this item is at least $w_i - \Delta$, so considering just the t heaviest items, $\sum_{i=1}^{t}(w_i - \Delta) \leq M$. Combining these two results, we have

$$\sum_{i=1}^{t}(w_i - \Delta) \leq W - \Delta(k + 1).$$

Rearranging, we obtain

$$\Delta \leq W^{\text{res}(t)}/(k + 1 - t).$$

In other words, for skewed distributions (where $W^{\text{res}(t)}$ is small compared to W), the accuracy guarantee is stronger.

Implementation Issues. A limitation of the MG summary is that the weight stored for an item may be considerably lower than the true count, due to weight reductions caused by many other items. A simple adjustment that can improve the accuracy at the expense of increasing the space used is to retain two weights for each item: the estimated weight as described previously, and a second observed weight, which is increased in accordance with the preceding procedures, but which is never decreased. This too is a lower bound on the true weight, but can be higher than the estimated weight that is used to determine when to retain the item. Note that this can still underestimate the true weight, since the item might be ejected from the summary at various points, and then the accrued weight of the item is lost.

The estimates provided are lower bounds. To turn these to upper bounds, we can add on a sufficient amount. It is straightforward to track W, the total weight of the whole input. Trivially, adding $W/(k + 1)$ to any estimated count provides an upper bound over any input. We can give a better bound in some cases by using $(W - M)/(k + 1)$, where M is the sum of the weights stored in the summary, as described earlier.

There has been much discussion in the research literature about how best to implement the MG summary to ensure that operations on the structure can be performed very quickly. When processing large sequences of UPDATE operations, we need to quickly determine whether x is currently stored in the structure (and if so, retrieve and modify its count), and also quickly find the minimum weight item and reduce all items by this amount. The question of tracking whether an item is currently stored is a standard *dictionary* data structure question. It can be addressed deterministically, by keeping the current set of items T in a search-tree data structure, or via a randomized hash-table data structure. The former supports insertion, deletion, and lookup of items in worst-case time $O(\log k)$, and the latter supports these operations in expected time $O(1)$.

Tracking the minimum value and modifying all the others is a less standard step. The simplest solution is just to iterate among all the stored counts to find the minimum, and then a second time to reduce them by this amount. This however takes time $O(k)$, which would slow down UPDATE operations. Instead, we can optimize this step (at the cost of slowing down QUERY operations) by storing the items in sorted order of their weights, and representing their weights in terms of the *difference* in weight between the next heaviest item. That is, we store the lightest-weight item first, then the next lightest and the amount by which it is heavier, and so on. To reduce the weights by the m value, it suffices to modify the weight of the lightest item or remove it entirely. However, to insert a new item means stepping through this sorted list to find where the item belongs – which requires linear time $O(k)$ in the worst case. We can reduce this time cost, since we do not strictly require that the items are kept in sorted order of weight, only that we can find (and possibly remove) the item of least weight. As a result, it is possible to adopt a min-heap data structure for this purpose. In the heap, we still store weights in terms of differences between the item and its parent in the heap. Using this representation, the heap operations to add a new item, modify the weight of an existing item, or remove the minimum weight item (and, implicitly, reduce the weights of the other items in the heap) can all be performed efficiently. In particular, these can all be done in time $O(\log k)$, proportional to the height of the heap. However, these are typically not supported in standard heap implementations, and so need to be implemented specially for this purpose. When we present the closely related SpaceSaving algorithm in Section 3.3, we will see how this summary can be implemented using an off-the-shelf heap structure.

In the special case when the updates are always 1 (so we are just counting the number of occurrences of each item), it is possible to reduce the UPDATE cost to constant time. In this case, we again represent the weight of items in terms of the difference between their weight and lighter items. However, we also group together all items that have the same weight and arrange the groups in order of increasing weight. Now observe that when we increase the weight of an item, due to an arrival of weight 1, then the item must move from its current group, to the next group if this has a weight difference of 1, or to a new group in between the current group and the next group, if the weight difference to the next group is greater than 1. Working through all the stages in UPDATE, all these steps can be performed in $O(1)$ time, if we maintain the items in groups via doubly linked lists. However, the number of cases to handle is quite large, and many pointer operations are required. Careful use of hash tables and arrays can simplify this logic and give a more compact representation [22].

History and Background. The history of this summary spans at least three decades. Initial interest arose from the question of finding the majority choice from a collection of votes. This problem and a candidate solution was described by Boyer and Moore [35]. The technical core of the solution is essentially the MG summary with $k = 1$ and all input weights set to 1, which therefore finds if there is one item that occurs more than half the time (a strict majority).

A generalization of this approach to process sequences of items with unit weight, and find all those that occur more than a $1/k$ fraction of the time, was first proposed by Misra and Gries [183]. The time cost of their algorithm is dominated by the $O(1)$ dictionary operations per update and the cost of decrementing counts. Misra and Gries described the use of a balanced search tree, and argued that the decrement cost is amortized $O(1)$. Refinements of this approach emerged two decades later, due to renewed interest in efficient algorithms for processing large streams of data. Karp et al. proposed a hash table to implement the dictionary [156]; and Demaine et al. show how the cost of decrementing can be made worst case $O(1)$ by representing the counts using offsets and maintaining multiple linked lists [85]. Bose et al. [34] observed that executing this algorithm with $k = 1/\epsilon$ ensures that the count associated with each item on termination is at most ϵW below the true value.

The extension to allow a MERGE operation, in addition to UPDATE, was made more recently [26], where the bounds in terms of $W^{\text{res}(k)}$ were also shown. The strong bounds on the effect of MERGE are due to Agarwal et al. [2]. Additional historical context for this summary is provided in [68]. An optimized implementation of MG is discussed by Anderson et al. [12], with particular attention paid to handling weighted updates and MERGE operations efficiently.

Available Implementations. The MG summary forms the basis of the Frequent Items implementation within the DataSketches library, https://datasketches.github.io/docs/Frequency/ FrequentItemsOverview.html. Items within the summary are stored in a hash table, and the compression of the summary to decrement counts is performed with a linear pass through the current structure. Optimizations due to Anderson et al. [12] are included. These ensure that the implementation is easily capable of processing over ten million UPDATE operations per second.

3.3 SpaceSaving

Brief Summary. The SpaceSaving summary retains a subset of items from a multiset v, with an associated weight for each. It answers point queries approximately: the answer to a query x is the weight associated with x in the summary, if x is stored, and 0 otherwise. Given a parameter ε, the summary stores $1/\varepsilon$ items and counts, and answers point queries with additive error at most $\varepsilon \|v\|_1$. It only supports updates with positive weights. Conceptually, the SpaceSaving summary is very similar to the MG summary (Section 3.2), with a few operational differences, and in fact the two structures can be considered almost identical.

Algorithm 3.5: SpaceSaving: UPDATE (x, w)

---

1 **if** $x \in T$ **then**
2 | $w_x \leftarrow w_x + w$;
3 **else**
4 | $y \leftarrow \arg\min_{j \in T} w_j$;
5 | $w_x \leftarrow w_y + w$;
6 | $T \leftarrow T \cup \{x\} \backslash \{y\}$;

Operations on the Summary. Like the MG summary, the SpaceSaving summary is represented as a collection of pairs of items drawn from the input x, and associated weights w_x. To INITIALIZE an empty summary, an empty set of $k = 1/\varepsilon$ tuples is created. It is sometimes convenient to think of these tuples being initialized to k distinct (dummy) values, each with associated count zero.

Each UPDATE operation of an item x with weight w tries to include x in the summary. If x is already stored with weight w_x, the UPDATE increases this weight to $w_x + w$. Otherwise, the operation identifies the stored tuple with the smallest weight, say y, and replaces it with the new item x. The corresponding weight is set to $w_y + w$. When there are multiple items stored in the summary with the same, least weight, an arbitrary one can be selected for replacement.

Algorithm 3.5 presents pseudocode for the UPDATE operation, where the set T holds the currently monitored items. This assumes that the summary is initialized with k "dummy" entries, so that each UPDATE preserves the size of the summary at k elements.

A MERGE operation is quite simple, and proceeds in the natural way, given two SpaceSaving summaries of the same size. The merged summary initially contains all items that occur in either of the input summaries. If an item x is stored in both summaries, then its weight in the new summary is the sum of its

---

Algorithm 3.6: SpaceSaving: MERGE (T_a, T_b)

1 $T \leftarrow T_a$;
2 **forall** $j \in T_b$ **do**
3   **if** $j \in T$ **then** $w_j \leftarrow w_j + w_{b,j}$;
4   **else**
5          $T \leftarrow T \cup \{j\}$;
6          $w_j \leftarrow w_{b,j}$;

7 **if** $|T| > k$ **then**
8      $w_{k+1} \leftarrow k + 1$st largest weight ;
9   **forall** $j \in T$ **do**
10   **if** $w_j \leq w_{k+1}$ **then** $T \leftarrow T \setminus \{j\}$;

---

weights in the previous summaries. Otherwise, its weight is the weight from whichever summary it was stored in. The intermediate result may have more than k tuples, so to reach a summary of bounded size, we retain only the k tuples with the largest weights (breaking any ties arbitrarily). Algorithm 3.6 shows the MERGE operation for the SpaceSaving summary. A subtlety not explicitly addressed in the pseudocode is that when multiple items share the same weight w_{k+1}, the algorithm should remove just the right number of them so that the resulting size of the summary is k.

To QUERY for the estimated weight of an item x, we look up whether x is stored in the SpaceSaving summary. If so, QUERY reports the associated weight as the estimate. This approximate answer is an overestimate of the true weight, as explained within the "Further Discussion" section. If x is not stored in the summary, then the QUERY operation can report the smallest weight value stored in the summary, n, as an upper bound on the true weight, or 0 as a lower bound on the true weight.

Example. Consider (again) the input sequence

$$a, \ b, \ a, \ c, \ d, \ e, \ a, \ d, \ f, \ a, \ d$$

interpreted as a sequence of items of weight 1. If we UPDATE each item in turn into a SpaceSaving summary of size $k = 4$, we may obtain at the end

a	d	e	f
4	3	2	2

Other instances of the summary are possible, depending on how we break ties when there are multiple items achieving the smallest frequency. For

concreteness, in this example, we break ties by overwriting the lexicograph-
ically smallest item.

Further Discussion. An important observation that simplifies the study
of this summary is that, despite differences in the description of the operations, it is essentially identical to the MG summary (Section 3.2). More
precisely, an MG summary with size parameter k and a SpaceSaving
summary with size parameter $k + 1$, subject to the same sequence of
UPDATE and MERGE operations over the same input contain the same
information. The correspondence between the two summaries is that the
estimated weight of x in the MG summary is the estimated weight of x
in the SpaceSaving summary, less the weight of the smallest item in the
summary, which we denote by n. For instance, comparing the example
(SpaceSaving with $k = 4$), with the corresponding example in the previous section (MG with $k = 3$), we see that after subtracting the minimum
value of 2 from the SpaceSaving example, we retain a with weight 2,
and d with weight 1, the same information as in the MG examples.

The proof that this holds in general proceeds inductively. The correspondence is certainly true initially, since all estimated weights in both
summaries are zero. Now consider the effect of an UPDATE operation
when the minimum value is denoted n, assuming that the correspondence
holds prior to this operation. If x is stored in both summaries, then the
correspondence holds after the UPDATE, since both estimated weights
increase by w. If x is not stored in the MG summary, but there is room to
store it, then its old estimated weight was 0 and its new estimated weight
is w. This means its estimated weight in SpaceSaving is n. Then either it
is stored in the SpaceSaving summary with weight n, or it is not stored,
and some item with weight n is overwritten. Either way, its new estimated
weight becomes $n + w$, preserving the correspondence. Lastly, if x is not
stored in the MG summary, and there is no room to store it, then all the
estimated weights there are reduced by the amount m. Using the assumed
correspondence, this means that there is a unique item with weight n in
the SpaceSaving summary, which is overwritten by x, and whose new
weight becomes $n + w$. Note that this has the effect of changing the
smallest weight in the SpaceSaving summary to either $n + w$ or the
smallest of the other estimated weights. Thus, the amount deducted from

the counts in MG, m, is exactly the amount by which the new smallest count in SpaceSaving differs from the old smallest count. Hence, the correspondence is preserved. By similar case-based reasoning, it follows that the MERGE operations also preserve this correspondence.

Thus the information provided by both summaries is essentially the same. The upper bound estimate stored by SpaceSaving can be transformed to the lower bound estimate, by subtracting n, the smallest of the stored counts.

Implementation Issues. The duality between the SpaceSaving and MG structures means that the same implementation issues affect both. However, the form of the SpaceSaving summary means that it is clearer to see an efficient way to process updates to the summary. Specifically, for an UPDATE we now only need to be able to find the smallest weighted item. This can be done using a standard min-heap data structure, with operations taking time $O(\log k)$. Merge operations requires summing up to k corresponding weights, and merging the structures, and so requires time $O(k)$.

History and Background. The SpaceSaving summary was first proposed as such by Metwally et al. for unit weight updates [182]. The generalization to weighted updates was given later by [26]. The observation of the correspondence between SpaceSaving and MG was made in [2], and used to provide an efficient MERGE operation. Efficient implementations of SpaceSaving with optimizations to allow constant time (amortized or worst-case) UPDATE operations is given by Basat et al. [23, 24]. These are based on using the (approximate) median weight element in the data structure to prune elements, similar to the concurrent work of Anderson et al. [12] – see the historical notes on the MG summary in the previous section. Parallel implementations have also been considered [80]. The summary was introduced in the context of counting clicks within Internet advertising, and more generally applies where we want to count popular items out of a very large number of possibilities.

Available Implementations. An implementation of the algorithm is presented in the Algebird library, https://twitter.github.io/algebird/datatypes/approx/space_saver.html, among others.

3.4 Count-Min Sketch for Frequency Estimation

Brief Summary. Like the MG and the SpaceSaving summary, the Count-Min Sketch summary also summarizes a multiset v and answers point queries with error at most $\varepsilon \|v\|_1$. But it is a linear sketch, in the sense that it can be written as the action of matrix on a vector (expanded in more detail in Section 9.3.4). It thus supports updates with both positive and negative weights. The Count-Min Sketch summary maintains an array of counts, which are updated with each arriving item. It answers point queries approximately by probing the counts associated with the item, and picking the minimum of these. It is a randomized algorithm. Given parameters ε and δ, the summary uses space $O(1/\varepsilon \log 1/\delta)$, and guarantees with probability at least $1 - \delta$ that any point query is answered with additive error at most $\varepsilon \|v\|_1$. A variant of the summary uses $O(1/\varepsilon^2 \log 1/\delta)$ space and has error at most $\varepsilon \|v\|_2$ with probability at least $1 - \delta$.

Operations on the Summary. The Count-Min Sketch summary is represented as a compact array C of $d \times t$ counters, arranged as d rows of length t. For each row, a hash function h_j maps the input domain U uniformly onto the range $\{1, 2, \ldots, t\}$. To INITIALIZE a new summary, the array of counters is created based on the parameters t and d, and every entry is set to 0. At the same time, a set of d hash functions is picked from a pairwise independent family (see Section 1.4.2). Algorithm 3.7 shows how to INITIALIZE the summary given parameters t and d, and randomly chooses the d hash functions (based on a suitable prime p).

Algorithm 3.7: Count-Min Sketch: INITIALIZE (t, d, p)

---
1 $C[1,1] \ldots C[d,t] \leftarrow 0$;
2 **for** $j \leftarrow 1$ **to** d **do**
3 $\quad \lfloor$ Pick a_j, b_j uniformly from $[1 \ldots p]$;

For each UPDATE operation to item i with weight w (which can be either positive or negative), the item is mapped to an entry in each row based on the hash functions, and the update applied to the corresponding counter. That is, for each $1 \leq j \leq d$, $h_j(i)$ is computed, and w is added to entry $C[j, h_j(i)]$ in the sketch array. Processing each update therefore takes time $O(d)$, since each hash function evaluation takes constant time. The pseudocode for UPDATE computes the hash function for each row of the update i, and updates the corresponding counter with the weight w (Algorithm 3.8).

Algorithm 3.8: Count-Min Sketch: UPDATE (i, w)

---

1 **for** $j \leftarrow 1$ **to** d **do**
2      $h_j(i) = (a_j \times i + b_j \mod p) \mod t$;
3      $C[j, h_j(i)] \leftarrow C[j, h_j(i)] + w$;

The Count-Min Sketch gets its name due to the two main operations used during a QUERY operation: counting of groups of items, and taking the minimum of various counts to produce an estimate. Specifically, we find all the locations where the queried item x is mapped, and retrieve the count from each such location. In the basic version of the summary, the estimated count is just the smallest of these counts. So the QUERY time is the same as the UPDATE time, $O(d)$. The procedure for QUERY in Algorithm 3.9 is quite similar to that for UPDATE: again, there is an iteration over the locations where x is mapped. A value e is maintained as the smallest of the values encountered, and returned as the final estimate.

Algorithm 3.9: Count-Min Sketch: QUERY (x)

---

1 $e \leftarrow \infty$;
2 **for** $j \leftarrow 1$ **to** d **do**
3      $h_j(x) = (a_j \times x + b_j \mod p) \mod t$;
4      $e \leftarrow \min(e, C[j, h_j(x)])$;
5 **return** e

To MERGE two Count-Min Sketch summaries, they must be built using the same parameters. That is, they must share the same t and d values, and use the same set of d hash functions. If this is the case, then we can merge two summaries directly by summing the corresponding entries in the arrays.

Example. Figure 3.1 shows the UPDATE process: an item i is mapped to one entry in each row j by the hash function h_j, and the update of c is added to each entry. It can also be seen as modeling the QUERY process: a query for the same item i will result in the same set of locations being probed, and the smallest value returned as the answer.

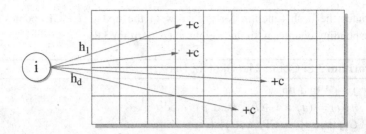

Figure 3.1 Count-Min Sketch data structure with $t = 9$ and $d = 4$.

Further Discussion. Let v denote the characteristic vector of the multi-set, so v_i is the total weight of all updates to entry i. The entries of the sketch C then obey

$$C[j,k] = \sum_{1 \leq i \leq M : h_j(i) = k} v_i.$$

That is, the kth entry in the jth row is the sum of frequencies of all items i that are mapped by the jth hash function to value k.

The effect of QUERY is to recover an estimate of v_i, for any i. Observe that for it to be worth keeping a sketch in place of simply storing v exactly, it must be that td is much smaller than the size of the input domain, U, and so the sketch will necessarily only approximate any v_i. The estimation can be understood as follows: in the first row, it is the case that $C[1, h_1(i)]$ includes the current value of v_i. However, since $t \ll U$, there will be many collisions under the hash function h_1, so that $C[1, h_1(i)]$ also contains the sum of all v_ℓ for ℓ that collides with i under h_1. Still, if the sum of such v_ℓs is not too large, then this will not be so far from v_i. In fact, we can state a bound in terms of $W = \sum_{1 \leq \ell \leq M} v_\ell$, the sum of all frequencies.

Fact 3.1 *The error in the estimate of v_i from a Count-Min Sketch is at most εW with probability $1 - \delta$ for a sketch with parameters $t = 2/\varepsilon$ and $d = \log 1/\delta$.*

We demonstrate this fact under the assumption that every entry in v is nonnegative (later, we discuss the case when this is not so). Then $C[1, h_1(i)]$ is an overestimate for v_i. The same is true for all the other rows: for each j, $C[j, h_j(i)]$ gives an overestimate of v_i, based on a different set of colliding items. Now, if the hash functions are chosen at random, the items will be distributed uniformly over the row. So the expected amount of "noise" colliding with i in any given row is just

$\sum_{1 \le \ell \le U, \ell \ne i} v_\ell / t$, a $1/t$ fraction of the total weight W. Moreover, by the Markov inequality (Fact 1.1 in Section 1.4), there is at least a 50% chance that the noise is less than twice this much.

Expressing this in probability terms, we have

$$\Pr\left[C[j, h_j(i)] - v_i > \frac{2W}{t} \right] \le \frac{1}{2}$$

Here, the probabilities arise due to the random choice of the hash functions. If each row's estimate of v_i is an overestimate, then the smallest of these will be the closest to v_i. By the independence of the hash functions, it is now very unlikely that this estimate has error more than $2 \sum_{1 \le \ell \le U} v_\ell / t$: this only happens if *every* row estimate is "bad," which happens with probability at most 2^{-d}. That is,

$$\Pr\left[\min_j C[j, h_j(i)] - v_i > \frac{2W}{t} \right] \le \left(\frac{1}{2} \right)^d.$$

Rewriting this, if we pick $t = 2/\epsilon$ and $d = \log 1/\delta$, then our estimate of v_i has error at most ϵW with probability at least $1 - \delta$. The value returned by QUERY is simply $\min_{j=1}^d C[j, h_j(i)]$.

For this analysis to hold, the hash functions are required to be drawn from a family of pairwise independent functions (Section 1.4.2). That is, over the random choice of the hash functions, for any i, ℓ and values x, y, $\Pr[h_j(i) = x \wedge h_j(\ell) = y] = \frac{1}{t}$. However, this turns out to be quite a weak condition: such functions are very simple to construct, and can be evaluated very quickly indeed [46, 219]. Hash functions of the form $((ax + b) \mod p) \mod t$, where p is a prime, and a, b are chosen randomly in the range 1 to $p - 1$ meet these requirements.

Residual Bound. The preceding analysis can be tightened to give a bound in terms of $\|v\|_1^{\text{res } k}$, the residual L_1 norm after removing the k largest entries. Consider the estimate of v_i for a row j. With probability $1 - 1/t$, the heaviest item is not mapped to $h_j(i)$. Taking a union bound over the k heaviest items, they all avoid $h_j(i)$ with probability $1 - k/t$. Picking $k = t/8$, say, ensures that this holds with constant probability. Conditioned on the event that all k avoid colliding with i, then we can apply the same expectation-based argument on the weight of the other colliding items, and show that this is $\|v\|_1^{\text{res}(k)} / t$ in expectation. Therefore, with constant probability, we have that none of the k heaviest items collide, and that the weight of items that do collide is at most a constant times

$\|v\|_1^{\text{res}(k)}/t$. Repeating over the d hash functions and taking the minimum estimate improves the probability of getting an estimate within $\varepsilon \|v\|_1^{\text{res}(k)}$ to $1 - \delta$.

Unbiased Estimator. The estimator $C[j, h_j(i)]$ is technically *biased*, in the statistical sense: it never underestimates but may overestimate, and so is not correct in expectation. However, it is straightforward to modify the estimator to be unbiased, by subtracting an appropriate quantity from the estimate. Specifically, we modify the QUERY procedure to compute

$$\hat{v}_{i,j} = C[j, h_j(i)] - \frac{1}{t-1} \sum_{k \neq h_j(i)} C[j, k] = \frac{t C[j, h_j(i)] - W}{t-1},$$

where W is the total weight of all updates. Since we have that the expectation of $C[j, h_j(i)] = v_i + (W - v_i)/t$, it follows that the expectation of this quantity is v_i, i.e., it is an unbiased estimator.

However, there is no way to preserve this unbiasedness across the d rows: ideas such as taking the median of estimators turn out not to work. One workaround is to convert the Count-Min Sketch to a Count Sketch, which produces an unbiased estimator across multiple rows – this is covered when we discuss the Count Sketch structure in Section 3.5.

L_2 Bound. The Count-Min Sketch can also produce an estimator whose error depends on $\|v\|_2$, the ℓ_2-norm of v. We use the unbiased estimator $\hat{v}_{i,j}$ as described earlier. Its variance can be bounded as follows, using standard properties of the variance (Section 1.4):

$$\text{Var}\left[\frac{t C[j, h_j(i)] - W}{t-1}\right] = \text{Var}\left[\frac{t}{t-1} C[j, h_j(i)]\right]$$

$$= \left(\frac{t}{t-1}\right)^2 \text{Var}\left[v_i + \sum_{k \neq i, h_j(k) = h_j(i)} v_k\right]$$

$$= \left(\frac{t}{t-1}\right)^2 \sum_{k \neq i} \text{Var}[v_k I(h_j(k) = h_j(i))]$$

$$= \left(\frac{t}{t-1}\right)^2 \sum_{k \neq i} v_k^2 \left(\frac{1}{t}\right)\left(1 - \frac{1}{t}\right)$$

$$= \frac{1}{t-1} \sum_{k \neq i} v_k^2 \leq \frac{\|v\|_2^2}{t-1},$$

where $I(E)$ is an indicator random variable for the event E. This analysis relies on the fact that whether two items are mapped to $h_j(i)$ can be treated as independent, over the choice of the hash function, and so the covariance of corresponding random variables is zero. We can apply the Chebyshev bound to this estimator (Fact 1.3 from Section 1.4), and obtain

$$\Pr\left[|\hat{v}_{i,j} - v_i| > \frac{2\|v\|_2}{\sqrt{t-1}}\right] \leq \frac{1}{4},$$

i.e., the estimate is within two standard deviations from its expectation, which is v_i, with probability at least $3/4$. Then we take the median of all the estimates (one from each row of the sketch) and return it as the final estimate. Note that the median of multiple unbiased estimators is not necessarily unbiased, but we can still obtain an (ε, δ) guarantee via the standard Chernoff bound argument (Section 1.4.1):

Fact 3.2 *The error in the (unbiased) estimate of v_i from a* Count-Min Sketch *with parameters $t = O(1/\varepsilon^2)$ and $d = O(\log 1/\delta)$ is at most $\varepsilon\|v\|_2$ with probability at least $1 - \delta$.*

To better contrast the two forms of guarantees from Facts 3.1 and 3.2, we may rewrite Fact 3.2 by substituting ε with $\sqrt{\varepsilon}$, so that the sketch size is the same $t = O(1/\varepsilon), d = O(\log 1/\delta)$. Then the L_2 error bound becomes $\sqrt{\varepsilon}\|v\|_2$. Note that this is in general incomparable to the L_1 error bound of $\varepsilon\|v\|_1$. When the frequency vector v is highly skewed, say with only one or two nonzero entries, then $\|v\|_1 = \|v\|_2$ and the L_1 bound is better. But when v is quite flat, say $v_1 = v_2 = \cdots = 1$, then $\|v_2\| = \sqrt{\|v\|_1} \ll \|v\|_1$, and the L_2 bound will be much better.

Negative Frequencies. The same sketch can also be used when the items have both positive and negative frequencies when the sketch is queried. In this case, the sketch can be built in the same way, but now it is not correct to take the smallest row estimate as the overall estimate: this could be far from the true value if, for example, all the v_i values are negative. However, an adaptation of the preceding argument shows that the error still remains bounded. Consider instead the sum of the *absolute* values of items that collide with i when estimating v_i. This is a positive quantity, and so can still be bounded by the Markov inequality (Fact 1.1) to be at most $\|v\|_1/t$ with constant probability, where $\|v\|_1$ denotes the 1-norm (sum of absolute values) of v. If this is the case, then the error in the estimate must lie between $-\|v\|_1/t$ (if all the colliding items are negative) and $+\|v\|_1/t$ (if all the colliding items are positive). So with constant probability, each estimate of v_i is within $2\|v\|_1/t$ additive error. To improve this to hold with high probability, we can take the *median* of the row estimates, and apply the Chernoff bounds argument described in Section 1.4 to obtain an accurate estimate. As a consequence, we have the following:

Fact 3.3 *The error in the estimate of v_i from a* Count-Min Sketch *over a multiset with both positive and negative frequencies is at most $\varepsilon\|v\|_1$ with probability $1 - \delta$, for a sketch with parameters $t = O(1/\varepsilon)$ and $d = O(\log 1/\delta)$.*

Conservative Update. The *conservative update* method can be applied on a Count-Min Sketch when there are many UPDATE operations in sequence. It tries to minimize overestimation by increasing the counters by the smallest amount possible given the information available. However, in doing so it breaks the property that the summary is a linear transform of the input, so it can no longer support updates with negative weights. Consider an update to item i in a Count-Min Sketch. The update function maps i to a set of entries in the sketch. The current estimate of v_i is given by the least of these, as $\hat{v}_i$: this has to increase by at least the amount of the update u to maintain the accuracy guarantee. But if other entries are larger than $\hat{v}_i + u$, then they do not need to be increased to ensure that the estimate is correct. So the conservative update rule is to set

$$C[j, h_j(i)] \leftarrow \max(\hat{v}_i + u, C[j, h_j(i)])$$

for each row j. The MERGE and QUERY operations under conservative update remain the same. However, to enjoy the maximum benefit from conservative update, we must expect a large amount of UPDATE operations: if the sketch is obtained from mostly MERGE operations rather than UPDATE operations, then the final sketch will be no different from the sketch obtained under the usual UPDATE operation.

History and Background. The central concept of the Count-Min Sketch is quite fundamental, and variations of the idea have appeared in several contexts. Variations of Bloom filters (see Section 2.7) have used the idea of hashing to counters to deal with set updates [101] and more specifically for count estimation [60]. In the context of networking, Estan and Varghese's multistage filters are a data structure that correspond to sketches, under assumptions of fully independent hash functions [100]. This work pioneered the idea of conservative update. The sketch was formally introduced with strong guarantees from weak hash functions in 2003 [73, 76], building on earlier work on retrieving heavy hitter items [74]. Kirsch and Mitzenmacher discuss how the hashing can be made faster, by performing arithmetic on combinations of hash values [158].

Several variations and extensions have been suggested. The approach of taking the minimum value as the estimate from Count-Min Sketch is appealing for its simplicity. But it is also open to criticism: it does not take full account of all the information available to the estimator. Lee et al. studied using a least-squares method to recover estimated frequencies of a subset of items from a Count-Min Sketch [168]. That is, using the fact that the sketch is a linear transform of the input, write the sketch as a multiplication between a version of the sketch matrix and a vector of the frequencies of the items of interest. Lu et al. use Message Passing, which also tries to find a distribution of counts that is consistent with the values recorded in the sketch of the observed data [174]. Jin et al. empirically measure the accuracy of an instance of a Count-Min Sketch [147]. They estimate the frequency of some items that are known to have zero count, say $U + 1, U + 2 \ldots$, etc. The average of these estimates is used as τ, the expected error, and all estimated counts are reduced by τ. This was sometimes referred to as Count-Mean-Min (CMM), by [86, 54]. Bianchi et al. [28] and Einziger and Friedman [96] both give an analysis of the conservative update method. A line of subsequent work has studied tighter bounds on estimation for Count-Min Sketch. Ting [222] provides new estimators with tight error bounds; Cai et al. [45] adopt a Bayesian perspective to analyze the sketch.

The sketch has been used for a variety of different tasks. Some examples include counting the frequency of particular strings in long genetic sequences [240]; tracking the popularity of different passwords, and warning if a chosen password is too common [207]; and a general technique to speed up machine learning in high-dimensional feature spaces [210]. The sketch has been used by Twitter to track the popularity of individual tweets across the web [30], and by Apple to reduce the size of information gathered under its private data collection tool [218].

Available Implementations. Many implementations of the Count-Min Sketch are available. Typically these are quite simple and straightforward: one example `https://github.com/rafacarrascosa/countminsketch` implements all methods in a few dozen lines of python. Other implementations listed on GitHub implement the summary in C, C++, Java, JavaScript, Go, Julia, and Clojure. Algebird provides code in Scala (`https://twitter.github.io/algebird/data types/approx/countminsketch.html`). The stream-lib implementation (`https://github.com/addthis/stream-lib/tree/master/src/main/java/com/clearspring/analytics/stream/frequency`) includes both the basic and conservative update variants.

3.5 Count Sketch for Frequency Estimation

Brief Summary. The Count Sketch summary is very similar to Count-Min Sketch. It also summarizes a multiset v and answers point queries approximately. It has asymptotically the same guarantees as the Count-Min Sketch, but with slightly worse hidden constant factors: given parameters ε and δ, the summary uses space $O(1/\varepsilon \log 1/\delta)$, and guarantees with probability at least $1 - \delta$ that any point query is answered with additive error at most $\varepsilon \|v\|_1$. Alternatively, with space $O(1/\varepsilon^2 \log 1/\delta)$, it has error at most $\varepsilon \|v\|_2$ with probability at least $1 - \delta$. The benefit of the Count Sketch is that it produces an unbiased estimator, which is important in certain applications (see, for example, Section 4.4).

Algorithm 3.10: Count Sketch: INITIALIZE (t, d, p)

---

1 $C[1,1] \ldots C[d,t] \leftarrow 0$;
2 **for** $j \leftarrow 1$ **to** d **do**
3 | Pick a_j, b_j uniformly from $[1 \ldots p]$;
4 | Pick c_j, d_j uniformly from $[1 \ldots p]$;

Operations on the Summary. The Count Sketch summary is represented as a compact array C of $d \times t$ counters, arranged as d rows of length t. It can be described as being similar in nature to the Count-Min Sketch summary, but with some key differences. For each row j, a *hash function* h_j maps the input domain U uniformly onto the range $\{1, 2, \ldots, t\}$. A second hash function g_j maps the input domain U uniformly on the range $\{-1, +1\}$. To INITIALIZE a new summary, the array of counters is created based on the parameters t and d, and every entry is set to 0. The two sets of d hash functions, g and h, are picked at the same time. Algorithm 3.10 shows the procedure to INITIALIZE a Count Sketch: the array is set to zero, and the parameters for the hash function are chosen randomly based on the prime p.

Algorithm 3.11: Count Sketch: UPDATE (i, w)

---

1 **for** $j \leftarrow 1$ **to** d **do**
2 | $h_j(i) = (a_j \times i + b_j \mod p) \mod t$;
3 | $g_j(i) = 2 \times ((c_j \times i + d_j \mod p) \mod 2) - 1$;
4 | $C[j, h_j(i)] \leftarrow C[j, h_j(i)] + w \times g_j(i)$;

For each UPDATE operation to item i with weight w (which can be either positive or negative), the item is mapped to an entry in each row based on the hash functions h, and the update applied to the corresponding counter, multiplied by the corresponding value of g. That is, for each $1 \le j \le d$, $h_j(i)$ is computed, and the quantity $wg_j(i)$ is added to entry $C[j, h_j(i)]$ in the sketch array. Processing each update therefore takes time $O(d)$, since each hash function evaluation takes constant time. Each UPDATE shown in Algorithm 3.11 computes $h_j(i)$ and $g_j(i)$ for each row j, and updates the corresponding entry of the array.

Algorithm 3.12: Count Sketch: QUERY (x)

---

1 **for** $j \leftarrow 1$ **to** d **do**
2 | $h_j(x) = (a_j \times x + b_j \mod p) \mod t$;
3 | $g_j(x) = 2 \times ((c_j \times x + d_j \mod p) \mod 2) - 1$;
4 | $e_j \leftarrow g_j(x) \times C[j, h_j(x)])$;
5 **return** median(e)

The QUERY operation on item x extracts the count associated with x in each row, and returns the median of these. That is, in row j it computes $g_j(i)C[j, h_j(i)]$ as the estimate for that row. This generates d estimates, and the median of these is the final estimate. Therefore, the QUERY time is also $O(d)$. For a QUERY operation in Algorithm 3.12, the procedure is quite similar to an UPDATE. A vector of estimates e is built, and the median of this vector is returned as the final answer.

To MERGE two Count Sketch summaries, they must have the same parameters, i.e., they must have the same t and d values, and use the same sets of hash functions h and g. Then they can be merged by summing the corresponding entries in the arrays. This works since the resulting sketch is identical to the one obtained if all UPDATE operations had been made to a single sketch.

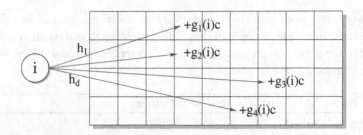

Figure 3.2 Count Sketch data structure with $t = 9$ and $d = 4$.

Example. Figure 3.2 shows an example of the Count Sketch: during an UPDATE operation, an item is mapped into one entry in each row by the relevant hash function, and multiplied by a second hash function g. The figure serves to emphasize the similarities between the Count Sketch and Count-Min Sketch: the main difference arises in the use of the g_j functions.

Further Discussion. As with the Count-Min Sketch summary, the accuracy of the estimate obtained is analyzed by considering the distribution of the "noise" of other items that affect the estimate. This is shown to be very likely to be small, under the random choice of the hash functions. Let v denote the characteristic vector of the multiset summarized, so that v_i is the total weight of all update to entry i. Then we can write the sketch C as

$$C[j,k] = \sum_{1 \leq i \leq M : h_j(i)=k} g_j(i)v_i.$$

So the kth entry in the jth row is a sum of frequencies of items i mapped to k by the jth hash function h_j, where each is multiplied by either $+1$ or -1, according to g_j. The intuition is that by hashing to different entries, i is unlikely to collide with too much "weight" from other items. Further, the use of g_j functions is intended to help the colliding items to "cancel" out with each other.

L_1 *error bound.* Formally, let $\hat{v}_{i,j} = g_j(i)C[j, h_j(i)]$ be the estimator in the jth row for v_i. We consider the random variable $|v_i - \hat{v}_{i,j}|$, which is the absolute error in the estimator. Its expectation is

$$\mathsf{E}[|v_i - \hat{v}_{i,j}|] = \mathsf{E}\left[\left|\sum_{\ell \neq i} I(h_j(\ell) = h_j(i)) \cdot v_\ell \cdot g_j(i) \cdot g_j(\ell)\right|\right]$$

$$\leq \sum_{\ell \neq i} \mathsf{E}[|I(h_j(\ell) = h_j(i)) \cdot v_\ell \cdot g_j(i) \cdot g_j(\ell)|]$$

$$= \sum_{\ell \neq i} |v_\ell| \cdot \mathsf{E}[I(h_j(\ell) = h_j(i))]$$

$$= \frac{1}{t} \sum_{\ell \neq i} |v_\ell| \leq \|v\|_1 / t.$$

Applying the Markov inequality to the (nonnegative) variable $|v_i - \hat{v}_{i,j}|$, we have that the error in this estimate is at most $3\|v\|_1/t$ with probability at least $2/3$. Taking the median of $O(\log 1/\delta)$ repetitions reduces this failure probability to δ, via a Chernoff bounds argument. So we have an L_1 error bound for the Count Sketch that is asymptotically the same as the Count-Min Sketch:

Fact 3.4 *The error in the estimate of v_i from a* Count Sketch *is at most $\epsilon\|v\|_1$ with probability $1 - \delta$ from a sketch with parameters $t = O\left(\frac{1}{\epsilon}\right)$ and $d = O(\log 1/\delta)$.*

Although the Count Sketch has asymptotically the same L_1 error guarantee as the Count-Min Sketch, the hidden constants are worse. This is due to the use of the *median* operator to select one out of the d rows to return as the final estimate. The estimate will be outside of the error interval as long as half of the d estimates are outside. This is to be contrasted with the Count-Min Sketch, which uses the *min* operator, and thus fails only if *all* the d estimates exceed the error limit. In addition, to be able to use the Chernoff bound argument, the success probability of each individual estimate has to be strictly greater than $1/2$, whereas in the case of the Count-Min Sketch, any constant will do.

L_2 *bound.* The Count Sketch can similarly provide an L_2 error guarantee. First, we show that the estimator from each row is unbiased:

$$\mathsf{E}[\hat{v}_{i,j}] = \mathsf{E}[g_j(i) \cdot C[j, h_j(i)]] = \mathsf{E}\left[g_j(i) \sum_{1 \leq \ell \leq M : h_j(i) = h(\ell)} g_j(\ell) v_\ell \right]$$

$$= (g_j(i))^2 v_i + \mathsf{E}\left[\sum_{\ell \neq i} g_j(i) g_j(\ell) v_\ell \right]$$

$$= v_i + \sum_{\ell \neq i} v_\ell (\Pr[g_j(i) g_j(\ell) = +1] - \Pr[g_j(i) g_j(\ell) = -1])$$

$$= v_i.$$

This analysis breaks the expectation of the result into two pieces: the contribution from v_i, and the contribution from the other items. Whatever the value of $g_j(i)$, we obtain a contribution of v_i from this term. For the second term, the expectation is multiplied by $g_j(i)g_j(\ell)$. Since we chose g_j from a pairwise independent family of hash functions, over this random choice, the product is $+1$ half the time, and -1 the rest of the time, and so is zero in expectation. Of course, while this product is zero in expectation, it is never actually zero (it is either $+1$ or -1), and so we consider the variance of the estimator from row j in order to study its accuracy.

$$
\begin{aligned}
\mathsf{Var}[\hat{v}_{i,j}] &= \mathsf{Var}[g_j(i) \sum_{1 \le \ell \le M : h_j(\ell) = h_j(i)} g_j(\ell)v_\ell] \\
&= \mathsf{Var}[v_\ell + g_j(i) \sum_{\ell \ne i} g_j(\ell)v_\ell I(h_j(\ell) = h_j(i))] \\
&= \sum_{\ell \ne i} \mathsf{Var}[g_j(i)g_j(\ell)v_\ell I(h_j(\ell) = h_j(i))] \\
&= \sum_{\ell \ne i} v_\ell^2 \mathsf{Var}[I(h_j(\ell) = h_j(i))] \le \frac{\|v\|_2^2}{t}.
\end{aligned}
$$

This analysis uses the standard properties of variance (Section 1.4), along with the fact that the events of two items both being mapped to $h_j(i)$ have zero covariance, due to the independence properties of the hash functions. Thus, applying a Chebyshev bound (Fact 1.3), we have (for any row j)

$$
\Pr\left[|\hat{v}_{i,j} - v_i| > \frac{2\|v\|_2}{\sqrt{t}}\right] \le \frac{1}{4},
$$

showing that the estimate is within two times the standard deviations of its expectation with probability at least $3/4$. Taking the median of $O(\log 1/\delta)$ repetitions and applying a Chernoff bounds argument (Section 1.4.1) reduces the probability to δ.

We can also observe that the random variable $\hat{v}_{i,j}$ has a pdf that is symmetric around its expectation, so the median of an odd number of such estimators retains the expectation. So the Count Sketch returns an unbiased estimator.

Fact 3.5 *The* Count Sketch *returns an unbiased estimator for any point query. The error in the estimate, with parameters $t = O(1/\varepsilon^2)$ and $d = O(\log 1/\delta)$, is at most $\varepsilon\|v\|_2$ with probability at least $1 - \delta$.*

Note that the Count Sketch achieves both the L_1 and the L_2 error guarantees with the same QUERY algorithm, namely, the estimate returned always obeys the smaller of the two error guarantees. This can be considered an additional benefit of the Count Sketch over the Count-Min Sketch, which needs to use different QUERY algorithms for achieving different error guarantees.

L_2 *Residual Bound.* We can also express the error in terms of $\|v\|_2^{\text{res}(k)}$, the residual L_2 norm, after removing the k largest (absolute) entries of v. This follows by adjusting the argument used to show Fact 3.5. Consider the estimate of $\hat{v}_{i,j}$ from row j. The probability that the heaviest item collides with i in row j of the sketch is at most $1/t$, using the pairwise independence of the hash functions. This also holds for the rest of the k heaviest items. The probability that all k of these items avoid i in row j is at least $1 - k/t$, using a union bound. So for $k = O(t)$, this holds with at least constant probability. If we condition on this event, then the variance of the estimator is reduced to $\|v\|_2^{\text{res}(k)}/t$. Applying the Chebyshev bound to this case, there is constant probability that the estimate is at most $\sqrt{\|v\|_2^{\text{res}(k)}/t}$ from its expected value. This constant probability captures the probability of avoiding collisions with the k heaviest items, and then of the conditioned random variable falling close to its expectation. Thus, with some rescaling of constants, we also have that a sketch of width $t = O(1/\varepsilon^2)$ and $d = O(\log 1/\delta)$ estimates v_i with error at most $\varepsilon\|v\|_2^{\text{res}(k)}/t$ for $k = O(t)$.

Converting Count-Min Sketch *to* Count Sketch. A different QUERY algorithm on the Count-Min Sketch can actually turn the Count-Min Sketch into a Count Sketch. We use the estimator:

$$\hat{v}_{i,j} = C[j,h_j(i)] - C[j,h_j(i) + 1 - 2(h_j(i) \mod 2)],$$

where the term $1 - 2(h_j(i) \mod 2)$ has the result of picking a neighboring entry in the sketch. The effect of this is to produce an estimate that is identical to that arising from the Count Sketch of size $t/2$: the effect of the subtraction is to mimic the role of the hash function g_j. Consequently, a Count-Min Sketch structure can simulate a Count Sketch and provide the same guarantees as the Count Sketch, though at the cost of twice the space.

Implementation Issues. The pairwise hash functions needed are very simple: picking parameters a and b uniformly in the range 1 to p for a prime p, then computing $((ax + b) \mod p) \mod t$ is sufficient (Section 1.4.2). Still, in some high-performance cases, where huge amounts of data are processed, we wish to make this part as efficient as possible. One way to reduce the cost of hashing is to compute a single hash function for row j that maps to the range $2t$, and use the last bit to determine g_j ($+1$ or -1), while the remaining bits determine h_j. This is essentially equivalent to the preceding observation that a Count Sketch is equivalent to taking a Count-Min Sketch of twice the width, and computing the differences of pairs of adjacent entries.

History and Background. The Count Sketch summary was first proposed by Charikar et al. in 2002 [51], although technically it can be thought of as an extension of the earlier AMS Sketch [10], which also used the idea of $+1/-1$ hash values to provide an unbiased estimator. The key innovation is the use of hashing in the Count Sketch to select a cell in each row, instead of averaging all cells. This means that the UPDATE operation is much faster than in the AMS sketch.

The Count Sketch has found many practical uses, due to its relative simplicity, and good accuracy. It is implemented in various tools for manipulating large data, such as the Sawzall system at Google for analyzing log structured data [203]. The simple structure has also allowed it to be extended to solve other problems. Pagh [199] showed that one could rapidly construct a Count Sketch of the product of two matrices, without explicitly performing the matrix multiplication; this is explained in Section 6.4. For similar reasons, it is possible to efficiently build a Count Sketch of polynomial kernels used in machine learning [202].

The Count Sketch is a key tool in the design of advanced algorithms for problems in high-dimensional data analysis. Many problems in randomized numerical linear algebra such as regression can be approximately solved using Count Sketch [205, 55]. Problems relating to compressed sensing – recovering approximately sparse vectors from few linear measurements – make use of the Count Sketch [117]. Lastly, the Count Sketch is the core part of a general approach to approximately computing functions over high-dimensional vectors [38].

3.6 (Fast) AMS Sketch for Euclidean Norm

Brief Summary. The AMS Sketch summary maintains an array of counts that are updated with each arriving item. It gives an estimate of the ℓ_2-norm of the vector v corresponding to the multiset being summarized, by computing the norm of each row, and taking the median of all rows. Given parameters ε and δ, the summary uses space $O(1/\varepsilon^2 \log 1/\delta)$, and guarantees with probability at least $1 - \delta$ that its estimate is within relative ε-error of the true ℓ_2-norm, $\|v\|_2$.

Algorithm 3.13: AMS Sketch: QUERY (x)

---

1 **for** $j \leftarrow 1$ **to** d **do**
2     $e_j \leftarrow 0$;
3   **for** $k \leftarrow 1$ **to** t **do**
4        $e_j \leftarrow e_j + (C[j,k])^2$;

5 **return** median(e)

Operations on the Summary. The AMS Sketch summary is almost identical to the Count Sketch summary, with one key difference: sometimes the terms Count Sketch and AMS Sketch are used interchangeably. It is represented as a compact array C of $d \times t$ counters, arranged as d rows of length t. In each row j, a hash function h_j maps the input domain U uniformly to $\{1, 2, \ldots t\}$. A second hash function g_j maps elements from U uniformly onto $\{-1, +1\}$. So far, this is identical to the description of the Count Sketch. An additional technical requirement is that g_j is *four-wise* independent (Section 1.4.2). That is, over the random choice of g_j from the set of all possible hash functions, the probability that any four distinct items from the domain get mapped to $\{-1, +1\}^4$ is uniform: each of the 16 possible outcomes is equally likely.

The INITIALIZE, UPDATE, and MERGE operations on the AMS Sketch summary are therefore identical to the corresponding operations on the Count Sketch summary (Section 3.5). Hence the algorithms for INITIALIZE and UPDATE match those given in Algorithms 3.10 and 3.11, the difference being the stronger requirements on hash functions g_j. Only QUERY is different. Here, the QUERY operation takes the sum of the squares of row of the sketch in turn, and finds the median of these sums. That is, for row j, it computes $\sum_{k=1}^{t} C[j,k]^2$ as an estimate, and takes the median of the d such estimates. Algorithm 3.13 gives code for the QUERY operation on AMS Sketch summaries: each estimate e_j is formed as the sum of squares of the jth row, and the median of these is chosen as the final estimate. The QUERY time is linear in the size of the sketch, $O(td)$. The time for INITIALIZE and MERGE operations is the same, $O(td)$. Meanwhile, UPDATE operations take time $O(d)$.

Further Discussion. To understand the accuracy of the estimates, consider the expectation and variance of the result obtained from each row. Let X_j denote the estimate obtained from row j, i.e., $X_j = \sum_{k=1}^{t} C[j,k]^2$. We have

$$\mathsf{E}[X_j] = \sum_{k=1}^{t} \mathsf{E}[C[j,k]^2]$$

$$= \sum_{k=1}^{t} \mathsf{E}\left[\left(\sum_{i:h_j(i)=k} v_i g_j(i)\right)^2\right]$$

$$= \sum_{k=1}^{t} \mathsf{E}\left[\sum_{i:h_j(i)=k} v_i^2 + 2 \sum_{i \neq \ell, h_j(i)=h_j(\ell)=k} g_j(i)g_j(\ell)v_i v_\ell\right]$$

$$= \sum_{k=1}^{t} \sum_{i:h_j(i)=k} v_i^2 = \sum_i v_i^2 = \|v_i\|_2^2,$$

because the expectation of terms in $g_j(i)g_j(\ell)$ is zero: this product is $+1$ with probability $1/2$ and -1 with probability $1/2$. For the variance, we have

$$\mathsf{Var}[X_j] = \mathsf{Var}\left[\sum_{k=1}^{t} C[j,k]^2\right]$$

$$= \mathsf{Var}\left[\|v\|_2^2 + 2\sum_{k=1}^{t}\sum_{i \neq \ell} g_j(i)v_i I(h_j(i) = k)\right.$$

$$\left. \times \, g_j(\ell)v_\ell I(h_j(\ell) = k)\right]$$

$$= \mathsf{Var}\left[2\sum_{i \neq \ell} g_j(i)v_i g_j(\ell)v_\ell I(h_j(i) = h_j(\ell))\right].$$

We will use random variables $Y_{i,\ell} = g_j(i)v_i g_j(\ell)v_\ell I(h_j(i) = h_j(\ell))$ to simplify this expression. Note that $\mathsf{E}[Y_{i,\ell}] = 0$, by the pairwise independence of g_j. We will use the fact that $Y_{i,\ell}$ is independent from $Y_{q,r}$ when all four of $\{i, \ell, q, r\}$ are different, using the four-wise independence property of g_j. That implies $\mathsf{Cov}[Y_{i,\ell}, Y_{q,r}] = 0$ under this condition. Then

$$\text{Var}[X_j] = \text{Var}\left[2\sum_{i\neq\ell} Y_{i,\ell}\right]$$

$$= 4 \sum_{i\neq\ell, q\neq r, h_j(i)=h_j(q)} \text{Cov}[Y_{i,\ell}, Y_{q,r}]$$

$$= 4 \sum_{i\neq\ell} \text{Cov}[Y_{i,\ell}, Y_{i,\ell}] + 4 \sum_{i\neq\ell, i\neq q} \text{Cov}[Y_{i,\ell}, Y_{i,q}]$$

$$= 4 \sum_{i\neq\ell} \text{E}[Y_{i,\ell}^2] + 0$$

$$= 4 \sum_{i\neq\ell} v_i^2 v_\ell^2 / t \leq \|v\|_2^4 / t.$$

Here, we use the fact that $\text{E}[Y_{i,\ell}Y_{i,q}] = 0$ when $i \neq q, \ell \neq q$ (again, using the four-wise independence of g_j), and hence $\text{Cov}[Y_{i,\ell}, Y_{i,q}] = 0$ also.

To summarize, we have that $\text{E}[X_j] = \|v\|_2^2$ and $\text{Var}[X_j] \leq 4\|v\|_2^4 \leq 4\text{E}[X_j]^2/t$. Thus, via the Chebyshev inequality, the probability that $|X_j - \text{E}[X_j]| \geq \|v\|_2^2/\sqrt{t}$ is at most a constant. Taking the median of d repetitions drives this probability down to δ. So we conclude as follows:

Fact 3.6 *The error in the estimate of* $\|v\|_2^2$ *from an* AMS Sketch *with parameters* $t = O(1/\varepsilon^2)$ *and* $d = O(\log 1/\delta)$ *is at most* $\varepsilon\|v\|_2^2$ *with probability at least* $1 - \delta$.

Equivalently, we have that the estimate is between $(1 - \varepsilon)\|v\|_2^2$ and $(1 + \varepsilon)\|v\|_2^2$. Taking the square root of the estimate gives a result that is between $(1 - \varepsilon)^{1/2}\|v\|_2$ and $(1 + \varepsilon)^{1/2}\|v\|_2$, which means it is between $(1 - \varepsilon/2)\|v\|_2$ and $(1 + \varepsilon/2)\|v\|_2$.

Note that since the input to AMS Sketch can be general, it can be used to measure the Euclidean distance between two vectors v and u: we can build an AMS Sketch of v and one of $-u$, and MERGE them together. Note also that a sketch of $-u$ can be obtained from a sketch of u by negating all the counter values.

Implementation Issues. For the analysis, we required that the random variables $Y_{i,\ell}$ and $Y_{q,r}$ have zero covariance. This requires that the expectation of terms in $g_j(i)g_j(\ell)g_j(q)g_j(r)$ are zero. For this to hold, we required that the hash functions g_j are drawn from a family of four-wise independent hash functions. This can be achieved by using polynomial hash functions, $g_j(x) = 2((ax^3 + bx^2 + cx + d \mod p) \mod 2) - 1$ (Section 1.4.2).

History and Background. The AMS Sketch was introduced in the work of Alon et al. in 1996 [10]. That version had the same size, but was structured differently. Instead of hashing into a row of t entries, all entries are used to make a single estimator (with hash functions g mapping to $+1/-1$ values). The average of $O(1/\varepsilon^2)$ estimates was taken to reduce the variance, then the median of $O(\log 1/\delta)$ repetitions used to drive down the error probability. The idea to use hashing instead of averaging to achieve the same variance but with a lower UPDATE time cost is seemingly inspired by the Count Sketch summary (the hashing-to-replace-averaging technique is also referred to as "stochastic averaging" in the earlier work of Flajolet and Martin [107]). Several works adopted this idea, notably that of Thorup and Zhang [221]. The version with hashing to a row of t counters is often referred to as the "fast AMS Sketch" summary (see Cormode and Garofalakis [66]). The AMS Sketch has many other applications, due to the importance of estimating the ℓ_2 norm (i.e., the length of a vector in Euclidean space). In particular, its application to estimating the inner product between pairs of vectors is discussed in Section 6.1.

3.7 L_p Sketch for Vector Norm Estimation

Brief Summary. An ℓ_p sketch gives an estimate of the ℓ_p-norm of the vector v corresponding to the multiset being summarized. It is similar in nature to the AMS Sketch, in that it builds a set of estimates, where each estimate is a projection of the input vector, and the median of all the estimates gives an approximation to the desired ℓ_p norm. Given parameters ϵ and δ, the summary uses space $O(1/\epsilon^2 \log 1/\delta)$, and guarantees that its estimate is within relative ϵ-error of the true ℓ_p norm, $\|v\|_p$.

Operations on the Summary. The ℓ_p sketch is based on taking projections with vectors whose entries are randomly chosen from so-called "stable" distributions. Each entry of the projection vector is drawn independently from an identically distributed symmetric and strictly stable distribution. Stable distributions are parameterized by α, where Gaussian distributions are stable with parameter $\alpha = 2$, and Cauchy distributions are stable with parameter $\alpha = 1$. The class of stable distributions are defined by the property that if X and Y are independent random stable variables with parameter α, then $aX+bY$ is distributed as a stable distribution scaled by $(|a|^\alpha + |b|^\alpha)^{1/\alpha}$. So to estimate

$\|v\|_p$, we take the inner product of v with a vector s whose entries are sampled iid p-stable. The result is then distributed as $\|v\|_p$ scaling a p-stable variable. We repeat this multiple times to estimate the scaling parameter, which we report as the answer.

To INITIALIZE the sketch, we initialize the seeds for $k = O\left(\frac{1}{\epsilon^2}\log\frac{1}{\delta}\right)$ independent repetitions, and create an empty sketch of k entries, all set to 0.

Algorithm 3.14: ℓ_p sketch: UPDATE (i, w, p)

---

1 **for** $j \leftarrow 1$ **to** k **do**
2 $\quad\lfloor \quad C[j] \leftarrow C[j] + w * \text{stable}_p(i, j)$

To process an UPDATE to the sketch, we make use of a function $\text{stable}_p(i, j)$, which consistently draws a random value from a stable distribution with parameter p. We assume that $\text{stable}_p(i, j)$ gives the same value every time it is called with the same values of i, j, and that $\text{stable}_p(i, j)$ is independent of $\text{stable}_p(i', j')$ if $i \neq i'$ or $j \neq j'$.

To QUERY a sketch, we compute the scaled median of the (absolute) stored values, i.e., $\text{median}_{j=1...k} |C[j]|/\beta_p$. Here, β_p is the median of absolute values drawn from the p-stable distribution.

Finally, to MERGE two sketches together that are built using the same $\text{stable}_p(i, j)$ values, we simply have to add together their sketch vectors C.

Example. Consider the input vector

$$v = [1, 2, 3, -4]$$

so we have that $\|v\|_1 = 10$.

We will sample from the Cauchy distribution, since this distribution is stable with parameter 1, and has $\beta_1 = 1$. We draw the following sets of four random values from iid Cauchy random variables for $k = 3$:

$$
\begin{array}{rrrr}
-1.639 & -1.722 & 0.338 & -0.238 \\
0.450 & -0.015 & -0.212 & -7.742 \\
-1.641 & 12.280 & -1.048 & 7.914
\end{array}
$$

Taking the inner product of v with each row of these draws generates $\{3.117, 30.752, -11.81\}$. We can observe that there is quite high variation among these three estimates, but that taking the median of the absolute values returns 11.81, which is tolerably close to the true value of 10.

Further Discussion. The sketch relies on the fact that linear scaling composes with the operations of taking absolute values and taking medians. That is, we have that for a random variable X,

$$\text{median}(|sX|) = s\,\text{median}(|X|).$$

In particular,

$$\text{median}(\|\|v\|_p X_p\|) = \|v\|_p\,\text{median}(|X_p|).$$

Combined with the defining properties of stable distributions, we have that each random projection yields an estimate centered on our target value of $\|v\|_p$.

The repetitions allow us to invoke concentration of measure results and give bounds on the repetitions. The analysis follows using an additive Chernoff–Hoeffding bound (Fact 1.4) in a variant of the standard median argument (Section 1.4.1). We outline the steps. Let τ be the value so that $\Pr[X \leq \tau] = \frac{1}{2} - \epsilon$, and consider the median of k copies of the estimator defined earlier. A necessary condition for this empirical median to fall below τ is for more than half the samples to fall below τ. The probability of each one falling below τ is captured by a Bernoulli random variable with probability $1/2 - \epsilon$. Applying the Chernoff–Hoeffding bound to these $k = O\left(\frac{1}{\epsilon^2} \log 1/\delta\right)$ Bernoulli variables gives us a probability of at most $\delta/2$ for this failure mode. The case for the estimate going above τ' such that $\Pr[X \leq \tau'] = 1/2 + \epsilon$ is symmetric. This ensures that, with probability at least $1 - \delta$, we obtain an estimate that is close to the true median.

This argument shows that the estimate is close to the true median in terms of the quantiles of the distribution. It is desirable to transform this into being close in absolute value; this is done by arguing that the relevant stable distribution is not flat close to the median; that is, that τ and τ' are both close to the median of the distribution. This can be verified analytically for the Cauchy distribution (stable with $p = 1$), and empirically for other values of p.

Implementation Issues. The key technical step needed is to sample from a stable distribution. We first observe that certain stable distributions have a closed form. The Gaussian distribution is 2-stable, while the Cauchy distribution is 1-stable. We can sample from the Cauchy distribution by transforming a uniform distribution. If U is a uniform random distribution over $[0, 1]$, then $\tan(\pi(U - 1/2))$ follows a Cauchy distribution.

For other p values in the range $0 < p < 2$, a transformation due to Chambers et al. [47] generates a sample from a stable distribution using two random variables. Let U and V be independent uniform variables from $[0, 1]$. Define the transform $\theta(U) = \pi(U - 1/2)$. Then the value

$$X_p = \frac{\sin(p\theta(U))}{\cos^{1/p}(\theta(U))} \left(\frac{\cos((1 - p)\theta(U))}{-\ln V} \right)^{\frac{1-p}{p}}$$

is distributed according to a p-stable distribution.

We also need to compute $\beta_p = \text{median}\,|X_p|$, the median of absolute values drawn from the p-stable distribution. For $p = 1$, the Cauchy distribution yields $\beta_1 = 1$ (and similarly, for $p = 2$, $\beta_2 = 1$ for the Gaussian distribution). For other values of p, β_p can be found with high accuracy by sampling a large enough number of values, and taking the median of them.

A practical consideration is that for very small values of p, approaching 0, the values sampled from stable distributions are typically very large in magnitude, and can exceed the capacity of fixed-size variables. Consequently, working with small p requires higher-precision arithmetic, and the true space cost grows larger as p gets asymptotically close to zero. Note that p close to zero is interesting, since it tends to flatten out the contribution of each nonzero value, and so approximately counts the number of nonzero values.

When k the number of projections is large, the UPDATE procedure can be rather slow, since $O(k)$ time is needed each update. Li [170] proposes a sparse random projection, where many entries in the projection matrix are chosen to be 0, and we only need to process the nonzero entries. Formally, Li shows that it suffices to ensure that only a $1/\sqrt{M}$ fraction of the entries need to be nonzero, where M is the dimensionality of the input vector. Li also shows that a modified estimation procedure based on taking the geometric mean of the individual estimates, rather than the median, provides accurate guarantees.

History and Background. Stable distributions have been extensively studied within the statistics literature – see the book by Zolotarev [243]. Their use in data summarization was pioneered by Indyk [138]. Experiments on the use of stable distributions with low p values are given in [64]. Extensions on the method for $p = 1$ to obtain fast, small summaries are due to Nelson and Woodruff [196].

3.8 Sparse Vector Recovery

Brief Summary. A SparseRecovery structure summarizes a multiset A of items under insertions and deletions of items. It allows the multiset to be recovered in its entirety, but only when the number of distinct items in the multiset is small. It is of value when at some intermediate point the multiset A may be very large, but due to deletions it later becomes small again. The structure is defined based on a parameter s, so that when the multiset has at most s distinct items, it will almost certainly recover them correctly; when the number of items is more than s, then no guarantee is made (the structure may return FAIL, indicating it could not recover the full multiset). The summary keeps structures similar to the sketches discussed previously, and uses extra information to retrieve the identity and count of items currently in the multiset.

Operations on the Summary. The sparse recovery structure resembles the BloomFilter as described in Section 2.7. As with the BloomFilter, we use k hash functions $h_1, \ldots, h_k$ to map each item to k locations in the array. For technical reasons, we will need these k hash functions to map any item to distinct locations. Unlike the BloomFilter, which uses a simple bit array, SparseRecovery uses an array C of t cells, where each cell stores more information about the elements that are mapped there. Specifically, each cell contains three pieces information: a *count* of the items that have been mapped to that location, a *sum* of all the item identifiers, and a *fingerprint* (Section 3.1) of the collection of items there.

Algorithm 3.15: SparseRecovery: INITIALIZE (t)

---

1 **for** $j \leftarrow 1$ **to** t **do**
2     $C[j]$.count $\leftarrow 0$;
3     $C[j]$.sum $\leftarrow 0$;
4     $C[j]$.fingerprint.INITIALIZE();

To INITIALIZE the structure (Algorithm 3.15), the array is created, with all counts and sums set to zero; the fingerprints are initialized to 0 or 1 depending on which version of Fingerprint is used (see Section 3.1).

Algorithm 3.16: SparseRecovery: UPDATE (i, w)

---

1 **for** $j \leftarrow 1$ **to** k **do**
2     $C[h_j(i)]$.count $\leftarrow C[h_j(i)]$.count $+ w$;
3     $C[h_j(i)]$.sum $\leftarrow C[h_j(i)]$.sum $+ w \cdot i$;
4     $C[h_j(i)]$.fingerprint.UPDATE(i, w);

Each UPDATE maps the given item to its corresponding locations in the array, and updates the sums, counts, and fingerprints there based on the weight

w (w can be either positive or negative). The count is modified by adding on w, while the sum is updated by adding on w times the item identifier i. We invoke the procedure to update the fingerprint as described in Section 3.1. Pseudocode is shown in Algorithm 3.16.

As with the BloomFilter, the procedure to MERGE two SparseRecovery structures requires that they are created with the same parameters (the same t and the same hash functions h_j). Then we merge the sets of sums, counts, and fingerprints. That is, pairs of corresponding sums are added, as are counts. The MERGE procedure for pairs of corresponding fingerprints is applied (Algorithm 3.2).

The QUERY process is a bit involved. The idea behind QUERY is that if the size of the multiset stored in the structure is small, then we can search the array and pick out the entries one by one, potentially uncovering more as we go. In particular, if there is some entry of the array that only stores information about a single item, then we use the information to retrieve the identifier and weight of that item. In this case, the total weight w can be read directly from the count value of the cell. Using standard arithmetic, since the sum contains $i \cdot w$, we can divide it by w to find i. However, there are additional issues to be concerned with: we need some way to know for sure whether a particular cell contains a single item, or contains a mixture of different items. Simply checking that the sum is an integral multiple of the count is not sufficient – it is possible that a mixture of different items add up to give the impression of a single one. A simple example is if one copy of each of items with identifiers 1 and 3 are placed in the same cell, then it would appear that there are two copies of the item with identifier 2 in the cell. This is why we also store the fingerprint: we attempt to recover an item from the cell, then compute the fingerprint corresponding to the conjectured item and weight. If it matches the stored fingerprint, then we are (almost) certain that this is a correct decoding, else we assume that it is an error.

The key observation behind the ability to recover many items is the following: once an item has been recovered, it can be removed from the other cells in which it has been placed. That is, we can perform the operation UPDATE $(i, -w)$ on the item i with weight w. This can cause more cells to become decodable (removing colliding items and leaving a single undecoded item left in the cell). This process is repeated until no more items can be identified and removed. At this point, either the structure is empty (i.e., all items have been recovered and every cell in the array is empty), or some items remain and have not been identified. In this case, the process might output FAIL. This approach is sometimes called "peeling," since once an item is found, it is "peeled" away from the structure. This peeling process can also

---

Algorithm 3.17: SparseRecovery: QUERY ()

1 $Q \leftarrow$ empty queue;
2 **for** $j \leftarrow 1$ **to** t **do**
3   **if** $C[j].count \geq 1$ **and**
    $(C[j].fingerprint = fingerprint\ of\ (C[j].sum\ /\ C[j].count,\ C[j].count))$
    then
4   Q.enqueue($C[j]$.sum$/C[j]$.count, $C[j]$.count)

5 **while** $Q \neq \emptyset$ **do**
6      $(i, w) \leftarrow Q$.dequeue();
7   output (i, w);
8   **for** $j \leftarrow 1$ **to** k **do**
9          $C[h_j(i)].count \leftarrow C[j, h_j(i)].count - w$;
10         $C[h_j(i)].sum \leftarrow C[j, h_j(i)].sum - w \cdot i$;
11         $C[h_j(i)].fingerprint$.UPDATE$(i, -w)$;
12   **if** $C[h_j(i)].count \geq 1$ **and**
        $(C[h_j(i)].fingerprint = fingerprint\ of\ (C[h_j(i)].sum/C[h_j(i)]$
                $.count, C[h_j(i)].count))$
        then
13   Q.enqueue($C[h_j(i)]$.sum$/C[h_j(i)]$.count, $C[h_j(i)]$.count)

---

be implemented to run efficiently in $O(t)$ time, and the full pseudocode is provided in Algorithm 3.17.

The analysis that follows argues that the size of the array C just needs to be $O(s)$ to allow this recovery to happen almost certainly, if no more than s items are stored in the structure. It has been suggested to use some k between 3 and 7, which will make the failure probability $O(t^{-k+2})$ as long as $t > c_k s$, where c_k is some constant depending on k. The precise values of c_k are known, and are actually quite small, as given in Table 3.1.

Example. A small example is shown in Figure 3.3, with six elements in an array with eight cells and $k = 3$. For simplicity, the figure shows in each

Table 3.1. *Values of c_k for $k = 3, 4, 5, 6, 7$.*

k	3	4	5	6	7
c_k	1.222	1.295	1.425	1.570	1.721

3, 4	1, 3, 4, 6	2	1, 5	2, 3, 5	1, 4	2, 6	5, 6	2 recovered
3, 4	1, 3, 4, 6		1, 5	3, 5	1, 4	6	5, 6	6 recovered
3, 4	1, 3, 4		1, 5	3, 5	1, 4		5	5 recovered
3, 4	1, 3, 4		1	3	1, 4			1, 3 recovered
4	4				4			4 recovered

Figure 3.3 An example on the peeling process.

cell the set of elements that are mapped there, rather than the corresponding sums, counts, and fingerprints. Successive rows show the state of the structure after successive steps of peeling have recovered one or more items from the structure. Initially, only item 2 can be recovered, as all other cells have more than one items mapped there. However, as the peeling proceeds, we are able to recover all items eventually.

Implementation Issues. Remember that we require the k hash functions to map each item to distinct locations. There are three ways to implement this.

The strictest way to follow this requirement is to have a single hash function h that maps the universe of items to the range $\{0, 1, \ldots, \binom{t}{k} - 1\}$. Note that there are a total of $\binom{t}{k}$ subsets of k distinct locations in an array of size t, so this hash function will pick one subset uniformly at random. For any item i, the k actual locations can be then extracted from the hash value $h = h(i)$ as follows. The first location is $h_1 = h \mod t$. Then we update $h \leftarrow h - t \cdot h_1$. The second location is $h_2 = h \mod (t - 1)$, counting from the beginning of the array but skipping location h_1. So we need to add 1 to h_2 if $h_1 \leq h_2$. Then we update $h \leftarrow h - (t - 1)h_2$. This process continues until we get h_k.

Alternatively, one can have k separate tables each of size t, with hash function h_j mapping items to the j-th table. This will also ensure that any item is hashed to k distinct locations. However, the downside is that the structure size is now k times larger. It is believed that using this version, the size of each table can be smaller than $c_k s$, but no formal analysis is known so far.

Finally, one can simply discard the duplicated hash values returned by the k hash functions, that is, an item may be mapped to fewer than k locations when there are duplicated hash values. Strictly speaking, the analysis that follows does not hold for this version, but empirically this may not lead to much difference for t not too small.

There are cases where the SparseRecovery structure can be further simplified. If we are not dealing with a multiset but a set, i.e., at most one copy of each item can exist in the structure, then the *sum* field can be replaced by the XOR of all the item identifiers mapped there. This eliminates any concern of bit overflow. Second, if we are dealing with a set and we are guaranteed that there will be no extraneous deletions, i.e., deleting a nonexistent item, then the *fingerprint* field is not needed. We simply check if the count is 1 for a cell, and recover the item from the cell if it is.

Further Discussion. The analysis relies on the connection between the peeling process and the existence of a 2-core in a random hypergraph. A *hypergraph* $G = (V, E)$ is similar to a standard graph, the only difference being that an edge in a standard graph connects two vertices but a hypergraph edge (or "hyperedge") may connect any number of vertices, i.e., each edge is now any subset of V.

To make the preceding connection, think of the cells as being vertices in the hypergraph, and the items as being hyperedges, with the vertices for an edge corresponding to the cells that the item is mapped to. In our case, each edge covers k randomly chosen vertices in the hypergraph. The *2-core* is the largest subhypergraph that has minimum degree at least 2, i.e., each vertex must be covered by at least two edges. The peeling process for SparseRecovery is then exactly the same as the standard peeling algorithm to find the 2-core of a hypergraph: while there exists a vertex with degree 1, delete it and the corresponding hyperedge. The equivalence between the peeling process and the QUERY algorithm for SparseRecovery is thus immediate. ·

We can recover the vector completely if the 2-core of the corresponding hypergraph is empty. This is determined by the random choice of the hash functions, which we can treat as generating a random hypergraph. Prior studies on the 2-core in a random hypergraph have established tight bounds on its existence probability. Let t be the number of vertices and s the number of hyperedges. If $t > (c_k + \varepsilon)s$ for any constant $\varepsilon > 0$ and the values of c_k in Table 3.1, then the probability that a nonempty 2-core exists is $O(t^{-k+2})$, which yields the aforementioned claimed bounds.

A full analysis on the existence probability of 2-cores is rather technical and can be found in [87, 187]; here we just provide some intuition. First let us consider the probability that any two given hyperedges form (part of) a 2-core. For this to happen, they must cover exactly the same set of k vertices, which happens with probability $O(t^{-k})$. As there are $O(s^2) = O(t^2)$ pairs of hyperedges, by the union bound, the probability that there exists a 2-core with two hyperedges is $O(t^{-k+2})$.

The full analysis will similarly examine the probability that there exists a 2-core with j hyperedges, for $j = 3, 4, \ldots, s$, and the calculation is quite involved. What has been shown is that, when $t > (c_k + \varepsilon)s$, these larger 2-cores are unlikely to occur, and the total probability of their existence is dominated by that of a 2-hyperedge 2-core.

History and Background. Structures that allow the recovery of a small number of items have appeared in many different problems within computer science. For example, many problems in coding theory relate to sending information (a bit string), which is corrupted in a small number of places. The difference between the transmitted and received bit string can be interpreted as a set of locations and the goal of error correction is to identify these locations, and correct them. Hence, many techniques from coding theory, such as Reed–Solomon and Reed–Muller codes [190], can be adapted to solve this sparse recovery problem.

More recently, interest in problems of "compressed sensing" have also produced algorithms for sparse recovery. The area of compressed sensing is concerned with defining a matrix M so that given the product Mx for a vector x, x can be recovered accurately. Note that exactly recovering x is impossible unless M has many rows, in which case simply setting M to be the identity matrix would solve the problem. Instead, it is usually assumed that x is "sparse" in some sense, in which case much more compact matrices M can be defined. This sparsity could manifest in the sense that few entries of x are large and most are small (but non-zero). The case when only k entries are nonzero and the rest are zero is known as the *strict k-sparsity* or *exactly k sparse* case. The idea of using sum and count in this way to simply decode an isolated item seems to have appeared first in the work of Ganguly [109]. This technique can also be understood as a limiting case of Reed–Solomon coding, when two polynomial extensions of the input are taken, corresponding to the sum and count of the symbols.

Most recently, there has been a line of work developing "invertible Bloom look-up tables" (IBLT) [98, 122]. The goal of these is to function as a BloomFilter but with the additional property of being able to recover the encoded set when the number of items is small enough. In some cases, the focus can be limited to where the input describes a set rather than a multiset (i.e., the multiplicity of each item is restricted to 1); this slightly simplifies the problem. Our description of the SparseRecovery structure is close to that of Eppstein and Goodrich [98], though the simple (slightly weaker) analysis was presented in [65]. A distillation of these ideas appears in the form of "Biff codes," whose name acknowledges the Bloom filter [186]. The key idea is to use an IBLT data structure to act as the error correcting part of a code, to handle character errors (or erasures). The resulting code is considered to be attractive, as encoding and decoding is very fast – encoding is essentially linear in the size of the input, while error correction takes time proportional to the number of errors. Although the constant factors that result for using the Biff code are not the smallest possible, the fast operation and simple algorithm make the code attractive for settings where there are large volumes of data in large blocks, and quite low error rates, which is a common scenario.

3.9 Distinct Sampling/ℓ_0 Sampling

Brief Summary. An ℓ_0-sampler structure summarizes a multiset A of items under insertions and deletions. It allows one (or more) items to be sampled uniformly from those items currently in A, i.e., those that have nonzero count. Formally, if $|A|$ denotes the distinct cardinality of the multiset, that is, the number of items with nonzero count, then the summary promises to sample each item with probability $(1 \pm \varepsilon)/|A| \pm \delta$, for parameters ε and δ. With ε and δ sufficiently small, this sampling is approximately uniform. The structure is based on multiple instances of a SparseRecovery structure, where each instance samples its input with decreasing probability.

Operations on the Summary. The sampling process is applied to items drawn from a known universe of possibilities, denoted U. The ℓ_0-sampler structure consists of m SparseRecovery data structures, where $m = \log n$ and $n = |U|$ is the size of the set of possible items in the multiset A (or a bound on the largest value of $|A|$). The ith SparseRecovery structure is applied to a subset of U where items are included in the subset with probability 2^{-i+1}, which we call "level i." If we write S_i to denote the i'th SparseRecovery structure, then S_1 applies to all possible items, S_1 applies to half, S_3 to a quarter, and so on. Let U_i be the subset of the universe selected at level i, and we write A_i to denote the input multiset restricted to U_i. The idea is that there is some level i where $0 < |A_i| < k$, where k is the parameter of the SparseRecovery structures. At this level, we can recover A_i exactly, and from this we can sample an item. The subsequent analysis shows that this is sufficiently close to uniform.

Algorithm 3.18: ℓ_0-sampler: INITIALIZE (n, δ)

---

1 $m \leftarrow \log n$;
2 **for** $j \leftarrow 1$ **to** m **do**
3 $\quad\lfloor\; S_j \leftarrow$ SparseRecovery.INITIALIZE $(\log^2 1/\delta)$;
4 $h \leftarrow$ randomly chosen hash function ;

To INITIALIZE the structure, we fix the value of m, and INITIALIZE m SparseRecovery data structures. We also initialize the mechanism that will be used to determine the mapping of items to subsets. This is done with a hash function (so the same item is mapped consistently). Picking a hash function h that maps to the range $[0 \ldots 1]$, we define A_i to contain all those items j so that $h(j) \leq 2^{-i+1}$.

Algorithm 3.19: ℓ_0-sampler: UPDATE (j, w)

---

1 **for** $i \leftarrow 1$ **to** m **do**
2 $\quad$ **if** $h(j) \leq 2^{-i+1}$ **then**
3 $\quad\quad\lfloor\; S_i.$UPDATE(j, w)

The UPDATE procedure applies the hash function to map to levels. Given an update to an item j and a change in its weight w, we apply the hash function h to determine which levels it appears in, and update the corresponding SparseRecovery structures. Algorithm 3.19 makes this explicit: $h(j)$ is evaluated and compared against 2^{-i+1} to determine if $j \in U_j$.

Algorithm 3.20: ℓ_0-sampler: QUERY ()

---

1 **for** $i \leftarrow 1$ **to** m **do**
2 $\quad A_i \leftarrow S_i.$QUERY();
3 $\quad$ **if** $A_i \neq$ FAIL **and** $A_i \neq \emptyset$ **then**
4 $\quad\quad\lfloor\; j \leftarrow$ random item from A_i ;
5 $\quad\quad\lfloor\;$ **return** (j) ;

To QUERY the structure, we iterate over each level and find the first level at which we can successfully retrieve the full set A_i (i.e., the size of A_i is not too large). Then a random element from this set is returned (Algorithm 3.20). For this to work, we have to ensure that there is some A_i for which A_i is not too large and is not empty. This is determined by the analysis. Lastly, to MERGE two ℓ_0-sampler structures (provided they were initialized with the same parameters and share the same h function), we just have to MERGE corresponding pairs of SparseRecovery structures.

| Level 4: 14 |
| Level 3: 3, 10, 14 |
| Level 2: 3, 8, 10, 14, 20 |
| Level 1: 3, 6, 7, 8, 10, 14, 18, 19, 20 |

Figure 3.4 Example of ℓ_0-sampler structure with four levels.

Example. Figure 3.4 shows a schematic of how the ℓ_0-sampler structure stores information. Each level is shown with the list of items that are stored at that level. The input describes the set $A = \{3, 6, 7, 8, 10, 14, 18, 19, 20\}$, which is also represented as A_1. About half of these elements are also represented in $A_2 = \{3, 8, 10, 14, 20\}$. At level 5 and above, no elements from A are selected, so $A_5 = \emptyset$ (not shown).

Suppose we set the parameter k of the SparseRecovery structure to be 4. Then it is not possible to recover A_1 or A_2 — their cardinality is too large. However, A_3 can be recovered successfully, and one of these items can be picked as the sample to return.

If occurrences of items $3, 10$, and 14 happened to be deleted, then level A_4 and A_3 would become empty. However, it would now be the case that $|A_2| = 3$, and so A_2 could be recovered and sampled from. The analysis detailed in the following argues that it will be possible to return a sample with good probability whatever the pattern of updates.

Further Discussion. The analysis has two parts. The first part is to argue that with a suitable setting of the parameter k for the SparseRecovery structures, there will be a level at which recovery can succeed. The second is to argue that the item(s) sampled will be chosen almost uniformly from A.

Given a particular input A, consider the event that some item is returned by the structure in response to a QUERY. For a level i, let the random variable $N_i = |A_i|$ be the number of (distinct) elements from the input that are mapped there. For the structure to succeed, we need that $1 \leq N_j \leq k$. Observe that

$$\mathsf{E}[N_i] = \sum_{j \in A} \Pr[j \in A_i] = \sum_{j \in A} 2^{-i+1} = \frac{|A|}{2^{i-1}},$$

by linearity of expectation since the chance that any item is included in A_i is 2^{-i+1}.

To ensure that there is at least one level with sufficiently many items, consider the level i such that

$$\frac{k}{4} \leq \mathsf{E}[N_i] \leq \frac{k}{2}.$$

We will be able to successfully recover A_i if its actual size is not too different from its expected size. Specifically, the absolute difference between N_i and $\mathsf{E}[N_i]$ must be at most $\mathsf{E}[N_i]$. If we assume that the choices of which items get included in A_i are fully independent, then we can apply Chernoff bounds of the form stated in Fact 1.5, and obtain that the probability of this event is exponentially small in k, i.e., $\Pr[1 \leq N_i \leq k] \geq 1 - \exp(-k/16)$. We note that it is not necessary to assume that the choices are fully independent; similar results follow assuming only k-wise independence [208, 65].

For the second part, we want to show that the sampling is almost uniform. This requires an argument that the items that survive to level i or above are uniformly selected from all items. This is the case when the selection is done with full independence, and this also holds approximately when limited independence is used. The fact that the sampling may fail with some small probability may also bias the distribution, but this gives only a very small distortion. Consequently, it holds that each item is sampled with probability $(1 \pm \varepsilon)/|A| \pm \delta$, where both ε and δ are exponentially small in k [65]. Equivalently, if we pick k to be $\log 1/\delta$, then the sampling probability is $1/|A| \pm \delta$.

Implementation Issues. As discussed in the analysis, an implementation must use hash functions to select items to level i that have only limited independence. The analysis shows that it is sufficient to have small $(\log 1/\delta)$ independence for the guarantees to hold. Further, rather than map to $\{0 \ldots 1\}$, it is more common to have hash functions that map to integers and select items that hash to a 2^{-i+1} fraction of the range. However, provided the range of the integers is sufficiently large (say, more than n^3 given the bound n on the size of the input), this does not affect the selection probabilities. For the analysis to hold, it seems that we should select the level i such that $k/4 \leq |A|/2^{i-1} \leq k/2$ to perform the recovery. This requires knowing a good estimate of $|A|$. However, it is seen that simply greedily picking the first level where recovery succeeds does not substantially affect uniformity and does not decrease the failure probability [65].

The discussion and analysis has assumed the case where the goal is to recover a single sample. However, when the goal is to recover a larger set of size s, the structure is almost identical. The only changes needed are to increase the size of k proportional to s [21].

History and Background. The notion of ℓ_0-sampling was first introduced under the name of distinct sampling, in order to solve problems in geometric data analysis [108] and to capture properties of frequency distributions [78]. Variations on the basic outline followed earlier have been presented, based on how sampling to levels is performed, and what kind of sparse recovery is applied. The underlying concept, of hashing items to levels and using recovery mechanisms, is universal [78, 108, 188, 150]. More recently, the variant where multiple items must be recovered has also been studied using similar constructions [21].

The notion has a surprising number of applications in computer science, although mostly these are more theoretical than practical. The chief surprise is that graph connectivity can be tracked in near-linear space, as edges are added and removed. This construction, reliant on ℓ_0 sampling, is described in Section 7.1. Other applications of ℓ_0 sampling appear in computational geometry, where they can be used to track the width (a measure of spread) of a pointset [15] and the weight of a spanning tree in Euclidean space [108], and for clustering high-dimensional data [36].

3.10 L_p Sampling

Brief Summary. An ℓ_p-sampler structure summarizes a multiset A of items under insertions and deletions. It allows items to be sampled from those currently in A according to the ℓ_p distribution, where each item is weighted based on the p'th power of its current frequency. Formally, the objective is to sample each element j whose current frequency is v_j with probability proportional to $(1 \pm \epsilon)\frac{v_j^p}{\|v\|_p^p} \pm \delta$, where ϵ and δ are approximation parameters. The structure is built on top of the Count Sketch data structure, which allows items to be selected based on the ℓ_2 distribution. With appropriate reweighting, this achieves the desired sampling distribution.

Operations on the Summary. The ℓ_p-sampler structure uses a hash function u to re-weight the input, where each hash value $u(j)$ is treated as a uniform random real number in the range 0 to 1. We describe the method that works for $0 < p < 2$.

Algorithm 3.21: ℓ_p-sampler: INITIALIZE (p, ϵ, δ)

---

1 $k \leftarrow 2\lceil \log(2/\epsilon) \rceil$;
2 $u \leftarrow$ random k-wise independent hash function to $[0, 1]$;
3 **if** $p = 1$ **then**
4      $m \leftarrow O(\log 1/\epsilon)$
5 **else**
6      $m \leftarrow O(\epsilon^{-\max(0, p-1)})$
7 Count Sketch.INITIALIZE($m, \log 1/\delta$);
8 ℓ_p sketch.INITIALIZE()

To INITIALIZE the structure (Algorithm 3.21), we sample the necessary hash function u and initialize the sketches that will be used to track the frequencies.

Algorithm 3.22: ℓ_p-sampler: UPDATE (j, w)

---

1 Count Sketch.UPDATE($j, u(j)^{-1/p} \cdot w$) ;
2 ℓ_p sketch.UPDATE (j, w, p)

To UPDATE the structure (Algorithm 3.22), we update the associated sketches: we use the hash function u to adjust the update to the Count Sketch, and we update the ℓ_p sketch to estimate the ℓ_p norm of the (unadjusted) input.

To query the structure and attempt to draw a sample according to the ℓ_p distribution, we try to identify the largest element in the rescaled vector. If the input defines a vector v, let z be the vector so that $z_j = v_j / u(j)^{1/p}$. We use the Count Sketch to find the (estimated) largest entry of z, as z_i, and also estimate $\|v\|_p$ by setting $r = \ell_p$sketch.QUERY(). We also use the Count Sketch to find the m largest entries of z, and estimate the ℓ_2 norm of the vector z after removing these (approximated) entries as s. We apply two tests to the recovered values, whose purpose is explained further later in this section. These tests require $s \leq \epsilon^{1-1/p} m^{1/2} r$ and $|z_i| \geq \epsilon^{-1/p} r$. If these tests pass, we output i as the sampled index; otherwise, we declare that this instance of the sampler failed. To ensure sufficiently many samples are generated, this process is repeated independently in parallel multiple times.

Example. Consider the vector $v = [1, 2, 3, -4]$, so that $\|v\|_1 = 10$. We consider trying to ℓ_1 sample from this vector with $\epsilon = 1/2$. For simplicity of presentation, we assume that we obtain $m = 1$, and the sketch correctly finds the largest items.

Suppose that the hash function u gives us a random vector

$$u = [0.919, 0.083, 0.765, 0.672].$$

Then we have the rescaled vector z as

$$z = [1.08, 24.09, 3.92, -5.95].$$

The largest magnitude entry of z is $z_2 = 24.09$. Suppose our estimate of $\|v\|_1$ gives $r = 11.81$, and we find s (the 2-norm of z after removing z_2) as 6.67. Our two tests are that $\|1.08, 3.92, -5.45\|_2 = 6.67 \leq 11.81$, and $24.09 \geq 2 \cdot 11.81$. Consequently, both tests pass, and we output 2 as the sampled index.

Further Discussion. The essence of the ℓ_p sampling algorithm is that the values of $u(j)^{1/p}$ give a boost to the probability that a small value becomes the largest entry in the rescaled vector z. It is chosen so that this probability corresponds to the desired sampling distribution. However, reasoning directly about an element becoming the largest in the rescaled vector is a little tricky, so we modify the requirement to considering the probability that any given element takes on a value above a threshold τ, and that no other element also exceeds that threshold.

We start by observing that the probability that the reciprocal of a uniform random value u_i in $[0, 1]$ exceeds a threshold τ is exactly $1/\tau$. That is, $\Pr[u_i^{-1} \geq \tau] = 1/\tau$. Now set $\tau = \|v\|_p^p / |v_i|^p$ and substitute this in: we get

$$\Pr[u_i^{-1} \geq \|v\|_p^p / |v_i|^p] = |v_i|^p / \|v_i\|_p^p.$$

Rearranging, we have

$$\Pr[|v_i|^p / u_i \geq \|v\|_p^p] = |v_i|^p / \|v_i\|_p^p$$

and so $\Pr[|v_i| / u_i^{1/p} \geq \|v\|_p] = |v_i|^p / \|v_i\|_p^p.$

This looks promising: the quantity $|v_i| / u_i^{1/p}$ corresponds to the entries of the rescaled vector z, while $|v_i|^p / \|v_i\|_p^p$ is the desired ℓ_p sampling probability for element i.

However, there are some gaps to fill, which the formal analysis takes account of. First, we are not working with the exact vector of $v_i / u_i^{1/p}$ values, but rather a Count Sketch, with u given by a hash function. This is addressed in the analysis, using similar arguments based on properties of limited independence hash function and concentration of measure that we have seen already. Secondly, it turns out that using the threshold of

$\|v\|_p$ is not desirable, since it could be that multiple indices pass this threshold once rescaled by u. This is handled by raising the threshold from $\|v\|_p$ to a higher value of $\|v\|_p/\epsilon^{1/p}$. This decreases the chance that multiple indices exceed the threshold. However, this also lowers the chance that any one index does pass the threshold. The analysis shows that the probability of returning any index from the structure is approximately proportional to ϵ. By repeating the procedure $O(1/\epsilon \log 1/\delta)$ times, the method returns a sample according to the desired distribution with probability at least $1 - \delta$.

The formal analysis is rather lengthy and detailed, and can be found in the references that follow.

History and Background. The notion of ℓ_p sampling was foreshadowed in some early works that provided algorithms for ℓ_0 sampling by Cormode et al. [78] and Frahling et al. [108]. The first solution to the more general problem was given by Monemizadeh and Woodruff [188], and subsequently simplified by Jowhari et al. [150]. More recently, Jayaram and Woodruff [142] showed that ℓ_p-sampling can be done perfectly, i.e., achieving $\varepsilon = 0$ in the sampling distribution, only using polylogarithmic space, although the summary is allowed to fail (i.e., not returning a sample) with a small probability.

ℓ_p sampling has numerous applications for computational problems. It can be applied to sampling rows and columns of matrices based on their so-called *leverage scores*, which reduces to ℓ_2 sampling [90], allowing the solution of various regression problems. More complex norms of data, known as "cascaded norms," can be approximated by ℓ_p sampling [188]. ℓ_2 sampling can also be used as the basis of estimating ℓ_q norms for $q > 2$, as first observed by Coppersmith and Kumar [62]. In graph algorithms, ℓ_2 sampling can be used to sample "wedges" nearly uniformly, as part of an algorithm to count triangles: a wedge is a pair of edges that share a vertex [180]. For a more comprehensive survey of ℓ_p sampling and its applications, see [70].

4

Summaries for Ordered Data

This chapter continues to work on multisets, but in addition we assume that the items are drawn from an ordered universe U (in this chapter, we will use U to denote both the domain and its size). As in Chapter 3, we use a vector representation for the multiset, and the input consists of (x, w) pairs, where x is an item from U and w is its integer weight. Some summaries only allow the input to have positive weights, while others allow both positive and negative weights. Some summaries allow only unweighted input, which means w is always taken to be 1. The multiplicity of x, v_x, is the sum of all the weights of x in the input. We require every v_x to be nonnegative.

Queries to the summaries will exploit the ordering of items, e.g., finding the median of the multiset. Formally, for an element x, either in the dataset or not, we define $\text{rank}(x) = \sum_{y<x} v_y$ to be the total weight of elements from the data that are strictly less than x. This allows the computation of various "order statistics." For example, the median will be the largest element whose rank is no greater than $W/2$, where W is the total weight of all elements. The summaries discussed in this chapter support two types of queries. A *rank query* finds the rank of a given element x, while a *quantile query* returns an element with a given rank. These queries are important in describing the distribution of the underlying data. As the summaries are lossy, they do not return the exact ranks. Let ε be an error parameter. For a rank query with a given element x, the summary will return an approximate rank $\tilde{r}$, such that $\text{rank}(x) - \varepsilon W \le \tilde{r} \le \text{rank}(x) + \varepsilon W$. Similarly, for a quantile query with a given rank r, the summary will return an element x such that $r - \varepsilon W \le \text{rank}(x) \le r + \varepsilon W$. Note that in a multiset, such an element may not exist, when there is an x with $\text{rank}(x) < r - \varepsilon W$ and $\text{rank}(x) + v_x > r + \varepsilon W$. In this case, the summary returns x.

In this chapter, we consider four quite distinct approaches to this problem, which apply to different restrictions on the input data.

- The Q-Digest summary (Section 4.1) is based on maintaining a subset of simple counters of ranges, when the input is drawn from a fixed integer domain and can be weighted.
- The GK summary (Section 4.2) can be viewed as maintaining a (deterministic) sample of the input. It is a comparison-based summary, meaning that it can be applied to any data type for which a comparator is defined, such as real numbers, user-defined types, etc., so it has a wider applicability than Q-Digest. However, it can only handle items with unit weights.
- The KLL summary (Section 4.3) is a randomized summary and provides a probabilistic guarantee, i.e., it answers queries within the ε-error bound with a high probability, which can be controlled by appropriate parameters. There is always a small chance that the error may exceed ε. This summary can also handle weighted items.
- The DCS summary (Section 4.4) is a sketching-based summary, so it can handle both insertion and deletion of items, which is its distinctive feature. However, it is also a randomized summary with a probabilistic guarantee. It also requires the input be drawn from a fixed integer domain. This summary can handle weighted items.

The following table summarizes the various features of these four quantile summaries:

Summary	Domain	Guarantee	Weights	Deletions
Q-Digest	Integer	Deterministic	Yes	No
GK	Comparison	Deterministic	No	No
KLL	Comparison	Probabilistic	Yes	No
DCS	Integer	Probabilistic	Yes	Yes

4.1 Q-Digest

Brief Summary. The Q-Digest provides a compact summary for data drawn from a fixed discrete input domain U, represented by the integers 0 to $U - 1$.

Each input is an (x, w) pair where w must be positive. The summary takes space at most $O\left(\frac{1}{\varepsilon} \log U\right)$, which is fixed and independent of the input. Summaries can be easily merged together. The summary works by maintaining a tree structure over the domain U: nodes in the tree correspond to subranges of U, and simple statistics are maintained for a small set of nodes.

Operations on the Summary. The Q-Digest structure is represented as a collection of nodes within a binary tree whose leaves are the ordered elements of U. Each node v is associated with a weight w_v. Only nodes with nonzero weight are explicitly stored. The maintenance procedures on the data structure ensure that the number of nodes stored is bounded by $O\left(\frac{1}{\varepsilon} \log U\right)$. The sum of all weights of nodes is equal to the total weight of the input items summarized, W. The INITIALIZE operation creates an empty Q-Digest, i.e., all the nodes in the binary tree have (implicit) weight 0.

At any time, there is a notion of the "capacity" C of the nonleaf nodes in the structure. This capacity is set to be $\varepsilon W / \log U$. The intuition is that error in answering queries will come from a bounded number of nodes in the tree. By bounding the weight associated with each node, this will lead to a bound on the error.

UPDATE. Each UPDATE operation of an item x performs a walk down the tree structure, starting from the root, with the aim of adding the weight w associated with x to nodes in the tree. The algorithm proceeds recursively: given a current node v, if the current weight associated with the node w_v is equal to the capacity C, then it finds which child node x belongs to (either the left or right child) and recurses accordingly. When the node is below capacity, the algorithm tries to store the new weight there. If v is a leaf node, since leaf nodes do not have to enforce a capacity, we can add w to w_v, and finish. For a nonleaf node v, if the sum of the weights, $w_v + w$ is at most the capacity C, then we can safely update the weight of node v to $w_v + w$ and finish. Otherwise, adding the full weight would take v over capacity. In that case, we update the weight of v to $w_v \leftarrow C$. This leaves $w - (C - w_v)$ of the weight of the update x still unassigned, so we recurse on the appropriate child of v as before. This procedure will take at most $\log U$ steps, since the length of a path from the root to the leaf level is $\log U$, and the procedure will always stop when it reaches the leaf level, if not before.

Algorithm 4.1 shows the pseudocode to update the data structure with an item x of weight w. The central while-loop determines what to do at a given node v. If v is below capacity, then lines 5 through 8 put as much of the weight w there as possible, and adjust w accordingly. If this reduces w to zero, then the algorithm can break out of the loop. Otherwise, it recurses on either the left or right subtree of v (denoted by v.left and v.right, respectively). Finally, any remaining weight is assigned to node v in line 14: if v is not a leaf, then w will be 0 at this point.

Algorithm 4.1: Q-Digest: UPDATE (x, w)

---

1 $W \leftarrow W + w$;
2 $C \leftarrow \varepsilon W / \log U$;
3 $v \leftarrow$ root ;
4 **while** v *is not a leaf node* **do**
5   **if** $(w_v < C)$ **then**
6           $d \leftarrow \min(C - w_v, w)$;
7           $w_v \leftarrow w_v + d$;
8           $w \leftarrow w - d$;
9   **if** $w = 0$ **then** break;
10   **if** x *is in left subtree of* v **then**
11          $v \leftarrow v$.left
12   **else**
13          $v \leftarrow v$.right

14 $w_v \leftarrow w_v + w$;

QUERY. A rank query for an element x is answered by computing the sum of weights of all nodes in the structure that correspond to ranges of items that are (all) strictly less than x. Note that all the weights stored in such nodes arose from the insertion of items that were strictly less than x, so this gives a correct lower bound on the answer. Similarly, nodes in the structure corresponding to ranges of items that are (all) strictly more than x do not contribute to rank(x). This only leaves nodes in the structure that include x: the weight of these nodes may have arisen from items that were below, above, or equal to x. These lead to the approximation in the answer. Note however that there are only $\log U$ such nodes: only nodes on the root-to-leaf path for x contain x. As the weight of each nonleaf node is bounded by the capacity C, we have that the error in the answer is bounded by at most $C \log U$. Since we require that $C \leq \varepsilon W / \log U$, this error is in turn bounded by εW.

Algorithm 4.2 shows code for the query procedure. The algorithm proceeds down from the root. It assumes that the values of W_v, the total weight of all nodes below (and including) node v have already been calculated.

This can be done with a single depth-first walk over the data structure. The
algorithm computes the sum of weights of all nodes that are strictly less than
x. The algorithm walks the path from the root down to x. At each step,
if x belongs to the right subbranch of the current node v, then it adds in
the count of all nodes in the left subbranch as W_u (line 8) to the running
sum r.

Algorithm 4.2: Q-Digest: QUERY (x)

---

1 $v \leftarrow$ root ;
2 $r \leftarrow 0$;
3 **while** v *is not a leaf node* **do**
4      $u \leftarrow v.\text{left}$;
5   **if** x *is in left subtree of* v **then**
6         $v \leftarrow u$
7   **else**
8         $r \leftarrow r + W_u$;
9         $v \leftarrow v.\text{right}$

10 **return** (r)

COMPRESS. If we only follow the above procedures, then the number of nodes
stored in the structure can grow quite large. This is because the capacity
$C = \varepsilon W / \log U$ is growing as more elements are inserted into the summary, so
nodes that are full will become underfull over time. To counter this, we shall
COMPRESS the structure from time to time. The COMPRESS operation ensures
that the number of nodes stored in the structure is bounded by $O(\log U / \varepsilon)$,
while retaining all the properties needed to give the accuracy guarantees. The
first step is to update the capacity C as $\varepsilon W / \log U$. Then the central idea of
COMPRESS is to ensure that as many nodes in the structure as possible are at
full capacity, by moving weight from nodes lower down in the tree up into
their ancestors.

First, we compute for each node v the total weight of the subtree at v, as W_v.
This can be done with a single depth-first walk over the tree. Then COMPRESS
proceeds recursively, starting from the root. Given a current node v, if it is
below capacity, i.e., $w_v < C$, then we seek to increase its weight by "pulling
up" weight associated with its descendants. If W_v is sufficient to bring the node
up to capacity, then we can adjust w_v up to C. This incurs a "debt" of $(C - w_v)$,
which must be passed on to the descendants of v. This debt is apportioned to

the left and right children of v so that neither child is given a debt that exceeds
the weight of their subtree. One way to do so is to assign as much of the debt
as possible to one of the children (e.g., always the left child), while respecting
this condition. The procedure continues recursively, although now the weight
W_v of a subtree has to be reduced by the debt inherited from the parents. If this
causes the weight of the subtree to be 0, then the node and all its descendants
now have zero weight, and so do not have to be retained. The recursion halts
when a leaf node is reached: leaf nodes have no descendants, so no further
weight can be pulled up from them.

Algorithm 4.3: Q-Digest: COMPRESS (v, d)

---

1 **if** $w_v = 0$ **then return**;
2 **if** v *is a leaf node* **then**
3      $w_v \leftarrow w_v - d$
4 **else**
5   **if** $W_v - d > C$ **then**
6          $d \leftarrow d + C - w_v$;
7          $w_v \leftarrow C$;
8          $u \leftarrow v.$left ;
9   COMPRESS$(v.$left$, \min(d, W_u))$;
10   COMPRESS$(v.$right$, \max(d - W_u, 0))$;
11   **else**
12         $w_v \leftarrow W_v - d$;
13   Set weight of all descendants of v to 0 ;

Algorithm 4.3 outlines the procedure for performing a COMPRESS. Again,
we assume that the values W_v have been computed for each node as the sum
of all weights in the subtree rooted at v. The algorithm is called initially with
COMPRESS$(v = $ root$, d = 0)$, where v indicates the node for the algorithm to
work on, and d indicates the current debt inherited from ancestor nodes. At the
leaf level, the current debt is applied to the weight of the current node (line 3).
The test at line 5 determines whether the current weight of the subtree, less the
inherited debt, exceeds the capacity of the node v. If so, then the weight of v is
increased to the capacity, and the debt adjusted to reflect this. Then as much of
the debt as possible is passed on to the left subtree (rooted at u), which can be
up to W_u, by the recursive call in line 9. The remainder of the debt is passed on
to the right subtree in line 10. In the case that the weight of the tree rooted v less

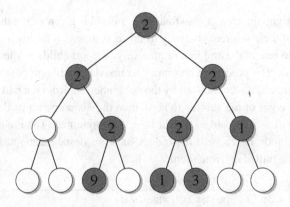

Figure 4.1 Example Q-Digest summary over $U = 0 \ldots 7$.

the current debt is below the current capacity, then line 12 updates the weight of v accordingly. All descendants of v have had all their weight assigned to ancestors, so their weight is now set to zero.

It is clear that this COMPRESS operation preserves the property that the weight associated with each node v is due to input items from the leaves of the subtree of v: since we can view the movement of weights in the tree as going toward the root, it is always the case that the weight of an input item x is associated with a node that is an ancestor of x in the tree. The COMPRESS operation can be implemented to take time linear in the number of nodes, since each node is visited a constant number of times and is processed in constant time.

MERGE. It is straightforward to perform a MERGE operation on two Q-Digest summaries over the same domain U. We simply merge the nodes in the natural way: the weight of node v in the new summary is the sum of the weights of node v in the two input summaries. Following a MERGE, it may be desirable to perform a COMPRESS to ensure that the space remains bounded.

Example. Figure 4.1 shows a schematic illustration of an example Q-Digest summary. It shows a binary tree structure over the domain $0 \ldots 7$. Shaded nodes have nonzero counts, while empty nodes are associated with zero counts and are not explicitly represented. Currently, the capacity of nodes is set to $C = 2$. If we perform a rank query operation for $x = 5$, we obtain an answer of 14, which is the sum of all nodes strictly to the left of the sixth leaf (the one with a weight of 3 in the example of Figure 4.1). The uncertainty in this answer is 6, given by the sum of weights on the path from the root to x. Suppose we

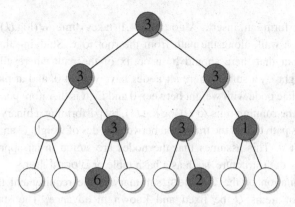

Figure 4.2 Example Q-Digest summary after COMPRESS operation with $C = 3$.

UPDATE the summary with an item with $x = 6$ and $w = 1$. Then the algorithm would walk down from the root until it reached the internal node with weight 1. This is below capacity, and so the weight can be increased to 2. Lastly, suppose we perform a COMPRESS operation on the version of the summary shown in Figure 4.1 after setting the capacity of nodes $C = 3$. Then we obtain the result shown in Figure 4.2. Three units of weight are taken from the third leaf to bring its ancestors up to the new capacity. One unit of weight is taken from each of the fifth and sixth leaves to give to their ancestors. This uses up all of the weight of the fifth leaf, so it is no longer stored. Thus, the COMPRESS operation has reduced the number of nodes stored by one.

Further Discussion. Following a COMPRESS operation, the number of nodes with nonzero count is bounded by $O(\log U/\varepsilon)$. This holds because, where possible, nodes now have a weight of C. Some nodes will have weight below capacity, but these nodes have no descendants with positive weight: if they did have such descendants, then the COMPRESS algorithm would have taken all this weight and distributed it to the ancestors. Consequently, each node below capacity can be associated with its parent that is at capacity; and each node at capacity has at most two children that are below capacity. Suppose there are n_c nodes that are at capacity $C = \varepsilon W/\log U$. Then n_c can be at most $\log U/\varepsilon$, since the weights of all nodes sum to W. Thus there can be at most $O(\log U/\varepsilon)$ nodes with nonzero count in total. This bounds the space of the data structure following a COMPRESS operation.

To perform an insert, Algorithm 4.1 takes time $O(\log U)$, as it performs a walk along the path from the root to x. Studying this path, it turns out that there should be a prefix of the path where all nodes have weight C, a suffix where all nodes have weight 0, and at most one intermediate node with weight between 0 and C. It is therefore possible to improve the running time to $O(\log \log U)$, by performing a binary search along this path to find the transition between nodes of weight C and nodes of weight 0. This assumes that the nodes are stored in an appropriate dictionary data structure, such as a hash table or BloomFilter.

A limitation of the Q-Digest summary is the requirement that the domain of items U be fixed and known in advance. The summary is suitable for dealing with items from a well-understood, structured domain, such as 32-bit integers or IP addresses. However, it does not easily apply to arbitrary text strings or arbitrary precision real numbers. For these cases, other summaries such as the GK summary can be used.

Implementation Issues. In the initial phase of the algorithm, it is not sensible to directly follow the UPDATE procedure, since this will lose too much information. Instead, while $W < \frac{1}{\varepsilon} \log U$, it is better to simply buffer the input items (and so provide exact answers to queries). Only when W exceeds this bound is it suitable to switch from buffering to using the approximate Q-Digest structure.

For a given element x, let r be the sum of the weights of all nodes that are strictly less than x, and Δ be the sum of the weighs of all ancestor nodes of x. As discussed, we have $r \leq \text{rank}(x) \leq r + \Delta$ and $\Delta < \varepsilon W$, and we use r to estimate $\text{rank}(x)$. But $r + \Delta/2$ is a better estimate, whose (two-sided) error is at most $\Delta/2$. Using this estimator, we may double the threshold C and thus make the summary even more compact.

When there are a series of QUERY operations, we may preprocess the summary in order to speed up the query process. For each node in the summary, we calculate the estimated rank of the largest value in the range represented by that node. All these ranks can be calculated with a postorder traversal, which can be done in time linear in the size of the summary. Now to find the rank of a given element x, we return the estimated rank of the largest value that is no greater than x; to find the element with a given rank, we return the item in the list whose estimated rank is closest to the given one. Both operations can be done efficiently with binary search.

The summary as defined in the preceding does not specify exactly when to perform a COMPRESS operation. This can be done whenever needed, without affecting the guarantees of the structure. For example, one could even perform a COMPRESS after every UPDATE operation, although this would slow down performance considerably. To keep the space bounded at $O(\log U/\varepsilon)$, we could only COMPRESS every time the weight W doubles: using the analysis from the discussion of COMPRESS, we still have that each node below capacity C is the child of a node whose weight is C, and we can have only $O(\log U/\varepsilon)$ such parents.

An intermediate strategy is to perform a compress operation every time the capacity C can increase by 1, i.e., every time W increased by $\log U/\varepsilon$. In this case, the amortized cost of an update is dominated by the cost of the UPDATE procedure, since the amortized cost of COMPRESS is $O(1)$ per step. However, in some high-throughput applications, we may want to ensure a worst-case time performance per update. In this case, the periodic execution of COMPRESS (as well as the need to switch over from buffering updates to using the Q-Digest) may cause an unacceptable delay. This can be resolved by performing small pieces of the COMPRESS operation with every UPDATE, at the cost of significantly complicating the implementation.

History and Background. The Q-Digest summary was first proposed by Shrivastava et al. in 2004 [211]. This version did not require that the nodes formed a tree: instead, it was proposed to maintain just a set of nodes and associated weights. Cormode et al. [71] observed that the same guarantees could be provided while additionally requiring that the nodes formed a tree. This simplifies the COMPRESS operation, and ensures that the space bounds are met following each execution of COMPRESS. This "top-down" version of the Q-Digest is then quite similar to a data structure proposed to track the "hierarchical heavy hitters" in streaming data by Zhang et al., also in 2004 [241].

Available Implementations. Several implementations of Q-Digest are available across various languages, differing in how they choose to implement the COMPRESS operation. The implementation from stream-lib (`https://github.com/addthis/stream-lib/tree/master/src/main/java/com/clearspring/analytics/stream/quantile`) uses a similar root-to-leaf version of COMPRESS as discussed here.

4.2 Greenwald–Khanna (GK)

Brief Summary. The GK summary provides a compact summary of data drawn from an ordered input domain U. In contrast with Q-Digest, the GK summary does not need U to be a domain of integers. It is a comparison-based algorithm, i.e., it works on any ordered domain U where a comparison operator is defined. But it only accepts insertions of unweighted elements. So here the total number of elements inserted into the summary, N, is the same as the total weight W. This summary can be merged, but its size grows after each MERGE.

Operations on the Summary. The GK summary stores information about its input as a list of triples, of the form (x_i, g_i, Δ_i). Here, x_i is an item from the input, g_i indicates the total number of items that are represented by this triple, and Δ_i records information about the uncertainty in the position of x_i in the sorted order of the input. The summary ensures that, at any time, for each triple (x_i, g_i, Δ_i), we have that

$$\sum_{j=0}^{i} g_j \leq \text{rank}(x_i) + 1 \leq \Delta_i + \sum_{j=0}^{i} g_j, \tag{4.1}$$

$$g_i + \Delta_i < 2\varepsilon N. \tag{4.2}$$

As a result, we have that the number of input items between x_{i-1} and x_i is at most $2\varepsilon N - 1$.

To INITIALIZE a new GK summary, we create a list that contains only one triple $(\infty, 1, 0)$.

To UPDATE the summary with an item x, we find the smallest i such that $x < x_i$. If $g_i + \Delta_i + 1 < 2\varepsilon N$, we simply increase g_i by 1, in which case no extra space is used. Otherwise we insert a new triple $(x, 1, g_i + \Delta_i - 1)$ right before the ith triple. Then we try to find an adjacent pair of triples (x_j, g_j, Δ_j) and $(x_{j+1}, g_{j+1}, \Delta_{j+1})$ such that $g_j + g_{j+1} + \Delta_{j+1} < 2\varepsilon N$. If such a pair can be found, we remove the first triple, and increase g_{j+1} by g_j, such that the size of the list will remain the same despite the new element. If there is not such a pair, the size of the list is increased by 1. The pseudocode for UPDATE is shown in Algorithm 4.4.

To MERGE two GK summaries, we perform a merge of the sorted lists of triples. Let the head of the two lists be (x, g, Δ) and (x', g', Δ'), and assume that $x \leq x'$. Then we remove the first triple from its list, and create a new triple in the output GK structure with $(x, g, \Delta + g' + \Delta')$. When one list is

---

Algorithm 4.4: GK : UPDATE (x)

---

1 $N \leftarrow N + 1$;
2 Find the smallest i such that $x < x_i$;
3 **if** $g_i + \Delta_i + 1 < 2\varepsilon N$ **then**
4      $g_i \leftarrow g_i + 1$;
5 **else**
6   Insert $(x, 1, g_i + \Delta_i - 1)$ before the ith triple ;
7   **if** $\exists j : (g_j + g_{j+1} + \Delta_{j+1} < 2\varepsilon N)$ **then**
8          $g_{j+1} \leftarrow g_j + g_{j+1}$;
9   remove the jth triple ;

Algorithm 4.5: GK : MERGE (S, T)

---

1 $i \leftarrow 0$;
2 $j \leftarrow 0$;
3 $R \leftarrow \emptyset$;
4 **while** $i < |S|$ *and* $j < |T|$ **do**
5   **if** $S_i.x \leq T_j.x$ **then**
6          $R \leftarrow R \cup (S_i.x, S_i.g, S_i.\Delta + T_j.\Delta + T_j.g - 1)$;
7          $i \leftarrow i + 1$;
8   **else**
9          $R \leftarrow R \cup (T_j.x, T_j.g, S_i.\Delta + T_j.\Delta + S_i.g - 1)$;
10          $j \leftarrow j + 1$;
11 **while** $i < |S|$ **do**
12      $R \leftarrow R \cup (S_i.x, S_i.g, S_i.\Delta)$;
13      $i \leftarrow i + 1$;
14 **while** $j < |T|$ **do**
15      $R \leftarrow R \cup (T_j.x, T_j.g, T_j.\Delta)$;
16      $j \leftarrow j + 1$;
17 **while** *there is j such that* $g_j + g_{j+1} + \Delta_{j+1} < 2\varepsilon N$ **do**
18      $g_{j+1} \leftarrow g_j + g_{j+1}$;
19   remove the jth triple ;

---

exhausted, we just copy over the tail of the other list. This has the effect of combining the bounds on the ranks in the correct way. In the end, we try to reduce the size by removing some tuples as in UPDATE. This is spelled out in Algorithm 4.5.

To QUERY a GK summary to find the estimated rank of a given item y, we scan the list of triples to find where it would fall in the summary. That is, we find triples (x_i, g_i, Δ_i) and $(x_{i+1}, g_{i+1}, \Delta_{i+1})$ so that $x_i \leq y < x_{i+1}$. We have

$$\sum_{j=0}^{i} g_j - 1 \leq \text{rank}(x_i) \leq \text{rank}(y) \qquad \text{and}$$

$$\text{rank}(y) \leq \text{rank}(x_{i+1}) \leq \sum_{j=0}^{i+1} g_j + \Delta_{i+1} - 1.$$

This bounds the rank of y, and leaves uncertainty of at most $g_{i+1} + \Delta_{i+1}$. So we return $\sum_{j=0}^{i} g_j - 1 + (g_{i+1} + \Delta_{i+1})/2$ as the approximate rank of y. Therefore, the maintenance algorithms ensure that this quantity is bounded. Similarly, suppose we want to QUERY to find an item of rank approximately r. Then we seek for a triple (x_i, g_i, Δ_i) so that

$$\text{rank}(x_i) \geq \sum_{j=0}^{i} g_j - 1 \geq r - \varepsilon N \text{ and } \text{rank}(x_i) \leq \Delta_i + \sum_{j=0}^{i} g_j - 1 \leq r + \varepsilon N.$$

For such an i, we report x_i as the item with approximate rank r: from (4.1), we have that

$$r - \varepsilon N \leq \text{rank}(x_i) \leq r + \varepsilon N.$$

Note that we can always find such an x_i in the summary. If $r + 1 \leq N - \varepsilon N$ (otherwise, picking the maximum value will suffice), then we consider the first triple such that $\Delta_i + \sum_{j=0}^{i} g_j > r + 1 + \varepsilon N$. Then, necessarily, $\text{rank}(x_{i-1}) \leq r + \varepsilon N$, and

$$\text{rank}(x_{i-1}) \geq \sum_{j=0}^{i-1} g_j - 1$$

$$= \Delta_i + \sum_{j=0}^{i} g_j - 1 - (g_i + \Delta_i) \geq (r + \varepsilon N) - (2\varepsilon N) = r - \varepsilon N.$$

Example. Table 4.1 shows how a GK summary works with input 1, 4, 2, 8, 5, 7, 6, 7, 6, 7, 2, 1. In this example, we set $\varepsilon = 1/5$, and after each insertion, we always remove the first triple that can be removed. In the end, we have six triples, and Table 4.2 shows the accuracy of this summary. We need to estimate each rank within error of $\varepsilon N = 2.4$, and indeed the summary can estimate all ranks well.

Table 4.1. *Example of a* GK *summary,* $\varepsilon = 1/5$.

Input	N	$\lceil 2\varepsilon N\rceil$	GK summary
	0	0	$(\infty, 1, 0)$
1	1	1	$(1, 1, 0), (\infty, 1, 0)$
4	2	1	$(1, 1, 0), (4, 1, 0), (\infty, 1, 0)$
2	3	2	$(1, 1, 0), (2, 1, 0), (4, 1, 0), (\infty, 1, 0)$
8	4	2	$(1, 1, 0), (2, 1, 0), (4, 1, 0), (8, 1, 0), (\infty, 1, 0)$
5	5	2	$(1, 1, 0), (2, 1, 0), (4, 1, 0), (5, 1, 0), (8, 1, 0), (\infty, 1, 0)$
7	6	3	$(1, 1, 0), (2, 1, 0), (4, 1, 0), (5, 1, 0), (7, 1, 0), (8, 1, 0), (\infty, 1, 0)$
			$(1, 1, 0), (2, 1, 0), (4, 1, 0), (5, 1, 0), (8, 2, 0), (\infty, 1, 0)$
6	7	3	$(1, 1, 0), (2, 1, 0), (4, 1, 0), (5, 1, 0), (6, 1, 1), (8, 2, 0), (\infty, 1, 0)$
			$(2, 2, 0), (4, 1, 0), (5, 1, 0), (6, 1, 1), (8, 2, 0), (\infty, 1, 0)$
7	8	4	$(2, 2, 0), (4, 1, 0), (5, 1, 0), (6, 1, 1), (7, 1, 0), (8, 2, 0), (\infty, 1, 0)$
			$(2, 2, 0), (4, 1, 0), (5, 1, 0), (6, 1, 1), (8, 3, 0), (\infty, 1, 0)$
6	9	4	$(2, 2, 0), (4, 1, 0), (5, 1, 0), (6, 1, 1), (6, 1, 2), (8, 3, 0), (\infty, 1, 0)$
			$(4, 3, 0), (5, 1, 0), (6, 1, 1), (6, 1, 2), (8, 3, 0), (\infty, 1, 0)$
7	10	4	$(4, 3, 0), (5, 1, 0), (6, 1, 1), (6, 1, 2), (7, 1, 2), (8, 3, 0), (\infty, 1, 0)$
			$(4, 3, 0), (6, 2, 1), (6, 1, 2), (7, 1, 2), (8, 3, 0), (\infty, 1, 0)$
2	11	5	$(2, 1, 2), (4, 3, 0), (6, 2, 1), (6, 1, 2), (7, 1, 2), (8, 3, 0), (\infty, 1, 0)$
			$(4, 4, 0), (6, 2, 1), (6, 1, 2), (7, 1, 2), (8, 3, 0), (\infty, 1, 0)$
1	12	5	$(1, 1, 3), (4, 4, 0), (6, 2, 1), (6, 1, 2), (7, 1, 2), (8, 3, 0), (\infty, 1, 0)$
			$(1, 1, 3), (4, 4, 0), (6, 2, 1), (7, 2, 2), (8, 3, 0), (\infty, 1, 0)$

Table 4.2. QUERY *with the example* GK *summary.*

x	Rank(x)	$\tilde{r}(x)$	Error
1	0	2	2
2	2	2	0
4	4	5.5	1.5
5	5	5.5	0.5
6	6	8	2
7	8	9.5	1.5
8	11	11.5	0.5

Further Discussion. The original paper [123] introduced two versions of the GK summary, a complicated one with a strict bound on the summary size, and a simplified one without proven guarantees on its size (hence also update and query time). The version introduced in this section is the second version. Despite the lack of a proof bounding its size, this version of the GK summary performs very well in practice, with size often smaller than the strict version. It is also faster since it is much simpler.

In the strict version, the new triple inserted on the arrival of x is always $(x, 1, \lfloor 2\varepsilon N - 1 \rfloor)$ regardless of the successor triple. And the UPDATE algorithm does not attempt to removed tuples immediately. Instead, a COMPRESS procedure is introduced that guarantees to reduce the space of the summary to $O\left(\frac{1}{\varepsilon}\log(\varepsilon N)\right)$. The COMPRESS procedure essentially takes the search through the data structure for triples that can be combined out of the UPDATE procedure, but also enforces some additional restrictions on which triples can be merged. Interested readers may find the proof and more details about the strict version in the original paper [123].

The MERGE operation is always guaranteed to be correct, in that it allows us to answer queries with the required accurate. However, performing a MERGE operation doubles the size of the summary. We can then perform a COMPRESS to reduce the size if there is redundancy, but it is not clear that the size will always be reduced substantially. It remains an open question whether the GK summary can be merged while keeping a small size.

Implementation Issues. The list of triples can be kept sorted in a binary tree (e.g., using std::map in C++), such that in line 2 of Algorithm 4.4, we may find i by performing a binary search.

The naive implementation of line 7 of Algorithm 4.4 requires a linear scan of the whole list. Alternatively, we may also maintain an auxiliary min-heap, which manages the values of $g_j + g_{j+1} + \Delta_{j+1}$. Now, we can simply check the minimum value in the heap, and remove the corresponding triple if possible; otherwise, it would be safe to claim that no triples can be merged. For each incoming element, the heap may be updated in the same time as UPDATE, so it will not introduce much overhead. Additional speed improvements can be achieved (at the expense of adding some complexity) by standard techniques, such as buffering the most recent set of new items to add to the structure, then sorting them and performing a bulk UPDATE at the same time as a COMPRESS. This will reduce the amortized cost of maintaining the data structure. To answer multiple queries, we can calculate the prefix sums of the g_is with a linear scan. Subsequently, a query can be answered easily by binary search.

History and Background. The GK summary was introduced by Greenwald and Khanna in 2001 [123]. It has been widely used: for example, in systems for large-scale log analysis [203], or for summarizing data arising from networks of sensors [124]. The limitations that no strong guarantees hold for the size of summaries subject to many MERGE operations, and requirement for unit weight input, have led to much interest in generalizations and variations that can overcome these limitations.

While very effective in practice, the bound of $O\left(\frac{1}{\epsilon} \log \epsilon n\right)$ is unsatisfying. A lower bound of $\Omega\left(\frac{1}{\epsilon} \log \frac{1}{\epsilon}\right)$, due to Hung and Ting [136], applies to any deterministic, comparison-based algorithm. The lower bound takes advantage of the assumed deterministic algorithm, to generate input sequences that force the algorithm to keep track of a sufficient amount of information if it is to give an acceptable algorithm. As shown in the next section, if a small probability of failure is allowed, then this lower bound can be broken with a randomized summary whose size is only $O\left(\frac{1}{\varepsilon} \log \log \frac{1}{\varepsilon}\right)$.

Available Implementations. Several implementations of GK are available online, across a variety of languages.

4.3 Karnin–Lang–Liberty (KLL)

Brief Summary. The KLL summary provides a summary of data drawn from an ordered domain U. It is a comparison-based summary, just like GK. The size of the summary is $O\left(\frac{1}{\varepsilon} \sqrt{\log \frac{1}{\varepsilon}}\right)$ after any number of UPDATE and MERGE operations. It is more space and time efficient than the GK summary, but it is a randomized algorithm that may exceed the ε error bound with a small probability. The version of KLL described in this section assumes unweighted items; weighted items can also be handled, and a pointer is given under "History and Background".

Algorithm 4.6: KLL: UPDATE (x)
---
1 $B[0] \leftarrow B[0] \cup \{x\}$;
2 COMPRESS;

Operations on the Summary. The KLL summary consists of a list of buffers B of varying capacities. Buffer $B[l]$ is said to be at level l, and all items in $B[l]$ have weights 2^l. Intuitively, each item in $B[l]$ represents 2^l original input items. The capacity of buffer $B[l]$ is defined to be $c^{h-l}k$ (but at least 2), where h is the highest level with a nonempty buffer, $k = O\left(\frac{1}{\varepsilon} \sqrt{\log(1/\varepsilon)}\right)$, and $c \in (0.5, 1)$ is a constant. Note that with $c < 1$, the buffer capacities decrease as we go down the levels.

The UPDATE procedure is shown in Algorithm 4.6. To UPDATE the summary with an item x, we simply add it to $B[0]$. At this point, there is no loss of information. When $B[0]$ reaches its capacity, we perform an operation called *compaction*, (i.e., a COMPRESS routine), which moves half of the items of $B[0]$ to $B[1]$ while resetting $B[0]$ to empty. This in turn may cause $B[1]$ to reach or exceed its capacity, and a series of compaction operations might be triggered as a result, as shown in Algorithm 4.7. Each compaction introduces some error to the rank estimation, but we will show that the accumulated error for any rank is at most εN with high probability, where N is the number of items summarized.

Algorithm 4.7: KLL: COMPRESS

---

1 **for** $l = 0, \ldots, h$ **do**
2   **if** $|B[l]| \geq \max\{2, c^{h-l}k\}$ **then**
3   Sort $B[l]$;
4          $i \leftarrow$ a fair coin toss;
5   **if** i *is heads* **then**
6              $B[l + 1] \leftarrow B[l + 1] \cup \{\text{items at odd positions in } B[l]\}$;
7   **else**
8              $B[l + 1] \leftarrow B[l + 1] \cup \{\text{items at even positions in } B[l]\}$;
9          $B[l] \leftarrow \emptyset$;

10 **if** $B[h + 1]$ *has been created* **then**
11      $h \leftarrow h + 1$;

The compaction operation is spelled out in lines 3 through 9 of Algorithm 4.7, where we compact $B[l]$ and move half of items to $B[l + 1]$. First, we sort all items in $B[l]$ (ties can be broken arbitrarily). Then with probability $1/2$, we take all items at odd positions, and with probability $1/2$ take all items at even positions. These items are added to $B[l + 1]$, while $B[l]$ is reset to empty.

To MERGE two KLL summaries S_1 and S_2, we first merge the two buffers at the same level (if they exist). Then we perform a series of compaction operations in a bottom-up fashion, just like in the UPDATE algorithm, to make sure that every buffer is below its capacity. See Algorithm 4.8.

To QUERY about rank(x) of an element x, we return the value

$$\tilde{r}(x) = \sum_l 2^l \, \text{rank}_l(x),$$

Algorithm 4.8: KLL: MERGE (S_1, S_2)

---

1 **for** $l = 0, \ldots, \max\{S_1.h, S_2.h\}$ **do**
2 $\quad \lfloor \; S.B[l] \leftarrow S_1.B[l] \cup S_2.B[l];$
3 S.COMPRESS;

---

where $\text{rank}_l(x)$ denotes the number of elements in the buffer $B[l]$ that are strictly less than x. This can be done with a single pass over the summary, as shown in Algorithm 4.9. Recall that each item in $B[l]$ represents 2^l original items, so $\tilde{r}(x)$ is really just the rank of x among the weighted items in all the buffers.

Algorithm 4.9: KLL: QUERY (x)

---

1 $r \leftarrow 0;$
2 **foreach** l **do**
3 $\quad$ **foreach** $y \in B[l]$ *such* $y < x$ **do**
4 $\quad \quad \lfloor \; r \leftarrow r + 2^l$

5 **return** r

On the other hand, to QUERY for an element whose rank is r, we return an element x in the summary whose estimated rank $\tilde{r}(x)$ is closest to r.

Example. Suppose that the following table represents the current status of the KLL summary, where we use $k = 8, c = 1/\sqrt{2}$.

l	Weight	Capacity	$B[l]$
5	32	8	33, 71, 105, 152, 165, 184
4	16	6	61, 112, 123, 175
3	8	4	23, 81, 134
2	4	3	92, 142
1	2	2	16
0	1	2	84

First consider a query that asks for the estimated rank of 100. This is estimated as

$$\tilde{r}(100) = 1 \cdot 1 + 2 \cdot 1 + 4 \cdot 1 + 8 \cdot 2 + 16 \cdot 1 + 32 \cdot 2 = 103.$$

Next, consider the operation UPDATE(44). We first add 44 to $B[0]$, which causes a compaction on $B[0] = \{44, 84\}$. Suppose we take the odd-positioned items. Then $B[0] = \emptyset$, $B[1] = \{16, 44\}$ after the compaction. This in turn will trigger a series of compaction operations, as follows.

1. Compact $B[1]$: Suppose we take the even-positioned items. Then
   $B[1] = \emptyset, B[2] = \{44, 92, 142\}$.
2. Compact $B[2]$: Suppose we take the odd-positioned items. Then
   $B[2] = \emptyset, B[3] = \{23, 44, 81, 92, 142\}$.
3. Compact $B[3]$: Suppose we take the even-positioned items. Then
   $B[3] = \emptyset, B[4] = \{44, 61, 92, 112, 123, 175\}$.
4. Compact $B[4]$: Suppose we take the even-positioned items. Then
   $B[4] = \emptyset, B[5] = \{33, 61, 71, 105, 112, 152, 165, 175, 184\}$.
5. Compact $B[5]$: Suppose we take the odd-positioned items. Then
   $B[5] = \emptyset, B[6] = \{33, 71, 112, 165, 184\}$.

After UPDATE(4), h has increased by one, so the capacities of the buffers will change (but the weights do not), as follows.

l	Weight	Capacity	$B[l]$
6	64	8	33, 71, 112, 165, 184
5	32	6	$\emptyset$
4	16	4	$\emptyset$
3	8	3	$\emptyset$
2	4	2	$\emptyset$
1	2	2	$\emptyset$
0	2	2	$\emptyset$

Now on this summary, the result of a rank QUERY for item 100 will result in $64 * 2 = 128$, increased somewhat from before.

Further Discussion. *Error Analysis.* As seen in the preceding discussion, each item in buffer $B[l]$ represents 2^l original, potentially different, items, so there will be some loss of information after each compaction operation. Consider, e.g., the compaction operation on $B[4] = \{44, 61, 92, 112, 123, 175\}$ in the example by taking the even-positioned items and moving them to $B[5]$. Before this operation, $B[4]$ contributed three items to the computation of $\tilde{r}(100)$, each with a weight of 16. After this operation, only one item, 61, has survived with a weight of 32, so we have incurred an error of -16. On the other hand, if we had taken the odd-positioned items, then two items would survive and we would incur an error of $+16$. So, we accumulate an error of $+2^l$ or -2^l from this compaction, each with equal probability. More importantly, the expected error is 0, meaning that if $\tilde{r}(100)$ was an unbiased estimator, it would remain so. On the other hand, no new error will be introduced for queries like $\tilde{r}(120)$, whether the odd- or even-positioned items are taken.

Before doing any compaction operations, $\tilde{r}(x)$ is obviously accurate. The preceding observations then imply that, for any x, $\tilde{r}(x)$ is always an unbiased estimator, with error equal to

$$\text{Err} = \sum_{l=0}^{h-1} \sum_{i}^{m_l} 2^l X_{i,l}, \tag{4.3}$$

where the $X_{i,l}$s are independent random variables, each taking $+1$ or -1 with equal probability. Here m_l is the number of compaction operations done on level l, and it can be shown [155, 141] that $m_l = O((2/c)^{h-l})$. This is quite easy to understand: the top level must have not seen any compactions (otherwise level $h+1$ would have been created), so $m_h = 0$. Level $h-1$ have had at most $2/c$ compactions, because each compaction at level $h-1$ promotes $ck/2$ items to level h, so $2/c$ compactions will make level h overflow. In general, because the capacities of two neighboring levels differ by a factor of c, and each compaction on the lower level promotes half of it capacity to the higher level, so every $2/c$ compactions on the lower level trigger one compaction on the higher level, hence $m_l = O((2/c)^{h-l})$. This simple analysis ignores rounding issues (the capacities of the bottom levels are all 2; see the preceding example), which are handled in [141].

Next, we apply the Chernoff–Hoeffding bound (Fact 1.4) on (4.3):

$$\Pr[|\text{Err} > \varepsilon N|] \le 2\exp\left(\frac{-2(\varepsilon N)^2}{\sum_{l=0}^{h-1} O((2/c)^{h-l}2^{2l})}\right)$$

$$= 2\exp\left(\frac{-2(\varepsilon N)^2}{\sum_{l=0}^{h-1} O((2/c)^h (2c)^l)}\right)$$

$$= 2\exp\left(\frac{-2(\varepsilon N)^2}{O((2/c)^h) \cdot O((2c)^h)}\right) \quad \text{(Recall } c \in (0.5, 1))$$

$$= 2\exp\left(\frac{-2(\varepsilon N)^2}{O(2^{2h})}\right).$$

Since each item on level h represents 2^h original items, and $B[h]$ has a capacity of k, h will be the smallest integer such that $N \leq 2^h k$, or $h \leq \log_2(N/k) + 1$. Thus,

$$2^{2h} \leq 2^{2\log_2(N/k)+2} = 4 \cdot 2^{\log_2(N/k)^2} = 4(N/k)^2.$$

Thus, setting $k = O\left(\frac{1}{\varepsilon}\sqrt{\log(1/\varepsilon)}\right)$ will reduce the failure probability $\Pr[|\text{Err} > \varepsilon N|]$ to $O(\varepsilon)$. By the union bound, with at least constant probability, the estimated ranks are accurate (within error of εN) for all the $1/\varepsilon - 1$ elements that rank at $\varepsilon N, 2\varepsilon N, \ldots, (1-\varepsilon)N$, which is enough to answer all rank queries within 2ε error. Rescaling ε can bring the error down to ε. When all rank queries can be answered within ε error, all the quantile queries can also be answered with the desired error guarantee.

Space and Time Analysis. Because the buffer capacities decrease geometrically, the total space is dominated by the capacity of the largest buffer at level h, which is $O(k) = O\left(\frac{1}{\varepsilon}\sqrt{\log(1/\varepsilon)}\right)$. However, since the smallest meaningful buffer capacity is 2, there might be a stack of such small buffers at the lower end, as illustrated in the preceding example, so the total space is $O\left(\frac{1}{\varepsilon}\sqrt{\log(1/\varepsilon)} + h\right) = O\left(\frac{1}{\varepsilon}\sqrt{\log(1/\varepsilon)} + \log(\varepsilon N)\right)$.

To analyze the time costs, observe that if we keep all buffers sorted, the merge in line 6 or 8 of Algorithm 4.7 can be performed in time proportional to $|B[l]|$. After this compact operation, $|B[l]|/2$ items have been promoted one level higher, so we can change the cost of each compact operation to the promotion of these items. Overall, half of the items have been promoted to level 1, $1/4$ to level 2, $1/8$ to level 3, $\ldots$, k to level h. Thus, the total cost of processing N items is $\sum_{l=1}^{h} \frac{N}{2^l} = O(N)$, and the amortized cost per item is $O(1)$. Furthermore, as all the algorithm does is merging of sorted arrays, this makes the summary very fast in practice due to good cache locality.

By keeping all buffers sorted, a QUERY can also be done more efficiently, by doing a binary search in each buffer. The time needed will be $O\left(\log^2 \frac{1}{\varepsilon}\right)$. For multiple QUERY operations without UPDATE or MERGE, we may preprocess the summary by assigning each element x from $B[l]$ with a weight 2^l, sorting elements from all buffers and calculating prefix sums of the weights. After that a QUERY can be done by a single binary search, which takes only $O\left(\log \frac{1}{\varepsilon}\right)$ time.

Further Improvements. One can reduce the size of the summary, by observing that the stack of capacity-2 buffers is not really necessary.

Every time we compact such a buffer, we simply promote one of its two items randomly, so the stack of buffers can be replaced by a simple sampler, which samples one item out of $2^{h'}$ items uniformly at random, where h' is the level of the highest capacity-2 buffer. This reduces the size of the summary to $O(k) = O\left(\frac{1}{\varepsilon} \sqrt{\log(1/\varepsilon)}\right)$. However, this makes the MERGE algorithm more complicated, as discussed in detail in [155].

Furthermore, by replacing the top $O(\log \log(1/\varepsilon))$ buffers with the GK summary, the size of KLL can be reduced to $O\left(\frac{1}{\varepsilon} \log \log \frac{1}{\varepsilon}\right)$ [155]. This improvement in theory may be of less interest in practice: for $\varepsilon = 2^{-16}$ (i.e., less than 1 in 65,000), the absolute values of $\sqrt{\log 1/\varepsilon} = \log \log 1/\varepsilon = 4$. Hence, the overhead in costs for the GK summary are such that we will not see much improvement in space efficiency unless ε is much, much smaller than this already small value. Consequently, this optimization may be considered only of theoretical interest.

Implementation Issues. As described in [141], there are several techniques that can be applied to improve the practical accuracy and efficiency of KLL. We mention two simple but effective ones here.

First, as observed in the preceding example, the actual size of the summary fluctuates over time. In most practical scenarios, we are given a fixed space budget. Thus, instead of compacting a buffer as soon as it reaches its capacity, we only have to do so if the total space budget is also exceeded. This means that sometimes buffers may exceed their capacities. Note that this will not affect the error analysis; in fact, this will reduce the error even more, because each compaction will compact a larger buffer, resulting in smaller m_l's.

The second technique reduces randomness via anticorrelation. Again consider the error introduced when compacting $B[4] = \{44, 61, 92, 112, 123, 175\}$ in the preceding example. As the example shows, this compaction introduces an error of ± 16 to $\tilde{r}(100)$, each with equal probability. Suppose at a later time $B[4]$ becomes $\{34, 50, 90, 101, 135, 145\}$, which is about to be compacted again. Now, instead of making a random choice here, we deterministically choose the opposite decision, i.e., if the last compaction chose odd-positioned items, we would choose the even-positioned items this time, and vice versa. This has the effect of canceling the previous error, resulting in a net error of 0. On the other hand, if the contents of $B[4]$ are $\{34, 50, 90, 95, 135, 145\}$, then this compaction will not cancel the previous error, but will not introduce new error, either. So, the total error of the every two compactions is at most ± 16, effectively reducing m_l by half. More precisely, we flip a fair coin for every two consecutive compactions: with probability $1/2$, we do even $\rightarrow$ odd, and with probability $1/2$, we do odd $\rightarrow$ even.

History and Background. Quantile summaries based on the compaction operation date back to Munro and Paterson [193], who gave a simple algorithm that made multiple passes over the data. By considering the guarantee from the first pass of the Munro–Paterson algorithm, Manku et al. [177] showed that this offered an ε accuracy guarantee with a space bound of $O\left(\frac{1}{\varepsilon} \log^2(\varepsilon N)\right)$. Manku et al. [178] combined this with random sampling, giving an improved bound of $O\left(\frac{1}{\varepsilon} \log^2 \frac{1}{\varepsilon}\right)$. By randomizing the compaction operation (choose odd- and even-position items with equal probability), Agarwal et al. [2] pushed the space down to $O\left(\frac{1}{\varepsilon} \log^{1.5} \frac{1}{\varepsilon}\right)$, and they also show how to merge their summaries. The space was then further improved to $O\left(\frac{1}{\varepsilon} \log \frac{1}{\varepsilon}\right)$ by Felber and Ostrovsky [103], and finally to $O\left(\frac{1}{\varepsilon} \log \log \frac{1}{\varepsilon}\right)$ by Karnin et al. [155]. The algorithm described in this section is a simpler version of their algorithm, which instead obtains $O\left(\frac{1}{\varepsilon} \sqrt{\log \frac{1}{\varepsilon}}\right)$. The extra $O\left(\log \log \frac{1}{\varepsilon}\right)$ factor is due to the requirement that all queries must be correct with a constant probability. If only a single quantile (say, the median) is required with probability $1 - \delta$, then the space needed is $O\left(\frac{1}{\varepsilon} \log \log \frac{1}{\delta}\right)$, which is known to be optimal [155].

Finally, the KLL summary can also handle weighted items. The size remains $O\left(\frac{1}{\varepsilon} \sqrt{\log(1/\varepsilon)}\right)$ but the time to UPDATE the summary becomes $O\left(\log(1/\varepsilon)\right)$ [141].

Available Implementations. Implementations of KLL are available across multiple languages. There is a reference implementation from the authors themselves in Python (https://github.com/edoliberty/streaming-quantiles), which shows how the COMPRESS operation can be written very concisely. There is a more robust implementation in the DataSketches library in Java (https://datasketches.github.io/docs/Quantiles/KLLSketch.html). The DataSketches implementation is compared with the antecedent method from Agarwal et al. [2], as well as to various heuristic approaches. Heuristic methods for quantile tracking, such as t-digest and moment sketch, have been widely implemented, but are shown to have poor performance on some input datasets that can occur. The implementation of KLL is shown to have strong accuracy in practice, while performing tens of millions of updates per second.

4.4 Dyadic Count Sketch (DCS)

Brief Summary. The DCS summary provides a compact summary of data drawn from an integer domain $[U] = [0, 1, \ldots, U - 1]$. It takes (x, w) pairs as input, where w can be an integer that is either positive or negative. But the multiplicity of x for any x in the dataset must remain non-negative when the summary is queried for it to be meaningful. It is a randomized algorithm. This summary takes space $O\left(\frac{1}{\varepsilon} \log^{1.5} U \log^{1.5} \frac{\log U}{\varepsilon}\right)$, and returns all ranks within εW error with constant probability, where W is the total weight of input integers. The summary works upon a *dyadic* structure over the universe U and maintains a Count Sketch structure for frequency estimation in each level of this dyadic structure.

Operations on the Summary. The DCS structure is represented as $\log U$ levels of substructures. Each one supports point queries over a partition of $[U]$ into subsets, which we refer to as a "reduced domain of $[U]$." These $\log U$ levels make up a dyadic structure imposed over the universe. More precisely, we decompose the universe U as follows. At level 0, the reduced domain is $[U]$ itself; at level j, the universe is partitioned into intervals of size 2^j, and the projected domain consists of $U/2^j$ elements, which are intervals in $[U]$: $[0, 2^j - 1], [2^j, 2 \cdot 2^j - 1]], \ldots, [U - 2^j, U - 1]$; the top level thus consists of only two intervals: $[0, U/2 - 1], [U/2, U - 1]$. Each interval in every level in this hierarchy is called a *dyadic interval*. Each level keeps a frequency estimation sketch that should be able to return an estimate of the weight of any dyadic interval on that level. Specifically, the DCS makes use of a Count Sketch at each level but with a different set of parameters. Note that in the jth level, an element is actually a dyadic interval of length 2^j, and the frequency estimation sketch summarizes a reduced universe $[U/2^j]$. So for j such that the reduced universe size $U/2^j$ is smaller than the sketch size, we should directly maintain the frequencies exactly, rather than using a sketch. We call a level a *lower level* if it maintains a Count Sketch, and an *upper level* if it maintains the frequencies exactly.

Recall that the Count Sketch consists of an array C of $\omega \times d$ counters. For each row, we use pairwise independent hash functions: $h_i : [U] \to \{0, 1, \ldots, \omega - 1\}$ maps each element in $[U]$ into a counter in this row, and $g_i : [U] \to \{-1, +1\}$ maps each element to -1 or $+1$ with equal probability. To update with (x, w) in the sketch, for each row i, we add $g_i(x) \cdot w$ to $C[i, h_i(x)]$. To estimate the frequency of x, we return the median of $g_i(x) \cdot C[i, h_i(x)], i = 1, \ldots, d$. Note that the Count Sketch has size $\omega \cdot d$, which can be large. For the highest (upper) levels of aggregation, it is more space efficient to simply keep exact counts. So we only use such a sketch for levels $0, 1, 2, \ldots, s = \lfloor \log(\frac{U}{\omega \cdot d}) \rfloor$.

The INITIALIZE operation creates a dyadic structure over the universe U. For each upper-level j, we allocate an array $D_j[.]$ of $U/2^j$ counters for recording frequencies of all dyadic intervals. For each lower-level j, we allocate a Count Sketch structure, i.e., an array $C_j[.,.]$ with parameters $\omega = \frac{1}{\varepsilon} \sqrt{\log U \log \left(\frac{\log U}{\varepsilon}\right)}, d = \log \left(\frac{\log U}{\varepsilon}\right)$.

The UPDATE operation of item x with weight w performs an update on each of the $\log U$ levels. An update operation on level j consists of two steps: (1) map x to an element on this level, denoted by k; and (2) update the element k in the Count Sketch or the frequency table. In step (1), the element on level j corresponding to x is simply encoded by the first $\log U - j$ bits of x. In step (2), when level j is an upper level, we add the weight w to the counter $D_j[k]$; otherwise, we add $w \cdot g_i(x)$ to each $C_j[i, h_i(k)]$ for $1 \le i \le d$ just as performing an update in the Count Sketch.

Algorithm 4.10: DCS: UPDATE (x, w)

---

1 **for** $j \leftarrow 0$ **to** $\lceil \log U \rceil$ **do**
2   **if** $(j > s)$ **then**
3        $D_j[x] \leftarrow D_j[x] + w$;
4   **else**
5   **for** $0 \le i \le d$ **do**
6           $C_j[i, h_i(x)] \leftarrow C_j[i, h_i(x)] + w \cdot g_i(x)$;
          // UPDATE the jth Count Sketch
7     $x \leftarrow \lfloor x/2 \rfloor$;

Algorithm 4.10 shows the pseudocode to update the data structure with an item x of weight w. The for-loop traverses the dyadic levels from bottom to top. Within this loop, it updates the structures on each level. At the start, x is the full item identifier; after each step, it updates x to be the index for the next level, by halving it and ignoring any remainder. If the level index $j > s$, it simply adds the weight w to the xth counter of D, else it updates d counters in the sketch array C.

Rank Queries. The routine "rank QUERY" takes a parameter $x \in U$, and returns the (approximate) rank of x. We first decompose the interval $[0, x - 1]$ into the disjoint union of at most $\log U$ dyadic intervals, at most one from each level; then we estimate the weight of the interval from each level, and add them up. More precisely, we can view this dyadic structure as a binary tree. The rank QUERY procedure can be carried out by performing a binary search for x, which yields a root-to-leaf path in the binary tree. Along this path, if and only if a node is a right child, its left neighbor corresponds to a dyadic interval in the dyadic decomposition of range $[0, x)$. For these dyadic intervals, we can query them from the corresponding frequency estimation structures: for the kth dyadic interval on an upper-level j, its frequency is $D_j[k]$; and for the kth dyadic interval on a lower-level j, its frequency is $\text{median}_{1 \leq i \leq d}\{C_j[i, h_i(k)]g_j(k)\}$.

Algorithm 4.11: DCS: rank QUERY (x)

---

1 $R \leftarrow 0$;
2 **for** $i \leftarrow 0$ **to** $\lceil \log U \rceil$ **do**
3   **if** x *is odd* **then**
4   **if** $j > s$ **then**
5 | $R \leftarrow R + D_j[x - 1]$;
6   **else**
7 | $R \leftarrow R + \text{median}_{0 \leq i \leq d}\{C_j[i, h_i(x - 1)] \cdot g_i(x - 1)\}$;
8      $x \leftarrow \lfloor x/2 \rfloor$;
9 **return** R;

Algorithm 4.11 shows the pseudocode to query for the rank of x for an given item x. The algorithm proceeds down from the top level. It uses a variable R recording the sum of weights of all dyadic intervals in the dyadic decomposition of $[0, x - 1]$. When this algorithm halts, R gives an estimate of the rank of the queried item.

Quantile Query. However, for a quantile query, we want to find which item achieves a particular rank. So we provide a second "quantile QUERY" function that takes parameter $\phi \in [0, W - 1]$ as the desired rank, and returns the integer x whose rank is approximately ϕ. We still view this dyadic structure as a binary tree. The quantile QUERY can be carried out by performing a binary search. More precisely, supposing the procedure arrives at a node u, it computes the rank of u's right child in the reduced universe on that level from the corresponding frequency estimation structures and checks whether it is smaller than ϕ. If yes, it visits u's right child; otherwise, it visits u's left child. At the end, this procedure reaches a leaf corresponding to an integer x at the bottom level, which is then returned.

Algorithm 4.12: DCS: quantile QUERY (ϕ)

---

1 $x \leftarrow 0$;
2 $R \leftarrow 0$;
3 **for** $j \leftarrow \lceil \log U \rceil$ **down to** 0 **do**
4      $x \leftarrow 2 \cdot x$;
5   **if** $j > s$ **then**
6          $M \leftarrow D_j[x]$;
7   **else**
8          $M \leftarrow \text{median}_{0 \leq i \leq d}\{C_j[i, h_i(x)]g_i(x)\}$;
9   **if** $R + M < \phi$ **then**
10         $x \leftarrow x + 1$;
11         $R \leftarrow R + M$;

12 **return** x;

Algorithm 4.12 shows the pseudocode to query for the integer x whose (approximate) rank interval contains the given rank ϕ. The algorithm proceeds down from the top level. It uses a variable x to indicate the index of the node visited by it, and uses another variable R recording the rank of the visited node in its reduced universe. In addition, another variable M is used to store the (approximate) weight of the left child of the current visited node. Obviously, if $R + M < \phi$, the rank of its right child is smaller than ϕ and it should go to the right child, i.e., update x and R; else it goes to the left child with no change to x and R.

Example. Figure 4.3 shows a DCS summary. It maintains a dyadic structure over the domain $0 \ldots 7$. The jth row consists of all dyadic intervals of the form $[b \cdot 2^j, (b+1)2^j - 1]$ for $b = 0, 1, \ldots, 8/2^j - 1$, and maintains a Count Sketch for the reduced universe consisting of all the dyadic intervals. Each rectangle in the figure corresponds to a dyadic interval, labeled by its dyadic range and its

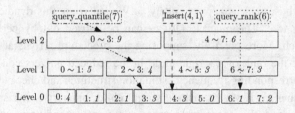

Figure 4.3 Example DCS summary over $U = 0 \ldots 7$.

estimated weight from the Count Sketch and the stored counts in arrays D_j. Suppose we UPDATE the summary with an item 4 with weight 1. The algorithm walks down the levels, and at each level it finds the rectangle where the item 4 falls into. In this example, the dyadic intervals that need to be updated are those labeled $(4 \sim 7)$ on level 2, labeled $(4 \sim 5)$ on level 1, and labeled 4 on level 0. Suppose we QUERY the rank of a given integer $x = 6$ on the summary. The algorithm again walks down these levels and visits the rectangles labeled $(4 \sim 7)$ on level 2, labeled $(6 \sim 7)$ on level 1, and labeled 6 on level 0. For each rectangle, the algorithm checks whether it corresponds to an odd number in the reduced universe. If yes, it adds the weight of its left neighbor to the final estimation. In this example, the rectangles on level 2 and 1 satisfy this condition, so it adds the weights of rectangle labeled $(0 \sim 3)$ on level 2 and rectangle labeled $(4 \sim 5)$ on level 1 together and returns 12 as the estimation. Suppose we QUERY the quantile of a given rank $\phi = 7$ on this summary. This algorithm walks down these levels by performing a binary search and visits the rectangles labeled $(0 \sim 3)$ on level 2, labeled $(2 \sim 3)$ on level 1 and labeled 3 on level 0, and reaches element 3 on the bottom level.

Further Discussion. In principle, any summary that provides good count estimation for multisets could be used in place of the Count Sketch, such as the Count-Min Sketch. However, the Count Sketch is chosen as the workhorse of this summary as it has additional properties that allow it to obtain a better space/accuracy trade-off. Specifically, rather than just add up the accuracy bounds of the different sketches pessimistically, we combine them together to give a tighter analysis of the distribution of the errors.

It should be clear that the DCS summary has space cost $O(\omega \cdot d \cdot \log U) = O(\frac{1}{\varepsilon} \log^{1.5} U \log^{1.5}(\frac{\log U}{\varepsilon}))$ and its update time is $O(\log U \log(\frac{\log U}{\varepsilon}))$. Next we analyze its accuracy when answering a rank QUERY. At each level, note that the Count Sketch produces an unbiased estimator. Since we add up the estimates from $\log U$ sketches, it is likely that some of the positive and negative errors will cancel each other out, leading to a more accurate final result. In the following discussion, we formalize this intuition. Let us consider the estimator $Y_i = g_i(x) \cdot C[i, h_i(x)]$ on each level. Clearly each Y_i is unbiased, since $g_i(x)$ maps to -1 or $+1$ with equal probability. Let Y be the median of $Y_i, i = 1 \ldots, d$ (assuming d is odd). The median of independent unbiased estimators is not necessarily unbiased, but if each estimator also has a symmetric pdf, then this is the case. In our case, each Y_i has a symmetric pdf, so Y is still unbiased. To keep the subsequent analysis simple, we let $\varepsilon' = \varepsilon \bigg/ \sqrt{\log U \log\left(\frac{\log U}{\varepsilon}\right)}$. Then using the same Markov inequality-based argument as for the Count-Min Sketch, we have

$$\Pr[|Y_i - \mathsf{E}[Y_i]| > \varepsilon'W] < 1/4.$$

Since Y is the median of the Y_is, by a Chernoff bound, we have

$$\Pr[|Y - \mathsf{E}[Y]| > \varepsilon'W] < \exp(-O(d)) = O\left(\frac{\varepsilon}{\log U}\right).$$

Now consider adding up $\log U$ such estimators; the sum must still be unbiased. By the union bound, the probability that every estimate has at most $\varepsilon'W$ error is at least $1 - O(\varepsilon)$. Conditioned upon this event happening, we can use Hoeffding's inequality (Fact 1.4) to bound the probability that the sum of $\log U$ such (independent) estimators deviate from its mean by more than $t = \varepsilon W$ as

$$2\exp\left(-\frac{2t^2}{(2\varepsilon'W)^2 \log U}\right) = 2\exp\left(-\frac{2t^2 \log\left(\frac{\log U}{\varepsilon}\right)}{(2\varepsilon W)^2}\right) = O\left(\frac{\varepsilon}{\log U}\right).$$

We can understand a quantile query in terms of this analysis of rank queries: we obtain a sufficiently accurate approximation of each quantile under the same conditions that a rank query succeeds, and so each quantile is reported accurately except with probability $O(\varepsilon/\log U)$. Applying another union bound on the $1/\varepsilon$ different quantiles, the probability that they are all estimated correctly is at least a constant. We can further increase d by a factor of $\log 1/\delta$ to reduce this error probability to δ.

Implementation Issues. In a DCS structure, at each level, it uses a Count Sketch that is $\omega \times d$ array of counters. The preceding settings of ω and d are chosen to ensure that the analysis will go through. In practice, it is usually sufficient to set parameters smaller, with $\omega = \frac{\sqrt{\log U}}{\varepsilon}$ and $d = 5$ or 7.

History and Background. The general outline of using a dyadic structure of aggregations and expressing a range in terms of a sum of a bounded number of estimated counts has appeared many times. The choice of which summary to use to provide the estimated counts then has knock-on effects for the costs of the compound solution. Gilbert et al. [118] first proposed the *random subset sum* sketch for this purpose, which results in an overall size of $O\left(\frac{1}{\varepsilon^2}\log^2 U \log\left(\frac{\log U}{\varepsilon}\right)\right)$. The disadvantages of this method are that the time to update was very slow, and the leading factor of $\frac{1}{\varepsilon^2}$ is very large, even for moderate values of ε. Cormode and Muthukrishnan introduced the Count-Min Sketch and showed how when used within the dyadic structure it can reduce the overall size by a factor of $1/\varepsilon$ [76]. This use of DCS was proposed and analyzed in [231]. Directly placing the Count Sketch in the dyadic structure and applying its standard bounds would not provide the right dependence in terms of ε, so a new analysis was made that reduced the overall size to $O\left(\frac{1}{\varepsilon}\log^{1.5} U \log^{1.5}\left(\frac{\log U}{\varepsilon}\right)\right)$. Further applications of dyadic decompositions with summaries are discussed in Section 9.3.

Available Implementations. Compared to the other summaries surveyed in this chapter, the DCS has attracted fewer implementations, to the extent that there do not appear to be any conveniently available online. Code generally implementing dyadic sketches for range queries is available, for example in the Apache MADlib library, `https://github.com/apache/madlib`.

PART II

Advanced Summaries and Extensions

5

Geometric Summaries

This chapter deals with data in a multidimensional space, that is, how to summarize a point set P in the d-dimensional Euclidean space $\mathbb{R}^d$. As many geometric summaries are just (carefully chosen) subsets of the points in P that approximately preserve certain properties of P, they are often called the *coresets* of P (for the respective properties).

We assume that the coordinates of the points in the dataset are real numbers. For simplicity, we will assume that all computations involving real numbers are exact; in actual implementation, using floating-point numbers (single- or double-precision) usually works fine; when rounding errors may cause robustness issues, or a higher precision is desired, some exact computation package (such as the one provided in CGAL) can be used. In this chapter, $\| \cdot \|$ always denotes the Euclidean norm.

5.1 ε-Nets and ε-Approximations

Brief Summary. ε-nets and ε-approximations are small summaries about a set of points P with respect to a certain class of ranges $\mathcal{R}$. In the plane, for example, $\mathcal{R}$ can be all the orthogonal rectangles, or all the halfplanes.[1] Let $|P| = n$. Given $0 < \varepsilon < 1$, a set $N \subseteq P$ is called an ε-net for P with respect to $\mathcal{R}$ if, for any range R of $\mathcal{R}$ with $|R \cap P| \geq \varepsilon n$, we have $N \cap R \neq \emptyset$, i.e., N "hits" every range in $\mathcal{R}$ that contains at least a fraction of ε of the points of P. This allows us to perform one-sided threshold tests for the ranges in $\mathcal{R}$: For any $R \in \mathcal{R}$, we simply check if R contains any point of N. If no, we are certain that R contains less than εn points of P; but if yes, R may or may not contain

---

[1] A *halfplane* is the region on either side of an infinite straight line.

at least εn points of P. In other words, an ε-net can be used to detect all the "heavy" ranges on P, although it might return some false positives.

A set $A \subseteq P$ is called an ε-*approximation* for $(P, \mathcal{R})$ if, for any $R \in \mathcal{R}$,

$$\left| \frac{|R \cap P|}{|P|} - \frac{|R \cap A|}{|A|} \right| \leq \varepsilon,$$

i.e., the fraction of points of P contained in R is approximately the same (at most ε apart) as that of A. Therefore, we can approximately count the number of points of P inside any range R by simply counting the number of points in $R \cap A$ and scaling back. The additive error will be at most εn.

Note that an ε-approximation is also an ε-net, but not vice versa.

The easiest way to construct ε-nets and ε-approximations is by simply drawing a random sample from P, and remarkably, the sample size only depends on ε and d, but not n, for almost all natural geometric range spaces (the notion will be made more precise later in this chapter).

Operations on the Summary. Suppose the range space $\mathcal{R}$ has VC-dimension d (see the precise definition in the "Further Discussion" section), a random sample of size $\frac{d}{\varepsilon}\left(\log \frac{1}{\varepsilon} + 2 \log \log \frac{1}{\varepsilon} + 3\right)$ from P is an ε-net for $(P, \mathcal{R})$ with probability at least $1 - e^{-d}$, and a random sample of size $O\left(\frac{1}{\varepsilon^2}\left(d + \log \frac{1}{\delta}\right)\right)$ is an ε-approximation with probability at least $1 - \delta$. Then one can simply use the random sampling algorithms to CONSTRUCT, UPDATE, or MERGE ε-nets or ε-approximations. Please refer to Section 2.2.

Note that although a random sample of a certain size is an ε-net or an ε-approximation with high probability, it is very expensive to actually verify that the obtained sample is indeed one [112]. In practice, we can only increase the sample size to reduce the probability of failure. Alternatively, there are deterministic algorithms for constructing ε-nets and ε-approximations, but they are also expensive and complicated, as mentioned in the "History and Background" section.

Further Discussion. The proofs for the preceding claimed bounds are quite technical; here we give proofs for slightly weaker results, which nevertheless still capture all the basic ideas.

Consider ε-nets first. For any particular range R with $|R \cap P| \geq \varepsilon n$, a randomly sampled point from P hits R with probability at least ε, thus if we sample s points to form N, then N misses R with probability at most $(1 - \varepsilon)^s \leq e^{-\varepsilon s}$. This means that with a sample size of $O(1/\varepsilon)$, we can hit R with constant probability. However, the challenge is that there are infinitely many ranges in $\mathcal{R}$. A first observation is that if two ranges R and R' contain the same set of points in P, the two can be considered as the same. Let $\pi_\mathcal{R}(n)$ be the maximum number of distinct ranges for any P with $|P| = n$. Clearly, $\pi_\mathcal{R}(n)$ depends on $\mathcal{R}$: For halfplanes, $\pi_\mathcal{R}(n) = O(n^2)$, as each distinct halfplane must be uniquely defined by two points on its boundary; for ellipses, the problem is more complicated. In order to derive a general result, we need the concept of VC-dimensions for range spaces.

Consider a range space $\mathcal{R}$. A set of points $X \subset \mathbb{R}^d$ is *shattered* by $\mathcal{R}$ if all subsets of X can be obtained by intersecting X with members of $\mathcal{R}$, i.e., for any $Y \subset X$, there is some $R \in \mathcal{R}$ such that $Y = X \cap R$. For example, if $\mathcal{R}$ consists of all the halfplanes in two dimensions, then the following figure shows three point sets that can be either shattered or not shattered, respectively. On the other hand, if $\mathcal{R}$ is all the ellipses, then all three point sets can be shattered. Thus intuitively, ellipses are more powerful, hence have higher complexity, than halfplanes.

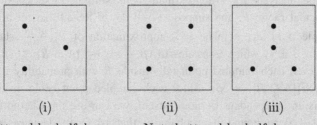

(i)   (ii)   (iii)

Shattered by halfplanes   Not shattered by halfplanes

The *Vapnik–Chervonenkis dimension*, or *VC-dimension*, of a range space $\mathcal{R}$ captures this complexity, and is defined to be the size of the largest point set X that can be shattered by $\mathcal{R}$. It can be verified that no four-point set can be shattered by halfplanes, so the range space of halfplanes has VC-dimension 3. On the other hand, the range space of all ellipses has VC-dimension at least 4. (To be precise, the actual VC-dimension of ellipses is 5: the five points on a regular pentagon is shattered by ellipses, and no six points can be shattered.) Figuring out the exact VC-dimension for any given range space may not be easy, but luckily for most natural geometric range spaces, the problem has already been studied. As a rule of thumb, if the ranges are defined by some shape of constant description size (e.g., simplices of balls, but not, say, arbitrary convex sets), then the VC-dimension is also a constant.

If there is no assumption on $\mathcal{R}$, $\pi_{\mathcal{R}}(n)$ can be as high as 2^n. It turns out if $\mathcal{R}$ has bounded VC-dimension, $\pi_R(n)$ can be effectively bounded.

Fact 5.1 *For any range space $\mathcal{R}$ of VC-dimension d, $\pi_{\mathcal{R}}(n) = O(n^d)$.*

A proof of this fact can be found in [227]. Intuitively, each distinct range can be characterized by up to d points in P, so $\pi_{\mathcal{R}}(n) \leq \binom{n}{0} + \binom{n}{1} + \cdots + \binom{n}{d} = O(n^d)$. Note that, however, Fact 5.1 may not give the tightest bound on $\pi_{\mathcal{R}}(n)$. For example, halfplanes have VC-dimension 3, but $\pi_{\mathcal{R}}(n)$ is actually only $O(n^2)$. Nevertheless, this does not affect the bounds on ε-nets and ε-approximations asymptotically.

Now with Fact 5.1, we can continue the analysis on the size of ε-net from before. Since a random sample of size s misses any particular heavy range with probability at most $e^{-\varepsilon s}$, it misses any one of the $\leq \pi_{\mathcal{R}}(n)$ heavy ranges with probability at most $n^d e^{-\varepsilon s}$, by a simple union bound. Thus, setting $s = O\left(\frac{d}{\varepsilon} \log \frac{n}{\delta}\right)$ suffices for the random sample to hit all heavy ranges, i.e., become an ε-net, with probability at least $1 - \delta$.

The analysis for ε-approximations is similar. First, consider any particular range R, and suppose $\frac{|R \cap P|}{n} = \beta$. Recall that for a random sample A of size s to be an ε-approximation of P, $\frac{|A \cap R|}{s}$ should be within $\beta \pm \varepsilon$, which translates to $(\beta - \varepsilon)s \leq |A \cap R| \leq (\beta + \varepsilon)s$. However, each sampled point falls inside R with probability β, so we have $\mathsf{E}[|A \cap R|] = \beta s$. Since each sampled point being inside R or not is an independent Bernoulli event, we can use the Chernoff bound (Fact 1.5) to bound its probability that $|A \cap R|$ deviates from its expectation by more than εs as

$$\exp\left(-O\left(\left(\frac{\varepsilon}{\beta}\right)^2 \beta s\right)\right) = \exp\left(-O\left(\frac{\varepsilon^2 s}{\beta}\right)\right) \leq \exp(-O(\varepsilon^2 s)).$$

By the union bound, the probability that A deviates from the correct fraction for any of the $\pi_{\mathcal{R}}(n)$ ranges is at most $n^d \exp(-O(\varepsilon^2 s))$. Thus, choosing $s = O\left(\frac{d}{\varepsilon^2} \log \frac{n}{\delta}\right)$ gives us an ε-approximation with probability at least $1 - \delta$.

To get the tighter bound as mentioned previously, one has to use more careful analysis than simply applying the union bound. In particular, to remove the dependency on n, one has to more carefully bound the number of distinct ranges where two ranges should be considered the same if they differ by no more than εn points. Some pointers are given in the "History and Background" section.

Finally, it is worth pointing out that all the analysis in this section can be carried over to any set system $(P,\mathcal{R})$, where P is any set of objects and $\mathcal{R}$ is a collection of subsets of P. For instance, we can define P to be all lines in the plane, and define $\mathcal{R}$ to be all the subsets of the following form: each subset P_s included in $\mathcal{R}$ is the set of lines intersected by some segment s. This set system has VC-dimension 4, and all the results in this section continue to hold with $d = 4$.

History and Background. The notion of VC-dimension originated in statistics, introduced by Vapnik and Chervonenkis [227], who also established initial random sampling bound for ε-approximations. It has been subsequently applied and further developed in many areas such as computational learning theory, computational geometry, and combinatorics. The $O\big(\frac{1}{\varepsilon^2}(d + \log\frac{1}{\delta})\big)$ bound was proved by Talagrand [217] and Li et al. [171], who also showed that it is optimal within a constant factor.

The notion of ε-net is due to Haussler and Welzl [131]. The dependence on d was subsequently improved by Blumer et al. [32] and by Komlós et al. [162], who gave the result mentioned earlier, which is almost tight.

The easiest way to construct an ε-net or an ε-approximation is by random sampling. By using more careful constructions and/or exploiting the special properties of the range space, asymptotically smaller ε-nets and ε-approximations can be obtained. In one dimension with all the intervals as the range space, we can simply sort all the points of P and take every (εn)-th point. It is easy to see that this gives us an εnet as well as an ε-approximation. So for this range space, the size of ε-net or an ε-approximation is $\Theta(1/\varepsilon)$. Note that such an ε-approximation is also a summary that supports ε-approximate rank and quantile queries as in Chapter 4, but this summary cannot be updated or merged.

In two and higher dimensions, asymptotically smaller ε-nets and ε-approximations are also known, but these results are mostly of a theoretical nature and the corresponding algorithms are quite complicated. For orthogonal rectangles in the plane, an ε-net of size $O\big(\frac{1}{\varepsilon}\log\log\frac{1}{\varepsilon}\big)$ can be constructed [16, 198], while an ε-approximation of size $O\big(\frac{1}{\varepsilon}\log^{2.5}\frac{1}{\varepsilon}\big)$ exists [213]. For a general range space with VC-dimension d, the size of an ε-net cannot be improved, but ε-approximations can be reduced to size $O\big(1/\varepsilon^{2-2/(d+1)}\big)$ [179], where the hidden constant depends on d. With some extra logarithmic factors, such ε-approximations can be updated and merged [2, 214].

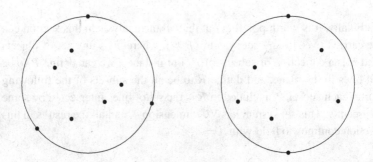

Figure 5.1 The minimum enclosing ball in two dimensions is defined by either three points (the example on the left) or two points (the example on the right) of P, assuming no four points are on the same circle.

5.2 Coresets for Minimum Enclosing Balls

Brief Summary. Let $B_{o,r}$ be the ball of radius r centered at point $o \in \mathbb{R}^d$, i.e., $B_{o,r} = \{p \in \mathbb{R}^d : \|p - o\| \le r\}$. Let P be a set of n points in $\mathbb{R}^d$. The *minimum enclosing ball* (MEB) of P, denoted as MEB(P), is the minimum-radius ball containing P. Note that the center of MEB(P) may not be a point of P. Figure 5.1 gives two examples of MEBs in two dimensions. In general, in d dimensions, the MEB is defined by up to $d + 1$ points of P. As it turns out, if some approximation is allowed, this number can be made independent of d, which is captured by the notion of an ε-coreset.

Given $\varepsilon > 0$, a subset $K \subseteq P$ is an *ε-coreset* (for MEB) of P if $P \subset B_{o,(1+\varepsilon)r}$, where $B_{o,r} = \text{MEB}(K)$, i.e., the $(1 + \varepsilon)$-factor expansion of the MEB of K contains P. It turns out that such a coreset of size $O(1/\varepsilon)$ exists, which is independent of both n and d. This makes it especially appealing for large high-dimensional data. In particular, many kernel methods in machine learning can be equivalently formulated as MEB problems in high dimensions, and much faster machine learning algorithms have been designed by using this coreset [226].

Operations on the Summary. For a ball B, we use $(1 + \varepsilon)B$ to denote its $(1 + \varepsilon)$-expansion, and use $r(B)$ to denote the radius of B. To CONSTRUCT the ε-coreset of P, we start with $K = \{p\}$, where p is an arbitrary point in P. Then we add points from P into K iteratively. In each iteration, we first check if $(1+\varepsilon) \text{MEB}(K)$ encloses all points of P. If yes, we are done and the current K must be an ε-coreset of P. Otherwise, we pick the farthest point in P from the center of MEB(K) and add it to K. The pseudocode of this algorithm is given in Algorithm 5.1. It has been shown that the algorithm always finishes in at most $2/\varepsilon$ iterations, so the resulting coreset has size at most $2/\varepsilon$ [41].

Algorithm 5.1: ε-coreset for MEB: CONSTRUCT (P)

---

1 $K \leftarrow \{p\}$, where p is an arbitrary point in P;
2 **while** *true* **do**
3      $B_{o,r} \leftarrow \text{MEB}(K)$;
4   **if** $P \subset B_{o,(1+\varepsilon)r}$ **then return** K;
5      $q \leftarrow \arg\max_{x \in P} \|o - x\|$;
6      $K \leftarrow K \cup \{q\}$;

Algorithm 5.2: ε-coreset for MEB: UPDATE (p)

---

1 $A \leftarrow A \cup \{p\}$;
2 **if** A *is not full* **then return**;
3 **if** $A \not\subseteq \bigcup_{i=1}^{u}(1 + \varepsilon)B_i$ **then**
4      $K' \leftarrow \text{CONSTRUCT}(\bigcup_{i=1}^{u} K_i \cup A)$;
5      $B' \leftarrow \text{MEB}(K')$;
6   **foreach** $K_i \in \mathcal{K}$ **do**
7   **if** $r(K_i) \leq \varepsilon/4 \cdot r(B')$ **then** Remove K_i from $\mathcal{K}$;
8   Renumber the indexes of $\mathcal{K}$ if necessary;
9   Append K' to $\mathcal{K}$;
10 $A \leftarrow \emptyset$;

To be able to UPDATE the ε-coreset, we maintain a sequence of coresets $\mathcal{K} = (K_1, \ldots, K_u)$. We maintain their MEBs explicitly $B_i = \text{MEB}(K_i)$ for $i = 1, \ldots, u$. The sequence is ordered such that $r(B_i) < r(B_j)$ for all $i < j$. There is also a buffer A for new points. Initially, the buffer is empty and $u = 0$. To UPDATE the summary with a new point p, we first add it to the buffer A. When the size of the buffer reaches a certain limit, we perform the following procedure. If all the points in A are inside $\bigcup_{i=1}^{u}(1 + \varepsilon)B_i$, we just clear A and we are done. Otherwise, we CONSTRUCT an $(\varepsilon/3)$-coreset K' on $\bigcup_{i=1}^{u} K_i \cup A$, and add it to $\mathcal{K}$. Let $B' = \text{MEB}(K')$. Then we clear A. Finally, we delete all K_is in $\mathcal{K}$ for which $r(B_i) \leq \frac{\varepsilon}{4}r(B')$. This removes a prefix of $\mathcal{K}$, so we need to renumber the indexes of the K_is. The pseudocode of this algorithm is given in Algorithm 5.2. The limit on the buffer A controls the trade-off of the size of the summary and update time, and can be usually set to $\frac{1}{\varepsilon}\log\frac{1}{\varepsilon}$. To query the summary for the MEB of all the points P that have ever been added, we first flush the buffer A by following the preceding procedure, and then return $\text{MEB}\left(\bigcup_{i=1}^{u} B_i\right)$. However, this only returns an $(1.22 + O(\varepsilon))$-approximation of $\text{MEB}(P)$, namely, we no longer have an ε-coreset for P. In fact, there is a lower bound stating that any summary that maintains an ε-coreset under insertions must have size $\Omega(\exp(d^{1/3}))$ [4].

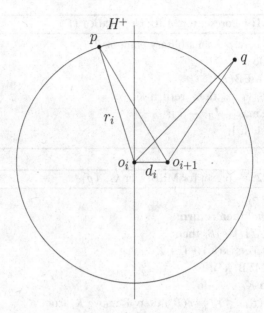

Figure 5.2 Algorithm 5.1 in the $(i + 1)$th iteration.

It is not known if this summary can be merged.

Further Discussion. Now we show that Algorithm 5.1 always terminates in at most $2/\varepsilon$ iterations, resulting in a coreset of size at most $2/\varepsilon$.

Fact 5.2 *For any set of n points P in $\mathbb{R}^d$, Algorithm 5.1 terminates in at most $2/\varepsilon$ iterations.*

Proof: We follow the argument in [41]. Let K_i be the coreset after the ith iteration, let $B_{o_i,r_i} = \text{MEB}(K_i)$, and let $B_{o^*,r^*} = \text{MEB}(P)$. In the $(i + 1)$th iteration, the algorithm adds q, the farthest point in P from o_i, to K_i. Please refer to Figure 5.2. We must have $\|q - o_i\| > r^*$, otherwise $B_{o_i, \|q - o_i\|}$ would have been the MEB of P. Consider the distance that the center o_i moves in this iteration $d_i = \|o_{i+1} - o_i\|$. If $d_i = 0$, then the algorithm terminates, since $\text{MEB}(K_{i+1}) = B_{o_i, \|q - o_i\|}$ encloses all points of P. If $d_i > 0$, consider the hyperplane H that passes through o_i and is orthogonal to $\overline{o_i o_{i+1}}$. Let H^+ be the closed halfspace bounded by H that does not contain o_{i+1}. Since B_{o_i,r_i} is the MEB of K_i, there must be a point $p \in K_i \cap H^+$ that lies on the surface of B_{o_i,r_i} (see, e.g., [120] for a proof for this property of MEBs). So we have $\|o_i - p\| = r_i$ and $r_{i+1} \geq \|o_{i+1} - p\| \geq \sqrt{r_i^2 + d_i^2}$. In addition, $r^* \leq \|o_i - q\| \leq d_i + \|o_{i+1} - q\| \leq d_i + r_{i+1}$. Therefore,

$$r_{i+1} \geq \max\left\{r^* - d_i, \sqrt{r_i^2 + d_i^2}\right\}. \tag{5.1}$$

The right-hand side (RHS) of (5.1) is minimized when

$$r^* - d_i = \sqrt{r_i^2 + d_i^2},$$

or

$$d_i = \frac{r^* - r_i^2/r^*}{2}.$$

So we have

$$r_{i+1} \geq r^* - \frac{r^* - r_i^2/r^*}{2} = \frac{r^* + r_i^2/r^*}{2}. \tag{5.2}$$

Setting $r_i = \lambda_i r^*$ for all i, (5.2) becomes

$$\lambda_{i+1} \geq \frac{1 + \lambda_i^2}{2}. \tag{5.3}$$

Substituting $\lambda_i = 1 - \frac{1}{\gamma_i}$ in recurrence (5.3), we get

$$\gamma_{i+1} \geq \frac{\gamma_i}{1 - \frac{1}{2\gamma_i}} = \gamma_i\left(1 + \frac{1}{2\gamma_i} + \frac{1}{4\gamma_i^2} + \cdots\right) \geq \gamma_i + \frac{1}{2}.$$

Since $\lambda_0 = 0, \gamma_0 = 1$, so $\gamma_i \geq 1 + i/2$ and $\lambda_i \geq 1 - \frac{1}{1+i/2}$. Therefore, to get $\lambda_i > 1 - \varepsilon$, it is enough that $1 + i/2 \geq 1/\varepsilon$, or $i \geq 2/\varepsilon$. □

The analysis of Algorithm 5.2 is more involved. For the proofs of the following fact, we refer the reader to [4, 49].

Fact 5.3 *Algorithm 5.2 maintains* $O(\log(1/\varepsilon))$ *coresets* $K_1, K_2, \ldots,$ *such that* $P \subset \text{MEB}\left(\bigcup_i \text{MEB}(K_i)\right)$, *whose radius is at most* $1.22 + O(\varepsilon)$ *times that of* $\text{MEB}(P)$.

Implementation Issues. There are various ways to implement the algorithm efficiently with little or no impact on the quality of the resulting coreset. To start with, instead of initializing the algorithm with an arbitrary point p (line 1 of Algorithm 5.1), we can find the farthest neighbor of p in P, i.e., the point that maximizes the distance from p, say q, and start the algorithm with $K = \{q\}$. This usually reduces the size of the resulting coreset by 1.

Computing the MEB (line 3 of Algorithm 5.1) can be formulated as a quadratic programming problem, for which many efficient solvers are available. Most of them use some iterative method to gradually approach the optimal solution, which is the MEB in our case. For the purpose of this algorithm, finding the exact MEB is unnecessary. Kumar et al. [163] proved that it suffices to find the MEB in each iteration of the algorithm up to error $O(\varepsilon^2)$ to still guarantee that the resulting K is an ε-coreset, while in practice it seems that an error of ε works just fine. Moreover, since only one point is added to K in each iteration, the corresponding quadratic program only changes slightly. So one can use the MEB solution obtained from the previous iteration as the starting point, so that the quadratic programming solver can converge quickly.

Finally, instead of finding the farthest neighbor from the center of $\text{MEB}(K)$ (line 5 of Algorithm 5.1), which requires $O(n)$ time, we can take a random sample of the points in P, and choose the farthest one in the sample. This may increase the size of the resulting coreset slightly, but can significantly improve the running time. When all the sampled points are within the $(1+\varepsilon)$-expansion of $\text{MEB}(K)$, we still have to examine all points in P. But when this happens, the algorithm will usually soon terminate in a few more iterations.

History and Background. The notion of ε-coreset for MEBs, as well as Algorithm 5.1 for constructing ε-coresets, was proposed by Bădoiu et al. [43], who showed that this algorithm terminates in $O(1/\varepsilon^2)$ rounds. Later, Bădoiu and Clarkson [41] improved the bound to $2/\varepsilon$ as described above. Independently, Kumar et al. [163] also showed an $O(1/\varepsilon)$ bound, as well as an efficient implementation with some experimental results. Their experimental results suggest that for typical inputs, the algorithm returns coresets that are much smaller than the $2/\varepsilon$ bound. Bădoiu and Clarkson [42] later gave an example on which the coreset has size $1/\varepsilon$, and presented an algorithm that always finds a coreset at most this size, so this problem can be considered as completely solved even up to the constant. But the new algorithm usually returns the same coreset as the one produced by Algorithm 5.1.

Algorithm 5.2 was proposed by Agarwal and Sharathkumar [4]. They showed that this algorithm maintains a sequence of $O\left(\log\frac{1}{\varepsilon}\right)$ coresets (thus using space $O\left(\frac{d}{\varepsilon}\log\frac{1}{\varepsilon}\right)$) and returns a $\frac{1+\sqrt{3}}{2}+\varepsilon = (1.366+\varepsilon)$-approximation to the MEB. The approximation ratio (of the same algorithm) was subsequently improved to $1.22+\varepsilon$ by Chan and Pathak [49]. On the other hand, Agarwal and Sharathkumar [4] proved that any summary that returns a $\frac{1+\sqrt{2}}{2}(1-2/d^{1/3})$-

approximation of the MEB while being able to support the addition of new points has to have size $\Omega(\exp(d^{1/3}))$, which rules out any small ε-coresets for MEBs in high dimensions. For low dimensions, ε-coresets that support addition of new points are known; please see the next section.

5.3 ε-Kernels

Brief Summary. Let P be a set of n points in $\mathbb{R}^d$. The ε-kernel is an approximation of the convex hull of P. Unlike the convex hull itself, which can have as many as n points, its ε-kernel has a small size that is independent of n. In this section, d is assumed to be a constant.

Let u be a unit directional vector in d dimensions, i.e., $u \in \mathbb{R}^d$ with $\|u\| = 1$. For any direction u, define the *directional width* of P in direction u, denoted by $\omega(u, P)$, to be

$$\omega(u, P) = \max_{p \in P}\langle u, p \rangle - \min_{p \in P}\langle u, p \rangle,$$

where $\langle \cdot, \cdot \rangle$ is the inner product. The directional width of P is thus the span of P when projected onto u. Let $\varepsilon > 0$ be an error parameter. A subset $Q \subseteq P$ is called an *ε-kernel* of P if for every direction u,

$$(1 + \varepsilon)\omega(u, Q) \geq \omega(u, P).$$

Clearly, $\omega(u, Q) \leq \omega(u, P)$. Please refer to Figure 5.3 for an example.

The ε-kernel is a coreset for many measures on P that depend on the convex hull of P, such as diameter (the distance between the two farthest points), width (maximum directional width), radius of the minimum enclosing ball, and the volume of the minimum enclosing box, etc.

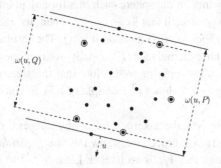

Figure 5.3 An example of a point set P and its ε-kernel (circled points). For any direction u, the width of the circled points (spanned by the two dashed lines) is only a $(1 + \varepsilon)$-factor smaller than the width of the whole point set.

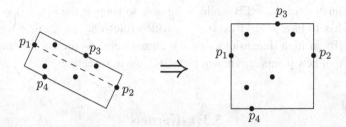

Figure 5.4 Transforming P into a fat point set in two dimensions. First, identify the two farthest points p_1 and $p_2 \in P$, which defines the first side of C. Then project all points onto the line $\overline{p_1 p_2}$ and find the two farthest points on this line, p_3 and p_4, which defines the second side of C. Finally, we take the affine transformation π that maps C to the unit square, and apply it to all points of P.

Operations on the Summary. There are two steps to CONSTRUCT an ε-kernel. In step one, we compute an affine transformation π so that $\pi(P)$ is an α-*fat* point set, namely, P is contained in $[-1, 1]^d$ but its convex hull encloses $[-\alpha, \alpha]^d$, where $0 < \alpha < 1$ is a constant. This is done by finding a bounding box C (not necessarily orthogonal) of P, as follows. Find the two farthest points $p, q \in P$. The segment pq defines the direction and length of one side of C. Then project all points in P into the $(d - 1)$-dimensional hyperplane perpendicular to $\overline{pq}$, and repeat the preceding process to find the remaining sides of C. The affine transformation π is thus the one that maps C to $[-1, 1]^d$. Please see Figure 5.4 for an example in two dimensions. This transformation gives a fatness α of at least $1/2$.

In step two, we compute the ε-kernel of $\pi(P)$. To compute the ε-kernel of an α-fat point set, we set $\delta = \sqrt{\varepsilon\alpha}$, and consider the sphere S of radius $\sqrt{d}+1$ centered at the origin. We place a set R of $O(1/\delta^{d-1}) = O(1/\varepsilon^{(d-1)/2})$ "equally spaced" points on the sphere such that for any point x on the sphere S, there is a point $y \in R$ such that $\|x - y\| \leq \delta$. Then, for each point in R, we find its nearest neighbor in $\pi(S)$ and add it to Q. The resulting set of chosen points Q becomes the ε-kernel of $\pi(P)$. Finally, we map the points in Q back to the original space by applying π^{-1}. Note that the size of the ε-kernel is $O(1/\varepsilon^{(d-1)/2})$. Figure 5.5 shows an example of how to construct an ε-kernel for a fat point set.

To be able to UPDATE the ε-kernel, we apply a general method that only relies on the CONSTRUCT procedure, known as the *logarithmic method*. For simplicity, we assume that $1/\varepsilon$ is an integer. Let $a/\varepsilon^{(d-1)/2}$ be the maximum size of the ε-kernel built by the previous CONSTRUCT algorithm, for some constant a. For $i \geq 1$, define $\rho_i = \varepsilon/i^2$. Instead of maintaining one kernel,

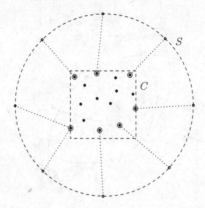

Figure 5.5 Constructing the ε-kernel for a fat point set in two dimensions: the points on the circle S are equally spaced and the distance between any two of them is at least δ. Each point on S picks its nearest neighbor in $\pi(P)$ (the circled points) and they form the ε-kernel of P. Note that multiple points in R on the sphere S can pick the same point in P as their nearest neighbor. In this case, it is stored only once in the ε-kernel.

we maintain a series of kernels, each associated with a *rank*. To INITIALIZE the summary, we create only one kernel $Q_0 = \emptyset$ and set its *rank* to be 0. To UPDATE the summary with a new point p, we first add it to Q_0. If $|Q_0| \leq a/\varepsilon^{(d-1)/2}$, we are done. Otherwise we CONSTRUCT a ρ_1-kernel of Q_0, denoted by Q', and set its rank to 1. Then we clear $Q_0 = \emptyset$. Next we check if there is another kernel Q'' in the summary with rank 1. If not, we are done; otherwise, we union Q' and Q'' together, and construct a ρ_2-kernel of their union, set its rank to 2, and delete Q' and Q''. We carry out this procedure iteratively: whenever there are two kernels Q' and Q'' of the same rank i, we CONSTRUCT a ρ_{i+1}-kernel of their union, set its rank to $i + 1$, and delete Q' and Q''. Eventually, there is at most one kernel left for each rank. It should be clear that there are at most $O(\log n)$ kernels in the summary after n points have been inserted. To extract a kernel for all these points, we can simply return the union of these $O(\log n)$ kernels, of total size $O(\log n/\varepsilon^{(d-1)/2})$. If a smaller size is desired, we can CONSTRUCT an ε-kernel of the union of these $O(\log n)$ kernels.

Two ε-kernel summaries that we have described can be similarly merged. We first merge the two kernels of rank 0 in the two summaries. If the resulting kernel has size more than $a/\varepsilon^{(d-1)/2}$, we CONSTRUCT a ρ_1-kernel for it and assign it rank 1. Next, we consider each rank i in the increasing order iteratively. For each rank i, there can be zero, one, two, or three (in case a new kernel of rank i has just been constructed by merging two kernels of rank $i - 1$)

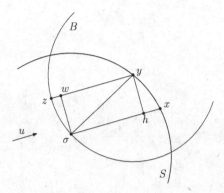

Figure 5.6 Correctness proof of the CONSTRUCT algorithm.

kernels. Whenever there are two or three kernels of rank i, we merge them together, and construct a ρ_{i+1}-kernel on their union. In the end, we still have at most one kernel at each rank.

Further Discussion. Here we briefly sketch the proof that the CON-STRUCT algorithm computes a subset $Q \subseteq P$ that is an ε-kernel of P, following the argument in [238]. We assume that P is α-fat for some constant α. We also assume that in the last step of the algorithm, we find the exact nearest neighbors of the points in R. Fix a direction $u \in \mathbb{S}^{d-1}$. Let $\sigma \in P$ be the point that maximizes $\langle u, p \rangle$ over all $p \in P$. Suppose the ray emanating from σ in direction u hits the sphere S at a point x. We know that there exists a point $y \in R$ such that $\|x - y\| \le \delta$. Let $\varphi(y)$ denote the nearest neighbor of y in P. If $\varphi(y) = \sigma$, then $\sigma \in Q$ and

$$\max_{p \in P} \langle u, p \rangle - \max_{q \in Q} \langle u, q \rangle = 0.$$

Now suppose $\varphi(y) \ne \sigma$. Let B be the d-dimensional ball of radius $\|y - \sigma\|$ centered at y. Since $\|y - \varphi(y)\| \le \|y - \sigma\|, \varphi(y) \in B$. Let us denote by z the point on the sphere ∂B that is hit by the ray emanating from y in direction $-u$. Let w be the point on zy such that $zy \perp \sigma w$ and h the point on σx such that $yh \perp \sigma x$; see Figure 5.6.

The hyperplane perpendicular to u and passing through z is tangent to B. Since $\varphi(y)$ lies inside B, $\langle u, \varphi(y) \rangle \ge \langle u, z \rangle$. Moreover, it can be shown that $\langle u, \sigma \rangle - \langle u, \varphi(y) \rangle \le \alpha \varepsilon$. Thus, we can write

$$\max_{p \in P} \langle u, p \rangle - \max_{q \in Q} \langle u, q \rangle \le \langle u, \sigma \rangle - \langle u, \varphi(y) \rangle \le \alpha \varepsilon.$$

Similarly, we have $\min_{p \in P} \langle u, p \rangle - \min_{q \in Q} \langle u, q \rangle \geq -\alpha\varepsilon$.

The preceding two inequalities together imply that $\omega(u, Q) \geq \omega(u, P) - 2\alpha\varepsilon$. Since $[-\alpha, \alpha]^d$ is contained in the convex hull of P, $\omega(u, P) \geq 2\alpha$. Hence $\omega(u, Q) \geq (1 - \varepsilon)\omega(u, P)$. For sufficiently small ε (and also by scaling ε slightly), this is essentially $(1 + \varepsilon)\omega(u, Q) \geq \omega(u, P)$.

Analysis of the UPDATE *and* MERGE *Algorithm.* We will only need the following two properties of kernels.

1. If P_2 is an ε_1-kernel of P_1, and P_3 is an ε_2-kernel of P_2, then P_3 is an $(1 + \varepsilon_1)(1 + \varepsilon_2) - 1 = (\varepsilon_1 + \varepsilon_2 + \varepsilon_1\varepsilon_2)$-kernel of P_1;
2. If P_2 is an ε-kernel of P_1, and Q_2 is an ε-kernel of Q_2, then $P_2 \cup Q_2$ is an ε-kernel of $P_1 \cup Q_1$.

By simple induction, we can show that the kernel at rank i has error

$$\prod_{l=1}^{i}(1 + \rho_i) - 1 = \prod_{l=1}^{i}\left(1 + \frac{\varepsilon}{l^2}\right) - 1 \leq \exp\left(\sum_{l=1}^{i}\frac{\varepsilon}{l^2}\right) - 1$$

$$\leq \exp\left(\frac{\pi^2\varepsilon}{6}\right) - 1 = O(\varepsilon).$$

So, the union of all the $O(\log n)$ kernels, or after another CONSTRUCT algorithm, still has error $O(\varepsilon)$.

The total size of the data structure is

$$\sum_{i=0}^{\lfloor\log\varepsilon^{(d-1)/2}n\rfloor+1} O\left(1/\rho_i^{(d-1)/2}\right) = \sum_{i=0}^{\lfloor\log\varepsilon^{(d-1)/2}n\rfloor+1} O\left(\frac{i^{d-1}}{\varepsilon^{(d-1)/2}}\right)$$

$$= O\left(\frac{\log^d n}{\varepsilon^{(d-1)/2}}\right).$$

Implementation Issues. The CONSTRUCT algorithm can be implemented with different choices in the various steps that can significantly reduce its running time without affecting the quality of the resulting kernel too much. In computing the bounding box C, we do not have to find the exact diameter of P (two farthest points), which takes $O(n^2)$ time, in deciding each side of C. Instead, one can use the following simple $O(n)$-time algorithm to find a constant approximation of the diameter [95]. Pick an arbitrary point $p \in P$. Find its farthest neighbor $q \in P$. Then find the farthest neighbor of q in P, denoted by q'. Note that q, q' must be the two farthest points along the direction $\overline{qq'}$, which can then be used to decide one side of C.

Placing equally spaced points on a circle in 2D is easy, but the problem becomes nontrivial in higher dimensions. A good way is to start with an arbitrary set of k points on the sphere, regarding each point as an electron, and then using the gradient descent method to minimize the total potential energy of the point set by repeatedly fine-tuning the position of each point. The final configuration tends to be a regular distribution on the sphere. This method also gives us an explicit control on the kernel size, and there is no need to compute the actual value of α. The weaknesses of this approach are that it does not give a guarantee on the error of the resulting ε-kernel, and that it can be slow in high dimensions or when k is large. But since this procedure is independent of the point set, it just needs to be performed once, possibly in an offline stage, for each desired kernel size.

Finally, in the last step of the CONSTRUCT algorithm, we do not have to find the exact nearest neighbors of the points in R; some approximation can be tolerated. One can for example use the ANN package [192] for approximate nearest neighbor search.

History and Background. The notion of ε-kernels was introduced by Agarwal et al. [3]. The construction algorithm described previously was proposed independently by Chan [48] and Yu et al. [238]. The $O(1/\varepsilon^{(d-1)/2})$ size of the resulting ε-kernels is optimal in the worst case. The practical methods presented here are from [238], while theoretically, an ε-kernel can be constructed in time $O(n + 1/\varepsilon^{d-3/2})$ [48]. The experimental results in [238] show that the algorithm works extremely well in low dimensions (≤ 4) both in terms of the kernel size/error and running time. However, it does not scale to high dimensions due to the exponential dependency on d.

The UPDATE algorithm is also described in [3], which is a modification of the logarithmic method of Bentley and Saxe [25]. This algorithm is simple and practical, but it raises the theoretical question whether it is possible to maintain an ε-kernel using space that is independent of n. Chan [48] answered the question in the affirmative, by presenting an algorithm that uses $1/\varepsilon^{O(d)}$ space. This result has been subsequently improved by Agarwal and Yu [5] and Zarrabi-Zadeh [239], ultimately yielding an algorithm using $O(1/\varepsilon^{(d-1)/2} \log(1/\varepsilon))$ space.

5.4 k-Center Clustering

Brief Summary. Let $B_{o,r}$ be the ball of radius r centered at point $o \in \mathbb{R}^d$. Let P be a set of n points in $\mathbb{R}^d$. In the k-center clustering problem, we wish to find the minimum radius r and k balls with radius r centered at $o_1, \ldots, o_k \in \mathbb{R}^d$, such that $B_{o_1, r} \cup \cdots \cup B_{o_k, r}$ contain all points in P. Note that when $k = 1$, this degenerates to the minimum enclosing ball problem discussed in Section 5.2. However, unlike the minimum enclosing ball problem, which can be solved in polynomial time, the k-center clustering problem is NP-hard. There is a simple 2-approximation algorithm for the k-center clustering problem: let $O = \emptyset$ be a collection of centers. In each step, find the point $p \in P$ with the largest $d(p, O)$ and add it to O, where $d(p, O)$ denotes the minimum distance from p to any center in O. This step is repeated k times so that we have k centers in O in the end. This algorithm requires us to keep the entire set of points P. Later we show how to turn this idea into a small summary of size $O(k/\varepsilon \cdot \log(1/\varepsilon))$ that maintains a $(2 + \varepsilon)$-approximation of the optimal k-center clustering.

Operations on the Summary. If we knew the optimal radius r_{OPT}, we could turn the previous 2-approximation algorithm into a summary of size k, as shown in Algorithm 5.3. It is easy to see why the summary size, $|O|$, never exceeds k when $r \geq r_{\text{OPT}}$. This is because all points can be covered by k balls with radius r, and the algorithm never adds more than one point from each ball into O. Meanwhile, we must not have seen any point that is $2r$ away from any center in O (otherwise the algorithm would have added it to O), so all points can be covered by balls with radius $2r$ centered at the centers in O. Thus, if we ran Algorithm 5.3 with $r = r_{\text{OPT}}$, we would find a 2-approximation of the optimal k-center clustering.

Algorithm 5.3: k-center-with-r: CONSTRUCT (r, P)

---

1   $O \leftarrow \emptyset$;

2   **for** $p \in P$ **do**

3   **if** $d(p, O) > 2r$ **then** $O \leftarrow O \cup \{p\}$;

4   **return** O;

However, the problem is that we do not know r_{OPT} in advance. Furthermore, when more points are added to the set of points on which we wish to summarize, r_{OPT} will gradually increase. Therefore, the idea is to run multiple instances of Algorithm 5.3 with different values of r. For $j = 0, 1, \ldots, j_{\text{max}} - 1$, where $j_{\text{max}} = \lceil \log_{1+\varepsilon}(1/\varepsilon) \rceil$, instance j maintains a collection of centers O_j with radius r_j. The r_j's will be a $(1 + \varepsilon)$-factor apart from each other. When more points are added, r_{OPT} will increase, and some instances will fail, i.e., having more than k centers. When $|O_j| > k$ for some j, we rerun the algorithm with a larger $r_j \leftarrow r_j/\varepsilon$ on O_j. If with the new r_j, O_j still has more than k centers, we increase r_j again.

A technical problem is from what value of r we should start. If $n \leq k$, then the optimal clustering is just to put each point in a cluster on its own. When $n = k + 1$, we find the closest pair of points, say p_1, p_2, and set $r_0 = d(p_1, p_2)/2, r_j = (1 + \varepsilon)^j r_0$ to start running the algorithm.

The complete algorithm is shown in Algorithm 5.4. The algorithm starts with $n = 0$ and $P = \emptyset$. Upon a QUERY, we return the O_j with the smallest r_j.

Algorithm 5.4: k-center: UPDATE (p)

---

1 $n \leftarrow n + 1$;
2 **if** $n \leq k + 1$ **then** $P \leftarrow P \cup \{p\}$;
3 **if** $n = k + 1$ **then**
4 $p_1, p_2 \leftarrow$ the two closest points in P;
5 $r_0 \leftarrow d(p_1, p_2)/2$;
6 $O_0 \leftarrow$ CONSTRUCT(r_0, P);
7   **for** $j = 1, \ldots, j_{\max} - 1$ **do**
8 $r_j = (1 + \varepsilon) r_{j-1}$;
9 $O_j \leftarrow$ CONSTRUCT(r_j, P);

10 **else**
11   **for** $j = 0, \ldots, j_{\max} - 1$ **do**
12   **if** $d(p, O_j) > 2r_j$ **then** $O_j \leftarrow O_j \cup \{p\}$;
13   **while** $|O_j| > k$ **do**
14 $r_j \leftarrow r_j/\varepsilon$;
15 $O_j \leftarrow$ CONSTRUCT(r_j, O_j);

It is not known if this summary can be merged.

Further Discussion. Now we show that Algorithm 5.4 returns a $(2 + \varepsilon)$-approximation of the optimal k-center clustering. It is sufficient to prove the following:

Fact 5.4 *For any O_j maintained by Algorithm 5.4, $\bigcup_{o \in O_j} B_{o,(2+3\varepsilon)r_{\mathrm{OPT}}}$ covers all points.*

Proof: Algorithm 5.4 is actually running $j_{\max}$ instances independently. Instance j starts with $r_j = (1 + \varepsilon)^j r_0$, and increases $r_j \leftarrow r_j/\varepsilon$ and reconstructs O_j from O_j itself whenever $|O_j| > k$. Suppose

$$r_0(1 + \varepsilon)^{j-1}/\varepsilon^i \leq r_{\mathrm{OPT}} < r_0(1 + \varepsilon)^j/\varepsilon^i,$$

for some integers $0 \leq j \leq j_{\max} - 1$, and $i \geq 0$. Note that such i, j must exist as we set $j_{\max} = \lceil \log_{1+\varepsilon}(1/\varepsilon) \rceil$. Then instance j must succeed, i.e., $|O_j| \leq k$ when it reaches $r_j = r_0(1 + \varepsilon)^j/\varepsilon^i$. In the following, we argue that the balls centered O_j must be able to cover all points with a certain radius. Recall the earlier argument. If we had run the instance with $r_j = r_0(1 + \varepsilon)^j/\varepsilon^i$ from the beginning, then a radius of $2r_j$ is enough. However, every time we rebuild O_j with $r_j = r_0(1 + \varepsilon)^j/\varepsilon^t$, we do not have all points available, so have only built it from O_j itself. Nevertheless, observe that any point must be within a distance of $2r_0(1 + \varepsilon)^j/\varepsilon^{t-1}$ of the centers in O_j. Carrying out this argument inductively and using the triangle inequality, we will need in total a radius of

$$\sum_{t=0}^{i} 2r_0(1 + \varepsilon)^j/\varepsilon^t = 2r_0(1 + \varepsilon)^j \frac{1/\varepsilon^i - 1}{1/\varepsilon - 1}$$

$$\leq 2r_0(1 + \varepsilon)^{j-1}/\varepsilon^i \cdot (1 + \varepsilon)\frac{1}{1/\varepsilon - 1}$$

$$\leq 2r_{\text{OPT}} \cdot \frac{1 + \varepsilon}{1 - \varepsilon}$$

$$\leq 2(1 + 3\varepsilon)r_{\text{OPT}}, \qquad (\text{assuming } \varepsilon < 1/4)$$

to cover all points. $\qquad\qquad\qquad\qquad\qquad\qquad\qquad\qquad\qquad\qquad$ □

If we replace ε with $\varepsilon/3$ to run the algorithm, then a $(2 + \varepsilon)$-approximation is guaranteed.

History and Background. The algorithm presented in this section and its analysis is from [126]. Many other theoretical papers have considered summaries for clustering under different clustering objective functions. Early work due to Guha et al. [127] and Charikar et al. [52] provides results for the k-median (sum of distances) function.

5.5 The (Sparse) Johnson–Lindenstrauss Transform

Brief Summary. The (Sparse) Johnson–Lindenstrauss transform (Sparse JLT) transforms a set of n points in $\mathbb{R}^d$ to a set P' of n points in $\mathbb{R}^k$ for $k = \Theta(1/\varepsilon^2 \log n)$, such that the pairwise distance of the points are preserved up to a multiplicative error of $1 + \varepsilon$. More precisely, it states that for any $\varepsilon > 0$, there exists a linear transform $f : \mathbb{R}^d \to \mathbb{R}^k$ such that for all $x, y \in P$,

$$(1 - \varepsilon)\|x - y\| \leq \|f(x) - f(y)\| \leq (1 + \varepsilon)\|x - y\|.$$

It is thus a summary that reduces dimensionality, not the number of points in the dataset P. It is a fundamental result concerning low-distortion embeddings [139] of points from high-dimensional to low-dimensional Euclidean space.

It turns out that the linear transform f can be obtained by simply picking a random $k \times d$ matrix S from a properly designed probability distribution. It can be shown that for such a random S and $k = \Theta(1/\varepsilon^2 \log(1/\delta))$, we have

$$\Pr[(1 - \varepsilon)\|x\| \le \|Sx\| \le (1 + \varepsilon)\|x\|] > 1 - \delta \tag{5.4}$$

for any $x \in \mathbb{R}^d$. Note that the transform S is independent of P and (5.4) holds for any $x \in \mathbb{R}^d$. Therefore, we can set $\delta = 1/n^2$, pick an S, and apply (5.4) to each of the $\binom{n}{2}$ pairs of the points in P so that all pairwise distances are preserved with probability at least $1/2$.

Operations on the Summary. We now specify how the Sparse JLT linear transform S is decided. Let $x_1, \ldots, x_d$ denote the d coordinates of a point $x \in \mathbb{R}^d$. We use y to denote the transformed point $y = Sx$, which has k coordinates, for some $k = \Theta(1/\varepsilon^2 \log(1/\delta))$. Set $r = \Theta(1/\varepsilon \log(1/\delta))$ such that it divides k. We will view the k coordinates of y as an $r \times k/r$ array, i.e., r rows each of size k/r. The array is initialized to all 0. For each row j of the array, we use a $2 \log(1/\delta)$-wise independent hash function $h_j : [d] \to [k/r]$, and a $\log(1/\delta)$-wise independent hash function $g_j : [d] \to \{-1, +1\}$. For each coordinate x_i of x and for each row j of the array, we add $x_i g_j(i)/\sqrt{r}$ to $y_{j,h_j(i)}$. From the right perspective, the Sparse JLT of a single point is essentially the same as the Count Sketch summary for that point, except that (1) the array has dimension $\Theta(1/\varepsilon \log(1/\delta)) \times \Theta(1/\varepsilon)$ as opposed to $\Theta(\log(1/\delta)) \times \Theta(1/\varepsilon^2)$ for Count Sketch; (2) we use hash functions of a higher degree of independence; and (3) we divide the values by $\sqrt{r}$ to give the correct scaling factor, as we do not take a median across rows but (effectively) average. Thus, this summary of a point can be updated and merged in basically the same way as with the Count Sketch, covered in Section 3.5. Finally, the QUERY function provides an estimate of $\|x\|$ by simply computing the norm of y, i.e., taking the squared sum of all entries in the array, as opposed to taking the median of the rows as in Count Sketch. Distances between points can similarly be computed by performing the corresponding operations between their Sparse JLT transformations, then applying the QUERY function.

Note that the Count Sketch also provides a summary that preserves pairwise Euclidean distances between points with the same sketch size. The time to perform an update is actually faster (it does not have the factor of $1/\varepsilon$), but since it uses the median operator to produce an estimate, it does not offer an embedding in to a lower-dimensional Euclidean space, which is needed in certain applications such as nearest-neighbor search and some machine learning applications. For this reason, the Sparse JLT may often be preferred due to its stronger mathematical guarantees, even though the cost of UPDATE operations is higher.

Further Discussion. The analysis of this technique is not hugely difficult to understand, but involves some concepts from combinatorics and coding theory that go beyond the scope of this volume. Consequently, we choose to sketch out the outline.

A first step is to assume that we are dealing with an input vector x with $\|x\|_2 = 1$. This is because the transformation is linear, so any scalar multiple of x is passed through the estimation process. Assuming $\|x\|_2 = 1$ threatens to make the analysis redundant, since the objective is to form an estimate of $\|x\|_2$, but of course, the algorithm does not rely on this assumption, and so we can proceed.

As noted previously, this version of a Sparse JLT transform is very similar in operation to the Count Sketch and the AMS Sketch. Consequently, we use the same notation to describe its analysis. As in Section 3.6, we can define a random variable X_j as the estimate obtained of $\|x\|_2^2$ from the jth row, as

$$X_j = \sum_{p=1}^{k/r} C[j, p]^2$$

$$= \sum_{p=1}^{k/r} \frac{1}{r} \left(\sum_{i:h_j(i)=p} x_i^2 + 2 \sum_{i\neq\ell, h_j(i)=h_j(\ell)=p} g_j(i)g_j(\ell)x_i x_\ell \right)$$

where $C[j, p]$ denotes the contents of the pth cell in the jth row of the sketch; x_i are the entries of vector x; h_j is the hash function assigning indices to cells in row j; and g_j provides the $\{+1, -1\}$ value for each index in row j.

Observe that by the assumption that $\|x\|_2 = 1$, we can write a random variable Z for the total error in estimation as

$$Z = \frac{1}{r} \sum_{j=1}^{r} (X_j - 1) = \frac{2}{r} \sum_{j=1}^{r} \sum_{p=1}^{k/r} \sum_{i\neq\ell, h_j(i)=h_j(\ell)=p} g_j(i)g_j(\ell)x_i x_\ell.$$

The analysis proceeds by bounding this random variable Z. For the analogous quantity in the analysis of AMS Sketch, it was possible to bound the second moment (i.e., to bound $E[Z^2]$) in order to show a constant probability of deviating far from zero error. This was done by expanding out the square of Z and arguing that terms were bounded due to the independence properties of the hash functions. The approach in this case is essentially the same, but now we need to show a bound directly in terms of δ, rather than a constant probability. This requires taking a higher moment of Z — we apply Markov's inequality to show that

$$\Pr[|Z| > \epsilon] < \epsilon^{-q} E[Z^q],$$

where q is chosen to be an even number greater than $\log(1/\delta)$.

However, Z^q does not lend itself to direct expansion and bounding, and so instead, we need a much more involved argument. The high-level idea is to use a graph representation of the polynomial to encode the terms that arise: nodes represent indices, and edges link indices that appear in the expansion of the polynomial Z^q. This allows a more convenient notation and bounding of the terms that arise, so the desired inequality can be proven.

History and Background. The JL lemma was established by Johnson and Lindenstrauss [148] in 1984. There have been a number of different proofs of this lemma, based on different constructions of the transform matrix S. Early constructions had S very dense – for example, where every entry is drawn independently from a Gaussian or Rademacher (Bernoulli with $+1$ or -1 values) distribution [140]. In this case UPDATE operations take time $O(k)$ for each coordinate that is updated. This construction remains of importance, as it leads to results in the relatively new area of compressed sensing [89]. For a concise proof for this Johnson–Lindenstrauss transform, see the proof of Dasgupta and Gupta [82].

Due to the importance of the transform, considerable effort has been invested in making it fast, by sparsifying the matrix S. We avoid a complete history, and highlight some key points along the way. An initial effort was by Achlioptas [1], whose construction had entries chosen independently from $\{-1, 0, +1\}$. This achieved a constant degree of sparsity, i.e., a constant fraction of the entries were nonzero. Ailon and Chazelle achieved a much faster result by introducing more structure into the transformation. The "fast Johnson–Lindenstrauss" transform [8] writes the matrix S as the product of three matrices, $S = PHD$. P is a sparse matrix where only a roughly

$\log^2 n/d$ fraction of the entries are non-zero: the nonzero entries are chosen independently from a Gaussian distribution. If we applied P directly on the input, we would achieve the desired result (preservation of the Euclidean norm) — if the input vector was dense (i.e., had few zero entries, and no particularly large entries). The other parts of the transform are designed to preserve the Euclidean norm of the vector, while (almost certainly) giving the dense property. D is a diagonal matrix whose entries are randomly chosen as $\{-1, +1\}$. Observe that this does not change the norm of the vector, and is very similar to steps in the Count Sketch and Sparse JLT described previously that randomly flip signs of entries. H is the Hadamard transform — this is an instance of a Fourier transform and so has some useful properties: (1) it is an orthonormal basis transformation, so again does not change the Euclidean norm of the vector; (2) it can be computed quickly using a Fast Fourier Transform algorithm, in time $O(d \log d)$. The Hadamard transform ensures that if x was sparse in the original space, it will be dense in the transformed space. The result of this construction is an instance of a Johnson–Lindenstrauss transform that can be computed for a vector of dimension d in time $O(d \log d)$. However, this relies on computing the transformation for a whole vector in one go. When the vector is being defined incrementally, the cost of a single UPDATE operation is not guaranteed to be fast.

This limitation prompted the study of sparse JL matrices. The version presented here is given by Kane and Nelson [152]. They also describe alternative approaches based on how the mapping to the sketch allows overlaps, with differing guarantees and proofs. It is natural to ask whether the sparsity can be reduced below the $1/\varepsilon$ dependency, or whether the number of dimensions k can be reduced below $1/\varepsilon^2$. Both questions have been answered in the negative. The number of dimensions of the reduced space $k = \Theta(1/\varepsilon^2 \log(1/\delta))$ has been shown to be optimal [146]. Nelson and Nguyen show no construction can achieve sparsity less than $1/\varepsilon$, as this would give too high a probability that significant entries of the input vector are not picked up by the transform [195].

6

Vector, Matrix, and Linear Algebraic Summaries

In this chapter, we show how ideas from the summaries described previously can be applied directly or adapted to solve problems that arise in the context of linear algebra: computations on vectors, matrices, and their generalizations to tensors.

For vectors, many of the summaries apply directly. We can often think of a vector as being synonymous with a frequency distribution, where the ith entry in the vector corresponds to the frequency of an element i. Queries for a particular element of a vector then correspond to a point query in the frequency distribution. Frequency moments have a natural interpretation in terms of vector norms. However, there are some problems over vectors that do not correspond to a natural question over frequency distributions, and so require some additional work.

In the case of matrices, many of the ideas and techniques from vector summaries carry over – in the extreme case, we can think of matrices as ordered collections of vectors. We typically describe results in terms of the Frobenius norm $\|M\|_F$ of a matrix M, an "entrywise" norm which measures the (square root of the) sum of squares of entries, i.e., $\|M\|_F = \sqrt{\sum_{i,j} M_{i,j}^2}$.

6.1 Vector Computations: Euclidean Norm and Inner Product Estimation

Given a high-dimensional vector v, we would like to find its Euclidean norm, $\|v\|_2$. This problem is by now very well understood, and several techniques directly solve it: the AMS Sketch (Section 3.6) in particular addresses this problem, but more generally, methods that implement the

176

Johnson–Lindenstrauss transform by computing an appropriate "sketch" of the vector can be applied. These find an ϵ-relative error approximation of $\|v\|_2$.

Equipped with such an approximation, we can solve a number of other problems on vectors. Most immediately, given vectors v and w we can find the Euclidean distance between them, defined as $\|v - w\|_2$. Functionally, this can be achieved by building a summary of v, and a summary of the vector $(-w)$ and applying a MERGE operation to these two. Because the summaries are linear transformations of the input vectors, one can more directly think of the summary of v as $sk(v)$, where $sk(\cdot)$ denotes the operation of building the (sketch) summary. Then $sk(v - w) = sk(v) - sk(w)$, and so we can obtain the sketch of the difference by taking the difference of the sketches. The Euclidean distance can therefore be estimated with relative error.

We can also use this property to find an estimate of the inner product between two vectors, albeit with additive error. The inner product between u and v is given by the sum of products of corresponding indices, defined as

$$u \cdot v = \sum_i u_i v_i$$

This can also be written in terms of Euclidean norm, using some algebra. Observe that

$$\|u + v\|_2^2 = \|u\|_2^2 + \|v\|_2^2 + 2(u \cdot v).$$

To see this, note that the contribution to the sum represented by the left-hand side from any index i is $u_i^2 + v_i^2 + 2u_i v_i$. Therefore, we can write $(u \cdot v) = \frac{1}{2}(\|u + v\|_2^2 - \|u\|_2^2 - \|v\|_2^2)$. Using sketches, we can estimate the right-hand side as our approximation to the inner product.

This estimate does *not* provide overall relative error. Each of the component quantities is found with relative error, but the additions and subtractions mean that the error stays of the magnitude of $\|u\|_2^2 + \|v\|_2^2$ (at least, this gives a quick bound). It is reasonable to ask whether a relative error can be obtained. In particular, there are many applications where a relative error guarantee for inner product would be most helpful. However, there are strong lower bounds (see Section 10.3) showing that such a result cannot be obtained in general. In essence, this is because such a sketch would allow us to distinguish between vectors that have inner product zero (i.e., are orthogonal) and that have inner product very close to zero (almost orthogonal).

A more careful use of summaries can obtain an improved additive error bound. Suppose, for the sake of concreteness, that we are using the AMS Sketch to summarize u and v. Each summary is formed as an array of

$d \times t$ counters. A QUERY operation for the inner product takes the inner product of each of the d rows of the pair of summaries, then finds the median of these. Then a similar analysis to the original use of the sketches shows that the result gives an estimate of $u \cdot v$ with additive error proportional to $\frac{1}{\sqrt{t}} \cdot \|u\|_2 \|v\|_2$, with probability $1 - \exp(-d)$. With the usual setting of $t = O(1/\epsilon^2)$ and $d = O(\log 1/\delta)$, the result gives error $\epsilon \|u\|_2 \|v\|_2$ with probability $1 - \delta$.

Further Discussion. We briefly sketch the outline of the proof, which can be viewed as a generalization of the proof for the estimator for the ℓ_2 norm. Recall the construction of the AMS Sketch, which is defined based on hash functions g and h, which map to arrays of counters C. As before, define X_j to be the estimate of $u \cdot v$ obtained from the jth row of the sketch, i.e., $X_j = \sum_{k=1}^{t} C_u[j,k]C_v[j,k]$. It follows quickly that

$$\mathsf{E}[X_j] = \sum_{k=1}^{t} \mathsf{E}[C_u[j,k]C_v[j,k]]$$

$$= \sum_{k=1}^{t} \sum_{h_j(i)=k} u_i v_i + \sum_{i \neq \ell, h_j(i)=h_j(\ell)=k} \mathsf{E}[g_j(i)]\mathsf{E}[g_j(\ell)]u_i v_\ell.$$

The first term in this sum is $u \cdot v$, and the second term is zero, due to the random properties of the g_j hash functions.

Similarly, for the variance, after expanding out and collapsing the terms that are zero in expectation, we obtain that

$$\mathsf{Var}[X_j] \leq 4\|u\|_2^2 \|v\|_2^2 / t$$

This bound on the variance ensures that the error is at most $\epsilon \|u\|_2 \|v\|_2$ with constant probability when we set the parameter t proportional to $1/\epsilon^2$. This error probability is reduced to δ when we choose $d = O(\log 1/\delta)$ and take medians, following the Chernoff bounds argument (Section 1.4).

History and Background. The use of the summary to estimate the inner product of vectors was described in a follow-up work by Alon et al. [9], and the analysis was similarly generalized to the fast version of the AMS Sketch by Cormode and Garofalakis [66].

6.2 ℓ_p Norms and Frequency Moments

Recall that, given a vector v, its ℓ_p norm is $\|v\|_p = \left(\sum_i v_i^p\right)^{1/p}$. For vectors formed as the frequency distribution of a series of updates, the kth frequency moment is defined as $F_k(v) = \sum_i v_i^k$. These definitions are sufficiently similar (up to taking the pth root) that we will use them interchangeably. In earlier sections, we have discussed summaries that allow estimating the ℓ_2 norm (AMS Sketch), and other ℓ_p norms for $p < 2$ (ℓ_p sketch). We now consider how to estimate the ℓ_p norm for $p > 2$.

An elegant solution is provided via the technique of ℓ_p sampling. We provide an outline here, since the details are rather more technical, and so this approach may be primarily of theoretical interest. In essence, the idea is to sample each element of vector v with probability proportional to its contribution to the (squared) ℓ_2 norm, i.e., apply an ℓ_2-sampling sketch. Then for each sampled element i, include a contribution as a function of its weight v_i so that in expectation its contribution is v_i^p. Summing expectations over all elements, we will obtain an estimate of $\|v\|_p^p$. The variance of this quantity can be bounded, and so the usual approach of taking sufficient repetitions via averaging and median can be used to provide an estimate with accuracy guarantees. The number of repetitions required is $O(n^{1-2/p}\epsilon^{-2})$, where n represents the dimensionality of the vector v. This polynomial dependence on n for $p > 2$ is known to be optimal and imposes a large space cost ($O(n^{1/3})$ for $p = 3$, for example), which is further compounded since each repetition of the ℓ_2 sampling requires multiple sketches to be kept. Consequently, this approach seems to need substantial engineering and careful parameter setting in order to be put into practice.

Further Discussion. We provide more details of the analysis, to give more insight into the method. Full details are provided in the references cited in the "History and Background" section.

Suppose we could sample perfectly according to the ℓ_2 distribution. Then the chance of picking index i from vector v is exactly $v_i^2/\|v\|_2^2$. Further, assume that our ℓ_p sampling summary allows us to estimate v_i and $\|v\|_2$ accurately. Then our estimator when we sample i is $X = v_i^{p-2}\|v\|_2^2$. Observe that this is correct in expectation:

$$E[X] = \sum_i \Pr[i \text{ is sampled}] \cdot v_i^{p-2} = \sum_i \frac{v_i^2}{\|v\|_2^2} v_i^{p-2} \|v\|_2^2$$

$$= \sum_i v_i^p = \|v\|_p^p.$$

The variance of this estimator can be computed similarly, as

$$\text{Var}[X] \le E[X^2] = \sum_i \frac{v_i^2}{\|v\|_2^2} (v_i^{p-2}\|v\|_2^2)^2 = \sum_i v_i^2 v_i^{2p-4} \|v\|_2^2$$

$$= \|v\|_{2p-2}^{2p-2} \|v\|_2^2.$$

In order to provide a more useful bound, we need to rewrite this last quantity in terms of $E[X]^2$. First, for any $p \ge 2$, we have that $\|v\|_{2p-2} \le \|v\|_p$. Via Hölder's inequality, we can show that $\|v\|_2^2 \le n^{(p-2)/p}\|v\|_p^2$. Combining these two facts, we obtain that

$$\|v\|_{2p-2}^{2p-2} \|v\|_2^2 \le n^{1-2/p}\|v\|_p^{2p}.$$

That is, we have that $\text{Var}[X] \le n^{1-2/p}E[X]^2$. Taking the average of $n^{1-2/p}/\epsilon^2$ repetitions reduces the variance by a corresponding factor. This allows us to apply the Chebyshev inequality to show that this mean is with an $1 + \epsilon$ factor of $E[X]$ with constant probability. Repeating $O(\log 1/\delta)$ times and taking the median amplifies this to probability $1-\delta$, via the Chernoff bounds argument.

In order to put this into practice, we need to remove the idealized sampling assumption. That is, rather than sampling with probability exactly $v_i^2/\|v\|_2^2$, we use an ℓ_p sampler to sample with approximately this probability. Similarly, we can only guarantee to find approximations of v_i and $\|v\|_2$. Putting these approximations into the analysis complicates the notation, but otherwise does not change the structure of the argument. Some care is needed in setting the accuracy parameters of the sampling and sketching in order to obtain an overall ϵ guarantee, but otherwise this is a straightforward exercise to analyze the algorithm's properties.

History and Background. The idea of using ℓ_p sampling to estimate ℓ_p norms and frequency moments is due to Coppersmith and Kumar [62], but it was not until Monemizadeh and Woodruff provided the first ℓ_2 sampling algorithm that this was possible [188]. A more detailed survey of ℓ_p sampling and its applications is given by Cormode and Jowhari [70]. The presentation here follows outlines that Andrew McGregor presented in slides on "sketches for ℓ_p sampling."

6.3 Full Matrix Multiplication

Perhaps the most fundamental problem in linear algebra is to perform matrix multiplication: given matrices A and B, compute their matrix product AB. Naive computation of the product for square $n \times n$ matrices takes time proportional to n^3, but faster computation is possible. Strassen's algorithm rewrites the computation in terms of a smaller number of terms to obtain $O(n^{2.807})$. Theoretical algorithms exist that have cost $O(n^{2.372})$, although these are considered far from practical. These approaches work with the full matrices and provide exact solutions. However, thanks to summaries, it is possible to provide approximate answers.

A starting point is to observe that each entry of the matrix product is an inner product: the entry $C_{i,j}$ is given by $A^{(i)} \cdot B_{(j)}$, where $A^{(i)}$ denotes the ith row of matrix A, and $B_{(j)}$ the jth column of B. We can then use sketches (such as AMS Sketch) to approximate these quantities. Assume we sketch every row of A and sketch every column of B. Then we can estimate (with constant probability of success) any desired entry of C, with error proportional to $\epsilon \|A^{(i)}\|_2 \|B_{(j)}\|_2$, for sketches of size $O(1/\epsilon^2)$. The space required is $O(n/\epsilon^2)$ to store the n sketches of each row of A and each column of B.

We can therefore take this approach to estimate every entry of C, as approximate matrix $\hat{C}$, using space $O(n/\epsilon^2)$ and taking time $O(n^2/\epsilon^2)$. The squared error in each entry is $\epsilon^2 \|A^{(i)}\|_2^2 \|B_{(j)}\|_2^2$. This may appear somewhat large, but if we sum this over all entries to get the total squared error, we obtain

$$\|(\hat{C} - AB)\|_F^2 \leq \sum_{i,j} \epsilon^2 \|A^{(i)}\|_2^2 \|B_{(j)}\|_2^2 = \epsilon^2 \left(\sum_i \|A^{(i)}\|_2^2 \right) \left(\sum_j \|B_{(j)}\|_2^2 \right)$$

$$= \epsilon^2 \|A\|_F^2 \|B\|_F^2$$

where $\| \cdot \|_F$ denotes the Frobenius norm as defined at the start of this chapter. Then we have that

$$\|(\hat{C} - AB)\|_F \leq \epsilon \|A\|_F \|B\|_F.$$

Further Discussion. Note that to have this property hold, we require each entry to meet its guarantee. This is achievable by increasing the size of the sketches by a factor of $O(\log n)$. Then each entry is estimated accurately with probability $1 - 1/n^3$, and so all n^2 entries are accurate with probability $1 - 1/n$, by a union bound.

Intuitively, this increased size of the sketches does not seem necessary: while some entries might exceed their permitted error bounds, others might lie comfortably within them, and we might expect this variation to cancel out on average. Essentially this is indeed the case, although proving it is rather more fiddly.

A first attempt is to consider the total squared error as a random variable, and apply error bounds to this, rather than each individual entrywise error. We have already calculated the expectation and variance of the entrywise errors, so we can immediately obtain expectation and variance of their sum. It might seem that we can then immediately apply the Chebyshev and Chernoff argument to this. However, there is a twist: previously, we were able to take the median of a (scalar) quantity to obtain an estimate with high probability of falling within our desired error bounds. But now, each sketch yields a candidate approximate matrix product: how should we take the median of a collection of matrices?

One approach is to use the fact that we can accurately estimate the norms of matrices, and the norm of differences between pairs of matrices. We can argue that with probability at least $1 - \delta$, one of our matrices is "central" among the estimates built from sketches: it is at most a distance of $\|A\|_F\|B\|_F/2$ to each of at least half of the other estimated matrices. This follows by arguing that there is a constant probability that each estimated matrix is "good" – that is, close (as a function of $\|A\|_F\|B\|_F$) to the target C; and therefore, by the triangle inequality, any pair of "good" matrices must also be close to each other. Performing this distance test helps to identify one good matrix, which can be reported as the approximate product.

A more direct approach is to go back to the original approach and argue that the sketches provide a stronger property: that they estimate not just one inner product accurately with constant probability, but that (with constant probability) they estimate *all* inner products accurately, and so we can work directly with the results of sketching. This stronger property is referred to as *subspace embedding*, and is discussed in more detail when we consider the regression problem.

History and Background. The observation that (dense) sketches allow us to estimate all entries is due to Sarlós [205] and uses an additional randomized trick to pick the estimate of C that is closest to C. Clarkson and Woodruff argue that sparse sketches are sufficient and introduce the technique based on finding one matrix that is close to a majority of the others [55]. They also show a stronger bound on sketch estimators, when constructed with more powerful hash functions. A more thorough survey that expands on the subspace embedding approach is given by Woodruff [235].

6.4 Compressed Matrix Multiplication

Given two matrices A and B, both of size $n \times n$, computing their product $C = AB$ is a fundamental problem. Despite years of extensive research, exact matrix multiplication remains an expensive operation. In this section, we present a method that allows us to compute C approximately in a compressed form. More precisely, we first compute the Count Sketch of each column of A and each row of B. Then from these sketches we will compute the Count Sketch of C, interpreted as a long vector of size n^2. As a result, all the properties of the Count Sketch from Section 3.5 apply here. For example, from this sketch, we can estimate any entry in C with error at most $\|C\|_F / \sqrt{t}$ with high probability, where, as before, $\| \cdot \|_F$ denotes the *Frobenius norm*, i.e., $\|C\|_F = \sqrt{\sum_{i,j} C_{i,j}^2}$.

Recall from Section 3.5 that (one row of) the Count Sketch of a vector v of size n is another vector $S(v)$ of size $t \ll n$ (both vectors are indexed starting from 0), where

$$S(v)[k] = \sum_{i \in [n]: h(i)=k} g(i) v_i, k = 0, \ldots, t - 1.$$

Here, $h : [n] \to [t]$ is a pairwise independent hash function, and $g : [n] \to \{-1, +1\}$ is also a pairwise independent hash function. Also recall that $S(v)$ can be constructed from v easily in one pass; in particular, this is still true if v is represented in a "compressed form," i.e., a list of (index, value) pairs consisting of all the nonzero entries of the vector.

Let u, v be two column vectors of size n. At the heart of the method is a nice way to compute $S(uv^T)$ from $S(u)$ and $S(v)$, where uv^T is the *outer product* of u and v, and $S(uv^T)$ is a Count Sketch built on uv^T interpreted as a vector of size n^2. Recall that the outer product of u and v is

$$uv^T = \begin{bmatrix} u_1 v_1 & u_1 v_2 & \cdots & u_1 v_n \\ u_2 v_1 & u_2 v_2 & \cdots & u_2 v_n \\ \vdots & \vdots & \ddots & \vdots \\ u_n v_1 & u_n v_2 & \cdots & u_n v_n \end{bmatrix}.$$

Let the two hash functions used in constructing $S(u)$ and $S(v)$ be h_u, g_u and h_v, g_v, respectively. The idea is to compute the *convolution* of $S(u)$ and $S(v)$. Recall that given two vectors a and b of size n, their convolution $a * b$ is vector of size $2n - 1$, where

$$(a * b)[k] = \sum_{j=0}^{k} a[j]b[k - j], k = 0, \ldots, 2n - 2.$$

The nice thing about convolution is that it can be computed efficiently using the Fast Fourier Transform (FFT) in $O(n \log n)$ time [63].

Next, we will interpret the convolution $S(u) * S(v)$ as a sketch of a new object. The convolution yields a vector of size $2t - 1$, where for $k = 0, 1, \ldots, 2t - 2$,

$$(S(u) * S(v))[k] = \sum_{j=0}^{k} S(u)[j]S(v)[k - j]$$

$$= \sum_{j=0}^{k} \left(\sum_{i \in [n]:h_u(i)=j} g_u(i)u_i \right) \left(\sum_{i \in [n]:h_v(i)=k-j} g_v(i)v_i \right)$$

$$= \sum_{i, j \in [n]:h_u(i)+h_v(j)=k} g_u(i)g_v(j)u_i v_j.$$

This is exactly a **Count Sketch** built on uv^T, but using hash functions $h(i, j) = h_u(i) + h_v(j)$ and $g(i, j) = g_u(i)g_v(j)$. Since both g_u and g_v are pairwise independent functions mapping $[n]$ to $\{-1, +1\}$, $g(i, j) = g_u(i)g_v(j)$ is still a pairwise independent function mapping $[n]$ to $\{-1, +1\}$. However, $h(i, j) = h_u(i) + h_v(j)$ is no longer a pairwise independent function. In particular, it is not uniform on $[2t - 1]$. The last trick is to fold $S(u) * S(v)$ into a vector of size t, getting a true **Count Sketch** on uv^T, where

$$S(uv^T)[k] = \begin{cases} (S(u) * S(v))[k] + (S(u) * S(v))[k + t], & k = 0, 1, \ldots, t - 2; \\ (S(u) * S(v))[k], & k = t - 1. \end{cases}$$

$$= \sum_{i \in [n]:h_u(i)+h_v(j) \bmod t=k} g_u(i)g_v(j)u_i v_j.$$

Observing that $h(i, j) = h_u(i) + h_v(j) \bmod t$ is a pairwise independent function from $[n]$ to $[t]$, we conclude that $S(uv^T)$ is a valid **Count Sketch** on uv^T.

Finally, to use this technique to compute a **Count Sketch** on $C = AB$, we write A in terms of column vectors $a_1, \ldots, a_n$ and B in terms of row vectors

$b_1, \ldots, b_n$. The matrix product AB can be written as a sum of n products of these vectors (effectively, these are outer products), as

$$AB = \sum_{i=1}^{n} a_i b_i^T,$$

and because of the fact that the Count Sketch is a linear sketch, we can compute the Count Sketch of $C = AB$ as

$$S(C) = \sum_{i=1}^{n} S(a_i b_i^T).$$

Further Discussion. In practice, one does not have to compute the convolution $S(u) * S(v)$ in full and then fold the result as described in this section. The Count Sketch $S(uv^T)$ can be computed more directly by slightly adjusting the FFT algorithm. In computing the full convolution, we use the *convolution theorem*:

$$S(u) * S(v) = \text{FFT}_{2t}^{-1}(\text{FFT}_{2t}(S(u)) \cdot \text{FFT}_{2t}(S(v))).$$

Here, we perform the FFT using the $(2t)$th root of unity. However, if we simply use the tth root of unity ω_t, then the result of the convolution will be the folded $S(uv^T)$ directly. This is also known as a circular convolution. The intuition is that since $\omega_t^t = 1$, it has exactly the effect of doing the $\bmod t$ operation. More detailed arguments can be found in [199].

The preceding algorithm also easily extends to nonsquare matrices. Suppose A is an $n_1 \times n_2$ matrix and B is an $n_2 \times n_3$ matrix, then $C = AB$ will be a sum of n_2 outer products. Although each outer product is between two vectors of different lengths, this does not affect the algorithm in any way, as the sketch sizes of the two vectors are always the same, which is t.

The running time of the algorithm is $O(N + n_2 t \log t)$, where N is the number of nonzero entries in A and B. Note that this can be even smaller than $O(n_1 n_3)$, which is the size of C. This is because we compute $C = AB$ in a compressed form, represented by the Count Sketch of C. Reconstructing the full C (approximately) still takes $O(n_1 n_3)$ time, since we have to query the Count Sketch for every entry of C. In [199], a method is given to extract the most significant entries of C more quickly.

History and Background. The algorithm described in this section is due to Pagh [199]. Subsequent work generalized the approach of taking convolutions of sketches to quickly build a sketch of the tensor product of a vector: essentially, a polynomial generalization of the outer product [202].

6.5 Frequent Directions

Other summaries of matrices are possible, depending on what properties of the matrix we would like to (approximately) preserve. The FrequentDirections summary captures information about the action of the summarized matrix on other matrices and vectors. It does so by iteratively using the singular value decomposition (SVD) on summaries computed so far to capture the information needed while keeping the summary small.

The summary applies to a data matrix A of dimension $n \times d$, where we assume that n will grow very large, while d is of moderate size. The matrix A is formed as the collection of n row vectors, each of dimension d, where each row vector is seen together, i.e., rows arrive one by one. The summary of A will be a smaller matrix B with up to ℓ rows of dimension d, so that B approximates A. We will focus on the action of A on approximating an arbitrary vector x of dimension d. That is, our objective is to show that our summary B of matrix A ensures that the norm of Bx is close to the norm of Ax.

Operations on the Summary. To INITIALIZE a new FrequentDirections summary B, we simply instantiate a new zero matrix of size $\ell \times d$. The UPDATE procedure for a new row vector a_i involves the computation of the SVD of B. We append the new row a_i to B to obtain B', and compute its SVD. This gives us the decomposition $U \Sigma V^T = B'$, so that $U^T U = I_\ell$ and $V^T V = I_d$, i.e., these (singular) vectors are orthonormal. The matrix Σ is diagonal, consisting of the singular values $\sigma_1 \cdots \sigma_\ell$, sorted by magnitude (i.e., $|\sigma_1| \geq |\sigma_2| \geq \ldots \geq |\sigma_\ell|$). We use these values to rescale the different "directions" in B, and to "forget" the least important direction. We define a new diagonal matrix Σ' as

$$\Sigma' = \text{diag}\left(\sqrt{\sigma_1^2 - \sigma_\ell^2}, \sqrt{\sigma_2^2 - \sigma_\ell^2} \cdots \sqrt{\sigma_\ell^2 - \sigma_\ell^2} \right).$$

Equivalently, we can write $\Sigma' = \sqrt{\Sigma - \sigma_\ell^2 I_\ell}$. This ensures that $\Sigma'_{\ell,\ell} = 0$. We use Σ' as a new set of singular values, and obtain an updated version of the summary B as $B = \Sigma' V^T$. Observe that since $\Sigma_\ell = 0$, the new B has at most $\ell - 1$ nonzero rows, so we drop row ℓ (which is all zeros).

The MERGE procedure builds on the approach of the UPDATE procedure. Given two summary matrices B and C, both of size $\ell \times d$, we can simply take each row of C in turn and UPDATE B with it. This is rather slow (requiring ℓ invocations of the SVD procedure), but we can observe that this is equivalent to the following method. We begin by appending B and C to get a new matrix D of size $2\ell \times d$. We then compute the SVD of D and obtain the corresponding $U\Sigma V^T$. We now compute Σ' based on σ_ℓ^2, noting that σ_ℓ is the ℓ'th largest of the 2ℓ singular values in Σ. Then

$$\Sigma' = \text{diag}\left(\sqrt{\max(\sigma_1^2 - \sigma_\ell^2, 0)}, \sqrt{\max(\sigma_2^2 - \sigma_\ell^2, 0)} \ldots \sqrt{\max(\sigma_{2\ell}^2 - \sigma_\ell^2, 0)} \right).$$

Observe that the first ℓ values of Σ' will be nonnegative, while the last $\ell + 1$ values are guaranteed to be zero. Then, as before, we compute the new summary as $B = \Sigma' V^T$, and keep only the (at most $\ell - 1$) nonzero rows.

Further Discussion. Recall that we want to show that the final summary we obtain, B, is similar to the input matrix A in its action on a vector x. In particular, we will consider the quantity $\|Ax\|_2^2 - \|Bx\|_2^2$. We can analyze the accuracy of the summary by considering the effect on the error of answering a particular query. Without loss of generality, let x be a vector of dimension d, with $\|x\|_2 = 1$. We will measure the error in terms of Euclidean norms (of vectors) and Frobenius norms (of matrices). Consider the quantity Ax, which we will approximate by Bx for the final summary B. We want to show that the difference in magnitude of these quantities is not too large, i.e., $\|Ax\|_2^2 - \|Bx\|_2^2$ is bounded. For simplicity, we will focus on the effect of a sequence of UPDATE operations.

A bound on this quantity follows by summing over the error introduced in each subsequent UPDATE operation. We first show that the error is nonnegative, i.e., that $\|Ax\|_2^2 - \|Bx\|_2^2 \geq 0$. We'll write $B_{[i]}$ for the summary obtained after the ith UPDATE row operation for row a_i. We also write $C_{[i]}$ to denote the value of $\sigma_{[i]} V_{[i]}^T$ computed from the SVD in step i. Finally, δ_i is the value of σ_ℓ^2 that is subtracted from the other singular values in the ith UPDATE operation.

Then we can expand

$$\|Ax\|_2^2 - \|B_{[n]}x\|_2^2 = \sum_{i=1}^n \left((a_i \cdot x)^2 + \|B_{[i-1]}\|_2^2 x - \|B_{[i]}x\|_2^2 \right)$$

$$= \sum_{i=1}^n \left(\|C_{[i]}x\|_2^2 - \|B_{[i]}x\|_2^2 \right) \geq 0$$

This makes use of the fact that $C_{[i]}$ preserves all the information about $B_{[i-1]}$ and a, so that $\|B_{[i-1]}x\|_2^2 + (a_i \cdot x)^2 = \|C_{[i]}x\|_2^2$. Meanwhile, $B_{[i]}$ loses information from $C_{[i]}$, so we have $\|C_{[i]}x\|_2^2 - \|B_{[i]}x\|_2^2 \geq 0$.

Next we consider placing an upper bound on the error $\|Ax\|_2^2 - \|Bx\|_2^2$. For step i, let $v_j[i]$ denote the j'th column of $V_{[i]}^T$. Then $C_{[i]}x = \sum_{j=1}^{\ell} \sigma_j v_j \cdot x$ and

$$\|C_{[i]}x\|_2^2 = \sum_{j=1}^{\ell} \sigma_j^2 (v_j \cdot x)^2$$

$$= \sum_{j=1}^{\ell} (\sigma_j'^2 + \delta_i)(v_j \cdot x)^2$$

$$= \sum_{j=1}^{\ell} \sigma_j'^2 (v_j \cdot x)^2 + \delta_i \sum_{j=1}^{\ell} (v_j \cdot x)^2$$

$$= \|B_{[i]}x\|_2^2 + \delta_i.$$

The final line substitutes the definition of $B_{[i]}$ using the reweighted values in Σ', and the fact that V^T is a unitary matrix while $\|x\|_2 = 1$. We can then sum this over every UPDATE step:

$$\|Ax\|_2^2 - \|B_{[n]}x\|_2^2 = \sum_{i=1}^{n} \left((a_i \cdot x)^2 + \|B_{[i-1]}x\|_2^2 - \|B_{[i]}x\|_2^2 \right)$$

$$= \sum_{i=1}^{n} \left(\|C_{[i]}x\|_2^2 - \|B_{[i]}x\|_2^2 \right)$$

$$\leq \sum_{i=1}^{n} \delta_i. \tag{6.1}$$

To bound δ_i, note that the squared Frobenius norm of a matrix is given by the sum of the squares of its singular values. Hence,

$$\|C_{[i]}\|_F^2 \geq \|B_{[i]}\|_F^2 + \ell\delta_i.$$

In each update, we start by appending the new row a_i, which causes the squared Frobenius norm to increase:

$$\|C_{[i]}\|_F^2 = \|B_{[i-1]}\|_F^2 + \|a_i\|_2^2.$$

Last, $\|A\|_F^2 = \sum_{i=1}^{n} \|a_i\|_2^2$. Rearranging and combining these three results, we obtain that $\|A\|_F^2 \geq \|B_{[n]}\|_F^2 + \ell \sum_{i=1}^{n} \delta_i$. Combining this with (6.1), we have our desired bound on the error,

$$0 \leq \|Ax\|_2^2 - \|B_{[n]}x\|_2^2 \leq (\|A\|_F^2 - \|B\|_F^2)/\ell \leq \|A\|_F^2/\ell.$$

Via a slightly longer argument, we can show stronger bounds in terms of A_k, which is the optimal k-rank approximation of A. A_k can be found via the SVD of $A = U \Sigma V^T$: defining U_k and V_k as the first k columns of U and V respectively, and Σ_k as the diagonal matrix containing k largest entries of Σ, we have $A_k = U_k \Sigma_k V_k^T$. Then we find

$$0 \leq \|Ax\|_2^2 - \|B_{[n]}x\|_2^2 \leq \|A - A_k\|_F^2/(\ell - k).$$

That is, provided ℓ is chosen suitably larger than k, we obtain a good approximation in terms of A_k.

Properties of the MERGE operation follow similarly, by considering the accuracy of two summaries, and arguing that the total error is bounded in terms of the sum of the local errors.

Implementation Issues. Computing the SVD of an $\ell \times d$ matrix (the central step in the UPDATE operation) takes time $O(d\ell^2)$. This is quite time consuming if carried out every step. The cost can be reduced by reducing the frequency with which SVD is found, but storing some extra space. Essentially, we keep a buffer of the most recent ℓ rows, then perform a MERGE operation with the running summary. This amortizes the cost of the SVD to $O(d\ell)$ time per update and keeps the space used to $O(d\ell)$ also.

History and Background. The FrequentDirections summary was introduced by Liberty [172], taking inspiration from the behavior of frequent items algorithms, particularly the MG summary. Additional results, including lower bounds and the extension to handling a MERGE operation, are due to Woodruff [234] and Ghashami and Phillips [111] respectively. Our presentation follows the outline of Ghashami et al. [110]. Due to its simplicity and flexibility, the summary has been widely used to summarize large datasets for machine learning, such as in feature selection, dimensionality reduction, and outlier detection.

Available Implementations. The FrequentDirections summary has garnered a lot of interest since it was first described, and several

6.6 Regression and Subspace Embeddings

The problem of regression can be expressed in terms of matrices and vectors. Given a "data" matrix A of size $n \times d$, and a corresponding "response" vector b of dimension n, the aim is to find a vector x of coefficients so as to minimize the quantity $\|Ax - b\|_p$. That is, our goal is to find

$$\arg \min_x \|Ax - b\|_p.$$

The norm p to minimize is a parameter of the problem. We will focus on the common case of $p = 2$, which gives the ordinary least squares regression problem.

We make use of a useful concept, an (oblivious) subspace embedding. Given an $n \times d$ matrix A, the matrix S is a subspace embedding for A if, for all $x \in \mathcal{R}^d$,

$$(1 - \epsilon)\|Ax\|_2^2 \leq \|SAx\|_2^2 \leq (1 + \epsilon)\|Ax\|_2^2. \tag{6.2}$$

In other words, (SA) approximates A in terms of the length of vectors x under the action of the matrix. We say that the embedding is *oblivious* if S is sampled at random from a distribution of matrices, independent of A. That is, we do not have to look at A to be (almost) certain that a sampled S gives a subspace embedding for A.

Observe that this definition appears quite similar to that for the Johnson–Lindenstrauss transform Sparse JLT (Section 5.5), except that transform does not specify a matrix A. It should therefore not be surprising that any Johnson–Lindenstrauss transform provides an oblivious subspace embedding, after some adjustment of parameters. The Count Sketch gives a weaker result than the Sparse JLT, but it can also be used for a subspace embedding via a different argument. The necessary size of the summary is somewhat larger, but we gain in terms of time cost: the Count Sketch is much faster to apply than even the Sparse JLT, due to its increased sparsity.

Given a subspace embedding, we can apply it immediately to approximately solve a regression problem. We apply the definition of the subspace embedding (Equation 6.2) to the $n \times (d + 1)$ matrix A' formed by concatenating A with b.

This means for any vector y in the $d + 1$-dimensional subspace spanned by A', we have $\|Sy\|_2^2 \in (1 \pm \epsilon)\|y\|_2^2$. In particular, we can consider only those y for which the final component is fixed to the value of -1. Rewriting, the problem of least squares regression is to find

$$\arg\min_x \|Ax - b\|_2^2 = \arg\min_{y:y_{d+1}=-1} \|A'y\|_2^2.$$

By the preceding discussion, we replace $A'y$ with $(SA')y$ and solve the (smaller) regression instance

$$\arg\min_{y:y_{d+1}=-1} \|(SA')y\|_2^2$$

using whatever method we prefer. For example, we could use the closed form $x = (A^T S^T S^T A)^{-1} A^T S^T b$ or apply gradient descent.

We can observe that this approach is quite general. For instance, the problem of constrained regression additionally imposes constraints on the solution. That is, $x \in C$ for some (usually convex) set C. Then the same approach works, since additionally constraining x does not affect the accuracy of S. Hence we just need to be able to solve the (smaller) constrained regression instance given by (SA) and (Sb) in place of A and b. For example, the popular LASSO regression model imposes the (L_1 regularization) condition $\|x\|_1 \leq \tau$, for some parameter τ. This can immediately be applied in this reduced dimensionality instance.

History and Background. The notion of using dimensionality reduction to speed up regression, and the demonstration of the subspace embedding property is due to Sarlós [205]. Clarkson and Woodruff showed that Count Sketch could give similar results in time proportional to the input sparsity [55]. Nelson and Nguyen [194] and Woodruff and Zhang [237] variously give improved bounds for oblivious subspace embeddings and their applications. A more detailed discussion, including omitted technical proofs, is given by Woodruff [235].

7

Graph Summaries

Graphs are a ubiquitous model for complex networks, with applications spanning biology, social network analysis, route planning, and operations research. As the data represented in these applications increase in size, so do the corresponding graphs. This chapter describes summaries that apply to graphs. A graph G is defined by its vertex set V and its edge set E. We assume that V is known, while the edges E can vary. For simplicity, we consider only simple graphs, that is, graphs that are undirected, do not have edge weights, and do not have self-loops.

The graph summaries that we describe tend to have the property that their size is at least proportional to $|V|$, the number of vertices. Although this quantity can still be offputtingly large in many applications, it is the case that there are often hard lower bounds that mean that no summary can exist with size that is asymptotically smaller than $|V|$. Lower bound techniques and some lower bounds for graph problems are discussed in Section 10.

Summaries differ, depending on what kinds of updates are allowed. Some problems that are straightforward when edges are only added to the graph (such as keeping track of the connected components of the graph) become more complex when edges can be added and removed.

7.1 Graph Sketches

Brief Summary. The Graph Sketch summary allows the connected components of a graph to be found. It makes clever use of the ℓ_0-sampler summary (Section 3.9) applied to inputs derived from graphs. The algorithm stores a number of ℓ_0-sampler summaries for each node. If the graph consists of only edge arrivals, then the problem is much easier: we can keep track of which nodes are in which components, and update this assignment as more information arrives. However, when there can be edge departures as well as arrivals, this simple approach breaks down, and a more involved solution is needed.

The idea behind the Graph Sketch summary is to allow a basic algorithm for connectivity to be simulated. The basic algorithm is to start with each node in a component of its own, then repeatedly find edges from the (current) edge set that connect two different components, and merge these components. If this is performed for all edges in parallel, then a small number of iterations is needed before the components have been found. The insight behind the Graph Sketch is to define an encoding of the graph structure to allow the summary to be built and for this algorithm outline to be applied.

Algorithm 7.1: Graph Sketch: INITIALIZE (r)

1 **for** $j \leftarrow 1$ **to** r **do**
2   **for** $i \leftarrow 1$ **to** n **do**
3       $S_{i,j} \leftarrow \ell_0$-sampler.INITIALIZE$(n, 1/n^2)$;

Operations on the Summary. To INITIALIZE a Graph Sketch, we create a set of $r = \log n$ ℓ_0-sampler summaries for each of the n nodes.

Algorithm 7.2: Graph Sketch: UPDATE $((u, v))$

1 $a \leftarrow \min(u, v)$;
2 $b \leftarrow \max(u, v)$;
3 **for** $j \leftarrow 1$ **to** r **do**
4    $S_{a,j}$.UPDATE$(a * n + b, + 1)$;
5    $S_{b,j}$.UPDATE$(a * n + b, - 1)$;

To UPDATE the Graph Sketch with a new edge (u, v), we first encode it as an update to the ℓ_0-sampler summaries for node u and node v. We can assume that u and v are both represented as integers, and we assume that $u < v$ (if not, interchange the roles of u and v). We also assume that we can treat the edge (u, v) as an item that can be processed by the ℓ_0-sampler summaries (for concreteness, we can think of (u, v) as being encoded by the integer $\min(u, v) * n + \max(u, v)$).

We UPDATE the ℓ_0-sampler summaries associated with node u with the item (u, v) and a weight update of $+1$. We also UPDATE the ℓ_0-sampler summaries associated with node v with the item (u, v) and a weight update of -1. Note that it is also straightforward to process edge deletions by swapping the $+1$ and -1 weights in the UPDATE procedure.

Algorithm 7.3: Graph Sketch: QUERY ( )

---

1   $C \leftarrow \emptyset$;

2   **for** $i \leftarrow 1$ **to** n **do**

3      $C_i = \{i\}$;

4      $C \leftarrow C \cup \{C_i\}$;

5      $T_i = i$;

6   **for** $j \leftarrow 1$ **to** r **do**

7   **forall** $C \in C$ **do**

8          $S \leftarrow \ell_0\text{-sampler}.\text{INITIALIZE}(n, 1/n^2)$;

9   **forall** $i \in C$ **do**

10            $\text{MERGE}(S, S_{i,j})$;

11          $(u, v) = S.\text{QUERY}()$;

12   **forall** $w \in C_{T_v}$ **do**

13            $T_w \leftarrow T_u$;
           /* Update the component information   */

14          $C_{T_u} \leftarrow C_{T_u} \cup C_{T_v}$;

15          $C \leftarrow C \setminus \{C_{T_v}\}$;

16 **return** C;

The QUERY procedure is rather involved. We begin by placing each node in a component of its own, with a unique label. We then repeat the following procedure for r rounds. In round j, create a sketch for each component by performing MERGE of the jth sketch of each of the nodes in the component. We then query this sketch to sample an edge. The crux of the process is that, because of the update procedure, the edge sampled is guaranteed to be outgoing from the component (if there are any such edges). This edge is used to combine the component with another. At the end of the rounds, the current set of components is returned as the set of connected components in the graph.

The pseudocode in Algorithm 7.3 introduces some extra notation to describe this procedure. Lines 3 to 5 initialize this by creating n initial components, $C_1 \ldots C_n$, and stores the set of components as C. For convenience of reference, it also instantiates a map from nodes to component identifiers, so that T_u means that node u is part of component C_{T_u}.

The main loop in the pseudocode is over component C in round j. The sketch S is built as the merger of all the sketches of nodes i in component C (line 10), from which an outgoing edge is found (line 11). Based on this edge

(u, v), we assign all the nodes in the component of v to be in the component of u (line 13). We then combine the components of u and v (line 14), and remove the component of v from the set of components C.

Example. For an example, we show a small graph, and study the way that its edges are encoded before being placed into the sketch. Consider the following graph:

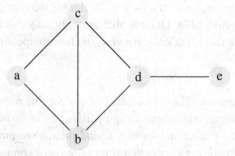

The initial encoding of the edges can be described in the following table:

	(a,b)	(a,c)	(a,d)	(a,e)	(b,c)	(b,d)	(b,e)	(c,d)	(c,e)	(d,e)
a	+1	+1								
b	−1				+1	+1				
c		−1			−1			+1		
d						−1		−1		+1
e										−1

Each node is associated with one row of the table that encodes its neighbors. Here, we index the rows by the identity of the edges (in the pseudocode description, we convert these to use a canonical integer representation). Node b is linked to three neighbors, a, c, and d. Since a comes before b in the (alphabetic) ordering of the node, edge (a, b) is represented by a -1 in the table, while edges (b, c) and (b, d) are encoded as $+1$ in b's row in the table. Observe that each edge is thus represented twice, with a $+1$ for one occurrence and a -1 for the other. Note that the table itself is not stored explicitly; rather, the summary keeps an instance of an ℓ_0-sampler for each row.

Now suppose that after one iteration of the algorithm, we have chosen to merge nodes a and c into one cluster, and b, d, and e into another. We now obtain the resulting table for the clusters:

	(a,b)	(a,c)	(a,d)	(a,e)	(b,c)	(b,d)	(b,e)	(c,d)	(c,e)	(d,e)
{a, c}	+1	0			−1			+1		
{b,d,e}	−1				1	0		−1		0

The row {a, c} in the new table is the result of summing the rows a and c from the first table (in the summary, we have obtain an ℓ_0-sampler of this sum). Here, we write 0 to denote where a +1 and −1 have co-occurred and annihilated each other. Similarly, the row {b, d, e} is the sum of the three rows b, d, e from the first table. Observe that the only edges that remain in this representation are those that cross between the two components: (a,b), (b,c), and (c,d).

Further Discussion. The correctness of the algorithm depends critically on the encoding of edges, and the properties of the ℓ_0-sampler structure. Consider a collection of nodes C and their corresponding merged ℓ_0-sampler structure. Observe that if an edge (u, v) connects two nodes $u \in C, v \in C$, then the contribution of this edge in the sketch is exactly 0: it is represented with +1 in the sketch of u and −1 in the sketch of v, so when these are merged together, the net contribution is zero. Therefore, this "internal" edge cannot be sampled from the merged sketch. Hence, only "outgoing" edges (where one node is in C and the other is not in C) can be drawn from the sketch.

The rest of the analysis then reduces to analyzing the algorithm that picks one outgoing edge from each component in each round, and merges the pairs of components. The number of components must at least halve in every round (excluding any connected components that have already been fully discovered), hence the number of rounds is at most $\log n$ since we start with n components (each containing a single node).

It remains to argue that, over all the accesses to sketches, the chance of failing to draw a sample from any is very low. From the preceding analysis, it follows that over the rounds we make no more than $n + n/2 + n/4 + \cdots < 2n$ calls to the QUERY routine for an ℓ_0-sampler structure. If we set the failure probability of each of these to be at most $1/n^2$, then the chance that there is any failure across all the whole operation of the Graph Sketch structure is still very small, $2/n$, by appealing to the union bound (Fact 1.6).

It is important for the correctness of the algorithm that independent sketches (using different random hash functions) are used in each round.

This ensures that we can correctly analyze the probability of success. For intuition, observe that if it were possible to use a single set of ℓ_0-sampler structures (one for each node), then we could use them to extract incident edges on each node, delete these edges from the summaries, and repeat until we have found all edges in the graph. That would allow the recovery of $O(n^2)$ edges from n summaries of small size – intuitively, this should be impossible! Indeed, this intuition can be formalized, and so we cannot hope to "recycle" the summaries so aggressively.

History and Background. The idea of graph sketches was introduced by Ahn et al. in [7]. They used variations of this idea to also establish k-connectivity of graphs (where the graph remains connected even up to the removal of k nodes) and bipartiteness (by expressing bipartiteness in terms of the number of connected components in a derived graph). However, since we need to keep multiple ℓ_0-sampler summaries for all n nodes, each of which is typically kilobytes in size [65], the space cost for this summary is quite large.

Similar summary ideas have been used for the problem of dynamic graph connectivity in polylogarithmic time [154]. Here, it is required to maintain an explicit representation of the connected components capable of answering whether a pair of nodes u and v are in the same component quickly.

7.2 Spanners

Brief Summary. A k-spanner of a graph G is a subgraph H (both defined over vertices V) so that for any pair of nodes u and v

$$d_G(u,v) \leq d_H(u,v) \leq k d_G(u,v).$$

That is, every distance in G is stretched by a factor of at most k in its Spanner. Spanners can be relatively easy to build, but come with some limitations. The first is that the values of k tend to be moderate constants, say 3 or 5 – whereas, in many cases we would prefer that k be close to 1 to preserve distances as much as possible. However, it is only with these larger k values that we can guarantee that the Spanner will be smaller than the original graph G. The second is that the Spanner we describe does not have a MERGE operation – they can only be built incrementally by a sequence of UPDATE operations. This restricts their applicability.

Algorithm 7.4: Spanner: INITIALIZE (V, k)

---

1 $H \leftarrow (V, \emptyset)$;
2 Record the value of k ;

Algorithm 7.5: Spanner: UPDATE $((u, v))$

---

1 **if** $d_H(u, v) > k$ **then**
2 $\quad \lfloor \quad E \leftarrow E \cup \{(u, v)\}$;

Operations on the Summary. To INITIALIZE a new Spanner based on stretch
parameter k, we create an empty graph on the vertex set V, and store k. To
UPDATE a Spanner with a new edge (u, v), we consider whether it is necessary
to add the edge. If the distance between u and v in the current version of the
stored graph H is at most the stretch parameter k, then we do not need to store
it. Otherwise, we do need to retain this edge to keep the promise, and so it is
added to H. This is shown in Algorithm 7.5.

The queries that the spanner supports are distance and reachability queries.
Given a pair of nodes (u, v), we approximate their distance in the input graph
G by returning their distance in the Spanner graph H, as $d_H(u, v)$.

Example. Consider the following graph, processed by the algorithm with
parameter $k = 3$:

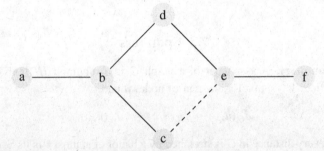

Suppose we have processed all edges up to the dashed edge (c, e). All edges
up to this point are retained in the summary, as none can be dropped without
disconnecting the graph. For edge (c, e), the graph distance between nodes c
and e is 3 – via c, b, d, e. So the edge (c, e) is not retained in the summary.

Now any distance in the graph is preserved up to a factor of (at most) 3.
The distance between c and f is 2 in the original graph, but is 4 in the spanner,
since the direct edge (c, e) is replaced by the path c, b, d, e.

Further Discussion. There are two steps to arguing that H provides a spanner of bounded size. First, we argue that the distances in H only stretch by a factor of k. Consider some path in G, which is a sequence of edges. In the worst case, none of these edges are retained in H. But if this is the case, then we know that for each edge that was discarded, there is a path in H of k edges. So the path in G is replaced by one at most k times longer.

The second part is to argue that the size of H does not grow too large. For this, we rely on some facts from the area of "extremal graph theory," regarding the graphs that lack some particular subgraph [33]. By construction, graph H has no cycles of size $k + 1$ (or smaller) – since the last edge to arrive in the cycle would be dropped by the summary construction algorithm. Such graphs can have at most $O(n^{1 + \frac{2}{k+1}})$ edges. For moderate values of k, say $k = 3$, we get guarantees that the size of H is certain to be much smaller than the theoretical maximum of n^2 possible edges in G.

Implementation Issues. A key implementation requirement is to be able to find $d_H(u, v)$ online as new edges are added to the Spanner. Efficient algorithms and data structures for this problem are beyond the scope of this volume, but this consideration has played into other algorithms for Spanner construction.

History and Background. The simple algorithm for Spanner construction described earlier is due to Feigenbaum et al. [102]. There has been much subsequent work on the problem of maintaining Spanners as edges are added. In particular, Elkin shows how to improve the time to process each edge with a randomized algorithm [97].

7.3 Properties of Degree Distributions via Frequency Moments

The degree distribution of a graph describes the number of nodes that have a particular degree. For many large graphs of interest (representing social networks, patterns of communication, etc.), the degree distribution can be approximately described by a small number of parameters. For example, in many cases, the distribution is heavily skewed: a small number of nodes have high degree, while the majority have very low degree (the long tail). Such behavior is often modeled by a power-law distribution: the fraction of nodes with degree d is taken to be proportional to d^{-z}, for a parameter z typically in the range 0.5 to 2.

Since the degree distribution can be captured as a vector, indexed by node identifiers, it is natural to apply many of the summaries seen previously to describe its properties. For example, we might naturally find the identifiers of the nodes with highest degree using summaries such as SpaceSaving or Count-Min Sketch (Chapter 3). Improved results are possible by mixing different sampling approaches: a KMV sample of the nodes to describe the behavior of the "head" of the frequency distribution, and a uniform RandomSample of the nodes to describe the behavior of the "tail" [212]. Tracking the sum of squares of degrees, i.e., F_2 via AMS Sketch, may allow the estimation of parameters of models such as a power-law distribution.

These analyses assume that the graph is presented so that each edge is observed only once. In some settings, we may see each edge multiple times (e.g., seeing multiple emails between a pair of communicating parties), but only wish to count it once. We can track the total number of distinct edges seen via HLL. For more complex queries, we can combine various of our summaries. For example, we can estimate the underlying degree of each node u, given by the number of distinct neighbors v of u seen among the edges. This can be done by nesting a distinct counting summary (e.g., HLL) within a frequent items structure (e.g., Count-Min Sketch). This approach is discussed at more length in Section 9.4.3.

7.4 Triangle Counting via Frequency Moments

Many analyses of graph-structured data rely on the notion of the triangle: a complete subgraph on three nodes. Detecting and counting such local structure can be hard when the graph to be analyzed is large, and possibly broken into multiple distributed pieces. Nevertheless, there has been a large amount of effort directed at problems to do with triangles: sampling a representative triangle, approximately counting the number of triangles, and so on.

Here we describe one method for estimating the number of triangles in a graph based on summaries described earlier. Given a graph $G = (V, E)$, each triangle is defined by a triple $(u, v, w) \in V^3$ such that $(u, v) \in E$, $(v, w) \in E$, and $(u, w) \in E$. We proceed by converting each edge into a list of the possible triangles that it can be a member of: from edge (u, v), we generate (u, v, w) for all $w \in V$. We then consider a vector x that encodes the total number of occurrences of each possible triangle: $x_{(u,v,w)}$ counts the number of times that possible triangle (u, v, w) is listed.

If each edge is seen exactly once in the description of G, then the number of triangles in G is the number of entries that are 3 in the vector x. A value of 3 can arise at index (u, v, w) only if all three edges (u, v), (v, w) and (u, w) are seen in the input. Tracking x exactly will require a lot of storage ($O(n^3)$ space to describe all possible triangles), and so we will use summaries. We have summaries that can approximate $F_2(x)$, i.e., $\sum_i x_i^2$, such as the AMS Sketch. We can also approximate $F_0(x)$, i.e., $\sum_{i:x_i \neq 0} 1$, such as the HLL. Lastly, we can compute $F_1(x)$ directly, as the sum of all entries in x.

Since the possible values in x are restricted to $\{0, 1, 2, 3\}$, we can use an algebraic trick to count only the entries that are 3. Observe that the polynomial $p(y) = 1 - 1.5y + 0.5y^2$ behaves as follows

$$p(1) = 0 \qquad p(2) = 0 \qquad p(3) = 1.$$

Now observe that $P(x) = F_0(x) - 1.5F_1(x) + 0.5F_2(x)$ is equivalent to counting 0 for each zero entry of x, and applying polynomial p to each nonzero entry of x. Consequently, $P(x)$ counts the number of triangles in G exactly.

By using summaries, we are able to approximate $P(x)$. We obtain an error of $\epsilon(F_0(x) + F_2(x))$ in our estimate – note that we can maintain $F_1(x)$ exactly with a counter. There's no immediate guarantee that the error term $\epsilon(F_0(x) + F_2(x))$ is related to the number of triangles T, and indeed, one can create graphs that have no triangles, but for which $F_0(x)$ and $F_2(x)$ are quite large. However, we can easily show that $F_0(x) \leq F_1(x)$ and $F_2(x) \leq 3F_1(x)$, and that $F_1(x) < mn$, where $m = |E|$ and $n = |V|$. Consequently, we obtain an error guarantee of at most $4\epsilon mn$.

A limitation of this approach is that the step of generating all possible triangles for edge (u, v) to feed into summaries would require $O(n)$ UPDATE operations if done explicitly. To make this efficient, we must adopt summaries for F_0 and F_2 that are efficient to update when presented with an implicit list of updates. That is, edge (u, v) implies a list of edges (u, v, w) for all $w \in V$. Such summaries are called *list efficient*.

History and Background. This approach to triangle counting is due to Bar-Yossef et al. [20]. This work introduced list-efficient summaries for F_0. They adapt prior work of Gilbert et al. on estimating F_2 to be list efficient for the lists of triangles that are generated [116]. Subsequent work has aimed to provide more efficient list-efficient summaries [201, 223]. Other approaches to counting triangles are based on sampling and counting, and so tend to imply summaries that can perform UPDATE but not MERGE operations (i.e., they process streams of edges). Some examples include the work of Jowhari and Ghodsi [149], Buriol et al. [44], Pavan et al. [200], and most recently McGregor et al. [180].

7.5 All-Distances Graph Sketch

The all-distances graph sketch (ADS) keeps information about the neighborhood of every node v in a graph G. It allows us to approximate functions based on the number of nodes at different distances from v. For example, a basic question would be, "how many nodes are within distance d from node v?" More generally, it can also answer questions such as, "how many red nodes are within distance d from node v?" (if each node has a different color), or, "compute the sum of the reciprocals of the distances of all nodes from v." Formally, we can compute arbitrary functions of the form $\sum_u f(u, d(u, v))$. The sum is over all nodes u in the same connected component as v, and allows the function f to specify a value based on the information of node u (e.g., color) and the graph distance between u and v, given as $d(u, v)$.

The summary can be instantiated based on a number of different summaries for counting distinct items, such as KMV and HLL. For concreteness, we describe a version that builds on KMV (Section 2.5). Recall that the KMV structure keeps a summary of a set by applying a hash function h to each member of the set, and retaining only the k elements that achieve the k lowest hash values. The ADS extends KMV by keeping additional information on graph distances as well. Assume for now that we have convenient access to $d(u, v)$ for all nodes u and v in the graph. For simplicity, let us assume that all distances are distinct (this can be achieved by breaking ties based on node IDs, for example). Now we keep node u in the ADS structure for v if its hash value (under hash function h) is among the k smallest for all nodes w whose distance from v is at most $d(u, v)$.

Algorithm 7.6: ADS: INITIALIZE (v,k)

---

1 Pick hash function h, and store k;
2 Initialize list $L_v = \emptyset$;

The INITIALIZE operation for a node v (Algorithm 7.6) is almost identical to that for KMV: it picks a hash function h mapping onto a range $1 \ldots R$, and creates an empty list that will hold information on nodes.

Algorithm 7.7: ADS: UPDATE $(u, d(u, v))$

1 **if** $u \notin L_u$ **then**
2     $L_v \leftarrow L_v \cup \{(u, d(u, v), h(u))\}$;
3   **if** $|\{w \in L_v | d(w, v) \leq d(u, v)\}| > k$ **then**
4        $x \leftarrow \arg\max_{w \in L_v, d(w,v) \leq d(u,v)} h(w)$;
5   Remove x from L_v ;

The UPDATE operation to add information about a node u to the summary for node v (Algorithm 7.7) automatically inserts the new node into the data structure for v. It then checks if the condition on the number of nodes at distance at most $d(u, v)$ is violated, and if so, deletes the node within that distance with the maximal hash value.

The consequence of this definition is to draw a sample (via the randomly chosen hash function h) where the inclusion probability for a node depends on its distance from v. The k closest nodes to v are certain to be included. Nodes very far from v have a lower chance to be included, essentially a k/n chance, when there are n nodes in the (connected) graph G. For the node that has the ith farthest distance from v, the chance that it is kept in the ADS is $\min(1, k/i)$. Then, we can quickly see that the expected size of the ADS is $k + \sum_{i=k+1}^{n} k/i \leq k \ln n$. That is, a moderate factor than the $O(k)$ size of a regular KMV summary.

To appreciate the power of the ADS, we first consider the query to estimate the number of nodes whose distance is at most d from v. In the ADS data structure, we extract all stored nodes that meet this distance restriction. Note that, provided that in the full graph G there are at least k such nodes, then we will recover at least k nodes from the summary. This follows by definition of which nodes are held in the summary. Furthermore, we can consider what would have happened if we had built a KMV summary applied to only those nodes that meet the distance restriction, using the same hash function h. Then we would have retained at least k of the nodes extracted from the ADS. That is, we have all the information necessary in the ADS in order to extract a KMV summary of this subset of the input. Consequently, we can apply the QUERY procedure for KMV, which is based on the hash values of the retained elements to estimate the cardinality of the set from which they were drawn. This provides a $(1 \pm \epsilon)$ guarantee for the number of nodes within distance d, provided that $k = O(1/\epsilon^2)$. In the case when there are fewer than k nodes at distance d from v, then the ADS is required to keep all of them, and so we obtain the exact result.

Algorithm 7.8: ADS: QUERY (v, P, d)

---

1 $Q \leftarrow \{u | u \in L_v, d(u,v) \le d\}$;
2 **if** $|Q| \le k$ **then**
3 $\quad | \quad r = k$
4 **else**
5 $\quad | \quad v_k \leftarrow \max_{w \in Q} h(w)$;
6 $\quad \lfloor \quad r \leftarrow (k-1) * R/v_k$;
7 **return** $r * |\{u | u \in L_v, d(u,v) \le d, P(u) = \textbf{true}\}|/|Q|$

This approach forms the basis of answering more general queries. For queries such as, "how many red nodes are within distance d of v?" we again extract all nodes in the ADS summary that are within distance d. We use this to estimate the total number of nodes at distance d. We then inspect the nodes extracted, and compute the fraction that meet the predicate (colored red), and give our estimate of the number as this fraction times the total number within distance d. The error in this estimate is proportional to $\epsilon|N_d|$, where N_d is the number of nodes within distance d. This follows by analogy with applying predicates to the KMV summary, discussed in Section 2.5. Algorithm 7.8 shows how to apply predicate P and distance bound d to the summary of node v, and estimate the number of nodes meeting this predicate within distance d from v.

For more general functions $F(v) = \sum_u f(u, d(u,v))$, we can proceed by (notionally) iterating over every node u in the graph. For any given node, we can use the ADS to estimate its contribution to the approximation of $F(v)$. This is given by $f(u, d(u,v))$, scaled by the estimate for the number of nodes within this distance. Observe that for nodes w not stored in the ADS summary, we have a contribution of 0 to the estimate. Therefore, it suffices to just iterate over every node that is stored in ADS, and compute its contribution to the estimate.

It remains to discuss how to build an ADS summary for nodes in a graph without exhaustively computing the all-pairs shortest path distances. Assume that we want to compute the ADS summary for all nodes in G. We start by instantiating an empty summary for each node. We fill each summary by creating a "self-referential" entry for node v at distance 0 from itself. Then each node v can follow a "gossip" style algorithm: every time it hears about a new node distance pair (u, d), it can test whether it should be included in its current ADS (possibly evicting some pair that now no longer meets the criterion for inclusion). If (u, d) is added to v's ADS, then v can inform all its neighbors w about the new node, at distance $d + d(v, w)$. Note that a node v

might hear about the same node u through different paths. If so, v can ensure that it only retains information about u with its shortest distance. It is possible to see that this process will converge to the correct result, after a number of "rounds" proportional to the diameter of the graph. It's less immediate how to bound the cost of this procedure, but we can observe that we do not expect many nodes to propagate very far through the graph, due to the definition of the ADS summary. The total number of operations to insert nodes into ADS structures across the whole graph can ultimately be bounded by the product of the size of each structure times the number of edges, m, as $O(km \log n)$.

Example. We give a small example of the QUERY procedure for ADS with $k = 3$. Consider the following set of nodes, where for each node we list its distance from the node v, and its hash value (an integer in the range 1 to 20).

Node ID	Distance from v	Hash value
a	1	19
b	2	5
c	3	12
d	4	8
e	5	15
f	6	3
g	7	9
h	8	2

Then for $k = 3$ we would retain the set of nodes $\{a, b, c, d, f, h\}$. We retain d since it has a lower hash value than a, which has closer distance. We omit e since there are already three nodes with lower hash values at closer distance. Likewise, g is dropped since b, d, and f have lower hash values and smaller distances.

To estimate the number of nodes with distance 4 or less, we can extract the k nodes in the ADS summary that form a KMV summary: that is, b, c, and d (a would be dropped from the KMV summary). Our estimate is given by $(k - 1) * R/v_k$, where $R = 20$ is the range of the hash function and $v_k = 12$ is the kth highest hash value (see Algorithm 7.8 and discussion for the KMV QUERY operation in Section 2.5). This gives the estimate of 3.33 elements, which is tolerably close to the true result of 4. Note that we could have made more use of the information available, since we also have knowledge of a and its hash value. This is discussed by Cohen [57], who defines an improved estimator based on the "inverse probability" of each node to be included in the summary.

History and Background. The central ideas for the ADS are due to Cohen [56], who introduced the summary to estimate the number of nodes reachable from a node, and the size of the transitive closure in directed graphs. Our presentation follows a later generalization by Cohen [57] that goes on to consider different constructions of the ADS and tight bounds on their estimation accuracy based in the notion of "Historic Inverse Probability (HIP)" estimators.

8

Summaries over Distributed Data

Big data is often distributed. This can be due to space concerns – a single machine just cannot hold all the data, or efficiency concerns. Even if the entire dataset can be stored on one machine, it is often more efficient to split it up into many pieces and process them in parallel. The UPDATE and MERGE algorithms that have been provided in the previous chapters serve this purpose well: for each piece, we repeatedly UPDATE the summary with each individual data record, and then send the resulting summary to a central entity, who can then perform MERGE operations on all the summaries received.

In a distributed setting, communication is usually considered as the most important measure of cost. The aforementioned approach incurs a communication cost of $k \times s$, where s is the individual summary size and k is the number of pieces. However, sometimes one can improve upon this standard approach, reducing the communication cost significantly. In this chapter, we will see a few important examples where this is the case. For some other cases, like distinct count (Sections 2.5 and 2.6) and F_2 estimation (Section 3.6), it is known that the approach of sharing summaries is already optimal [236].

To make the presentation more precise, we adopt the following simple communication model, also called the *flat model* or the *star network* in the literature. We assume that the whole dataset is partitioned into k pieces, each held by a node. There is a dedicated central node, or the *coordinator*, who has a two-way communication channel with each of the k nodes. These k nodes do not communicate to each other directly, but they can pass messages via the coordinator if needed. Note that algorithms designed in the flat model can usually be applied to more general network topologies, with a communication cost that is h times that in the flat model, where h is the diameter of the network. In some cases, more efficient algorithms are known for general network topologies than directly applying the flat model algorithms, and proper references are provided in the "History and Background" section.

8.1 Random Sampling over a Distributed Set

Brief Summary. Recall from Section 2.2 that the goal of random sampling is to draw a random sample of size s without replacement from a set of n items. In the distributed setting, the whole set A is partitioned into k subsets $A_1, \ldots, A_k$, each of size $n_1, \ldots, n_k$, respectively. If we draw a random sample of size s from each subset, and then MERGE them together using the algorithm in Section 2.2, the total communication cost will be $O(ks)$. Here, we describe an algorithm with communication cost $O(k + s)$.

Operations on the Summary. The k nodes first send the sizes of their subsets, i.e., $n_1, \ldots, n_k$, to the coordinator. Then the idea is for the coordinator to simulate the sampling process using only these counts, and then retrieve the actual sampled items from the nodes. Specifically, the coordinator first decides the number of sampled items from each node using the following procedure. Let $n = n_1 + \cdots + n_k$. For the first sampled item, with probability n_i/n, it should come from A_i. So we pick A_i with probability n_i/n. Then it decrement n_i by one, and repeat the process. After s steps, the coordinator knows s_i, the number of sampled items it should retrieve from A_i for $i = 1, \ldots, k$. Then it sends s_i to the ith node, who then returns a random sample of size s_i from A_i. Finally, the random sample of the entire set is simply the union of the random samples returned from the k nodes. The pseudocode is given in Algorithm 8.1.

Algorithm 8.1: Random sampling over distributed data

---

1 **foreach** i **do**
2   ⎿ Node i sends n_i to Coordinator;

3 $n \leftarrow n_1 + \cdots n_k$;
4 $s_i \leftarrow 0, i = 1, \ldots, k$;
5 **for** $j \leftarrow 1$ **to** s **do**
6   Pick r uniformly from $\{1, \ldots, n\}$;
7   Find i such that $\sum_{\ell=1}^{i-1} n_i < r \leq \sum_{\ell=1}^{i} n_i$;
8     $s_i \leftarrow s_i + 1$;
9     $n_i \leftarrow n_i - 1$;
10    $n \leftarrow n - 1$;

11 **foreach** i **do**
12   Coordinator sends s_i to node i;
13    $S_i \leftarrow$ a random sample of size s_i from A_i;
14   Node i sends S_i to Coordinator;

15 Coordinator returns $S = S_1 \cup \cdots \cup S_k$;

Further Discussion. The communication cost of this algorithm is clearly $O(k + s)$. The $O(k)$ part is due to the cost of communicating the subset sizes $n_1, \ldots, n_k$. If these are already known, e.g., when the algorithm is repeatedly executed to draw random samples multiple times, then the cost is only $O(s)$. The correctness of the algorithm can be easily established using the principle of deferred decisions.

8.2 Point Queries over Distributed Multisets

Brief Summary. In this section, we consider a multiset that is stored in a distributed fashion. We assume that the items in the multiset are drawn from a bounded universe $[u] = \{1, \ldots, u\}$. The multiset is partitioned into k pieces, held by k distributed nodes. We denote the *local count* of item i at node j by $x_{i,j}$, and the *global count* of item i is $y_i = \sum_j x_{i,j}$. Let $n = \|y\|_1 = \sum_i y_i$. A point query for item i returns an approximation of y_i. In Chapter 3, we have seen a number of summaries of size $O(1/\varepsilon)$ or $O(1/\varepsilon \log(1/\delta))$ that can answer point queries with additive error εn. Here, δ is the probability that any y_i is estimated with an error greater than εn. Constructing such a summary for each piece and then merging them together will lead to a communication cost of $O(k/\varepsilon)$ or $O(k/\varepsilon \log(1/\delta))$. Here we present an improved algorithm with communication cost $O(\sqrt{k}/\varepsilon \log(1/\delta))$ bits.

Operations on the Summary. The algorithms described in this section all return an unbiased estimator of y_i for any given i, with variance $O((\varepsilon n)^2)$. By the Chebyshev inequality, this gives us an estimate with additive εn error with a constant probability. If a higher success probability $1 - \delta$ is desired, one can use the standard technique of running $O(\log(1/\delta))$ independent instances of the algorithm, and returning the median estimate. We now describe a sequence of three increasingly complicated sampling algorithms for the distributed point estimation problem.

Uniform Coin-Flip Sampling. A very simple algorithm is for each node to sample each of its items with probability $p = 1/(\varepsilon^2 n)$. If an item i has local count $x_{i,j}$ at node j, it is treated as $x_{i,j}$ copies of i and each copy is sampled by node j independently. All the sampled items are sent to the coordinator. Then for a queried item i, we use the estimator $Y_i = X_i/p$, where X_i is the number of copies of item i received by the coordinator. It follows that $\mathsf{E}[Y_i] = y_i$ and $\mathsf{Var}[Y_i] = O((\varepsilon n)^2)$ (details presented in the following subsection).

The expected communication cost of this simple algorithm is $pn = O(1/\varepsilon^2)$. This method works well if $k > 1/\varepsilon^2$. Otherwise, the following algorithm works better.

Importance Sampling. The idea is still to use random sampling, but bias the sampling probability so as to favor heavy items, i.e., those with large local counts. The basic version of the algorithm is very simple. Let $g(x) = \min\{x \sqrt{k}/\varepsilon n, 1\}$ be the sampling function. We assume that the common parameters n, k, ε are known to all nodes; otherwise we can spend an extra $O(k)$ communication cost to broadcast them. If an item i has local count $x_{i,j}$ at node j, then the node with probability $g(x_{i,j})$ samples this item and sends the item together with its local count $x_{i,j}$ to the coordinator. Set $Y_{i,j} = x_{i,j}$ if the coordinator receives the item–count pair $(i, x_{i,j})$ from node j, and $Y_{i,j} = 0$ otherwise. Then for any given i, the coordinator can estimate y_i as (define $\frac{0}{0} = 0$)

$$Y_i = \frac{Y_{i,1}}{g(Y_{i,1})} + \cdots + \frac{Y_{i,k}}{g(Y_{i,k})}. \tag{8.1}$$

The full analysis shows that $\mathsf{E}[Y_i] = y_i$ and $\mathsf{Var}[Y_i] = O((\varepsilon n)^2)$, and this algorithm transmits a total of $O(\sqrt{k}/\varepsilon)$ item–count pairs.

An Advanced Version of the Importance Sampling Algorithm. One can be more careful with the exact number of bits communicated. Let u be the size of the universe where the items are drawn from. For example, if the items are IPv6 addresses, then $u = 2^{128}$. Note that an item thus needs $O(\log u)$ bits to represent, and a count needs $O(\log n)$ bits, so the basic version of the algorithm communicates $O(\sqrt{k}/\varepsilon(\log u + \log n))$ bits in total. A more advanced version of the algorithm can reduce this cost to just $O(\sqrt{k}/\varepsilon)$ bits. The idea is to encode the sampled items into a BloomFilter. Recall from Section 2.7 that a BloomFilter is a space-efficient encoding scheme that compactly stores a set of items S. We recall its properties that are needed for our purpose here. Given any item, the BloomFilter can tell us whether this item is in S or not. It does not have false negatives, but may have a false positive probability q for any queried item. More precisely, if the queried item is in S, the answer is always "yes"; if it is not in S, then with probability q it returns "yes," and with probability $1 - q$ returns "no." The false positive probability q can be made arbitrarily small by using $O(\log(1/q))$ bits per item, and the value of q can be computed as (2.6). Thus the BloomFilter uses $O(n \log(1/q))$ bits to store a total of n items, regardless of the size of the universe.

. We now describe the advanced version of the algorithm. First write each $x_{i,j}$ in a canonical form as

$$x_{i,j} = a_{i,j} \frac{\varepsilon n}{\sqrt{k}} + b_{i,j}, \tag{8.2}$$

where $a_{i,j}$ and $b_{i,j}$ are both nonnegative integers such that $a_{i,j} \leq \frac{\sqrt{k}}{\varepsilon}$ and $b_{i,j} < \frac{\varepsilon n}{\sqrt{k}}$. We assume $\frac{\varepsilon n}{\sqrt{k}}$ is an integer. Note that given these constraints, there is a unique way of expressing $x_{i,j}$ in the preceding form. Then we have

$$y_i = \frac{\varepsilon n}{\sqrt{k}} \sum_{j=1}^{k} a_{i,j} + \sum_{j=1}^{k} b_{i,j}. \tag{8.3}$$

Given a point query i, we will estimate the two terms of (8.3) separately.

The second term is easier to deal with. As in the basic version of the algorithm, the nodes sample each $b_{i,j}$ with probability $g(b_{i,j})$, and then estimate the second term of (8.3) similarly as before

$$B_i = \frac{B_{i,1}}{g(B_{i,1})} + \cdots + \frac{B_{i,k}}{g(B_{i,k})},$$

where $B_{i,j} = b_{i,j}$ if $b_{i,j}$ is sampled by node j, and 0 otherwise. The observation is that, since $g(x)$ is a linear function when $x \leq \varepsilon n / \sqrt{k}$, $\frac{B_{i,j}}{g(B_{i,j})}$ is either 0 or $\varepsilon n / \sqrt{k}$. Thus, the nodes do not need to send out the values of $b_{i,j}$s at all; they only need to inform the coordinator which items have had their $b_{i,j}$s sampled. So all these items can be encoded in a Bloom filter. But as the Bloom filter has a false positive rate q, this has to be accounted for. More precisely, for a point query i, suppose among the k Bloom filters that the coordinator has received, Z_i of them says "yes," then we use the estimator

$$B_i = \frac{\varepsilon n}{\sqrt{k}} \cdot \left(\frac{Z_i - kq}{1 - q} \right). \tag{8.4}$$

It can be shown that (8.4) is an unbiased estimator for the second term of (8.3) with variance $O((\varepsilon n)^2)$, for any constant q.

For the first term of (8.3), the idea is to consider each $a_{i,j}$ in its binary form and deal with each bit individually. Let $a_{i,j}[r]$ be the rth rightmost bit of $a_{i,j}$ (counting from 0). For each r, node j encodes all the items i where $a_{i,j}[r] = 1$ in a Bloom filter with false positive probability $q_r \leq 1/2^{3r+1}$. For any item i, suppose $Z_{i,r}$ is the number of Bloom filters that assert $a_{i,j}[r] = 1$. Then we use the following estimator for the first term of (8.3):

$$A_i = \frac{\varepsilon n}{\sqrt{k}} \sum_{r=0}^{\log(\sqrt{k}/\varepsilon)} 2^r \frac{Z_{i,r} - kq_r}{1 - q_r}. \tag{8.5}$$

Algorithm 8.2: Point queries over distributed multiset: Node j

---

1 Initialize empty Bloom filter F_j with any constant false positive rate q;
2 **for** $r \leftarrow 0$ **to** $\log(\sqrt{k}/\varepsilon)$ **do**
3 　Initialize empty Bloom filter $F_j[r]$ with false positive rate
　　$q_r \leq 1/2^{3r+1}$;
4 **foreach** i **do**
5 ' 　Let $x_{i,j} = a_{i,j}\frac{\varepsilon n}{\sqrt{k}} + b_{i,j}$, where $a_{i,j}$ and $b_{i,j}$ are non-negative

　　integers and $a_{i,j} \leq \frac{\sqrt{k}}{\varepsilon}, b_{i,j} < \frac{\varepsilon n}{\sqrt{k}}$;
6 　**for** $r \leftarrow 0$ **to** $\log(\sqrt{k}/\varepsilon)$ **do**
7 　　**if** $a_{i,j}[r] = 1$ **then** insert i into $F_j[r]$;
8 　With probability $g(b_{i,j})$, insert i into F_j;
9 Send $F_j, F_j[0], F_j[1], \ldots, F_j[\log(\sqrt{k}/\varepsilon)]$ to Coordinator;

Algorithm 8.3: Point queries over distributed multiset: Coordinator with query i

---

1 $Z_i \leftarrow$ the number of F_j's that assert containing i;
2 **for** $r \leftarrow 0$ **to** $\log(\sqrt{k}/\varepsilon)$ **do**
3 　$Z_{i,r} \leftarrow$ the number of $F_j[r]$'s that assert containing i;

4 **return** $\dfrac{\varepsilon n}{\sqrt{k}} \cdot \dfrac{Z_i - kq}{1-q} + \dfrac{\varepsilon n}{\sqrt{k}} \displaystyle\sum_{r=0}^{\log(\sqrt{k}/\varepsilon)} 2^r \dfrac{Z_{i,r} - kq_r}{1-q_r}$;

This is an unbiased estimator of the first term of (8.3) with variance $O((\varepsilon n)^2)$ (details in the "Further Discussion" section that follows).

The pseudocode for the nodes and the coordinator is given in Algorithms 8.2 and 8.3.

All the Bloom filters received by the coordinator constitute the summary for the entire multiset, on which any point query can be posed. The total size needed for all the BloomFilter instances can be shown to be $O(\sqrt{k}/\varepsilon)$ bits.

Further Discussion. *The uniform sampling algorithm.* The analysis of the uniform sampling algorithm is quite standard. Consider any given i, which has y_i copies in the entire multiset. For $\ell = 1, \ldots, y_i$, let $X_{i,\ell} = 1$ if the ℓ-th copy is sampled, and 0 otherwise. We have $\mathsf{E}[X_{i,\ell}] = p$, and $\mathsf{Var}[X_{i,\ell}] = p(1-p)$. Setting $p = 1/\varepsilon^2 n$, the estimator has expectation

$$\mathsf{E}[Y_i] = \mathsf{E}[X_i/p] = 1/p \cdot \mathsf{E}\left[\sum_{\ell=1}^{y_i} X_{i,\ell}\right] = 1/p \cdot py_i = y_i,$$

and variance

$$\mathsf{Var}[Y_i] = \mathsf{Var}[X_i/p] = 1/p^2 \cdot \mathsf{Var}\left[\sum_{i=1}^{y_i} X_{i,\ell}\right]$$

$$= 1/p^2 \cdot y_i p(1-p) \le y_i/p \le (\varepsilon n)^2.$$

The Basic Version of the Importance Algorithm. We now analyze the basic version of the biased sampling algorithm. Recall that the algorithm samples each local count $x_{i,j}$ with probability $g(x_{i,j})$, where $g(x) = \min\{x\sqrt{k}/\varepsilon n, 1\}$. The estimator given in (8.1) has expectation

$$\mathsf{E}[Y_i] = \sum_{j=1}^{k} \frac{\mathsf{E}[Y_{i,j}]}{g(Y_{i,j})} = \sum_{j=1}^{k} g(x_{i,j})\frac{x_{i,j}}{g(x_{i,j})} = \sum_{j=1}^{k} x_{i,j} = y_i.$$

Now we consider the variance of Y_i. Since we sample an item with probability one (i.e., zero variance) when the local count $x_{i,j} > \varepsilon n/\sqrt{k}$, it is sufficient to consider the worst case when all $x_{i,j} \le \varepsilon n/\sqrt{k}$. We have

$$\mathsf{Var}[Y_i] = \sum_{j=1}^{k} \frac{x_{i,j}^2(1 - x_{i,j}\sqrt{k}/\varepsilon n)}{x_{i,j}\sqrt{k}/\varepsilon n}$$

$$= \frac{\varepsilon n}{\sqrt{k}}\sum_{j=1}^{k} x_{i,j} - \sum_{j=1}^{k} x_{i,j}^2$$

$$\le \frac{\varepsilon n}{\sqrt{k}}y_i - \frac{1}{k}y_i^2 \quad \text{(Cauchy–Schwartz inequality)}$$

$$= -\left(\frac{y_i}{\sqrt{k}} - \frac{\varepsilon n}{2}\right)^2 + \frac{(\varepsilon n)^2}{4} \le \frac{1}{4}(\varepsilon n)^2.$$

For the communication cost, we can easily derive that this algorithm samples and transmits a total of $\sum_{i,j} g(x_{i,j}) \le \sum_{i,j} x_{i,j}\sqrt{k}/\varepsilon n = n \cdot \sqrt{k}/\varepsilon n = \sqrt{n}/\varepsilon$ item–count pairs (in expectation).

The Advanced Version of the Biased Sampling Algorithm. Recall that in the advanced version of the algorithm, we decompose the global count y_i

into two terms as in (8.3) and estimate each of them separately. The second term is easier to analyze, as it is similar to the basic version, except that we need to take into account the false positive rate q of the Bloom filters.

We define $Z_{i,j}$ to be the indicator random variable set to 1 if the Bloom filter from node j asserts that it contains the item i, and 0 otherwise. It is easy to see that $\Pr[Z_{i,j} = 1] = g(b_{i,j}) + (1 - g(b_{i,j}))q$, and thus $\mathsf{E}[Z_{i,j}] = g(b_{i,j}) + (1 - g(b_{i,j}))q$. Then we have

$$
\begin{aligned}
\mathsf{E}[B_i] &= \frac{\varepsilon n}{\sqrt{k}} \cdot \frac{\mathsf{E}[Z_i] - kq}{1 - q} \\
&= \frac{\varepsilon n}{\sqrt{k}} \cdot \frac{\sum_{j=1}^{k} \mathsf{E}[Z_{i,j}] - kq}{1 - q} \\
&= \frac{\varepsilon n}{\sqrt{k}} \cdot \frac{(1 - q)\sum_{j=1}^{k} g(b_{i,j}) + kq - kq}{1 - q} \\
&= \frac{\varepsilon n}{\sqrt{k}} \sum_{j=1}^{k} g(b_{i,j}) = \sum_{j=1}^{k} b_{i,j}.
\end{aligned}
$$

The variance of the estimator is

$$
\begin{aligned}
\mathsf{Var}[B_i] &= \frac{(\varepsilon n)^2}{k(1 - q)^2} \mathsf{Var}[Z_i] \\
&= \frac{(\varepsilon n)^2}{k(1 - q)^2} \sum_{j=1}^{k} \mathsf{Var}[Z_{i,j}] \\
&= \frac{(\varepsilon n)^2}{k(1 - q)^2} \sum_{j=1}^{k} \big((g(b_{i,j}) + (1 - g(b_{i,j}))q)(1 - g(b_{i,j}) \\
&\qquad\qquad - (1 - g(b_{i,j}))q) \big) \qquad\qquad\qquad (8.6) \\
&= \frac{(\varepsilon n)^2}{k(1 - q)^2} \left(\frac{k}{4} - \left(\frac{(1 - q)\sum_{j=1}^{k} b_{i,j}}{\varepsilon n} - \frac{(1 - 2q)\sqrt{k}}{2} \right)^2 \right) \\
&\leq \frac{(\varepsilon n)^2}{4(1 - q)^2}.
\end{aligned}
$$

Thus it is sufficient to set a constant q so that $\mathsf{Var}[Y_i] = O((\varepsilon n)^2)$. The communication cost for this part is the same as in the basic version, except that since now each sampled item–count pair only consumes $O(\log(1/q)) = O(1)$ bits, the total cost is $O(\sqrt{n}/\varepsilon)$ bits.

For the first term, we need to show that $E[A_i] = \dfrac{\varepsilon n}{\sqrt{k}} \displaystyle\sum_{j=1}^{n} a_{i,j}$, and bound $\mathsf{Var}[A_i]$. Let $Z_{i,r}$ be the number of Bloom filters that assert $a_{i,j}[r] = 1$. Let $c_{i,r} = \sum_{j=1}^{k} a_{i,j}[r]$. Since there are $k - c_{i,r}$ Bloom filters that may, with probability q_r, assert $a_{i,j}[r] = 1$ despite $a_{i,j}[r] = 0$, it is easy to see that $E[Z_{i,r}] = c_{i,r} + (k - c_{i,r})q_r$, and $\mathsf{Var}[Z_{i,r}] = (k - c_{i,r})q_r(1 - q_r) \le kq_r(1 - q_r)$. Thus we have

$$E[A_i] = \frac{\varepsilon n}{\sqrt{k}} \sum_{r=0}^{\log(\sqrt{k}/\varepsilon)} 2^r \frac{E[Z_{i,r}] - kq_r}{1 - q_r}$$

$$= \frac{\varepsilon n}{\sqrt{k}} \sum_{r=0}^{\log(\sqrt{k}/\varepsilon)} 2^r c_{i,r} = \frac{\varepsilon n}{\sqrt{k}} \sum_{j=1}^{k} a_{i,j},$$

and

$$\mathsf{Var}[A_i] = \frac{(\varepsilon n)^2}{k} \sum_{r=0}^{\log(\sqrt{k}/\varepsilon)} \frac{2^{2r}}{(1 - q_r)^2} \mathsf{Var}[Z_{i,r}]$$

$$\le (\varepsilon n)^2 \sum_{r=0}^{\log(\sqrt{k}/\varepsilon)} 2^{2r} \frac{q_r}{1 - q_r}.$$

So as long as we set $q_r \le 1/2^{3r+1}$, we can bound $\mathsf{Var}[A_i]$ by $O((\varepsilon n)^2)$, as desired. The cost for each $a_{i,j}[r] = 1$ is thus $O(\log(1/q_r)) = O(r)$ bits. Since each $a_{i,j}[r] = 1$ represents $2^r \frac{\varepsilon n}{\sqrt{k}}$ copies of an item, the amortized cost for every $\frac{\varepsilon n}{\sqrt{k}}$ copies is $O(r/2^r) = O(1)$ bits. Therefore, the total communication cost is $O(\sqrt{k}/\varepsilon)$ bits.

Implementation Issues. For the preceding analysis to go through, the nodes need to use independent random sources, including the randomness in the sampling and the random hash functions in their Bloom filters.

History and Background. The sampling framework and the idea to combine with Bloom filters were introduced by Zhao et al. [242]. Their algorithm was later simplified and improved by Huang et al. [135] to the version presented here. The $O(\sqrt{k}/\varepsilon)$-bit communication cost was later shown to be optimal for $k \le 1/\varepsilon^2$ [236], while the $O(1/\varepsilon^2)$-bit communication cost achieved by the simple random sampling algorithm is optimal for $k > 1/\varepsilon^2$.

8.3 Distributed Ordered Data

Brief Summary. In this section, we revisit the problem considered in Chapter 4, i.e., rank and quantile queries on a set A of n elements drawn from an ordered universe, except that here the set A is partitioned into k pieces, each held by a different node. In this section, we assume that there are no duplicates in the set A. Recall that for an element x, the rank of x in A (x may or may not be in A) is $\text{rank}(x) = |\{y < x : y \in A\}|$. An ε-approximate rank query for element x returns an estimated rank $\tilde{r}$ such that

$$\text{rank}(x) - \varepsilon n \leq \tilde{r} \leq \text{rank}(x) + \varepsilon n,$$

while an ε-approximate quantile query for a rank r returns an element x such that

$$r - \varepsilon n \leq \text{rank}(x) \leq r + \varepsilon n.$$

Using the summaries described in Chapter 4 and merging them requires a communication cost of at least $\Omega(k/\varepsilon)$. In the following subsection, we present an algorithm with communication cost $\tilde{O}(\sqrt{k}/\varepsilon)$.

Operations on the Summary. Let $t = \lfloor \varepsilon n / \sqrt{k \log(2/\delta)/2} \rfloor$, where δ will be the probability of exceeding the ε-error guarantee. The algorithm is very simple. Each node first sorts its own set of elements. Then it chooses an offset b uniformly at random between 0 and $t - 1$, and sends the $(at + b)$th element to the coordinator, for $a = 0, 1, 2, \ldots$. Since one out of every t elements is selected, the total communication cost is $O(n/t) = O(\sqrt{k \log(1/\delta)}/\varepsilon)$.

To answer a rank query for any given element x, the coordinator simply counts the number of elements received from all the nodes that are smaller than x, multiplied by t.

To answer a quantile query for a given rank r, the coordinator just sorts all the elements received and returns the one at position $\lfloor r/t \rfloor$.

Further Discussion. We first analyze the error in the rank query for any given element x. Let $\text{rank}(x, i)$ be the local rank of x at node i, i.e., the number of elements smaller than x stored at node i. It is clear that the global rank of x is $\text{rank}(x) = \sum_i \text{rank}(x, i)$. Effectively, the coordinator computes an estimate of $\text{rank}(x, i)$, denoted $\widehat{\text{rank}}(x, i)$, for each i and adds them up, whereas $\widehat{\text{rank}}(x, i)$ is simply the number of selected elements at node i that are smaller than x, multiplied by t. Recall that the algorithm chooses the offset b uniformly at random between 0 and $t - 1$, so we have

$$\widehat{\text{rank}}(x,i) = \begin{cases} \left\lfloor \frac{\text{rank}(x,i)}{t} \right\rfloor \cdot t, & \text{w.p. } 1 - \frac{\text{rank}(x,i) \bmod t}{t}; \\ \left(\left\lfloor \frac{\text{rank}(x,i)}{t} \right\rfloor + 1 \right) \cdot t, & \text{w.p. } \frac{\text{rank}(x,i) \bmod t}{t}. \end{cases}$$

One can check that

$$\mathsf{E}[\widehat{\text{rank}}(x,i)] = \left\lfloor \frac{\text{rank}(x,i)}{t} \right\rfloor \cdot t + (\text{rank}(x,i) \bmod t) = \text{rank}(x,i).$$

Therefore, $\widehat{\text{rank}}(x) = \sum_i \widehat{\text{rank}}(x,i)$ is an unbiased estimator of $\text{rank}(x)$. Since it is a sum of independent random variables, each of which has a bounded range of $t = \varepsilon n / \left(\sqrt{(k/2) \log(2/\delta)} \right)$, we can invoke the Chernoff–Hoeffding inequality 1.4 to obtain the following concentration results:

$$\Pr\left[\left| \widehat{\text{rank}}(x) - \text{rank}(x) \right| > \varepsilon n \right] \le 2 \exp\left(\frac{-2(\varepsilon n)^2}{kt^2} \right) = \delta,$$

i.e., the probability that the estimated rank deviates from the true rank by more than εn is at most δ.

To have a guarantee on quantile queries, we set $\delta = \varepsilon/3$ in the algorithm. This ensures that any rank query can be answered within error εn with probability at least $1 - \varepsilon/3$. Then, with at least constant probability, the estimated rank is accurate (within error of εn) for all the $1/\varepsilon - 1$ elements that rank at $\varepsilon n, 2\varepsilon n, \ldots, (1 - \varepsilon)n$, which is enough to answer all rank queries. When all rank queries can be answered within εn error, all the quantile queries can also be answered with the desired error guarantee.

History and Background. The algorithm presented in the preceding subsections is a simplification of the algorithm described in [134] for the 1D case. The general algorithm works in higher dimensions and computes an ε-approximation (see Section 5.1) for any range space with bounded discrepancy. However, in higher dimensions, the algorithm relies on discrepancy minimization [18], which is not known to be practical.

If we directly use this algorithm on a general communication network, the communication cost will be $O(h\sqrt{k}/\varepsilon)$, where h is the diameter of the network. In [133], a better algorithm with communication cost $O(\sqrt{hk}/\varepsilon)$ was presented.

9

Other Uses of Summaries

In this chapter, we discuss some other applications and manipulations for working with summaries. These include nearest-neighbor search; reducing the significance of older updates; ways to combine summaries with other data transformations; and operations on summaries such as reweighting and resizing.

9.1 Nearest-Neighbor Search

The *nearest-neighbor search* problem, also known as *similarity search*, is defined as follows: given a set P of n points in a metric space with distance function D, build a data structure that, given any query point q, returns its nearest neighbor $\arg\min_{p \in P} D(q, p)$. This problem has a wide range of applications in data mining, machine learning, computer vision, and databases. However, this problem is known to suffer the "curse of dimensionality," i.e., when the dimensionality of the metric space is high, there does not seem to be a method better than the naive solution, which, upon a query, simply scans all the points and computes $D(p, q)$ for every $p \in P$.

The past few decades have seen tremendous progress on this problem. It turns out that if some approximation is allowed, then the curse of dimensionality can be mitigated, and solutions significantly more efficient than the linear search method exist. Many of them are actually based on computing a small summary for each point in P, as well as for the query point q. If the summaries are "distance preserving," then the nearest neighbor of q can be found by searching through the summaries or performing a few index look-ups, which can be more efficient than searching over the original points in P.

Most solutions along this direction actually solve the approximate *near-neighbor* problem, which is parameterized by an approximation factor $c > 1$

218

and a radius $r > 0$. This problem asks the data structure to return a $p \in P$ such that $D(p,q) \leq cr$, provided that there exists a point p' with $D(p',q) \leq r$. If no such p' exists, the data structure may return nothing. This is in effect a "decision version" of the nearest-neighbor problem. Thus, to find the (c-approximate) nearest neighbor, one can build multiple copies of the data structure with $r = \Delta_{\min}, c\Delta_{\min}, c^2\Delta_{\min}, \ldots, \Delta_{\max}$, where $\Delta_{\min}$ and $\Delta_{\max}$ are the smallest and largest possible distances between the query and any point in P, respectively. In practice, this solution is often sufficient, as one does not have to set $\Delta_{\min}$ and $\Delta_{\max}$ to be the true minimum and maximum distances; instead, the user may use a range that is of his/her interest: a nearest neighbor with distance too large, even if found, may not be very interesting; on the other hand, neighbors with distances smaller than some $\Delta_{\min}$ may be equally good. Theoretically speaking, this approach leads to a space complexity that is not bounded by any function of n. However, more complicated reductions that incur a $\log^{O(1)} n$ loss do exist [129].

In this section, we review two types of solutions for the approximate near-neighbor (ANN) problem based on computing small summaries over the points. The first achieves logarithmic query time, but with a high requirement on space; the second one strikes a better balance between space and time, and is used more often in practice.

9.1.1 ANN via Dimension Reduction

The Johnson–Lindenstrauss transform as described in Section 5.5 is a summary over points in $\mathbb{R}^d$ that preserves the ℓ_2-distance up to a $(1 + \varepsilon)$-factor. Most importantly, by setting $\delta = 1/n^2$, we see from Section 5.5 that the size of the summary, i.e., the dimensionality of the transformed points, is only $k = O\left(\frac{\log n}{\varepsilon^2}\right)$, which is completely independent of d. Thus, it offers an efficient way to solve high-dimensional ANN, by searching over the transformed points in $\mathbb{R}^k$.

More precisely, we perform the Johnson–Lindenstrauss transform on every point $p \in P$. Let $f(p) \in \mathbb{R}^k$ be the transformed point of p. We build an ANN data structure over $f(P) = \{f(p) \mid p \in P\}$, as follows. For a given radius r, we discretize the space $\mathbb{R}^k$ into cubes of side length $\varepsilon r/\sqrt{k}$. Note that each cube can be identified by a k-integer tuple. For every $p \in P$, let $S(p)$ be the set of cubes that intersect the ball $B_{f(p),r}$. We build a dictionary data structure[1] mapping each cube to an arbitrary point p such that the cube is in

---

[1] A dictionary data structure stores a set S of elements from a discrete universe, each with some associated data. For any given x, the structure can return x and its associated data, or report that

$S(p)$. If there is no such p, this cube will not be stored in the dictionary. For a given query q, we just compute $f(q)$, locate the cube that contains $f(q)$, and use the dictionary structure to find the cube and report its associated point p. If the cube does not exist in the dictionary, we return nothing.

In the following subsection, we will show that the algorithm solves the ANN problem with an approximation ratio of $c = 1 + 3\varepsilon$. The space needed by the data structure is $O(dn) + n^{O(\log(1/\varepsilon)/\varepsilon^2)}$ and the query time is $O\left(\frac{d \log n}{\varepsilon}\right)$. Note that by replacing 3ε with ε, the approximation ratio can be scaled to $1 + \varepsilon$ with no change in the asymptotic bounds on space and query time.

Further Discussion. Now we analyze the approximation guarantee provided by the previous algorithm. Let q be the query point. We know from the Johnson–Lindenstrauss transform that, with probability at least $1/2$, we have

$$(1 - \varepsilon)D(p,q) \leq D(f(p), f(q)) \leq (1 + \varepsilon)D(p,q)$$

for all $p \in P$. The following analysis will all be based on this happening.

Let p' be a point in P with $D(p',q) \leq r$. We need to show that the algorithm returns some $p \in P$ with $D(p,q) \leq cr$ for some c. As described, the algorithm will try to find in the dictionary the cube containing q, and returns some p such that this cube is in $S(p)$. Note that this cube must exist in the dictionary; indeed, because $D(p',q) \leq r$, this cube must belong to $S(p')$. But the point associated with this cube may not be p', but some other p such that $B_{f(p),r}$ also intersects this cube. Note that the maximum distance between any two points inside the cube is $\sqrt{k \cdot (\varepsilon r / \sqrt{k})^2} = \varepsilon r$. So if $B_{f(p),r}$ intersects the cube, by the triangle inequality, we must have

$$D(f(p), f(q)) \leq r + \varepsilon r = (1 + \varepsilon)r.$$

Therefore, we have

$$D(p,q) \leq \frac{1}{1 - \varepsilon} D(f(p), f(q)) = \frac{1 + \varepsilon}{1 - \varepsilon} r \leq (1 + 3\varepsilon)r,$$

assuming $\varepsilon \leq \frac{1}{3}$. Thus, this algorithm solves the ANN problem with an approximation ratio of $c = 1 + 3\varepsilon$.

---

x does not exist in S. One concrete solution is a hash table [63], which uses linear space and answers a query in $O(1)$ time in expectation.

It remains to analyze the space and query time of this ANN data structure. The query time is dominated by the Johnson–Lindenstrauss transform. Using the Sparse Johnson–Lindenstrauss transform (Section 5.5), this can be done in time $O\left(\frac{d\log n}{\varepsilon}\right)$. The subsequent dictionary lookup takes time $O(k) = O\left(\frac{\log n}{\varepsilon^2}\right)$, which is asymptotically smaller than $O\left(\frac{d\log n}{\varepsilon}\right)$ when $d > \frac{1}{\varepsilon}$. Note that $d \le \frac{1}{\varepsilon}$ is considered low dimensional and there is no need to use this data structure.

The space needed by the data structure consists of two parts: we first need to store all the raw data points, which take space $O(dn)$. This is linear to the input size and is unavoidable. We also need to store the dictionary, which stores all the distinct cubes that appear in some $S(p)$. The number of such cubes is at most $\sum_{p\in P} |S(p)|$. Recall that $S(p)$ includes all cubes in $\mathbb{R}^k$ within a distance of r to p and each cube has side length $\varepsilon r/\sqrt{k}$. Using standard estimates on the volume of ℓ_2 balls, one can show that $|S(p)| \le (\frac{1}{\varepsilon})^{O(k)}$. Each cube needs space $O(k)$ to store in the dictionary, so the total space needed is

$$n \cdot \left(\frac{1}{\varepsilon}\right)^{O(k)} \cdot k = n^{O(\log(1/\varepsilon)/\varepsilon^2)}.$$

History and Background. The approaches described in the preceding subsection were introduced in [140, 129]. A similar approach was introduced in [165] in the context of the Hamming space.

The dimension reduction is needed only when $d = \Omega(\log n)$. For smaller values of d, the ANN data structure described by Arya et al. [17] is better, which uses $O(dn)$ space and answers a query in $O(c(d,\varepsilon)\log n)$ time, where $c(d,\varepsilon)$ is a function that exponentially depends on d.

9.1.2 ANN via Locality-Sensitive Hashing

For constant ε, the method described earlier achieves logarithmic query time, which is ideal, but at the cost of a high polynomial space, which is not practical. Next we describe an alternative approach that needs a smaller space of $O(dn + n^{1+\rho})$ for some $0 < \rho < 1$, although at the cost of increasing the query time from logarithmic to $O(dn^\rho)$.

This approach, known as *locality-sensitive hashing (LSH)*, restricts the summary of a point p to take a single value. But the "distance-preserving" requirement is also weaker: instead of preserving the distance up to a constant factor, the summary is only required to distinguish between large distances and small distances probabilistically. More precisely, the summary will be a function h, randomly chosen from a family $\mathcal{H}$, such that the following holds for any x, y in the metric space:

- if $D(x, y) \leq r$, then $\Pr[h(x) = h(y)] \geq p_1$;
- if $D(x, y) \geq cr$, then $\Pr[h(x) = h(y)] \leq p_2$.

For this framework to be of use, it is required that $p_1 > p_2$. Indeed, the parameter ρ mentioned earlier depends on the gap between p_1 and p_2, and will be shown to be $\rho = \frac{\log p_1}{\log p_2}$. Note that when $p_1 > p_2$, we must have $\rho < 1$.

When the data points are taken from $\{0, 1\}^d$ and the distance measure is the Hamming distance, a simple LSH family is *bit sampling*, which just picks a random $i \in \{1, \ldots, d\}$ and maps the point to its ith coordinate. More precisely, $\mathcal{H} = \{h_i(x) = x_i, i = 1, \ldots, d\}$. When the $D(x, y) \leq r$, x and y have at least $d - r$ equal coordinates, so $p_1 = 1 - \frac{r}{d}$. Similarly, when $D(x, y) > cr$, $\Pr[h(x) = h(y)] \leq p_2 = 1 - \frac{cr}{d}$. Thus, $\rho = \frac{\log(1 - \frac{r}{d})}{\log(1 - \frac{cr}{d})}$.

Another widely used LSH family is the *MinHash*. Here a data "point" is a set, and the distance measure is the Jaccard similarity $S(x, y) = \frac{|x \cap y|}{|x \cup y|}$. Because a "similarity" is high when two points are close, the definition of the LSH family is then restated as follows:

- if $S(x, y) \geq r$, then $\Pr[h(x) = h(y)] \geq p_1$;
- if $S(x, y) \leq r/c$, then $\Pr[h(x) = h(y)] \leq p_2$.

Let g be a function that maps each element in the universe to a real number in $[0, 1]$ independently. Then MinHash sets $h(x)$ to be the element that has the smallest $g(\cdot)$ value in the set x. It can be easily verified that $\Pr[h(x) = h(y)] = S(x, y)$, so we have $p_1 = r, p_2 = r/c$, and $\rho = \frac{\log r}{\log(r/c)}$. However, such a truly random function g cannot be practically constructed. Instead, an ℓ-wise independent function can be used instead, and it has been shown that with $\ell = O(\log(1/\varepsilon))$, the MinHash function can achieve $\Pr[h(x) = h(y)] = S(x, y) \pm \varepsilon$ [137]. Thus, this is essentially the same as the KMV summary described in Section 2.5, except that we set $k = 1$ and use a hash function with a higher degree of independence instead of pairwise independence.

In this section, we describe a data structure for the ANN problem, assuming we have an LSH family $\mathcal{H}$ for a distance function $D(\cdot, \cdot)$; the same approach also works for the case when $S(\cdot, \cdot)$ is a similarity function satisfying the revised LSH definition.

The first attempt would be to simply pick an $h \in \mathcal{H}$ randomly, and build a dictionary structure mapping each unique hash value to the list of points with that hash value. Upon a query q, we search the list of points p with $h(p) = h(q)$, and stop as soon as we find a p such that $D(p,q) \leq cr$. Due to the LSH property, points close to q are more likely to be found than those far away from q. However, the problem with this simple algorithm is that the probabilistic guarantee of the LSH family is quite weak, and we may end up with searching in a long list without finding any qualified p. Indeed, when using the bit-sampling LSH family, there are only two distinct hash values (0 and 1), and each list will have $\Omega(n)$ points!

We take two steps to fix the problem, which entail maintaining multiple independent summaries. First, we pick $k = \log_{1/p_2} n$ functions $h_1, \ldots, h_k \in \mathcal{H}$ independently at random, and form a composite hash function $g(x) = (h_1(x), \ldots, h_k(x))$. We build the dictionary structure using g. This effectively creates more distinct hash values, so it will reduce the lengths of the lists. But its also reduces the collision probability, i.e.,

- if $D(x, y) \leq r$, then $\Pr[g(x) = g(y)] \geq p_1^k$;
- if $D(x, y) \geq cr$, then $\Pr[g(x) = g(y)] \leq p_2^k$.

To make sure that close points will be found with high probability, we repeat the whole construction ℓ times, i.e., we pick a total of ℓk functions from $\mathcal{H}$ independently at random, and build ℓ dictionary structures, each using a composite g consisting of k functions. Note that each point will thus be stored ℓ times, once in each dictionary. To save space, we do not need to store the points in full (i.e., all d coordinates) every time. Instead, we just keep one copy of the points, while the lists can just store pointers to the full points. Upon a query q, we check the list of points with hash value $g(q)$ in each of the ℓ dictionaries, and stop as soon as we find a point p with $D(p,q) \leq cr$.

In the following subsection, we will show that by setting $\ell = O(n^\rho)$, the algorithm described can solve the ANN problem with at least constant probability, while achieving the claimed space/time bounds mentioned at the beginning of this subsection.

Further Discussion. First, with $\ell = O(n^\rho)$, it is immediate that the space needed is $O(dn + \ell n) = O(dn + n^{1+\rho})$, since we only store one copy of the full points, while only keeping pointers in the ℓ dictionaries.

In this subsection, we analyze the query cost and the probability that the data structure finds a point p with $D(p,q) \leq cr$, provided that there exists a point $p' \in P$ with $D(p',q) \leq r$. Consider the following two events:

$\mathcal{E}_1$: $g(p') = g(q)$ in at least one of the ℓ dictionaries;

$\mathcal{E}_2$: the total number of points p with $D(p,q) \geq cr$ and $g(p) = g(q)$ in all dictionaries is at most 10ℓ.

Note that under $\mathcal{E}_1$, the algorithm will succeed in finding a point p with $D(p,q) \leq cr$, because at least p' can be such a p. Under $\mathcal{E}_2$, we search through at most $O(\ell)$ points. Computing the distance between q and each of these points takes $O(d)$ time, so the total query time will be $O(d\ell) = O(dn^\rho)$. We will next show that $\mathcal{E}_1$ and $\mathcal{E}_2$ each happen with probability at least 0.9. Then by the union bound, they happen simultaneously with probability at least 0.8.

We first analyze $\mathcal{E}_1$. From earlier, we know that

$$\Pr[g(p') = g(q)] \geq p_1^k = p_1^{\log_{1/p_2} n} = n^{\log_{1/p_2} p_1} = n^{\frac{\log p_1}{\log(1/p_2)}}$$

$$= n^{-\frac{\log p_1}{\log p_2}} = n^{-\rho}.$$

By setting $\ell = c_1 n^\rho$ for some constant c_1, we have

$$\Pr[\mathcal{E}_1] \geq 1 - (1 - n^{-\rho})^{c_1 n^\rho} \geq 1 - e^{-c_1}.$$

It is clear that this can be made at least 0.9 by choosing a constant c_1 large enough.

Finally, we analyze $\mathcal{E}_2$. The expected number of points p with $g(p) = g(q)$ in one dictionary is at most

$$np_2^k = np_2^{\log_{1/p_2} n} = n^{1+\log_{1/p_2} p_2} = n^{1-1} = 1.$$

So the expected total number of such points in all ℓ dictionaries is at most ℓ. Then by the Markov inequality, we obtain that the probability of exceeding this expectation by a factor of ten or more is at most 0.1, and so $\Pr[\mathcal{E}_2] \geq 0.9$.

History and Background. The LSH framework follows from the work of Indyk and Motwani [140], and was further developed in [119]. It has since been significantly expanded in scope and applicability. Many metric spaces have been shown to admit LSH families. For Hamming space, the bit-sampling family can be shown to have $\rho < 1/c$, which is near-optimal [197]. For Euclidean space, an LSH family based on random projection is shown to achieve $\rho < 1/c$ [84], which has been improved to optimal $\rho = 1/c^2 + o(1)$ [13]. Another widely used LSH function is SimHash [53]. These LSH families are "data independent," i.e., their constructions depend only on the metric space, not the actual pointset P. The aforementioned LSH families are optimal when restricted to such data-independent constructions. Recently, significant progress has been made toward data-dependent LSH families, i.e., one is allowed to construct the family after seeing P. This approach is very popular in practice as real-world datasets often have some implicit or explicit structure.

LSH has been widely used for similarity search applications, for example over images and other digital signals. Basic implementations of MinHash are available in the Algebird library, while a broader set of algorithms is available in C++ in the FALCONN library (`https://github.com/FALCONN-LIB/FALCONN`).

Full coverage of this topic is beyond the scope of this volume, and interested readers are referred to excellent surveys [230, 14].

9.2 Time Decay

In our discussion of data summarization so far, we have assumed that while data may arrive incrementally, the importance placed on each update is equal. However, there are scenarios where we wish to down-weight the importance of some items over time: when computing statistics, we might want today's observations to carry more weight than last week's. This notion is referred to as "time decay." There is a large literature on combining summaries with different models of time decay. In this section, our aim is to introduce the key notions, and give some simple examples.

Timestamped Data. For time decay to apply, each data item must also have an associated timestamp. We can assume that timestamps correspond to particular times and give a total ordering of the data items. We further assume that items to be summarized are received in timestamp order. Note that in large, distributed systems, these assumptions may be questionable. For the exponential decay model, out of order arrivals can be fairly easily handled, while this is more challenging for sliding windows and other models.

9.2.1 Exponential Decay

The model of exponential decay stipulates that the weight of an item decreases as an exponential function of the difference between its time-stamp and the current time. That is, item x with timestamp t_x is considered to have a weight of $2^{(-\lambda(t-t_x))}$ at time t. Here, λ is a parameter that controls the rate of the time decay. It can be thought of as encoding the "half-life" of items: every $1/\lambda$ time units, the weight of the item halves again.

Exponential decay can be motivated by analogy with physical processes, such as radioactive decay, where the intensity of radioactive emissions decay according to an exponential pattern. However, exponential decay is popular as a time decay model in part because it is easy to implement. Consider for example a simple counter, where we wish to maintain the exponentially decayed sum of weights of items. Without exponential decay, we simply maintain the sum of all weights. With exponential decay, we similarly maintain a sum of (decayed) weights. Here, all the weights decay at the same (multiplicative) rate, so it suffices to apply the decay factor to the sum. If timestamps are kept as integers (say, number of seconds), then every timestep, we multiply the current counter by the factor $2^{-\lambda}$, and add on any new weights that have arrived in the new timestep. Merging two summaries is achieved by just adding the counters.

In the case that time-stamps are treated as arbitrary real values, we modify this approach by keeping a timestamp t_c with the counter c, which records the most recent timestamp of an update to the counter. When a new item with weight w_i and timestamp $t_i \geq t_c$ arrives, we update the counter in two steps. First, we decay the counter to the new timestamp: we update $c \leftarrow c2^{-\lambda(t_c - t_i)}$, and set $t_c \leftarrow t_i$. Then we add in the new item at full weight: $c \leftarrow c + w_i$. A convenient feature of exponential decay is that it can tolerate updates that arrive out of time-sorted order: if $t_i < t_c$, we instead down-weight the item weight, and add it to the counter, via $c \leftarrow c + w_i 2^{-\lambda(t_c - t_i)}$.

Further Discussion. The correctness of these procedures can be understood by expanding out the definitions of exponential decay. For a given time t, the correct value of the decayed count is given by $c_t = \sum_i w_i 2^{-\lambda(t - t_i)}$.

First, observe that to decay the counter to any desired timestamp t', we can simply multiply by an appropriate factor:

$$c_{t'} = \sum_i w_i 2^{-\lambda(t' - t_i)}$$

$$= \sum_i w_i 2^{-\lambda(t' - t + t - t_i)}$$

$$= \sum_i w_i 2^{-\lambda(t' - t)} 2^{-\lambda(t - t_i)}$$

$$= 2^{-\lambda(t' - t)} \sum_i w_i 2^{-\lambda(t - t_i)} = 2^{-\lambda(t' - t)} c_t.$$

It is also immediate from this sum expansion that if we want to update a summary with timestamp t with an item with timestamp t_i, the decayed weight of the item is given by $w_i 2^{-\lambda(t_c - t_i)}$, and this can be just added to the counter.

Exponential Decay for Other Summaries. Due to the simple way that exponential decay can be applied to a counter, we can apply exponential decay to other summaries by simply replacing their internal counters with decayed counters as appropriate. Some care is needed, since not all summaries preserve their guarantees with this modification. Some examples where exponential decay can be straightforwardly applied include the various "sketch" summaries, such as Count-Min Sketch, Count Sketch, AMS Sketch, and ℓ_p sketch. Here, since each count stored in the sketch summary is a (weighted) sum of item weights, they can be replaced with exponentially decayed counters, and we obtain a summary of the exponentially decayed input. This allows us to, for example, estimate the decayed weight of individual items, or the L_p norm of the decayed weight vector.

For other summaries, similar results are possible, although more involved. Replacing the counters in the Q-Digest structure with decayed counters allows a weighted version of quantiles and range queries to be answered, based on the decayed weights of items. Similarly, using decayed counters in the SpaceSaving structure allows a decayed version of point queries and heavy hitters to be answered. In both cases, the operations on the data structures are largely as before, with the addition of decay operations on the counters, but the analysis to show the correctness needs to be reworked to incorporate the decay. An implementation issue for both of these is to take a "lazy" approach to decaying counters. That is, we try to avoid requiring that all counters are decayed to reflect the very latest timestamp t, which may take time proportional to the size of the data structure for each update. Instead, we allow each counter to maintain a local timestamp t_c, and only apply the decay operation whenever that counter is accessed by an operation.

History and Background. The notion of exponential decay applied to statistics is one that has appeared in many settings, and does not appear to have a clear point of origin. For similar reasons, the idea of applying exponential decay to sketches seems to be "folklore." Initial efforts to extend exponential decay to other summaries is due to Manjhi et al. [176] for tracking item frequencies, and Aggarwal [6] for sampling with decaying weights.

The comments here about generalizing Q-Digest and SpaceSaving are based on a note by Cormode et al. [72].

9.2.2 Sliding Windows

A second approach to time decay is to consider only a window of recent updates as being relevant. That is, if every update has an associated timestamp, then we only want to answer queries based on those updates falling within the recent window. A window can be defined either time based – e.g., we only consider updates arriving within the last 24 hours – or sequence based – e.g., we only consider the most recent 1 billion updates. Following the trend in the scientific literature, we focus our main attention on the sequence-based model, where the size of the window is denoted W. The examples we give also allow queries to be posed in the time-based window model.

If the space needed is not an issue, then we could in principle just retain the most recent W updates in a buffer, and compute the desired function of interest on demand for this buffer. However, with the assumption that W is still a large quantity, we will discuss summary structures that use much smaller than W space.

We first consider an approach to computing the count of items falling within a sliding window, then see how this can be generalized to other problems.

Exponential Histograms for Windowed Counts. The *exponential histogram* method allows us to keep track of how many item arrivals occur within a recent window. Our input is defined by a sequence of timestamps t_i that record item arrivals. We assume that these are seen in time-stamp order. The structure will allow us to approximately determine how many items arrived within a recent time window of size w and, conversely, find the window size W containing approximately N recent items.

The structure divides the past into a sequence of buckets, with associated counts and timestamps. The most recent $k + 1$ buckets each contain a single item, and record the timestamp at which that item arrived as b_i. The next (upto) $k + 1$ buckets have a count of 2, corresponding to two items, and record the timestamp of the older item. Then, the jth collection of (upto) $k + 1$ buckets have each bucket holding a count of 2^j and recording the timestamp of the oldest item in each bucket.

Updating the structure is done so that the bounds on the number and weights associated with each bucket are maintained. A new item is placed in a bucket of weight 1 at the head of the list. If this causes there to be more than $k + 1$

buckets of weight 1, then we take the oldest two weight 1 buckets and merge them together to obtain a bucket of weight 2, whose timestamp is set to the older of the two timestamps. Similarly, if we obtain more than $k + 1$ buckets of weight 2^j, we merge the two oldest such buckets to obtain one new bucket of weight 2^{j+1}.

To find the number of items from timestamp t to the present (time-window model), we add up the weights of all buckets with timestamps more recent than t. Similarly, to estimate the duration of the time window containing N recent items (sequence-based model), we find the most recent timestamp such that the sum of all bucket weights from that point onward exceeds N.

To limit the space needed, we can delete all buckets whose weight is more than W/k, for a target window size of W. The space of the data structure is bounded by $O(k \log(W/k))$, and queries are answered with an uncertainty in the count of $1/k$, according to the following analysis.

A limitation of this data structure is that it does not allow the MERGE operation: if two exponential histograms have been kept over different inputs, it is likely that they have witnessed sufficiently different patterns of arrivals that we cannot combine their bucket structures and obtain a summary of the union of their inputs.

Further Discussion. According to the aforementioned invariants, we have at most $k + 1$ buckets of each weight class. Hence, if we only keep buckets of weight up to W/k, there are $\log_2(W/k)$ weight classes, each of which keeps at most $k + 1$ buckets. Hence the space needed is $O(k \log_2(W/k))$.

To understand the accuracy of the structure, observe that for the k most recent items, we know their timestamps exactly. For each weight class 2^j, note that there are at least k buckets in each smaller class. Hence, the total weight of more recent items is at least $\sum_{\ell=0}^{j-1} k2^\ell = k2^j$. So the uncertainty in the timestamps we have corresponds to 2^j out of at least $k2^j$ items, which is a $1/k$ fraction. If we set $1/k = \epsilon$ for a target accuracy ϵ, we obtain uncertainty in our queries of ϵ relative error, with space proportional to $O(\frac{1}{\epsilon} \log(\epsilon W))$.

Exponential Histograms for Summaries. As with exponential decay, the structure of the exponential histogram is sufficiently simple that it can be combined with other summary structures. In this case, the natural thing is to keep the overall structure of the histogram and its buckets, and augment the counts with instances of summaries that can be merged. For example, we could keep a SpaceSaving data structure in each bucket, and follow the merging rules. This would allow us to estimate item frequencies within a sliding window. To find item frequencies from (approximately) time-stamp t to the present, we would MERGE together all the summaries in histogram buckets with timestamps more recent than t. This would potentially omit a small number of the oldest updates, at most a $1/k$ fraction of those that do fall in the window. The space cost is then the product of the chosen summary size by the number of buckets. The method is suitably general that it can be applied to all summaries that possess a MERGE method. However, because of the blowup in space cost, there has been a lot of research to find algorithms for specific problems with reduced space bounds.

Timestamps in Summaries. A technique that can be used to introduce sliding windows to certain summaries is to replace binary flags that report the presence of an observation with a timestamp. Two such structures are the BloomFilter and HLL. In both of these, we use bits to record whether an update has been mapped there by a hash function. We can replace these bits with timestamps of the most recent item that has been mapped to that location (or a null value if no item has been mapped there). This allows us to query the summary for an arbitrary time window: given the window, we make a copy of the summary with a 1-bit value in a given location if there is a timestamp that falls within the time window at the corresponding location, and a 0-bit value otherwise. Thus, we obtain a version of the original summary with exactly the configuration as if we had only seen the items that fall within the queried time window. The space cost is a constant factor blowup, as we replace each bit with a timestamp (typically 32 bits).

History and Background. The exponential histogram was introduced by Datar et al. [83], where they also discussed how to generalize it to containing other summary structures. The paper also suggested the idea of replacing bits with timestamps. Other work has considered how to provide efficient solutions for specific problems under sliding windows. For example, Lee and Ting [169] adapt the MG summary to keep information on timestamps to allow sliding window frequency queries, while still only requiring $O(1/\epsilon)$ space. A naive approach that combined MG or SpaceSaving with the aforementioned exponential histogram would instead require $O(1/\epsilon^2 \log(\epsilon W))$ space.

Subsequent work by Braverman and Ostrovsky introduced the concept of *smooth histograms* [37]. These allow a broad class of functions to be approximated under the sliding windows model in a black box fashion, under some assumptions on the function being approximated. The high-level idea is to start a new summary data structure at each timestep to summarize all subsequent updates. Many of these summaries can later be deleted while still ensuring accurate answers. "Smoothness" properties of the target function are used to bound the total space needed.

9.2.3 Other Decay Models

We briefly mention other models of time decay.

Latched Windows. The effort needed to give strong algorithmic guarantees for sliding window queries may seem too large. A simpler approach, known as "latched windows," is to tolerate a weaker notion of approximation. For example, if the goal is to monitor the state of a system over the last 24 hours, it may suffice to create a summary for each hour, and merge together the last 24 summaries to approximately cover the last day. If there is no strong need to have the summaries cover the window to the last microsecond, this is a simple and practical approach.

Arbitrary Functions via Sliding Windows. Alternatively, if the desire is to approximate an arbitrary decay function on the data, this can be simulated by making multiple calls to a sliding window summary. We assume that the decay function is differentiable and is monotone non-increasing as the age increases. The observation is that we can rewrite the value of a decayed query as an integral over time of the derivative of the decay function times the result of the function for the corresponding window. This formulation can be accurately approximated by replacing the continuous integral with a sum over differences in the decay function value, scaled by approximate window queries.

History and Background. The term "latched window" was coined by Golab and Özu [121]. The observation about arbitrary function approximation for sums and counts is due to Cohen and Strauss [59] and applied to summaries by Cormode et al. [79].

9.3 Data Transformations

The applicability of summary techniques can be extended when they are applied not to raw data, but to a (usually linear) transformation of the input data. This provides most flexibility when the transformation can be computed on each individual update as it arrives, so the summary (or summaries) processes a sequence of transformed updates.

We have already seen examples of this, in the form of the Dyadic Count Sketch (DCS, Section 4.4). The method can be understood as first mapping each update into a collection of updates, each of which is processed by a separate summary. There are a number of uses of this approach to solve new problems by making use of existing solutions. Moreover, these can be chained together: we apply a sequence of transformations to each update, before it is summarized. The ability to MERGE the original summaries means that we can also MERGE summaries of transformed data.

9.3.1 Dyadic Decompositions for Heavy Hitters

Several of the summaries for multisets (Chapter 3) address the question of finding items from the input domain whose aggregate weight is heavy – often called the "frequent items" or "heavy hitters" problem. For example, the items kept by a MG or SpaceSaving summary include those whose weight is larger than an ϵ fraction of the total weight, $\|v\|_1$. Sketch-based methods, such as Count-Min Sketch and Count Sketch, can also solve this problem, with guarantees in terms of $\|v\|_1$ or $\|v\|_2$. However, these sketches do not directly make it convenient to find the heavy items. The most direct approach is to QUERY for the estimated weight of every item in the domain – which is very slow for large domains.

Instead, one can make use of the DCS for this problem. Recall that this applies a "dyadic decomposition" to the domain of the input items, $[U]$. A sketch is kept on the original items, on pairs of adjacent items in the domain, on items grouped into fours, and so on. This allows a recursive top-down search process to be applied to find the heavy items. We begin by querying the weight of the left half and the right half of the domain, using the statistics kept by the DCS. For each dyadic interval whose total weight (according to the DCS) exceeds a ε fraction of the total weight, we split the dyadic interval into its two constitute subintervals of half the length, and recursively proceed. If we reach an interval consisting of a single item, then this can be returned as a "heavy hitter." Provided all items have nonnegative weight, then every range containing a heavy hitter item will be a heavy range, and so we will not miss any heavy items.

Further Discussion. The guarantees of this search procedure follow from those for the DCS. Every query posed is transformed into a point QUERY to one of the Count Sketch data structures that make up the DCS structure. Consequently, the error is bounded with sufficient probability. The total number of queries is bounded: assuming that each query meets its accuracy bound, then the number of queries posed to a given level in the dyadic decomposition is bounded, since the total weight at each level is bounded in terms of the total weight of the input. For example, if we are seeking to find all items of weight at least $\varepsilon \|v\|_1$, then there are at most $O(1/\varepsilon)$ dyadic ranges at each level whose true weight exceeds $\varepsilon \|v\|_1$. Consequently, we can bound the time taken for the search as a function of $(1/\varepsilon)$ and the parameters of the sketch. Naively, this cost is poly-logarithmic in the size of the domain from which items are drawn, U, since we rescale the accuracy parameter by factors of $\log U$ (see Section 4.4). A slightly improved analysis is due to Larsen *et al.* [167, appendix E], who show that the expected time to search for all heavy hitters can be kept to $O(1/\varepsilon \log U)$ by keeping sketches of total size only $O\left(\frac{1}{\varepsilon} \log U\right)$.

9.3.2 Coding Transforms for Heavy Item Recovery

The problem becomes more challenging when items may have negative weights, which can happen in more general scenarios. Here, the divide and conquer approach can fail, since a heavy item can be masked by surrounding items with the opposite sign. An approach is to still make use of sketch summaries, but to arrange them based on ideas from coding theory.

A first example is based on the Hamming code. Given an m bit binary message, the Hamming code adds $\lceil \log m \rceil$ additional "parity" bits. The first parity bit is computed from the bits at odd locations in the message (i.e., indices $1, 3, 5, \ldots$). The jth parity bit is computed from the bits for which the jth bit of their binary index is a 1. That is, the second parity bit depends on indices 2, 3, 6, 7, 10, 11, ...

This structure can be adapted to give a data transformation. Given items drawn from a domain $[U]$, we map to $\lceil \log U \rceil + 1$ summaries — for concreteness, we will use a Count Sketch, where each instance uses the same parameters and the same set of hash functions. We follow the same pattern: only those items whose jth bit of their index is 1 are mapped into the jth sketch, and processed by the usual UPDATE routine. For the 0'th sketch, we process all updates without any exceptions.

To QUERY this modified summary, we can probe each cell of the sketches in turn. For each cell in the 0th sketch, we examine the magnitude of the count stored there, $|c|$. If it is above a threshold τ, then there is evidence that there could be a heavy item mapping to this cell — or there could be multiple items mapping there that sum to c. The process attempts to "decode" the identity of an item, using the sketches of the transformed data. The cell will be abandoned if it is not possible to clearly determine the identity of an item.

The aim is to recover each bit of the heavy item's identifier, if there is a heavy item. Consider first the least significant bit (index 1), which determines whether an item's identifier is odd or even. We can inspect the corresponding cell of the first sketch, which has included only the odd items. If the magnitude of this cell, c_1, is also above τ, and $|c - c_1|$ is less than τ, then we can conclude that there is potentially an odd item that is heavy. Meanwhile, if $|c - c_1| \geq \tau$ and $|c_1| < \tau$, we conclude that there is potentially an even item that is heavy. The other two cases are $|c - c_1| < \tau$ and $|c_1| < \tau$, which implies that there are no items in this cell above the threshold of τ; or $|c - c_1| \geq \tau$ and $|c_1| \geq \tau$, which implies that there could be more than one heavy item in this cell. In either of the last two cases, we abandon this cell, and move on to the next cell in the 0th sketch.

This process can be repeated for every sketch. If at the end we have not abandoned a cell, then we have a bit value (0 or 1) for each location, which can be concatenated to provide an item identifier for an item that is assumed to be heavy. This can be confirmed by, for example, keeping an additional independent Count Sketch to cross-check the estimated weight, and also by checking that the candidate item is indeed mapped to the cell it was recovered from.

Further Discussion. It's clear that the preceding process will recover some candidate items, but it is less clear whether items that are heavy will be successfully identified. Consider some item which is heavy (above the threshold τ), and assume that it is mapped by the hash function into the zeroth sketch so that the total (absolute) weight of other items in the same cell is less than the threshold τ. Then we can be sure that every test that is applied to determine the value of a particular bit in its item identifier will succeed – we will find the correct value for that bit. Consequently, we will recover the item correctly. Hence, the argument comes down to bounding the amount of weight from other items that collides with it in a particular cell. This can be done with a Markov-inequality argument, similar to the Count-Min Sketch: the expected amount of colliding mass is a $1/w$ fraction of the total mass (measured in terms of either $\|v\|_1$ or $\|v\|_2^2$), where w is the width of the sketch data structure. Choosing τ to be at least $2\|v\|_1/w$ (or at least $2\|v\|_2/\sqrt{w}$ in the ℓ_2 case) means that there is at least a constant probability to find a given heavy item in each row of the sketch. This probability is amplified over the rows of the sketches. If we ensure that the number of rows is $O(\log w/\delta)$, then we ensure that we can find all heavy items with probability at least $1 - \delta$.

History and Background. This Hamming code-inspired approach to finding heavy items is described by Cormode and Muthukrishnan [74, 75], with similar ideas appearing previously in [114]. It is possible to use the same approach with more complex code constructions; see for example [199]. Other approaches are based on the idea of applying an invertible remapping to item identifiers, and breaking these into smaller chunks for sketching, yielding "reversible sketches" [209]; and the counter-braids approach, which uses a random mapping to sketch entries of varying capacity, based on low-density parity check codes [174]. Similar ideas are used to construct algorithms with improved space bounds based on coding items so that heavy items appears as "clusters" within a graph [167].

9.3.3 Range Transformations

Given a data vector v indexed over the integer domain $[U]$, a range query $[l, r]$ is to find the quantity $\sum_{i=l}^{r} v_i$. With a summary that allows us to estimate entries of v, we can simply sum up the corresponding estimates. However, the query time, and the error, tends to scale proportional to the length of the range, $|r - l + 1|$. The dyadic decomposition allows us to answer range queries more efficiently, and with lower error. This is already provided by the DCS (Section 4.4), where the case of a rank query is discussed. Since a rank query for index x corresponds to the range query $[0, x - 1]$, we can answer range queries by computing $\text{rank}(r - 1) - \text{rank}(l)$, and obtain error $\epsilon\|v\|_1$.

Range queries generalize to higher dimensions. One approach discussed in Section 5.1, based on ϵ-nets and ϵ-approximations, is effective for a dataset of points arriving in d dimensions. However, when data points may arrive and depart, a different approach may be needed. The notion of dyadic decompositions can be extended to multiple dimensions: we perform a dyadic decomposition on each dimension, and summarize vectors of membership of the cross-product of these decompositions. Then each data point falls into $O(\log^d U)$ cells, and the space required to provide an $\epsilon\|v\|_1$ guarantee scales with $O(\log^{2d} U)$. This can be effective for small d, but is often too costly for more than two or three dimensions.

History and Background. The idea of dyadic decompositions is a ubiquitous idea in computer science and computational geometry, and has been independently suggested within the context of data summarization several times. An early example is due to Gilbert et al. [118]. Discussion and evaluation of different sketching approaches to range query estimation are given by Dobra and Rusu [88, section 6], in the context of estimating the join size between database relations (which is equivalent to inner products of vectors).

9.3.4 Linear Transforms

A large class of data transformations can be described as linear transformations. That is, if the data can be considered to define a vector, v, the transformation can be considered to be a (fixed) matrix A so that the transformed data are the vector Av. Note that our previous examples, such as the dyadic decomposition, meet this definition of a linear transformation.

Many other transformations meet this definition, in particular basis transformations, where in addition the (implicit) transformation A represents an (orthonormal) basis transformation, so that $AA^T = I$. That is, distinct rows of A are orthogonal, and the (Euclidean) norm of each row is one. These naturally compose with sketching techniques. Since many of the sketch summaries we have seen, such as Count-Min Sketch, Count Sketch, AMS Sketch, and Sparse JLT, are also linear transformations, we can write the joint action of a sketch S and a transformation A as the product SA. Further, the structure of the transform may allow it to be applied quickly. We give two examples that have been used in the context of data summaries.

Discrete Haar Wavelet Transform (DHT). The Discrete Haar Wavelet Transform (Haar transform, or wavelets for short) is used extensively in signal processing as a way of transforming the data to extract high-level detail. Similar to other transformations such as (discrete) Fourier transforms, it transforms an input vector of U entries into a vector of U wavelet coefficients. The inverse transform of a set of coefficients rebuilds the corresponding input vector. It is often used as the basis of data compression, since reducing the accuracy with which some coefficients are stored, or dropping some entirely, still allows a fairly accurate reconstruction of the original vector. Another useful feature of the transform is that (one-dimensional) range queries can be answered by combining only $O(\log U)$ wavelet coefficients (similar to the dyadic decomposition). Last, the transform is an orthonormal basis, as described previously, and so the Euclidean norm of of the coefficients is equal to the Euclidean norm of the input vector.

In more detail, each row in the Haar transform matrix is formed as the concatenation of two adjacent dyadic ranges (i.e., a range whose length is a power of two, beginning at an integer multiple of its length), where the first range is multiplied by +1, and the second by −1, normalized so that the row norm is 1. Hence, the transform is somewhat similar to the dyadic decomposition discussed previously. As a result, it can be combined with sketching: we can apply the Haar transform to each update, then take each result and use them to UPDATE a sketch, such as a Count Sketch. By combining this with methods such as the coding approach outlined earlier, it is possible to recover the wavelet transform accurately from the sketch. An important feature of the wavelet transform is that it is relatively sparse: each column of the $2^d \times 2^d$ transform matrix has only $d + 1$ nonzero entries, and these can be computed directly without storing the full matrix. Therefore, each data update translates into $d + 1$ wavelet coefficient updates.

Discrete Hadamard Transform. The Discrete Hadamard Transform (Hadamard, for short), is the Fourier transform when we consider the data to be indexed as a d-dimensional hypercube. Compared to other Fourier transforms, it is perhaps simpler to express. The $2^d \times 2^d$ Hadamard transform is given by $H_{i,j} = 2^{-d/2}(-1)^{\langle i,j \rangle}$, where $\langle i, j \rangle$ is the modulo-2 inner product of the binary representations of i and j. A sketch of the Hadamard transform of a dataset can be computed as for the DHT: each update is transformed to generate a set of updates to the Hadamard transform, which are then used to UPDATE the sketch. However, the Hadamard transform is very dense, so every update to the data produces 2^d updates to the transform. It may then be advantageous to buffer up some updates before computing their transformation, which can be added on to the sketch, using the properties of linearity: $SH(x + y) = SHx + SHy$. We have mentioned one application of Hadamard transform already, in our discussion of the Sparse JLT (Section 5.5).

History and Background. Computing the wavelet transform of a stream of data was one of the first problems actively studied in that area. Gilbert et al. [116] suggested first building a sketch of the original data, then estimating wavelet coefficients by building a sketch of each wavelet basis vector, and estimating the inner product. The idea to instead transform the input data into the wavelet domain as it arrives was suggested by, among others, Cormode et al. [67]. Computing summaries to find the (sparse) Fourier transform of data has also had a long history, going back to the start of the century [115]. As noted, the Hadamard transform specifically plays an important role in instantiations of the Johnson–Lindenstrauss transform [8]. More recently, there

has been a line of work to build summaries of the Fourier transform so that the
k biggest Fourier coefficients of data of size n can be found faster than the
(already quite fast) $O(n \log n)$-time Fast Fourier Transform [130].

9.4 Manipulating Summaries

Given different ways to summarize data as building blocks, there are many
possible ways to extend their applications by manipulating summary structures, such as combining or nesting them in ways beyond the basic UPDATE
and MERGE procedures.

9.4.1 Algebra on Summaries

Whenever we apply a MERGE operation on a pair of summaries, we are
relying on an algebraic property. This may be that MERGE(X, MERGE(Y, Z)) =
MERGE(MERGE(X, Y), Z), i.e., the MERGE operation is associative; or a weaker
statement that MERGE(X, MERGE(Y, Z)) $\approx$ MERGE(MERGE(X, Y), Z) – that is,
that the result of changing the merge order may not provide identical results,
but that the results are equivalent in terms of the approximation guarantees that
they promise (encoded by the $\approx$ relation).

For some summaries, we have stronger algebraic properties. In particular,
when the summary is a linear transform, as discussed in Section 9.3.4. Recall
that we say a summary is a linear transform when it can be written as Av,
when the input is described by a vector v. It then immediately follows from
properties of linear algebra that $A(\alpha v + \beta w) = \alpha Av + \beta Aw$. That is, we
can apply linear scaling to the inputs v and w by directly scaling the result of
summarizing. This gives flexibility in manipulating summaries. In particular,
it means that $A(v - w) = Av - Aw$: we can summarize inputs v and w
separately, then subtract the summaries to obtain a summary of this difference.
This allows, for example, using a Count Sketch to estimate the difference
in frequencies between two observations of a distribution (say, the difference
between the distribution yesterday and today). The error is proportional to $\|v -
w\|_2$, which can be much smaller than the alternative approach of separately
estimating the frequency of the two instances, which incurs error proportional
to $\|v\|_2 + \|w\|_2$.

9.4.2 Resizing a Summary

For traditional data structures that are initialized to a fixed size, it is common to
allow the structure to be "resized" to accommodate more or fewer items, even

if this requires emptying the structure of stored items, and filling a new instance from scratch. While many summaries we have seen are also initialized based on a fixed parameter, in order to provide a particular approximation guarantee ϵ, say, it is rarely straightforward to resize a summary.

In several cases, it is possible to reduce the size of a summary, say by halving the size parameter. For example, it is possible to resize a BloomFilter summary down, e.g., to go from m to $m/2$ bits (when m is even), by treating the left and right halves of the summary as the subjects of a MERGE operation, and ignoring the most significant bit of the hash values going forward. Similar results hold for sketches like Count-Min Sketch, Count Sketch, AMS Sketch, and Sparse JLT.

However, the inverse operation (doubling the size of the summary) does not lend itself to such tricks. In general, we would not expect summaries to be increased in size without some penalty in space or accuracy. To provide the approximation guarantees associated with the larger size would entail retrieving information that was previously "forgotten" in order to ensure a smaller space bound. The best one might hope for is that far in advance of the current structure filling up with information, we would start a new instance of the summary in parallel to summarize the subsequent updates. Then the total magnitude of those initial updates that were ignored would eventually be sufficiently small that they would not impact the approximation guarantee.

9.4.3 Nesting Summaries

A natural approach to building new summaries is to "nest" summaries inside one another. That is, we use one summary type as a substructure within another one. We have already seen some examples that meet this description. For example, the ℓ_0-sampler is built by nesting SparseRecovery summaries inside a sampling structure. We next describe some more examples where one summary type is "nested" inside another.

Summaries Using Probabilistic Counters. Many summaries (particularly sketch summaries) are based on collections of counters that count the number of items mapped to those counters by hash functions. In Section 1.2.2, we saw that a counter could be considered as a first example of a summary. It is natural to replace an exact counter with a MorrisCounter probabilistic counter. The result is to reduce the space required for the summary when dealing with inputs truly huge in volume, since the bit size of the counters is reduced to the logarithm of this amount. With careful argument, it can be shown that the resulting estimates remain approximately correct.

Summaries Using Distinct Counters. Consider the problem where our input is described by a sequence of pairs (x, y), and we want to find those x values that are associated with a large number of distinct y values. For example, the pairs (x, y) could be edges in a graph, and we want to find those nodes that have a high number of (distinct) neighbors. If there were only a few x values, then we would keep a distinct counter for each x (a KMV or HLL structure). If there were no duplicate (x, y) pairs, we would use a frequent items structure such as SpaceSaving or Count-Min Sketch summary. It therefore makes sense that to solve the general form of the problem when there are many x values and many repetitions that we can combine a frequent items structure with distinct counters. A simple instantiation comes from taking a Count-Min Sketch and replacing each counter with an HLL summary. Each (x, y) update uses the Count-Min Sketch hash functions to map x to a set of cells. Each cell contains an HLL, which is updated with the value of y. The analysis of the new nested summary is similar to that for the basic Count-Min Sketch: to estimate the number of distinct ys associated with a given x, we inspect the cells where that x is mapped. Each one counts (approximately) the number of distinct y's for that x along with other colliding items. Taking the smallest of these estimates minimizes the amount of noise from colliding items.

Summaries with Quantile Summaries. Last, we can use quantile summaries such as GK or Q-Digest as the nested summary. For example, consider replacing the counters in a Count-Min Sketch with a GK summary. We can now process data represented by pairs (x, y), where x is used to map into the Count-Min Sketch, and then y is used to update the corresponding GK summary in the mapped cell. This allows us to estimate the distribution of y values associated with a given x, by probing all the cells associated with x and interrogating the GK summary with the lowest total weight. For xs that are relatively rare, this will have a higher error, but fairly accurate answers can be provided for x's with high frequency.

History and Background. The idea of building sketches on top of probabilistic counters is explored by Gronemeier and Sauerhoff [125]. Considine et al. [61] describe combinations of the Count-Min Sketch and Q-Digest with the Flajolet–Martin sketch, a precursor to HLL. Motivation for this problem in the networking domain is given by Venkataraman et al. [228], which defines the notion of "superspreaders." These correspond to network addresses that communicate with a large number of distinct other addresses. Related problems, such as combining frequency moments with distinct counts, are covered by Cormode and Muthukrishnan [77]. Problems that require applying different stages of aggregation have been studied variously under the labels of "correlated aggregates" [224] and "cascaded norms" [145].

10
Lower Bounds for Summaries

The focus of this volume so far has been on what is possible to effectively summarize. Yet it should come as no surprise that there are some questions for which no summary exists. In this chapter, we look at cases where it is not simply that no summary is known to exist, but rather where it is mathematically impossible for any summary to be made that is less than some size. The intuition underlying these results are that certain settings require a large amount of information to be stored in order to allow a range of queries to be answered accurately. Where this information is comparable to the size of the data being stored, it effectively precludes the possibility of a useful summary for that problem. In other cases, summaries are possible, and the lower bounds tell us how small we can hope the summary to be.

Computational complexity is the area of computer science devoted to understanding the fundamental limits of what can be computed effectively. Most computer science degrees cover the time complexity of solving problems based on classes such as $\mathcal{P}$ and $\mathcal{NP}$. $\mathcal{P}$ is the class of problems that can be solved in a standard model of computation in time that is bounded by a polynomial in the input size, denoted n. $\mathcal{NP}$ is the class of problems (informally) where a conjectured solution can be *verified* in time polynomial in n. The notion of *hardness* in this setting is to show that a given problem is as hard as another, in the sense that a polynomial time algorithm for the former problem would yield a polynomial time algorithm for the latter.

These notions of complexity do not translate to the world of summaries for a number of reasons. Primarily, summaries are often relevant when bounds that are polynomial would be considered too lax. For the most part, the summaries described in this book address problems that can be easily solved in time polynomial in the input size n. Rather, we look for summaries that use time and space resources that are smaller than n, ideally strictly sublinear in n.

Techniques that provide lower bounds for summaries tend to be derived from the area of communication complexity. These study the cost of communication between two parties (traditionally, anthropomorphized as Alice and Bob) who each hold part of the input and wish to collaborate to compute a function of it. For example, suppose Alice and Bob hold strings x and y, and wish to compute whether $x = y$ or $x \neq y$. We refer to this as the EQUALITY problem. In this setting, a trivial protocol is for Alice to send her part of the input to Bob, which would take $O(n)$ communication. Therefore, the way to show bounds on summary size is to derive bounds on communication, up to linear in n.

There is a very natural mapping from bounds on communication to bounds on summaries. We can view the communication between Alice and Bob as a communication from the past to the present. That is, suppose we had a summary that addressed a particular problem that maps onto a particular communication problem. We could have Alice run the summary algorithm on her portion of the input to build the summary data structure in memory. This could then be communicated to Bob, who could subsequently put his portion of the input into the summary, either by performing a MERGE with a summary of his data, or applying repeated UPDATE operations. If the summary provides an answer via a QUERY operation that can be interpreted as an answer to the communication problem, then we have a communication protocol.

Therefore, any lower bound on the communication needed to solve the communication problem provides a corresponding lower bound on the size of a summary to solve the relevant summarization problem. We will see several examples of this outline being instantiated over the course of this chapter. The application of data summarization (particularly in the context of streaming data processing) has stimulated the area of communication complexity, and led to many novel techniques being developed in order to prove new lower bounds for summaries. The lower bounds tend to be on the size of the summary, rather than on the time necessary to UPDATE or QUERY them: this is a result of the focus on communication size from communication complexity. In other words, the techniques we have for proving hardness most naturally provide lower bounds on summary size; proving bounds on the time costs associated with data summarization would also be very important, but has proved to be more challenging with the tools currently available.

We will not provide proofs of the communication complexity lower bounds, which warrant a volume of their own to define (as a starting point, see the text of Kushilevitz and Nisan [164]). Rather, we focus on the ways that hard communication problems provide lower bounds on summary sizes. These tend to be *reductions*: for a given summary problem, we identify a suitable communication problem that would be solved if a small summary existed. For the remainder of this chapter, we describe some of the commonly used hard problems in communication complexity, and give examples of the summaries for which they provide lower bounds. An important concept is whether the communication bounds are one round (for protocols where Alice sends a single message to Bob), or multiround (the bounds still hold when Alice and Bob are allowed to have a conversation with many messages back and forth).

10.1 Equality and Fingerprinting

The most basic communication complexity problem is the EQUALITY problem. Here, Alice and Bob both possess binary strings of length n, denoted as x and y respectively. The problem is to determine whether or not $x = y$. It is straightforward to see that if Alice is to send a single message to Bob, then it must contain n bits, if Bob is to be guaranteed to give the correct answer. Suppose the contrary: Alice sends a message of $b < n$ bits in length. Alice has 2^n possible inputs, but only $2^b < 2^n$ possible messages to choose from. So by the pigeonhole principle, there must be two different inputs x and x' that Alice could have that would cause her to send the same message to Bob. Then Bob cannot guarantee to succeed, as he may have $y = x$ as his string, and be uncertain whether Alice held x (requiring a "yes" answer) or x' (requiring a "no" answer). Therefore, the problem must require a communication of at least n bits. Applying the preceding template, this also means that any summary that claims to answer the corresponding problem – summarizing two inputs to determine whether or not they are equal – must also require $\Omega(n)$ bits.

Connection to Fingerprinting. At first glance, this hardness may appear to cause a contradiction. We have studied a summary (Fingerprint) that claims to solve exactly this problem using a summary size that is much smaller than n bits. This apparent contradiction is resolved by observing that the preceding argument required Alice and Bob to be deterministic in their operation. That is, we have successfully shown that any *deterministic* summary must be linear in the input size if it allows equality to be tested and verified with certainty. However, if Alice and Bob are allowed to make random choices, and tolerate some small probability of error, then a much smaller summary is possible, as witnessed by the Fingerprint method. This serves to highlight the importance of randomization: for the majority of problems we consider, randomization is required to evade strong lower bounds on deterministic summaries.

The subsequent examples we consider provide lower bounds on communication schemes that allow randomization, which therefore provide lower bounds on randomized summary techniques.

10.2 Index and Set Storage

The INDEX problem in communication complexity is defined as follows:

Definition 10.1 (INDEX problem) *Alice holds a binary string x of n bits in length, while Bob holds an index y in $[n]$. The goal is for the players to follow a protocol to output $x[y]$, i.e., the y'th bit from the string x.*

If the players are allowed multiple rounds of communication between them, then there is a trivial protocol for INDEX: Bob communicates y to Alice, who then emits $x[y]$, requiring $\lceil \log n \rceil + 1$ total bits of communication. However, under the constraint that Bob does not communicate to Alice, the problem becomes much harder. That is, in the "one-way" communication complexity model, Alice sends a message to Bob, who must then output the answer. It is hard to imagine that one can find any solution appreciably better than Alice sending her entire string to Bob, who can then read off the required bit. Indeed, it is straightforward to adapt the previous proof for EQUALITY to show that no deterministic algorithm for this problem can communicate fewer than $\Omega(n)$ bits of information.

It is more involved to show that this remains the case when Alice and Bob are allowed to use randomization. Intuitively, it is not clear how randomization would help here, but a formal lower bound must rule out the possibility of some clever summary that encodes Alice's string in some nonobvious way. Such a proof was first shown in the early 1990s by Razborov [204]. A compact proof of this fact that uses the method of information complexity is provided by Jayram [143]. Formally, these results show that even when the randomized communication protocol is required to succeed only with some constant probability (say, 2/3), the players still need to communicate $\Omega(n)$ bits.

It is natural to apply this result to summary techniques. The constraint that Bob is not allowed to communicate his index y to Alice is a natural one: we can think of Alice as observing the data, from which she must construct her summary (message). Bob then receives the summary and wants to answer some query. However, if the answer to Bob's query could reveal the value of any one of n bits encoded into the summary by Alice, then we know that the summary must have size $\Omega(n)$.

Lower Bound for Set storage. A direct application of this is to show a size bound for any summary that encodes a set, such as a BloomFilter (Section 2.7). The argument proceeds as follows. Suppose we had a summary that could very compactly encode a set A of items from n possibilities. Now take an instance of INDEX. Alice could store her bitstring in the set summary, by storing each element i such that $x[i] = 1$. After the summary is sent to Bob, Bob looks up y in the summary. If y is present in the set, then Bob asserts that $x[y] = 1$, else he concludes $x[y] = 0$. Therefore, any summary that encodes a set in this way would provide a solution to the INDEX problem, and hence must use at least $\Omega(n)$ bits. In particular, this argument shows that the BloomFilter must use $\Omega(n)$ bits to represent sets whose size is proportional to n.

Lower Bound for Count Distinct. A slightly more elaborate argument can show a lower bound on the size of summaries to estimate the number of distinct members of a set, such as KMV and HLL. Consider again an instance of the INDEX problem, and a summary that claims to allow the estimation of the number of distinct elements in a set, up to an approximation factor of $1 \pm \epsilon$. Alice performs a similar reduction to the previous one: she performs an UPDATE operation on the distinct elements summary with each index i such that $x[i] = 1$. On receiving the summary, Bob first performs a QUERY operation to estimate the size of Alice's set, as m. Bob then performs an UPDATE with his index y, and makes a second QUERY to the summary, to obtain a second estimate m'. These two answers are compared as follows: if $(1-\epsilon)m' > (1+\epsilon)m$, then Bob concludes that the number of distinct elements has increased following the insertion of y. That is, y was not previously in the set, and so $x[y] = 0$; otherwise, Bob concludes that $x[y] = 1$. This argument works if the parameter ϵ is small enough so that a change of 1 in the size of the sets must lead to a different answer. That is, $\epsilon n < 1$, for a set size of n. The lower bound of $\Omega(n)$ then implies a lower bound in terms of ϵ as $\Omega(1/\epsilon)$ on the size of the summary.

Observe that this lower bound is somewhat unsatisfying, since both KMV and HLL are shown to have a space cost that depends on $O(1/\epsilon^2)$. A reduction to a stronger lower bound below (Section 10.4) removes this gap.

Lower Bound for Counting Triangles. The hardness of INDEX can also be used to show the hardness of the problem of counting triangles in a graph. Upper bounds for this problem are discussed in Section 7.4. Here, we formalize the problem of counting triangles as a problem parametrized by a scalar T. We are asked to distinguish between graphs that have no triangles at all, and those that have at least $T < n$ triangles. Given a summary technique that claims to solve this problem, we show how to use it to solve INDEX. We construct the graph over three sets, X, Y, and Z, where Z is chosen to be of size T. The bitstring x is encoded into the adjacency pattern between X and Y: index i is mapped in some canonical fashion to a pair of indices j and k, and edge (X_j, Y_k) is placed in the graph by Alice if the corresponding bit $x_i = 1$. This encoding allows Bob to probe for the value of a bit in x, as follows. Bob similarly finds the indices j and k from his index y, and inserts edges (X_j, Z_ℓ) and (Y_k, Z_ℓ) for all $1 \leq \ell \leq T$. Then, if there is the edge (X_j, Y_k) in the graph (corresponding to $x_i = 1$), there are a total of T triangles, whereas there are no triangles otherwise. This shows that the triangle counting problem requires space $\Omega(|X| \cdot |Y|)$. A nice feature of this reduction (due to Braverman et al. [39]) is that the sizes of X and Y can be chosen to generate an arbitrary number of edges as a function of n, so the problem is hard, whether the graph is sparse (has only $O(n)$ edges) or dense (has $\Omega(n^2)$ edges), or anywhere in between. The number of edges, m, is $O(nT)$, for an INDEX instance of size n, so the summary size lower bound in terms of m is $\Omega(m/T)$.

10.3 Disjointness and Heavy Hitters

The DISJOINTNESS problem is defined as follows:

Definition 10.2 (DISJOINTNESS problem) *Alice holds a binary string x of n bits in length, while Bob holds a binary string y, also of n bits in length. The goal is for the players to determine whether there exists an index i such that $x[i] = y[i] = 1$, or that no such index exists.*

The problem may appear tractable, but it is hard. Formally, any communication protocol for DISJOINTNESS requires the players to communicate a total of $\Omega(n)$ bits, even if randomization is allowed. This holds even when the players are allowed to have multiple rounds of interaction: Alice and Bob can send multiple messages. This relaxation does not help in proving stronger lower bounds for summary construction, but is useful for places where multiple rounds of communication could be allowed, such as in the distributed setting (Chapter 8). The hardness of the DISJOINTNESS problem is shown by a similar argument. It was first demonstrated by Kalyanasundaram and Schnitger [151], and simplified by Razborov [204].

Note that if we change the problem to ask whether there exists any index i such that $x[i] = y[i]$ (i.e., we remove the requirement that the bit at the index is 1), then the new problem becomes much simpler. If we have a "no" instance of this new problem, then we must have $x[i] \neq y[i]$ for all locations i. That is, $x[i] = (1 - y[i])$. Then we can compare fingerprints of x and the string y'

formed by flipping every bit of y, and output "no" if these fingerprints match. This protocol has communication cost $O(\log n)$. Thus the asymmetry in the problem definition is required to make it a difficult problem.

Lower Bound for multiset frequency. A first application of the DISJOINTNESS problem is to show the hardness of estimating the highest frequency in a multiset. That is, the input defines a multiset v, and the objective is to estimate $\max_i v_i$, the largest frequency in the multiset. Again, assume we had a compact summary for this problem, and we will show how it could be used to solve DISJOINTNESS. Given the instance of DISJOINTNESS, Alice takes her string x, and encodes it so that $v_i = x[i]$, i.e., inserts i into the summary if $x[i] = 1$. This summary is sent to Bob, who similarly encodes his string. This means that $v_i = x[i] + y[i]$. Suppose we could find $F = \max_i v_i$. Then $F = 2$ if and only if (iff) there is some i such that $x[i] = y[i] = 1$, and $F \leq 1$ otherwise. Hence, we can't hope to solve this maximum frequency problem with a summary of size less than $\Omega(n)$, even if we allow an approximate answer.[1] This explains why the various summaries that address this problem (MG, SpaceSaving, Count-Min Sketch, and Count Sketch) offer a different guarantee: they approximate frequencies not with relative error, but with an error that depends on $\|v\|_1$ or $\|v\|_2$.

Lower Bound for Inner Product Estimation. Section 6.1 shows how sketches can be used to estimate inner products between pairs of vectors u and v, with an error that is proportional to $\|u\|_2 \|v\|_2$. In many applications, we would prefer to have an error that scales proportional to the inner product $u \cdot v$ itself. This is not feasible in general for arbitrary inputs, by a reduction to the DISJOINTNESS problem.

Suppose that we had a summary that promised to answer inner product queries with error $\epsilon(u \cdot v)$. Then we could use it to solve DISJOINTNESS quite directly: simply set $u = x$ and $v = y$ for binary vectors x and y. Then observe that $(x \cdot y) = 0$ iff x and y are disjoint (a no instance of the problem), but $(x \cdot y) \geq 1$ iff x and y have any point of intersection. That is, the result counts the number of points of intersection. Then the space required by any summary must be $\Omega(n)$, else it could be used as the basis of a DISJOINTNESS communication protocol. In particular, this rules out any constant factor approximation of $(x \cdot y)$, since this would allow us to distinguish between the $x \cdot y = 0$ and $x \cdot y \geq 1$.

This argument also allows us to argue that error terms like $\epsilon \|u\|_2 \|v\|_2$ are reasonable. Consider the same interpretation of bitstrings from DISJOINTNESS

---

[1] That is, even if we only approximate F up to a constant factor less than 2.

as vectors. Then $\|u\|_2, \|v\|_2 = \Omega(\sqrt{n})$ in general, where n denotes the length of the bitstrings. Estimating their inner product with sufficient accuracy to distinguish a 0 from a 1 result would require the additive error to satisfy $\epsilon \|u\|_2 \|v\|_2 = \epsilon \Omega(n) < \frac{1}{2}$, i.e., $\epsilon = O(1/n)$, or $n = \Omega(1/\epsilon)$. This implies that the size of the summary must be $\Omega(1/\epsilon)$.

Multipass Lower Bound for Triangle Counting. In Section 10.2, we used the hardness of the INDEX problem to show that counting the number of triangles in a graph requires a summary of size proportional to the number of edges. Here, we describe a stronger lower bound [69], under the more demanding scenario that we are allowed to access the input data multiple times. This corresponds to a communication problem where Alice and Bob can exchange multiple messages. Note that INDEX is not helpful to us here: if Alice and Bob can have multiple rounds of communication, then we can easily solve INDEX instances with few bits: Bob just has to send the index to Alice, who can reply with the target value. Instead, we rely on problems like DISJOINTNESS, which remain hard even when multiple rounds of communication are allowed.

As before, we focus on the problem of distinguishing a graph G with no triangles from one with T or more triangles. We will construct a graph on $\theta(n)$ vertices with $\Omega(n\sqrt{T})$ edges and $1 \leq T \leq n^2$ triangles by encoding an instance of DISJOINTNESS. We define three sets of nodes, A with n nodes, and B and C, which each have $\sqrt{T}$ nodes. Given the binary string y over n bits, Bob creates edges from each a_i such that $y_i = 1$ to all nodes in B. Alice creates every edge (b, c) between $b \in B$ and $c \in C$. Last, she inserts edges from each a_i such that $x_i = 1$ to all nodes in C.

Observe from this construction that if strings x and y are disjoint, then there are no triangles in the graph, since there is no node a_i with an edge to B and an edge to C. However, for every intersection i between x and y there are triangles on nodes (a_i, b_j, c_k) for all $\sqrt{T}$ values of j and k, giving a total of T triangles. The bound $T \leq n^2$ ensures that the number of nodes is $O(n)$, and the number of edges is $T + (|x| + |y|)\sqrt{T} \leq 3n\sqrt{T}$ (using $\sqrt{T} \leq n$ from the assumption).

From the hardness of DISJOINTNESS, we know that any summary for this problem must use $\Omega(n)$ space. Rewriting the bound in terms of the number of edges, m, we obtain a bound of $\Omega(m/\sqrt{T})$. This is stronger than the corresponding bound of $\Omega(m/T)$ by using a reduction from INDEX.

10.4 Gap Hamming and Count Distinct, Again

To prove stronger bounds for some problems, a different problem is defined, based on the notion of Hamming distance: the number of places where a pair of binary strings differ.

Definition 10.3 (GAP-HAMMING problem) *Alice holds a binary string x of n bits in length, and Bob holds a binary string y of n bits in length. The Hamming distance, $H(x, y)$ is defined as $|\{i : x_i \neq y_i\}|$. We are promised that either $H(x, y) \leq n/2 - \sqrt{n}$ or $H(x, y) \geq n/2 + \sqrt{n}$. The goal is for the players to determine which case their input falls in.*

Note that we could solve this problem using summary techniques we have seen already. If we treat the binary strings x and y as vectors, then the vector $(x - y)$ has squared Euclidean norm equal to $H(x, y)$; that is, $H(x, y) = \|x - y\|_2^2$. We can obtain an estimate of the Euclidean norm (and hence the squared Euclidean norm) with relative error ϵ using space $O(1/\epsilon^2)$. We can answer the GAP-HAMMING problem if this relative error is small enough to distinguish the two cases. This requires $\epsilon \leq \sqrt{n}/H(x, y) \propto 1/\sqrt{n}$. That is, we can solve this problem using a method like **AMS Sketch** with ϵ chosen so that the space is $O(n)$. However, this is no significant improvement on the trivial approach, which simply has Alice send x to Bob, using $O(n)$ bits of communication.

Indeed, this is the best that can be done for this problem: GAP-HAMMING requires $\Omega(n)$ communication from Alice to Bob in the one-round communication complexity model. This result was shown by Woodruff [233], with a simplified proof due to Jayram et al. [144], who reduced the problem to an instance of INDEX.

Lower Bound for Count Distinct and Frequency Moments. The GAP-HAMMING problem allows a stronger lower bound to be shown for count distinct than the direct reduction from INDEX. Given an instance of GAP-HAMMING, Alice and Bob both code up their inputs in the natural way. Alice creates a set as follows: if $x_i = 0$, she inserts an item corresponding to the tuple $(i, 0)$; otherwise, she inserts a tuple $(i, 1)$. Bob similarly encodes his set. We can observe that this encoding generates $2H(x, y)$ tuples that occur once over the full input, and a further $n - H(x, y)$ that occur twice. In total, there are $n + H(x, y)$ distinct tuples generated. In one case, the total number of distinct elements is at least $3n/2 + \sqrt{(n)}$, and in the other it is at most $3n/2 - \sqrt{n}$. Thus, choosing ϵ for an approximate distinct counter to be $\propto 1/\sqrt{n}$ would be sufficient to distinguish these two cases. This implies a space requirement of $\Omega(1/\epsilon^2)$ for the count distinct problem, and hence **KMV** and **HLL** are optimal in their dependence on ϵ.

We note that a similar construction and analysis also shows the same $\Omega(1/\epsilon^2)$ space requirement to estimate $\|v\|_p$ vector norms for constant values of p. The hardness for estimating $\|v\|_2$ in turn shows the corresponding hardness for estimating inner product, due to the close connection of these problems: Euclidean norm ($\|v\|_2$) is a special case of inner product since $v \cdot v = \|v\|_2^2$. Hence, inner product $u \cdot v$ is shown to require $\Omega(1/\epsilon^2)$ space in order to estimate with additive error proportional to $\epsilon \|u\|_2 \|v\|_2$.

10.5 Augmented Index and Matrix Multiplication

The problem of AUGMENTEDINDEX is used to prove stronger bounds for summaries that allow items to be deleted, also referred to as "negative updates."

Definition 10.4 (AUGMENTEDINDEX problem) *Alice holds a binary string x of n bits in length, while Bob holds a string y of $0 \leq i < n$ bits in length, with the promise that $x_j = y_j$ for all $j \leq i$. The goal is for the players to follow a protocol to output $x[i + 1]$, the $i + 1$st bit from the string x.*

We can view this as equivalent to INDEX with the additional help that Bob knows the prefix of x up to (but not including) the vital bit of interest. As with the basic INDEX problem, the hardness derives from the fact that Alice does not know anything about the critical index $i + 1$, and Bob cannot communicate it to her. It turns out that the extra information available to Bob does not help: the communication complexity of this problem remains $\Omega(n)$. However, the extra information does allow us to encode slightly more complex instances of other problems, and hence show stronger lower bounds on summaries that allow deletions or negative updates.

Lower Bound for Matrix Multiplication. We now describe a lower bound for the matrix multiplication using a reduction to AUGMENTED INDEX, based on an approach of Clarkson and Woodruff [55]. Consider an instance of the Matrix multiplication (Section 6.3). We are given matrices A and B, both of n rows and c columns, specified with incremental updates to their entries. We suppose that we have a summary to estimate the product $A^T B$ with error at most $\epsilon \|A\|_F \|B\|_F$, where $\| \cdot \|_F$ denotes the Frobenius (entrywise) norm, $\|A\|_F = \sqrt{(\sum_{i,j} A_{i,j}^2)}$.

We use the supposed summary to allows us to solve an instance of AUGMENTEDINDEX. Alice will encode her string x into the matrix A by filling it with entries in some canonical fashion, say top to bottom and right to left. The sign of an entry is positive if the corresponding bit in x is 1, and negative if it is 0. The magnitude of the entries are increased from left to right. We set the parameter $r = \log(cn)/(8\epsilon^2)$. In the first $r/\log(cn)$ columns, the magnitude of all entries is 1; the next $r/\log(cn)$ columns, it is 2; and in the k'th group of $r/\log(cn)$ columns, the magnitude of all entries is 2^k. The remaining $n - r$ columns in A are set to all zeros.

On receiving the summary from Alice, Bob uses his knowledge of the prefix of x to "remove" all the information in the matrix A corresponding to this prefix. That is, Bob subtracts the quantity in each entry of A that Alice added that corresponds to a bit value that he knows about, since Alice's transformation is completely deterministic. Recall that Bob wants to retrieve the bit corresponding to $x[i + 1]$. Let (i^*, j^*) denote the coordinates in matrix A that correspond to $x[i+1]$. Bob then instantiates a matrix B that is entirely 0, except for a single entry of weight 1 in row j^*. Observe that the product $A^T B$ essentially "reads off" the j^*th column of A^T, which includes the target element.

The permitted error in the reconstruction of $A^T B$ is $\epsilon \|A\|_F \|B\|_F$. By construction, $\|B\|_F = 1$. Meanwhile, let k be such that the largest entry in A is 2^k (after Bob has removed the larger entries). Then $\|A\|_F^2 \le (cr/\log(cn) \cdot (1 + 4 + \cdots + 2^{2k})$, the size of each 'block' of A, times the squared weights for each block. Then $\|A\|_F^2 \le \frac{4}{3} cr 2^{2k}/\log(cn)$. Based on the choice of $r = \log(cn)/(8\epsilon^2)$, the permitted squared error is $\epsilon^2 \|A\|_F^2 \|B\|_F^2 \le c4^k/6$.

We now consider the reconstructed column of A^T found via $A^T B$, which has c entries. We say that an entry is "bad" if its sign is incorrect in the reconstruction compared to in the original. Observe that since each entry has squared magnitude 4^k, an error in sign contributed at least 4^k to the total squared error. The bound on error from above means that at most a one-sixth fraction of entries can be bad without violating the promise. We can assume that the index of interest is chosen independently of other choices, so the probability that the correct sign is found, and hence the correct value of the bit of interest is at least $5/6$.

This is sufficient to ensure that the instance of AUGMENTEDINDEX is solved with sufficient probability. The size of the instance encoded is the number of non-zero entries in A, which is $O(rc = (c/\epsilon^2)\log(cn))$. This means that any summary for approximate matrix multiplication on matrices of size $r \times c$ must use space $\Omega(c\epsilon^{-2}\log(cn))$.

The impact of using AUGMENTEDINDEX is that it allows us to introduce the additional factor of $\log(cn)$ into the hardness bound. If we were to try a similar reduction with an instance of INDEX, the bound would emerge as $\Omega(c\epsilon^{-2})$. The reduction would involve a matrix A with fewer rows, and all entries with magnitude 1.

References

[1] D. Achlioptas. Database-friendly random projections. In *ACM Symposium on Principles of Database Systems*, pages 274–281, 2001.

[2] P. K. Agarwal, G. Cormode, Z. Huang, J. Phillips, Z. Wei, and K. Yi. Mergeable summaries. *ACM Transactions on Database Systems*, 38(4), 2013.

[3] P. K. Agarwal, S. Har-Peled, and K. R. Varadarajan. Approximating extent measures of points. *Journal of the ACM*, 51:606–635, 2004.

[4] P. K. Agarwal and R. Sharathkumar. Streaming algorithms for extent problems in high dimensions. In *ACM-SIAM Symposium on Discrete Algorithms*, pages 1481–1489, 2010.

[5] P. K. Agarwal and H. Yu. A space-optimal data-stream algorithm for coresets in the plane. In *Symposium on Computational Geometry*, pages 1–10, 2007.

[6] C. C. Aggarwal. On biased reservoir sampling in the presence of stream evolution. In *International Conference on Very Large Data Bases*, pages 607–618, 2006.

[7] K. J. Ahn, S. Guha, and A. McGregor. Analyzing graph structure via linear measurements. In *ACM-SIAM Symposium on Discrete Algorithms*, pages 459–467, 2012.

[8] N. Ailon and B. Chazelle. Approximate nearest neighbors and the fast Johnson–Lindenstrauss transform. *SIAM Journal on Computing*, 39(1):302–322, 2009.

[9] N. Alon, P. Gibbons, Y. Matias, and M. Szegedy. Tracking join and self-join sizes in limited storage. In *ACM Symposium on Principles of Database Systems*, pages 10–20, 1999.

[10] N. Alon, Y. Matias, and M. Szegedy. The space complexity of approximating the frequency moments. In *ACM Symposium on Theory of Computing*, pages 20–29, 1996.

[11] N. Alon, Y. Matias, and M. Szegedy. The space complexity of approximating the frequency moments. *Journal of Computer and System Sciences*, 58:137–147, 1999.

[12] D. Anderson, P. Bevan, K. Lang, E. Liberty, L. Rhodes, and J. Thaler. A high-performance algorithm for identifying frequent items in data streams. In *Internet Measurement Conference*, pages 268–282, 2017.

253

[13] A. Andoni and P. Indyk. Near-optimal hashing algorithms for approximate nearest neighbor in high dimensions. In *IEEE Conference on Foundations of Computer Science*, pages 459–468, 2006.

[14] A. Andoni, P. Indyk, and I. Razenshteyn. Approximate nearest neighbor search in high dimensions. https://arxiv.org/abs/1806.09823, 2018.

[15] A. Andoni and H. L. Nguyên. Width of points in the streaming model. *ACM Transactions on Algorithms*, 12(1):5:1–5:10, 2016.

[16] B. Aronov, E. Ezra, and M. Sharir. Small-size ε-nets for axis-parallel rectangles and boxes. *SIAM Journal on Computing*, 39(7):3248–3282, 2010.

[17] S. Arya, D. Mount, N. S. Netanyahu, R. Silverman, and A. Y. Wu. An optimal algorithm for approximate nearest neighbor searching fixed dimensions. *Journal of the ACM*, 45(6):891–923, 1998.

[18] N. Bansal. Constructive algorithms for discrepancy minimization. In *IEEE Conference on Foundations of Computer Science*, 2010.

[19] Z. Bar-Yossef, T. Jayram, R. Kumar, D. Sivakumar, and L. Trevisian. Counting distinct elements in a data stream. In *Proceedings of RANDOM 2002*, pages 1–10, 2002.

[20] Z. Bar-Yossef, R. Kumar, and D. Sivakumar. Reductions in streaming algorithms, with an application to counting triangles in graphs. In *ACM-SIAM Symposium on Discrete Algorithms*, pages 623–632, 2002.

[21] N. Barkay, E. Porat, and B. Shalem. Feasible sampling of non-strict turnstile data streams. In *Fundamentals of Computation Theory*, pages 48–59, September 2013.

[22] R. Ben-Basat, G. Einziger, R. Friedman, and Y. Kassner. Heavy hitters in streams and sliding windows. In *IEEE INFOCOM*, page 1–9, 2016.

[23] R. Ben-Basat, G. Einziger, R. Friedman, and Y. Kassner. Optimal elephant flow detection. In *IEEE INFOCOM*, pages 1–9, 2017.

[24] R. Ben-Basat, G. Einziger, and R. Friedman. Fast flow volume estimation. In *Proceedings of the International Conference on Distributed Computing and Networking*, pages 44:1–44:10, 2018.

[25] J. L. Bentley and J. B. Saxe. Decomposable searching problems I: static-to-dynamic transformation. *Journal of Algorithms*, 1:301–358, 1980.

[26] R. Berinde, G. Cormode, P. Indyk, and M. Strauss. Space-optimal heavy hitters with strong error bounds. In *ACM Symposium on Principles of Database Systems*, pages 157–166, 2009.

[27] K. S. Beyer, P. J. Haas, B. Reinwald, Y. Sismanis, and R. Gemulla. On synopses for distinct-value estimation under multiset operations. In *ACM SIGMOD International Conference on Management of Data*, pages 199–210, 2007.

[28] G. Bianchi, K. Duffy, D. J. Leith, and V. Shneer. Modeling conservative updates in multi-hash approximate count sketches. In *24th International Teletraffic Congress*, pages 1–8, 2012.

[29] J. Błasiok. Optimal streaming and tracking distinct elements with high probability. In *ACM-SIAM Symposium on Discrete Algorithms*, pages 2432–2448, 2018.

[30] L. Bledaite. Count-min sketches in real data applications. https://skills matter.com/skillscasts/6844-count-min-sketch-in-real-data-applications, 2015.

[31] B. Bloom. Space/time trade-offs in hash coding with allowable errors. *Communications of the ACM*, 13(7):422–426, July 1970.

[32] A. Blumer, A. Ehrenfeucht, D. Haussler, and M. Warmuth. Learnability and the Vapnik–Chervonenkis dimension. *Journal of the ACM*, 36:929–965, 1989.

[33] B. Bollobás. *Extremal Graph Theory*. Academic Press, 1978.

[34] P. Bose, E. Kranakis, P. Morin, and Y. Tang. Bounds for frequency estimation of packet streams. In *SIROCCO*, pages 33–42, 2003.

[35] B. Boyer and J. Moore. A fast majority vote algorithm. Technical Report ICSCA-CMP-32, Institute for Computer Science, University of Texas, Feb. 1981.

[36] V. Braverman, G. Frahling, H. Lang, C. Sohler, and L. F. Yang. Clustering high dimensional dynamic data streams. In *the 34th International Conference on Machine Learning*, pages 576–585, 2017.

[37] V. Braverman and R. Ostrovsky. Smooth histograms for sliding windows. In *IEEE Conference on Foundations of Computer Science*, pages 283–293, 2007.

[38] V. Braverman and R. Ostrovsky. Zero-one frequency laws. In *ACM Symposium on Theory of Computing*, pages 281–290, 2010.

[39] V. Braverman, R. Ostrovsky, and D. Vilenchik. How hard is counting triangles in the streaming model? In *International Colloquium on Automata, Languages and Programming*, pages 244–254, 2013.

[40] A. Z. Broder and M. Mitzenmacher. Network applications of Bloom filters: a survey. *Internet Mathematics*, 1(4):485–509, 2004.

[41] M. Bădoiu and K. L. Clarkson. Smaller core-sets for balls. In *ACM-SIAM Symposium on Discrete Algorithms*, pages 801–802, 2003.

[42] M. Bădoiu and K. L. Clarkson. Optimal core-sets for balls. *Computational Geometry: Theory and Applications*, 40(1):14–22, 2008.

[43] M. Bădoiu, S. Har-Peled, and P. Indyk. Approximate clustering via core-sets. In *ACM Symposium on Theory of Computing*, pages 250–257, 2002.

[44] L. S. Buriol, G. Frahling, S. Leonardi, A. Marchetti-Spaccamela, and C. Sohler. Counting triangles in data streams. In *ACM Symposium on Principles of Database Systems*, pages 253–262, 2006.

[45] D. Cai, M. Mitzenmacher, and R. P. Adams. A Bayesian nonparametric view on count-min sketch. In *Advances in Neural Information Processing Systems*, pages 8782–8791, 2018.

[46] J. L. Carter and M. N. Wegman. Universal classes of hash functions. *Journal of Computer and System Sciences*, 18(2):143–154, 1979.

[47] J. Chambers, C. Mallows, and B. Stuck. A method for simulating stable random variables. *Journal of the American Statistical Association*, 71(354):340–344, 1976.

[48] T. M. Chan. Faster core-set constructions and data-stream algorithms in fixed dimensions. *Computational Geometry: Theory and Applications*, 35:20–35, 2006.

[49] T. M. Chan and V. Pathak. Streaming and dynamic algorithms for minimum enclosing balls in high dimensions. In *International Symposium on Algorithms and Data Structures*, pages 195–206, 2011.

[50] K. Chandra. View counting at reddit. https://redditblog.com/2017/05/24/view-counting-at-reddit/, 2017.

[51] M. Charikar, K. Chen, and M. Farach-Colton. Finding frequent items in data streams. In *Procdings of the International Colloquium on Automata, Languages and Programming*, pages 693–703, 2002.

[52] M. Charikar, L. O'Callaghan, and R. Panigrahy. Better streaming algorithms for clustering problems. In *Proceedings of the 35th Annual ACM Symposium on Theory of Computing*, pages 30–39, 2003.

[53] M. S. Charikar. Similarity estimation techniques from rounding algorithms. In *ACM Symposium on Theory of Computing*, pages 380–388, 2002.

[54] K. Chen and S. Rao. An improved frequent items algorithm with applications to web caching. Technical Report UCB/CSD-05-1383, EECS Department, University of California, Berkeley, 2005.

[55] K. L. Clarkson and D. P. Woodruff. Numerical linear algebra in the streaming model. In *ACM Symposium on Theory of Computing*, pages 205–214, 2009.

[56] E. Cohen. Size-estimation framework with applications to transitive closure and reachability. *Journal of Computer and System Sciences*, 55(3):441–453, 1997.

[57] E. Cohen. All-distances sketches, revisited: HIP estimators for massive graphs analysis. *IEEE Transactions on Knowledge and Data Engineering*, 27(9):2320–2334, 2015.

[58] E. Cohen, N. Duffield, H. Kaplan, C. Lund, and M. Thorup. Efficient stream sampling for variance-optimal estimation of subset sums. *SIAM Journal on Computing*, 40(5):1402–1431, 2011.

[59] E. Cohen and M. Strauss. Maintaining time-decaying stream aggregates. In *ACM Symposium on Principles of Database Systems*, 223–233, 2003.

[60] S. Cohen and Y. Matias. Spectral Bloom filters. In *ACM SIGMOD International Conference on Management of Data*, 241–252, 2003.

[61] J. Considine, M. Hadjieleftheriou, F. Li, J. W. Byers, and G. Kollios. Robust approximate aggregation in sensor data management systems. *ACM Transactions on Database Systems*, 34(1):6:1–6:35, 2009.

[62] D. Coppersmith and R. Kumar. An improved data stream algorithm for frequency moments. In *ACM-SIAM Symposium on Discrete Algorithms*, pages 151–156, 2004.

[63] T. H. Cormen, C. E. Leiserson, R. L. Rivest, and C. Stein. *Introduction to Algorithms*, 3rd edition. MIT Press, 2009.

[64] G. Cormode, M. Datar, P. Indyk, and S. Muthukrishnan. Comparing data streams using Hamming norms. *IEEE Transactions on Knowledge and Data Engineering*, 15(3):529–541, 2003.

[65] G. Cormode and D. Firmani. On unifying the space of ℓ_0-sampling algorithms. In *Algorithm Engineering and Experiments*, pages 163–172, 2013.

[66] G. Cormode and M. Garofalakis. Sketching streams through the net: distributed approximate query tracking. In *International Conference on Very Large Data Bases*, pages 13–24, 2005.

[67] G. Cormode, M. Garofalakis, and D. Sacharidis. Fast approximate wavelet tracking on streams. In *International Conference on Extending Database Technology*, pages 4–22, 2006.

[68] G. Cormode and M. Hadjieleftheriou. Finding frequent items in data streams. In *International Conference on Very Large Data Bases*, Pages 1530–1541, 2008.

[69] G. Cormode and H. Jowhari. A second look at counting triangles in graph streams (corrected). *Theoretical Computer Science*, 683:22–30, 2017.

[70] G. Cormode and H. Jowhari. l_p samplers and their applications: a survey, *ACM Computing Surveys*, pages 16:1–16:3, 2019.

[71] G. Cormode, F. Korn, S. Muthukrishnan, and D. Srivastava. Space- and time-efficient deterministic algorithms for biased quantiles over data streams. In *ACM Symposium on Principles of Database Systems*, pages 263–272, 2006.

[72] G. Cormode, F. Korn, and S. Tirthapura. Exponentially decayed aggregates on data streams. In *IEEE International Conference on Data Engineering*, pages 1379–1381, 2008.

[73] G. Cormode and S. Muthukrishnan. Improved data stream summary: the Count-Min sketch and its applications. Technical Report 2003-20, DIMACS, 2003.

[74] G. Cormode and S. Muthukrishnan. What's hot and what's not: tracking most frequent items dynamically. In *ACM Symposium on Principles of Database Systems*, pages 296–306, 2003.

[75] G. Cormode and S. Muthukrishnan. What's new: finding significant differences in network data streams. In *Proceedings of IEEE Infocom*, pages 1534–1545, 2004.

[76] G. Cormode and S. Muthukrishnan. An improved data stream summary: the Count-Min sketch and its applications. *Journal of Algorithms*, 55(1):58–75, 2005.

[77] G. Cormode and S. Muthukrishnan. Space efficient mining of multigraph streams. In *ACM Symposium on Principles of Database Systems*, pages 271–282, 2005.

[78] G. Cormode, S. Muthukrishnan, and I. Rozenbaum. Summarizing and mining inverse distributions on data streams via dynamic inverse sampling. In *International Conference on Very Large Data Bases*, pages 25–36, 2005.

[79] G. Cormode, S. Tirthapura, and B. Xu. Time-decaying sketches for sensor data aggregation. In *ACM Conference on Principles of Distributed Computing*, pages 215–224, 2007.

[80] S. Das, S. Antony, D. Agrawal, and A. E. Abbadi. Cots: a scalable framework for parallelizing frequency counting over data streams. In *IEEE International Conference on Data Engineering*, pages 1323–1326, 2009.

[81] A. Dasgupta, K. J. Lang, L. Rhodes, and J. Thaler. A framework for estimating stream expression cardinalities. In *International Conference on Database Theory*, pages 6:1–6:17, 2016.

[82] S. Dasgupta and A. Gupta. An elementary proof of a theorem of Johnson and Lindenstrauss. *Random Structures and Algorithms*, 22(1):60–65, 2003.

[83] M. Datar, A. Gionis, P. Indyk, and R. Motwani. Maintaining stream statistics over sliding windows. In *ACM-SIAM Symposium on Discrete Algorithms*, pages 635–644, 2002.

[84] M. Datar, N. Immorlica, P. Indyk, and V. S. Mirrokni. Locality-sensitive hashing scheme based on p-stable distributions. In *Symposium on Computational Geometry*, pages 253–262, 2004.

[85] E. Demaine, A. López-Ortiz, and J. I. Munro. Frequency estimation of internet packet streams with limited space. In *European Symposium on Algorithms (ESA)*, pages 348–360, 2002.

[86] F. Deng and D. Rafiei. New estimation algorithms for streaming data: Count-Min can do more. Unpublished manuscript.

[87] M. Dietzfelbinger, A. Goerdt, M. Mitzenmacher, A. Montanari, R. Pagh, and M. Rink. Tight thresholds for cuckoo hashing via XORSAT. In *International Colloquium on Automata, Languages and Programming*, pages 213–225, 2010.

[88] A. Dobra and F. Rusu. Sketches for size of join estimation. *ACM Transactions on Database Systems*, 33(3): 5:1–15:46, 2008.

[89] D. Donoho. Compressed sensing. *IEEE Transactions on on Information Theory*, 52(4):1289–1306, April 2006.

[90] P. Drineas, M. Magdon-Ismail, M. W. Mahoney, and D. P. Woodruff. Fast approximation of matrix coherence and statistical leverage. *Journal of Machine Learning Research*, 13:3475–3506, 2012.

[91] N. Duffield, C. Lund, and M. Thorup. Estimating flow distributions from sampled flow statistics. In *ACM SIGCOMM*, pages 325–336, 2003.

[92] N. Duffield, C. Lund, and M. Thorup. Priority sampling for estimation of arbitrary subset sums. *Journal of the ACM*, 54(6):32, 2007.

[93] M. Durand and P. Flajolet. Loglog counting of large cardinalities (extended abstract). In *European Symposium on Algorithms*, pages 605–617, 2003.

[94] R. Durstenfeld. Algorithm 235: random permutation. *Communications of the ACM*, 7(7):420, 1964.

[95] O. Eğecioğlu and B. Kalantari. Approximating the diameter of a set of points in the Euclidean space. *Information Processing Letters*, 32:205–211, 1989.

[96] G. Einziger and R. Friedman. A formal analysis of conservative update based approximate counting. In *International Conference on Computing, Networking and Communications*, pages 255–259, 2015.

[97] M. Elkin. Streaming and fully dynamic centralized algorithms for constructing and maintaining sparse spanners. *ACM Transactions on Algorithms*, 7(2):20, 2011.

[98] D. Eppstein and M. T. Goodrich. Straggler identification in round-trip data streams via Newton's identities and invertible Bloom filters. *IEEE Transactions on Knowledge and Data Engineering*, 23(2):297–306, 2011.

[99] Ú. Erlingsson, V. Pihur, and A. Korolova. RAPPOR: randomized aggregatable privacy-preserving ordinal response. In *Computer and Communications Security*, pages 1054–1067, 2014.

[100] C. Estan and G. Varghese. New directions in traffic measurement and accounting. In *ACM SIGCOMM*, volume 32, 4 of *Computer Communication Review*, pages 323–338, 2002.

[101] L. Fan, P. Cao, J. Almeida, and A. Broder. Summary cache: A scalable wide-area web cache sharing protocol. In *ACM SIGCOMM*, pages 254–265, 1998.

[102] J. Feigenbaum, S. Kannan, A. McGregor, S. Suri, and J. Zhang. Graph distances in the streaming model: the value of space. In *ACM-SIAM Symposium on Discrete Algorithms*, pages 745–754, 2005.

[103] D. Felber and R. Ostrovsky. A randomized online quantile summary in $O(1/\epsilon \log(1/\epsilon))$ words. In *APPROX-RANDOM*, pages 775–785, 2015.

[104] P. Flajolet. Approximate counting: a detailed analysis. *BIT*, 25:113–134, 1985.

[105] P. Flajolet, E. Fusy, O. Gandouet, and F. Meunier. Hyperloglog: the analysis of a near-optimal cardinality estimation algorithm. In *Analysis of Algorithms*, pages 127–146, 2007.

[106] P. Flajolet and G. N. Martin. Probabilistic counting. In *IEEE Conference on Foundations of Computer Science*, pages 76–82, 1983.

[107] P. Flajolet and G. N. Martin. Probabilistic counting algorithms for database applications. *Journal of Computer and System Sciences*, 31:182–209, 1985.

[108] G. Frahling, P. Indyk, and C. Sohler. Sampling in dynamic data streams and applications. In *Symposium on Computational Geometry*, pages 142–149, June 2005.

[109] S. Ganguly. Counting distinct items over update streams. In *International Sympoisum on Algorithms and Computation*, pages 505–514, 2005.

[110] M. Ghashami, E. Liberty, J. M. Phillips, and D. P. Woodruff. Frequent directions: simple and deterministic matrix sketching. *SIAM Journal on Computing*, 45(5):1762–1792, 2016.

[111] M. Ghashami and J. M. Phillips. Relative errors for deterministic low-rank matrix approximations. In *ACM-SIAM Symposium on Discrete Algorithms*, pages 707–717, 2014.

[112] P. Giannopoulos, C. Knauer, M. Wahlstrom, and D. Werner. Hardness of discrepancy computation and ε-net verification in high dimension. *Journal of Complexity*, 28(2):162–176, 2012.

[113] P. Gibbons and S. Tirthapura. Estimating simple functions on the union of data streams. In *ACM Symposium on Parallel Algorithms and Architectures*, pages 281–290, 2001.

[114] A. Gilbert, S. Guha, P. Indyk, Y. Kotidis, S. Muthukrishnan, and M. Strauss. Fast, small-space algorithms for approximate histogram maintenance. In *ACM Symposium on Theory of Computing*, pages 389–398, 2002.

[115] A. Gilbert, S. Guha, P. Indyk, S. Muthukrishnan, and M. Strauss. Near-optimal sparse Fourier representation via sampling. In *ACM Symposium on Theory of Computing*, pages 152–161, 2002.

[116] A. Gilbert, Y. Kotidis, S. Muthukrishnan, and M. Strauss. Surfing wavelets on streams: one-pass summaries for approximate aggregate queries. *IEEE Transactions on Knowledge and Data Engineering*, 15(3):541–554, 2003.

[117] A. C. Gilbert and P. Indyk. Sparse recovery using sparse matrices. *Proceedings of the IEEE*, 98(6):937–947, 2010.

[118] A. C. Gilbert, Y. Kotidis, S. Muthukrishnan, and M. J. Strauss. How to summarize the universe: dynamic maintenance of quantiles. In *International Conference on Very Large Data Bases*, pages 454–465, 2002.

[119] A. Gionis, P. Indyk, and R. Motwani. Similarity search in high dimensions via hashing. In *International Conference on Very Large Data Bases*, pages 518–529, 1999.

[120] A. Goel, P. Indyk, and K. Varadarajan. Reductions among high dimensional proximity problems. In *ACM-SIAM Symposium on Discrete Algorithms*, pages 769–778, 2001.

[121] L. Golab and M. T. Özsu. Issues in data stream management. *SIGMOD Record*, 32(2):5–14, June 2003.

[122] M. T. Goodrich and M. Mitzenmacher. Invertible Bloom lookup tables. In *Annual Allerton Conference on Communication, Control, and Computing*, pages 792–799, 2011.

[123] M. Greenwald and S. Khanna. Space-efficient online computation of quantile summaries. In *ACM SIGMOD International Conference on Management of Data*, pages 58–66, 2001.

[124] M. Greenwald and S. Khanna. Power-conserving computation of order-statistics over sensor networks. In *ACM Symposium on Principles of Database Systems*, pages 275–285, 2004.

[125] A. Gronemeier and M. Sauerhoff. Applying approximate counting for computing the frequency moments of long data streams. *Theory of Computer Systems*, 44(3):332–348, 2009.

[126] S. Guha. Tight results for clustering and summarizing data streams. In *International Conference on Database Theory*, pages 268–275, 2009.

[127] S. Guha, A. Meyerson, N. Mishra, R. Motwani, and L. O'Callaghan. Clustering data streams: theory and practice. *IEEE Transactions on Knowledge and Data Engineering*, 15(3):515–528, 2003.

[128] A. Hall, O. Bachmann, R. Büssow, S. Ganceanu, and M. Nunkesser. Processing a trillion cells per mouse click. *PVLDB*, 5(11):1436–1446, 2012.

[129] S. Har-Peled, P. Indyk, and R. Motwani. Approximate nearest neighbor: towards removing the curse of dimensionality. *Theory of Computing*, 8:321–350, 2012.

[130] H. Hassanieh, P. Indyk, D. Katabi, and E. Price. Simple and practical algorithm for sparse fourier transform. In *ACM-SIAM Symposium on Discrete Algorithms*, pages 1183–1194, 2012.

[131] D. Haussler and E. Welzl. Epsilon-nets and simplex range queries. *Discrete and Computational Geometry*, 2:127–151, 1987.

[132] S. Heule, M. Nunkesser, and A. Hall. Hyperloglog in practice: algorithmic engineering of a state of the art cardinality estimation algorithm. In *International Conference on Extending Database Technology*, pages 683–692, 2013.

[133] Z. Huang, L. Wang, K. Yi, and Y. Liu. Sampling based algorithms for quantile computation in sensor networks. In *ACM SIGMOD International Conference on Management of Data*, pages 745–756, 2011.

[134] Z. Huang and K. Yi. The communication complexity of distributed epsilon-approximations. In *IEEE Conference on Foundations of Computer Science*, pages 591–600, 2014.

[135] Z. Huang, K. Yi, Y. Liu, and G. Chen. Optimal sampling algorithms for frequency estimation in distributed data. In *IEEE INFOCOM*, pages 1997–2005, 2011.

[136] R. Y. S. Hung and H. F. Ting. An $\omega(1/\epsilon \log 1/\epsilon)$ space lower bound for finding ϵ-approximate quantiles in a data stream. In *Proceedings of the 4th International Conference on Frontiers in Algorithmics*, pages 89–100, 2010.

[137] P. Indyk. A small approximately min-wise independent family of hash functions. *Journal of Algorithms*, 38(1):84–90, 2001.

[138] P. Indyk. Stable distributions, pseudorandom generators, embeddings and data stream computation. *Journal of the ACM*, 53(3):307–323, 2006.

[139] P. Indyk, J. Matoušek, and A. Sidiropoulos. Low-distortion embeddings of finite metric spaces, In C. D. Toth, J. O'Rourke, and J. E. Goodman, eds., *Handbook of Discrete and Computational Geometry*, 3rd edition, pages 211–231. CRC Press, 2017.

[140] P. Indyk and R. Motwani. Approximate nearest neighbors: towards removing the curse of dimensionality. In *ACM Symposium on Theory of Computing*, pages 604–613, 1998.

[141] N. Ivkin, E. Liberty, K. Lang, Z. Karnin, and V. Braverman. Streaming quantiles algorithms with small space and update time. ArXiV CoRR abs/1907.00236, 2019.

[142] R. Jayaram and D. P. Woodruff. Perfect Lp sampling in a data stream. In *IEEE Conference on Foundations of Computer Science*, pages 544–555, 2018.

[143] T. S. Jayram. Information complexity: a tutorial. In *ACM Symposium on Principles of Database Systems*, pages 159–168, 2010.

[144] T. S. Jayram, R. Kumar, and D. Sivakumar. The one-way communication complexity of gap hamming distance. www.madalgo.au.dk/img/ SumSchoo2007_Lecture_20slides/Bibliography/p14_Jayram_ 07_Manusc_ghd.pdf, 2007.

[145] T. S. Jayram and D. P. Woodruff. The data stream space complexity of cascaded norms. In *IEEE Conference on Foundations of Computer Science*, pages 765–774, 2009.

[146] T. S. Jayram and D. P. Woodruff. Optimal bounds for Johnson–Lindenstrauss transforms and streaming problems with low error. In *ACM-SIAM Symposium on Discrete Algorithms*, pages 1–10, 2011.

[147] C. Jin, W. Qian, C. Sha, J. X. Yu, and A. Zhou. Dynamically maintaining frequent items over a data stream. In *CIKM*, pages 287–294, 2003.

[148] W. Johnson and J. Lindenstrauss. Extensions of Lipshitz mapping into Hilbert space. *Contemporary Mathematics*, 26:189–206, 1984.

[149] H. Jowhari and M. Ghodsi. New streaming algorithms for counting triangles in graphs. In *International Conference on Computing and Combinatorics*, pages 710–716, 2005.

[150] H. Jowhari, M. Saglam, and G. Tardos. Tight bounds for Lp samplers, finding duplicates in streams, and related problems. In *ACM Symposium on Principles of Database Systems*, pages 49–58, 2011.

[151] B. Kalyanasundaram and G. Schnitger. The probabilistic communication complexity of set intersection. *SIAM Journal on Discrete Mathematics*, 5(4):545–557, 1992.

[152] D. M. Kane and J. Nelson. Sparser Johnson–Lindenstrauss transforms. In *ACM-SIAM Symposium on Discrete Algorithms*, pages 1195–1206, 2012.

[153] D. M. Kane, J. Nelson, and D. P. Woodruff. An optimal algorithm for the distinct elements problem. In *ACM Symposium on Principles of Database Systems*, pages 41–52, 2010.

[154] B. M. Kapron, V. King, and B. Mountjoy. Dynamic graph connectivity in poly-logarithmic worst case time. In *ACM-SIAM Symposium on Discrete Algorithms*, pages 1131–1142, 2013.

[155] Z. Karnin, K. Lang, and E. Liberty. Optimal quantile approximation in streams. In *IEEE Conference on Foundations of Computer Science*, pages 41–52, 2016.

[156] R. Karp, C. Papadimitriou, and S. Shenker. A simple algorithm for finding frequent elements in sets and bags. *ACM Transactions on Database Systems*, 28:51–55, 2003.

[157] R. M. Karp and M. O. Rabin. Efficient randomized pattern-matching algorithms. *IBM Journal of Research and Development*, 31(2):249–260, 1987.

[158] A. Kirsch and M. Mitzenmacher. Less hashing, same performance: building a better Bloom filter. In *European Symposium on Algorithms (ESA)*, pages 456–467, 2006.

[159] D. E. Knuth. *The Art of Computer Programming, Vol. 1, Fundamental Algorithms*. Addison-Wesley, 2nd edition, 1998.

[160] D. E. Knuth. *The Art of Computer Programming, Vol. 2, Seminumerical Algorithms*. Addison-Wesley, 2nd edition, 1998.

[161] G. Kollios, J. Byers, J. Considine, M. Hadjieleftheriou, and F. Li. Robust aggregation in sensor networks. *IEEE Data Engineering Bulletin*, 28(1), March 2005.

[162] J. Komlós, J. Pach, and G. Woeginger. Almost tight bounds for ε-nets. *Discrete and Computational Geometry*, 7:163–173, 1992.

[163] P. Kumar, J. S. B. Mitchell, and E. A. Yildirim. Approximate minimum enclosing balls in high dimensions using core-sets. *ACM Journal of Experimental Algorithmics*, 8, 2003.

[164] E. Kushilevitz and N. Nisan. *Communication Complexity*. Cambridge University Press, 1997.

[165] E. Kushilevitz, R. Ostrovsky, and Y. Rabani. Efficient search for approximate nearest neighbor in high dimensional spaces. In *ACM Symposium on Theory of Computing*, pages 614–623, 1998.

[166] K. J. Lang. Back to the future: an even more nearly optimal cardinality estimation algorithm. Technical report, ArXiV, 2017.

[167] K. G. Larsen, J. Nelson, H. L. Nguyen, and M. Thorup. Heavy hitters via cluster-preserving clustering. In *IEEE Conference on Foundations of Computer Science*, pages 61–70, 2016.

[168] G. M. Lee, H. Liu, Y. Yoon, and Y. Zhang. Improving sketch reconstruction accuracy using linear least squares method. In *Internet Measurement Conference*, pages 273–278, 2005.

[169] L. Lee and H. Ting. A simpler and more efficient deterministic scheme for finding frequent items over sliding windows. In *ACM Symposium on Principles of Database Systems*, pages 290–297, 2006.

[170] P. Li. Very sparse stable random projections, estimators and tail bounds for stable random projections. Technical Report cs.DS/0611114, ArXiV, 2006.

[171] Y. Li, P. Long, and A. Srinivasan. Improved bounds on the sample complexity of learning. *Journal of Computer and System Sciences*, 62(3):516–527, 2001.

[172] E. Liberty. Simple and deterministic matrix sketching. In *ACM SIGKDD*, pages 581–588, 2013.

[173] R. J. Lipton. Fingerprinting sets. Technical Report CS-TR-212-89, Princeton, 1989.

[174] Y. Lu, A. Montanari, S. Dharmapurikar, A. Kabbani, and B. Prabhakar. Counter braids: a novel counter architecture for per-flow measurement. In *ACM SIGMETRICS*, pages 121–132, 2008.

[175] J. O. Lumbroso. How Flajolet processed streams with coin flips. Technical Report 1805.00612, ArXiV, 2018.

[176] A. Manjhi, V. Shkapenyuk, K. Dhamdhere, and C. Olston. Finding (recently) frequent items in distributed data streams. In *IEEE International Conference on Data Engineering*, pages 767–778, 2005.

[177] G. S. Manku, S. Rajagopalan, and B. G. Lindsay. Approximate medians and other quantiles in one pass and with limited memory. In *ACM SIGMOD International Conference on Management of Data*, pages 426–435, 1998.

[178] G. S. Manku, S. Rajagopalan, and B. G. Lindsay. Random sampling techniques for space efficient online computation of order statistics of large datasets. In *ACM SIGMOD International Conference on Management of Data*, pages 251–262, 1999.

[179] J. Matoušek. Tight upper bounds for the discrepancy of halfspaces. *Discrete and Computational Geometry*, 13:593–601, 1995.

[180] A. McGregor, S. Vorotnikova, and H. T. Vu. Better algorithms for counting triangles in data streams. In *ACM Symposium on Principles of Database Systems*, pages 401–411, 2016.

[181] D. McIlroy. Development of a spelling list. Technical report, Bell Labs, 1982.

[182] A. Metwally, D. Agrawal, and A. E. Abbadi. An integrated efficient solution for computing frequent and top-k elements in data streams. *ACM Transactions on Database Systems*, 31(3):1095–1133, 2006.

[183] J. Misra and D. Gries. Finding repeated elements. *Science of Computer Programming*, 2:143–152, 1982.

[184] M. Mitzenmacher. *Bloom Filters*, pages 252–255. Springer, 2009.

[185] M. Mitzenmacher and E. Upfal. *Probability and Computing: Randomized Algorithms and Probabilistic Analysis*. Cambridge University Press, 2005.

[186] M. Mitzenmacher and G. Varghese. Biff (Bloom filter) codes: fast error correction for large data sets. In *IEEE International Symposium on Information Theory*, pages 483–487, 2012.

[187] M. Molloy. Cores in random hypergraphs and Boolean formulas. *Random Structures and Algorithms*, 27(1):124–135, 2005.

[188] M. Monemizadeh and D. P. Woodruff. 1-pass relative-error l_p-sampling with applications. In *ACM-SIAM Symposium on Discrete Algorithms*, pages 1143–1160, 2010.

[189] R. Morris. Counting large numbers of events in small registers. *Communications of the ACM*, 21(10):840–842, 1977.

[190] S. Moser and P. N. Chen. *A Student's Guide to Coding and Information Theory*. Cambridge University Press, 2012.

[191] R. Motwani and P. Raghavan. *Randomized Algorithms*. Cambridge University Press, 1995.

[192] D. Mount and S. Arya. ANN: library for approximate nearest neighbor searching. Technical report, University of Maryland, 2010.

[193] J. I. Munro and M. S. Paterson. Selection and sorting with limited storage. *Theoretical Computer Science*, 12:315–323, 1980.

[194] J. Nelson and H. L. Nguyen. OSNAP: faster numerical linear algebra algorithms via sparser subspace embeddings. In *IEEE Conference on Foundations of Computer Science*, pages 117–126, 2013.

[195] J. Nelson and H. L. Nguyen. Sparsity lower bounds for dimensionality reducing maps. In *ACM Symposium on Theory of Computing*, pages 101–110, 2013.

[196] J. Nelson and D. Woodruff. Fast Manhattan sketches in data streams. In *ACM Symposium on Principles of Database Systems*, pages 99–110, 2010.

[197] R. O'Donnell, Y. Wu, and Y. Zhou. Optimal lower bounds for locality-sensitive hashing (except when q is tiny). *ACM Transactions on Computation Theory*, 6(1):5, 2014.

[198] J. Pach and G. Tardos. Tight lower bounds for the size of epsilon-nets. *Journal of the American Mathematical Society*, 26:645–658, 2013.

[199] R. Pagh. Compressed matrix multiplication. In *ITCS*, pages 442–451, 2012.

[200] A. Pavan, K. Tangwongsan, S. Tirthapura, and K. Wu. Counting and sampling triangles from a graph stream. *PVLDB*, 6(14):1870–1881, 2013.

[201] A. Pavan and S. Tirthapura. Range-efficient counting of distinct elements in a massive data stream. *SIAM Journal on Computing*, 37(2):359–379, 2007.

[202] N. Pham and R. Pagh. Fast and scalable polynomial kernels via explicit feature maps. In *ACM SIGKDD*, pages 239–247, 2013.

[203] R. Pike, S. Dorward, R. Griesemer, and S. Quinlan. Interpreting the data: parallel analysis with sawzall. *Dynamic Grids and Worldwide Computing*, 13(4):277–298, 2005.

[204] A. A. Razborov. On the distributional complexity of disjointness. *Theoretical Computer Science*, 106(2):385–390, 1992.

[205] T. Sarlós. Improved approximation algorithms for large matrices via random projections. In *IEEE Conference on Foundations of Computer Science*, pages 143–152, 2006.

[206] C.-E. Särndal, B. Swensson, and J. Wretman. *Model Assisted Survey Sampling*. Springer, 1992.

[207] S. E. Schechter, C. Herley, and M. Mitzenmacher. Popularity is everything: a new approach to protecting passwords from statistical-guessing attacks. In *5th USENIX Workshop on Hot Topics in Security*, pages 1–8, 2010.

[208] J. P. Schmidt, A. Siegel, and A. Srinivasan. Chernoff–Hoeffding bounds for applications with limited independence. In *ACM-SIAM Symposium on Discrete Algorithms*, pages 331–340, 1993.

[209] R. Schweller, Z. Li, Y. Chen, Y. Gao, A. Gupta, Y. Zhang, P. A. Dinda, M.-Y. Kao, and G. Memik. Reversible sketches: enabling monitoring and analysis over high-speed data streams. *IEEE Transactions on Networks*, 15(5):1059–1072, 2007.

[210] Q. Shi, J. Petterson, G. Dror, J. Langford, A. J. Smola, and S. V. N. Vishwanathan. Hash kernels for structured data. *Journal of Machine Learning Research*, 10:2615–2637, 2009.

[211] N. Shrivastava, C. Buragohain, D. Agrawal, and S. Suri. Medians and beyond: new aggregation techniques for sensor networks. In *ACM SenSys*, Pages 239–249, 2004.

[212] O. Simpson, C. Seshadhri, and A. McGregor. Catching the head, tail, and everything in between: a streaming algorithm for the degree distribution. In *IEEE International Conference on Data Mining*, pages 979–984, 2015.

[213] A. Srinivasan. Improving the discrepancy bound for sparse matrices: better approximations for sparse lattice approximation problems. In *ACM-SIAM Symposium on Discrete Algorithms*, pages 692–701, 1997.

[214] S. Suri, C. D. Tóth, and Y. Zhou. Range counting over multidimensional data streams. *Discrete and Computational Geometry*, 26(4):633–655, 2006.

[215] M. Szegedy. The DLT priority sampling is essentially optimal. In *ACM Symposium on Theory of Computing*, pages 150–158, 2006.

[216] M. Szegedy and M. Thorup. On the variance of subset sum estimation. In *European Symposium on Algorithms*, pages 75–86, 2007.

[217] M. Talagrand. Sharper bounds for Gaussian and empirical processes. *The Annals of Probability*, 22(1):28–76, 1994.

[218] D. P. Team. Learning with privacy at scale. *Apple Machine Learning Journal*, 1(8):1–25, December 2017.

[219] M. Thorup. Even strongly universal hashing is pretty fast. In *ACM-SIAM Symposium on Discrete Algorithms*, pages 496–497, 2000.

[220] M. Thorup. Equivalence between priority queues and sorting. *Journal of the ACM*, 54(6):1–27, 2007.

[221] M. Thorup and Y. Zhang. Tabulation based 4-universal hashing with applications to second moment estimation. In *ACM-SIAM Symposium on Discrete Algorithms*, pages 615–624, 2004.

[222] D. Ting. Count-min: optimal estimation and tight error bounds using empirical error distributions. In *ACM SIGKDD*, pages 2319–2328, 2018.

[223] S. Tirthapura and D. P. Woodruff. Rectangle-efficient aggregation in spatial data streams. In *ACM Symposium on Principles of Database Systems*, pages 283–294, 2012.

[224] S. Tirthapura and D. P. Woodruff. A general method for estimating correlated aggregates over a data stream. *Algorithmica*, 73(2):235–260, 2015.

[225] A. Tridgell and P. Mackerras. The rsync algorithm. Technical Report TR-CS-96-05, Department of Computer Science, The Australian National University, 1996.

[226] I. W. Tsang, J. T. Kwok, and P.-M. Cheung. Core vector machines: fast SVM training on very large data sets. *Journal of Machine Learning Research*, 6:363–392, 2005.

[227] V. N. Vapnik and A. Y. Chervonenkis. On the uniform convergence of relative frequencies of events to their probabilities. *Theory of Probability and Its Applications*, 16:264–280, 1971.

[228] S. Venkataraman, D. X. Song, P. B. Gibbons, and A. Blum. New streaming algorithms for fast detection of superspreaders. In *Network and Distributed System Security Symposium*, pages 149–166, 2005.

[229] J. S. Vitter. Random sampling with a reservoir. *ACM Transactions on Mathematical Software*, 11(1):37–57, March 1985.

[230] J. Wang, W. Liu, S. Kumar, and S.-F. Chang. Learning to hash for indexing big data: a survey. *Proceedings of the IEEE*, 104(1):34–57, 2016.

[231] L. Wang, G. Luo, K. Yi, and G. Cormode. Quantiles over data streams: an experimental study. In *ACM SIGMOD International Conference on Management of Data*, pages 737–748, 2013.

[232] K. Y. Whang, B. T. Vander-Zanden, and H. M. Taylor. A linear-time probabilistic counting algorithm for database applications. *ACM Transactions on Database Systems*, 15(2):208, 1990.

[233] D. Woodruff. Optimal space lower bounds for all frequency moments. In *ACM-SIAM Symposium on Discrete Algorithms*, pages 167–175, 2004.

[234] D. P. Woodruff. Low rank approximation lower bounds in row-update streams. In *Advances in Neural Information Processing Systems*, pages 1781–1789, 2014.

[235] D. P. Woodruff. Sketching as a tool for numerical linear algebra. *Foundations and Trends in Theoretical Computer Science*, 10(1–2):1–157, October 2014.

[236] D. P. Woodruff and Q. Zhang. Tight bounds for distributed functional monitoring. In *ACM Symposium on Theory of Computing*, pages 941–960, 2012.

[237] D. P. Woodruff and Q. Zhang. Subspace embeddings and ℓ_p-regression using exponential random variables. In *Conference on Learning Theory*, pages 546–567, 2013.

[238] H. Yu, P. K. Agarwal, R. Poreddy, and K. R. Varadarajan. Practical methods for shape fitting and kinetic data structures using coresets. *Algorithmica*, 52(3):378–402, 2008.

[239] H. Zarrabi-Zadeh. An almost space-optimal streaming algorithm for coresets in fixed dimensions. *Algorithmica*, 60(1):46–59, 2011.

[240] Q. Zhang, J. Pell, R. Canino-Koning, A. C. Howe, and C. T. Brown. These are not the k-mers you are looking for: efficient online k-mer counting using a probabilistic data structure. *PLoS ONE*, 9(7):1–13, July 2014.

[241] Y. Zhang, S. Singh, S. Sen, N. Duffield, and C. Lund. Online identification of hierarchical heavy hitters: algorithms, evaluation and applications. In *Internet Measurement Conference*, pages 101–114, 2004.

[242] Q. Zhao, M. Ogihara, H. Wang, and J. Xu. Finding global icebergs over distributed data sets. In *ACM Symposium on Principles of Database Systems*, pages 298–307, 2006.

[243] V. M. Zolotarev. *One dimensional stable distributions*, volume 65 of *Translations of Mathematical Monographs*. American Mathematical Society, 1983.

Index

Printed in the United States
By Bookmasters